Hana-Kimi

For You in Full Blossom

18

story and art by
HISAYA NAKAJO

HANA-KIMI
For You in Full Blossom
VOLUME 18

STORY & ART BY HISAYA NAKAJO

Translation & English Adaptation/David Ury
Touch-Up Art & Lettering/Primary Graphix
Design/Izumi Evers
Editor/Jason Thompson

Managing Editor/Megan Bates
Editorial Director/Elizabeth Kawasaki
Editor in Chief, Books/Alvin Lu
Editor in Chief, Magazines/Marc Weidenbaum
Sr. Director of Acquisitions/Rika Inouye
Sr. VP of Marketing/Liza Coppola
Exec. VP of Sales & Marketing/John Easum
Publisher/Hyoe Narita

Printed in the U.S.A.

Published by VIZ Media, LLC, P.O. Box 77010, San Francisco, CA 94107

Shôjo Edition
10 9 8 7 6 5 4 3 2 1

First printing, June 2007

www.viz.com
store.viz.com

RATED T+ FOR OLDER TEEN

PARENTAL ADVISORY
HANA-KIMI is rated T+ for Older Teen and is recommended for ages 16 and up. Contains strong language, sexual themes and alcohol and tobacco usage.

CONTENTS

Hana-Kimi Chapter 98 5

Hana-Kimi Chapter 99 37

Hana-Kimi Chapter 100 58

Hana-Kimi Chapter 101 83

Hana-Kimi Chapter 102 109

Hana-Kimi Chapter 103 141

Hana-Kimi Chapter 104 171

Don't Worry, Kadoma-kun! 191

About the Author.......................................195

Previews 196

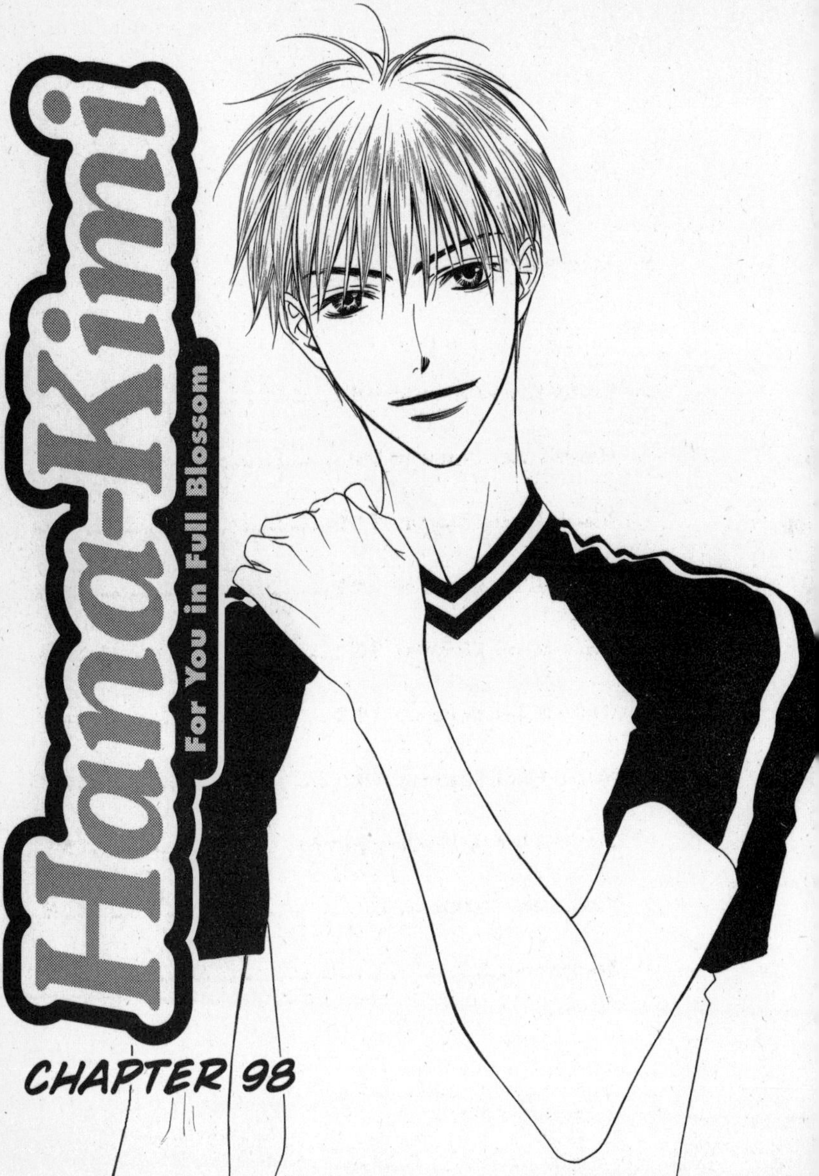
Hana-Kimi
For You in Full Blossom
CHAPTER 98

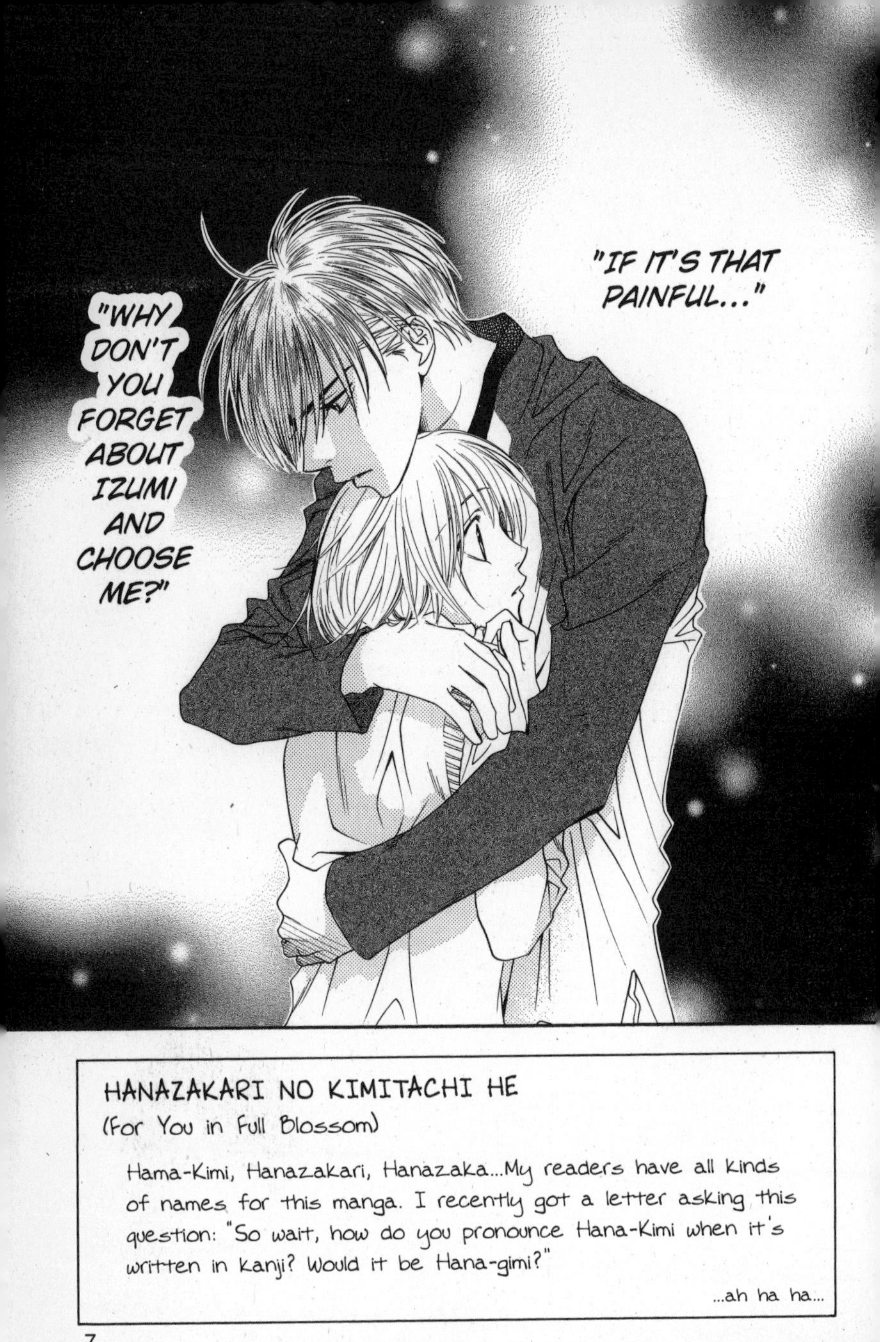
"IF IT'S THAT PAINFUL..."
"WHY DON'T YOU FORGET ABOUT IZUMI AND CHOOSE ME?"

HANAZAKARI NO KIMITACHI HE

(For You in Full Blossom)

Hama-Kimi, Hanazakari, Hanazaka...My readers have all kinds of names for this manga. I recently got a letter asking this question: "So wait, how do you pronounce Hana-Kimi when it's written in kanji? Would it be Hana-gimi?"

...ah ha ha...

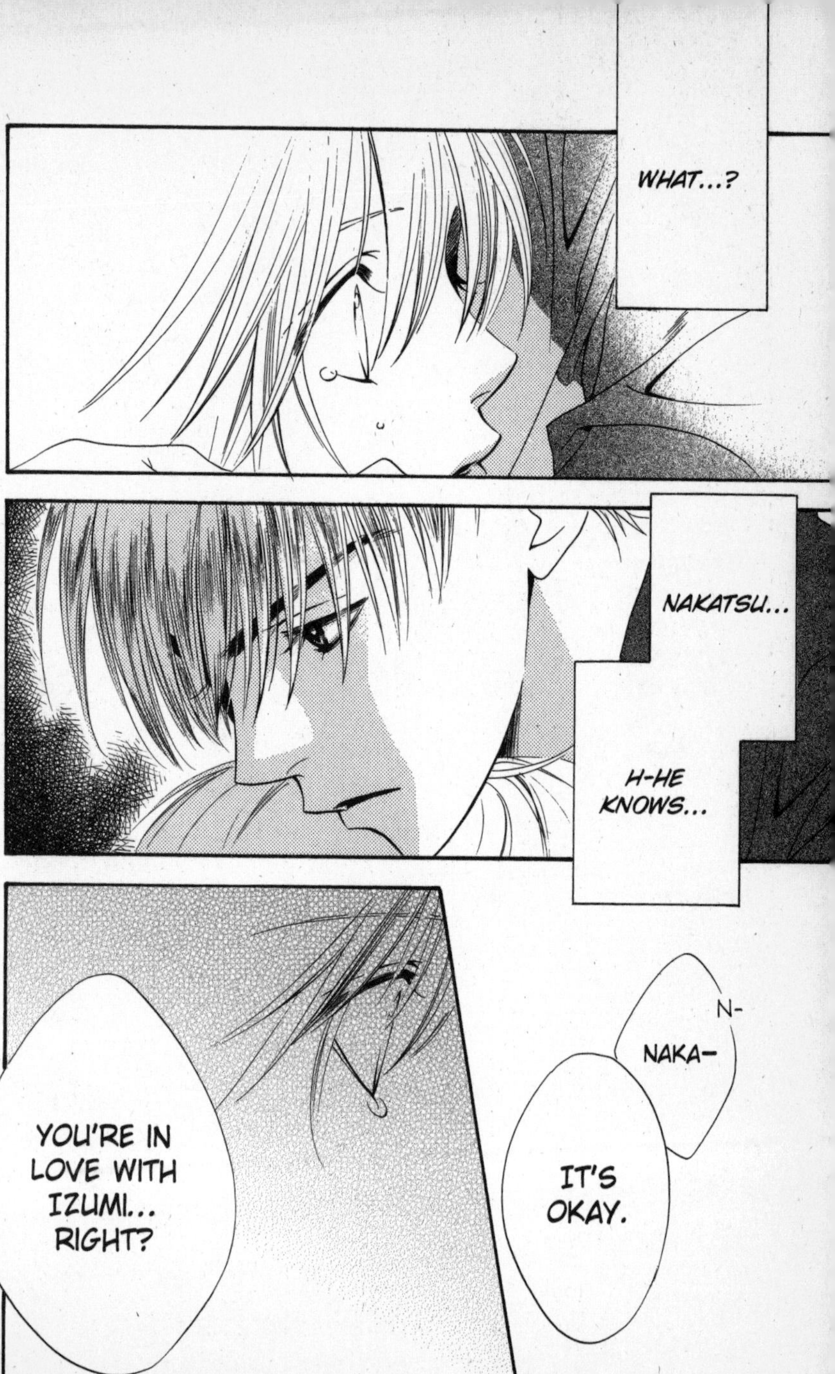
WHAT...?
NAKATSU...
H-HE KNOWS...
N- NAKA-
IT'S OKAY.
YOU'RE IN LOVE WITH IZUMI... RIGHT?

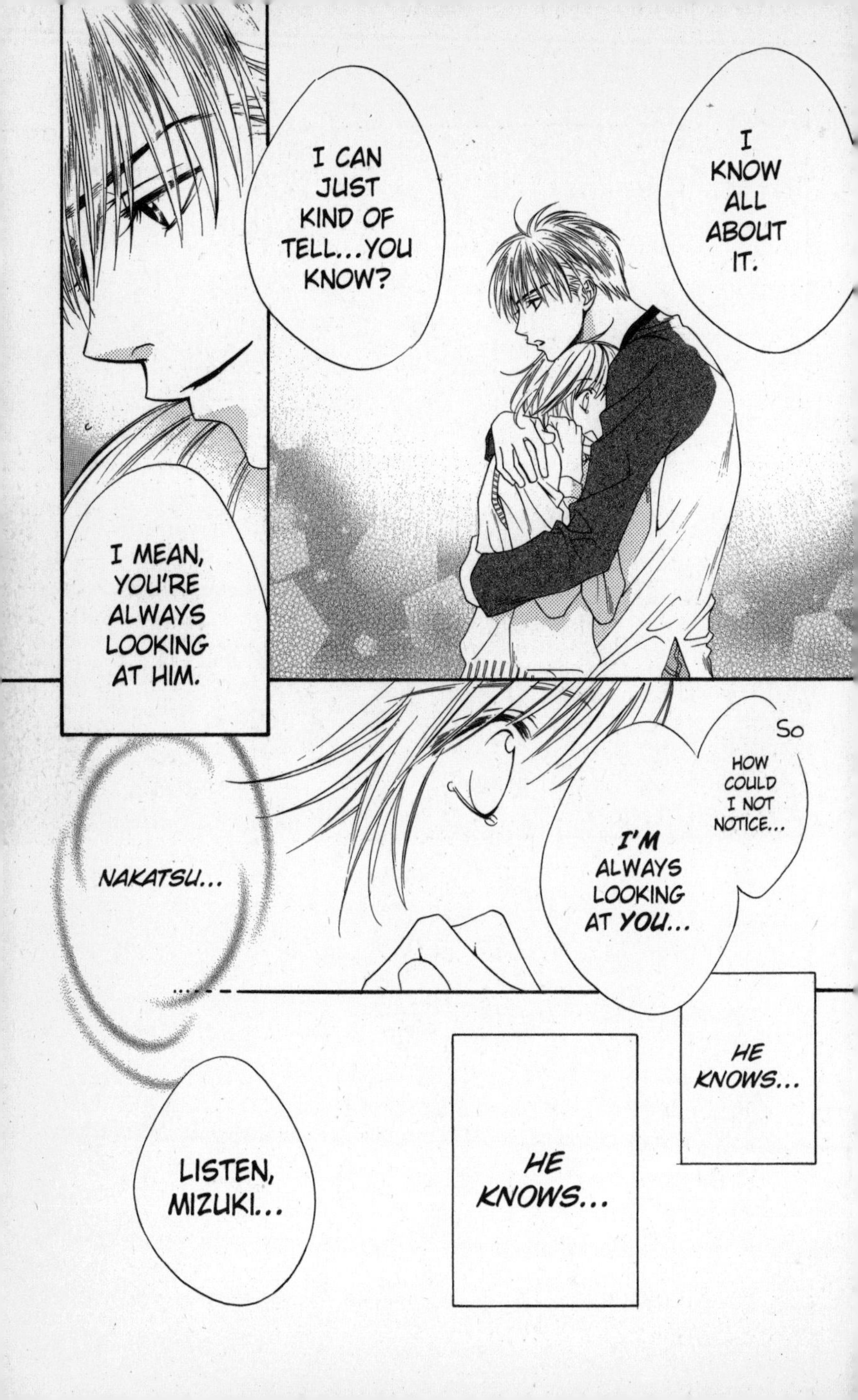

I KNOW ALL ABOUT IT.
I CAN JUST KIND OF TELL...YOU KNOW?
I MEAN, YOU'RE ALWAYS LOOKING AT HIM.
So
HOW COULD I NOT NOTICE...
I'M ALWAYS LOOKING AT *YOU*...
NAKATSU...
......
HE KNOWS...
HE KNOWS...
LISTEN, MIZUKI...

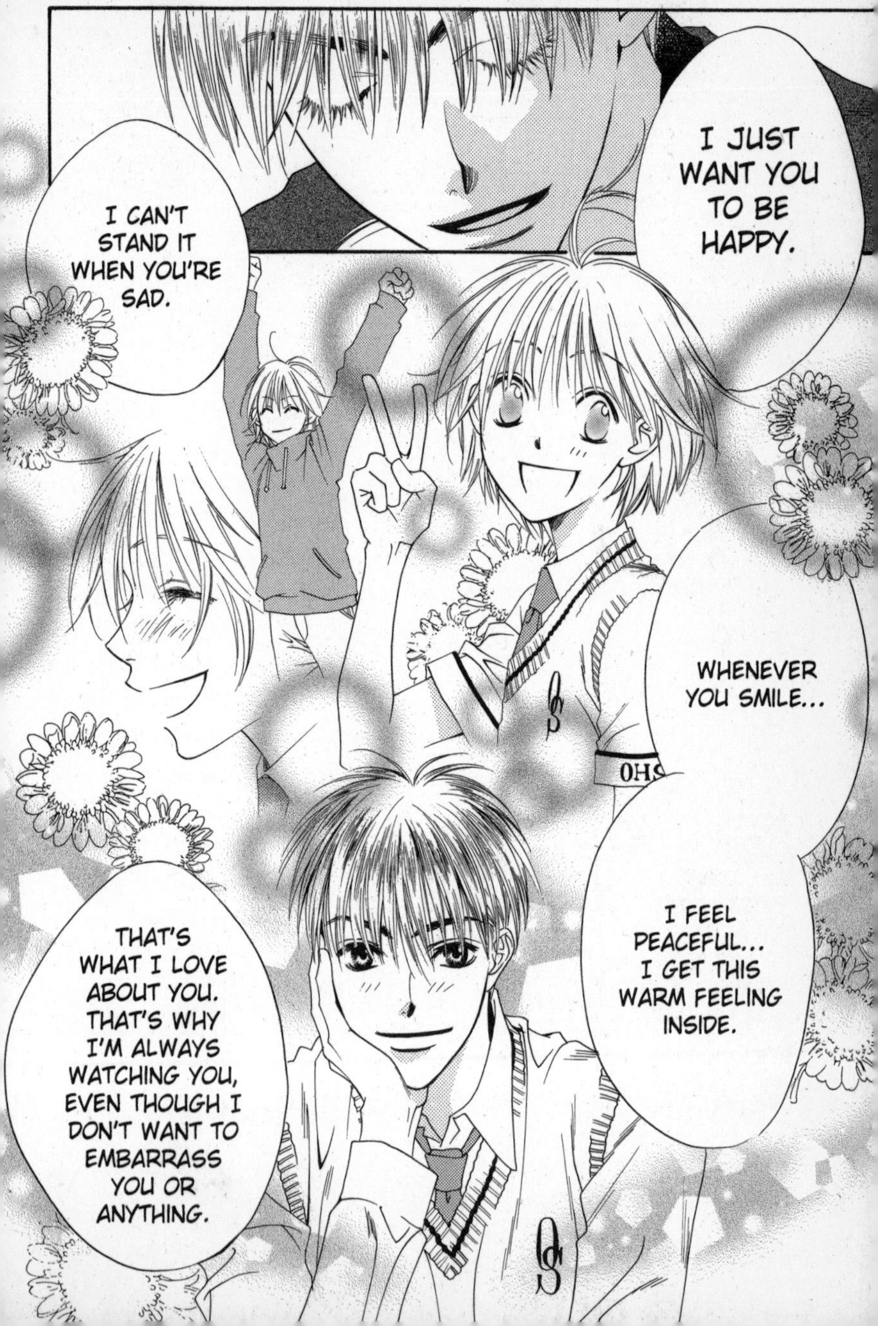
I JUST WANT YOU TO BE HAPPY.
I CAN'T STAND IT WHEN YOU'RE SAD.
WHENEVER YOU SMILE...
I FEEL PEACEFUL... I GET THIS WARM FEELING INSIDE.
THAT'S WHAT I LOVE ABOUT YOU. THAT'S WHY I'M ALWAYS WATCHING YOU, EVEN THOUGH I DON'T WANT TO EMBARRASS YOU OR ANYTHING.

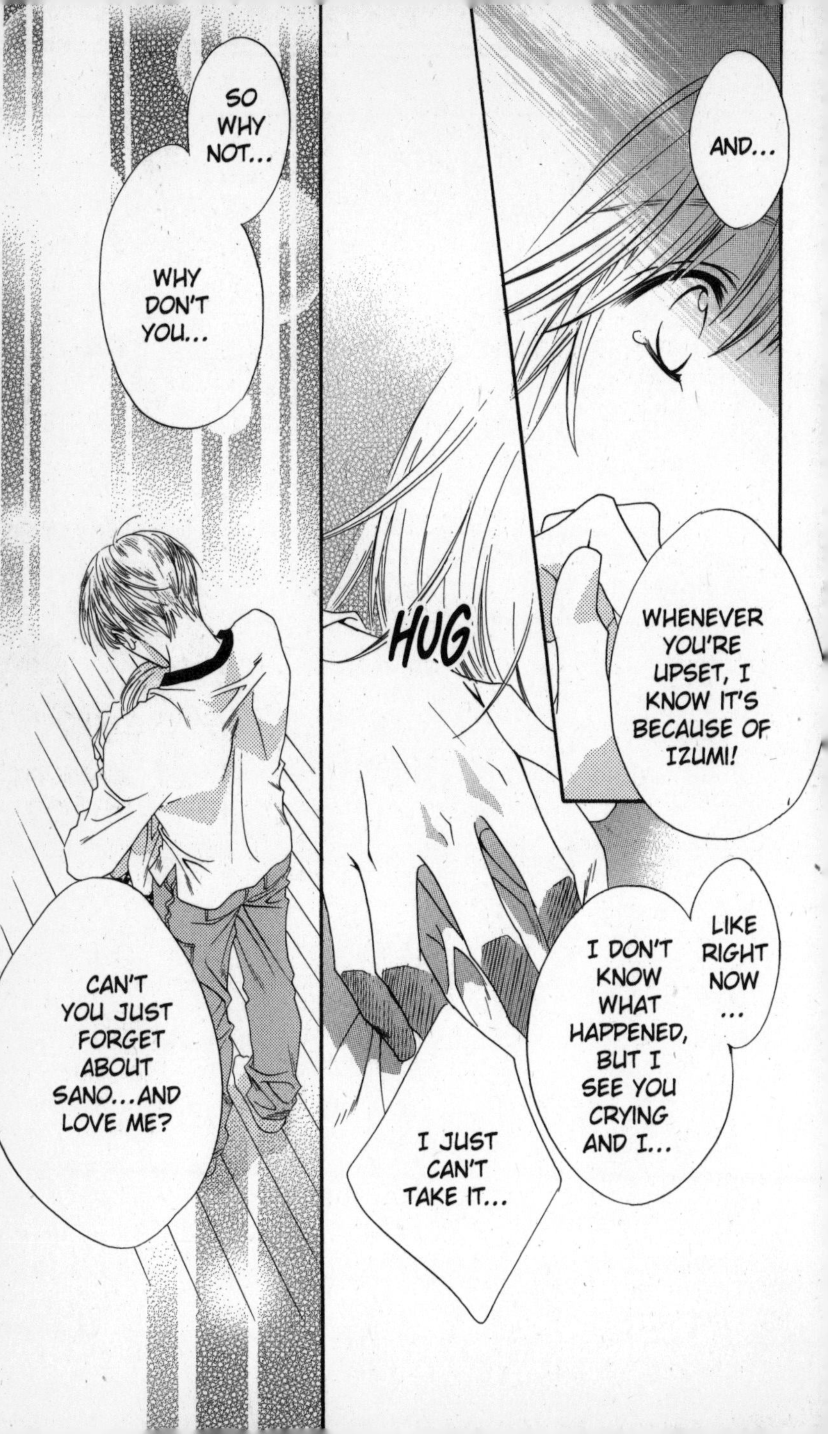
AND...
WHENEVER YOU'RE UPSET, I KNOW IT'S BECAUSE OF IZUMI!
HUG
LIKE RIGHT NOW...
I DON'T KNOW WHAT HAPPENED, BUT I SEE YOU CRYING AND I...
I JUST CAN'T TAKE IT...
SO WHY NOT...
WHY DON'T YOU...
CAN'T YOU JUST FORGET ABOUT SANO...AND LOVE ME?

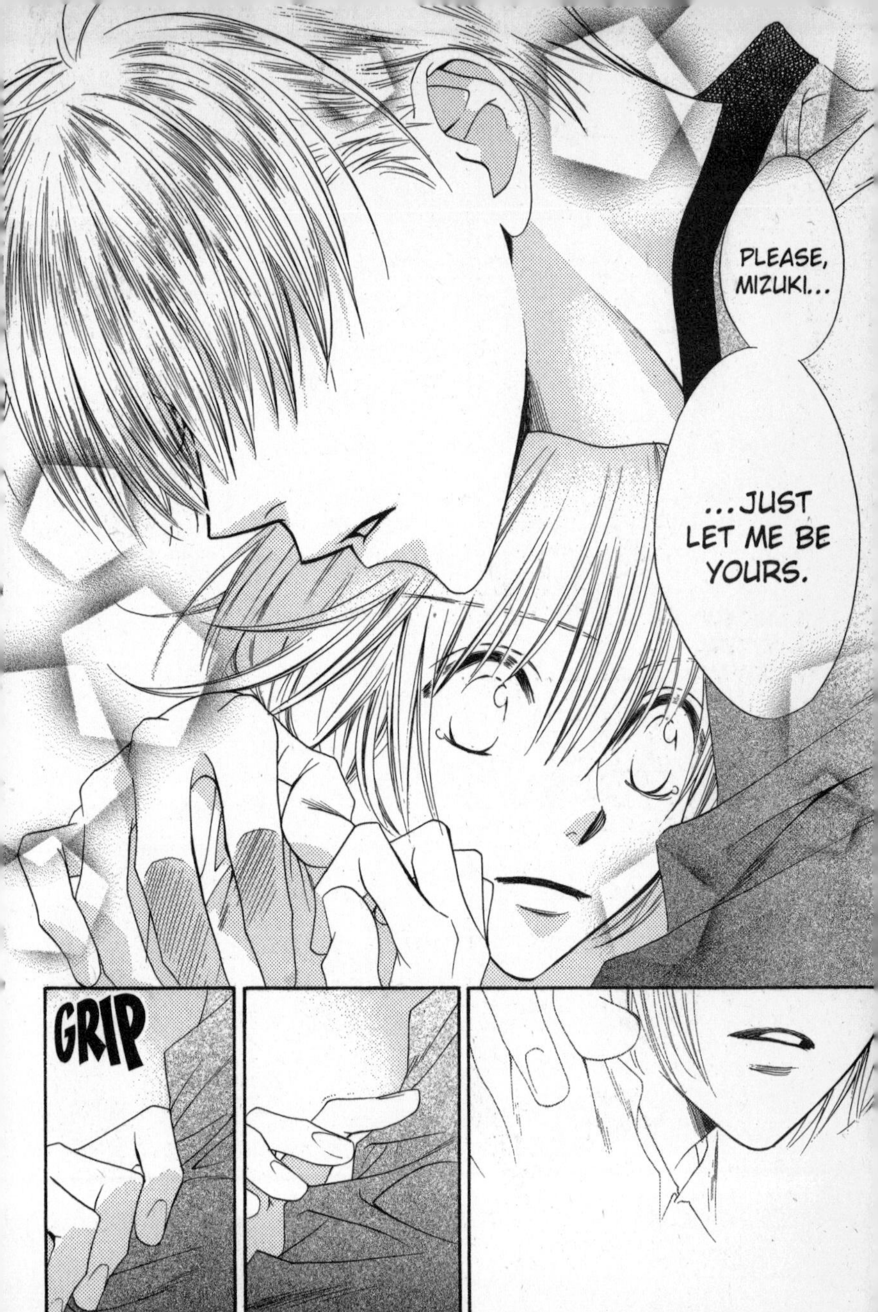
PLEASE, MIZUKI...
...JUST LET ME BE YOURS.
GRIP

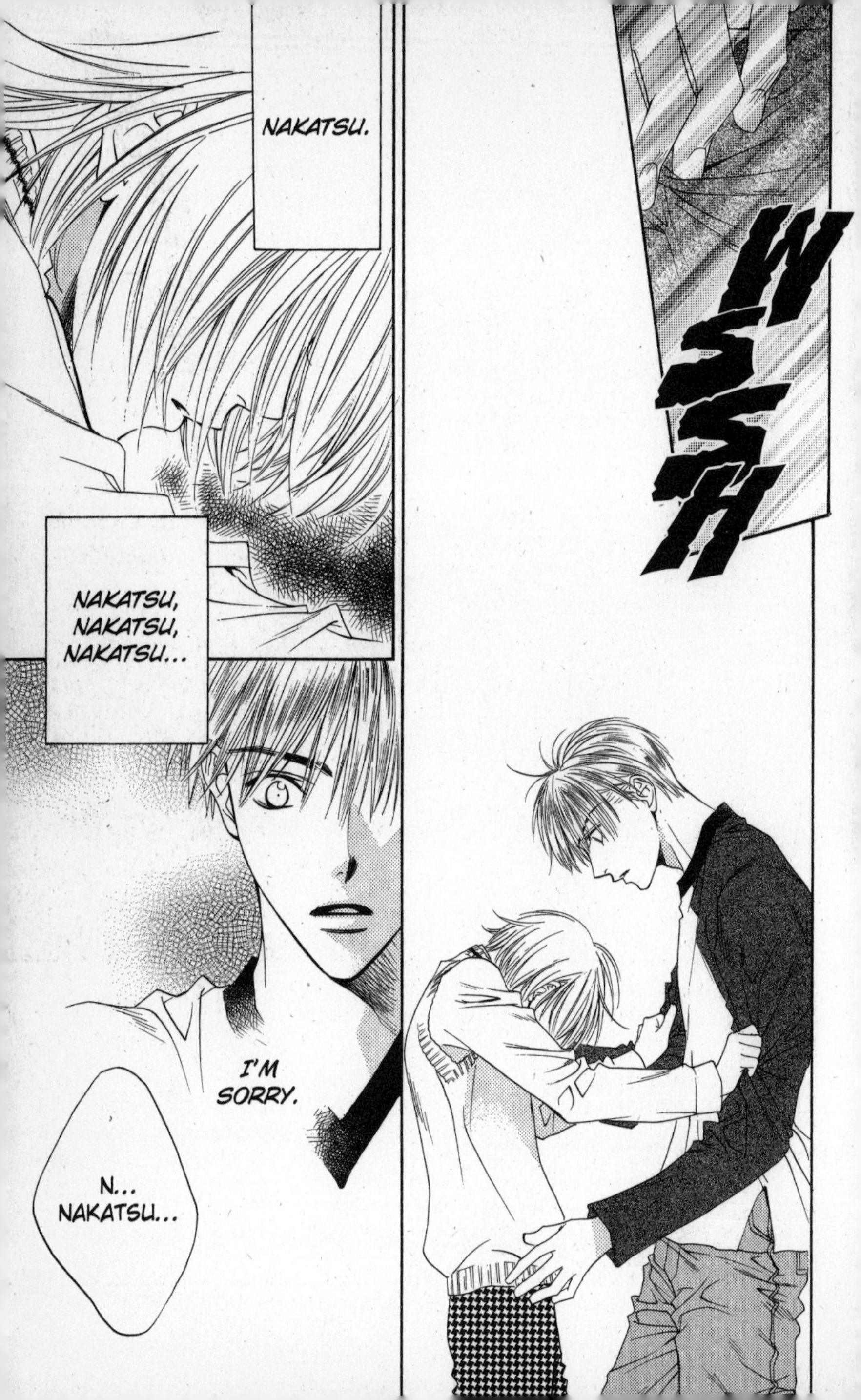
WSSH
NAKATSU.
NAKATSU, NAKATSU, NAKATSU...
I'M SORRY.
N... NAKATSU...

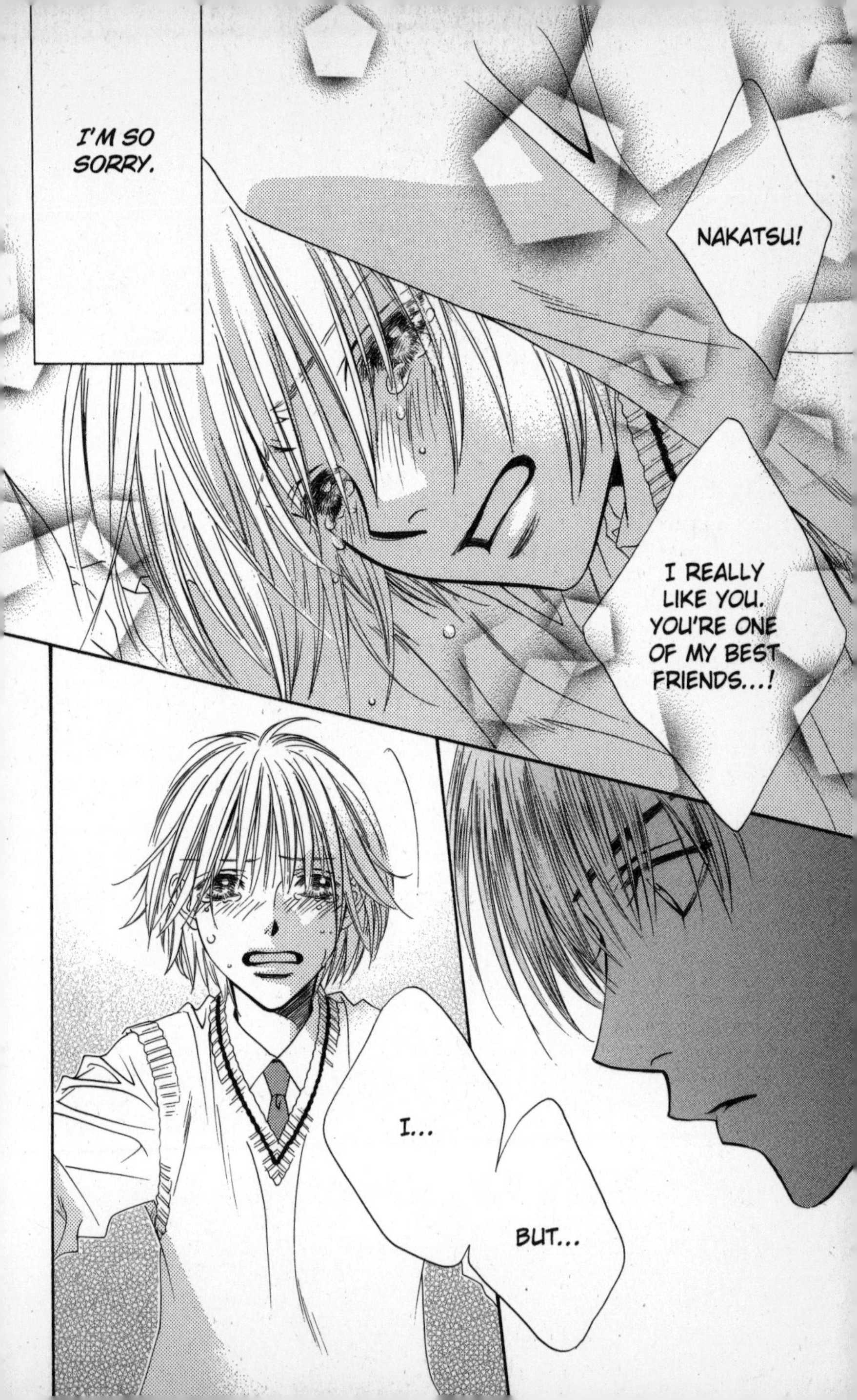
NAKATSU!
I REALLY LIKE YOU. YOU'RE ONE OF MY BEST FRIENDS...!
I'M SO SORRY.
I...
BUT...

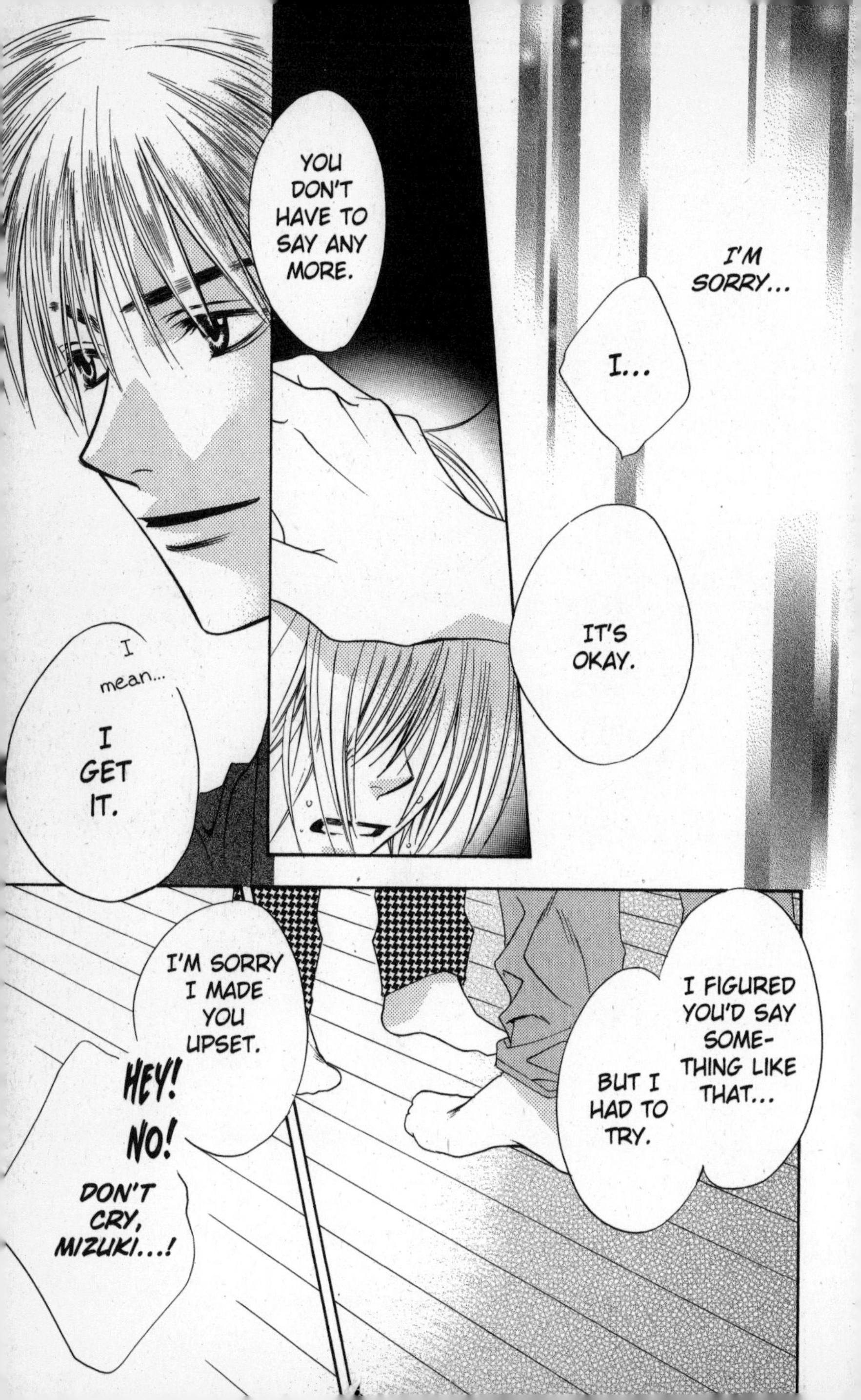
I'M SORRY...
I...
IT'S OKAY.
YOU DON'T HAVE TO SAY ANY MORE.
I mean...
I GET IT.
I FIGURED YOU'D SAY SOME-THING LIKE THAT...
BUT I HAD TO TRY.
I'M SORRY I MADE YOU UPSET.
HEY!
NO!
DON'T CRY, MIZUKI...!

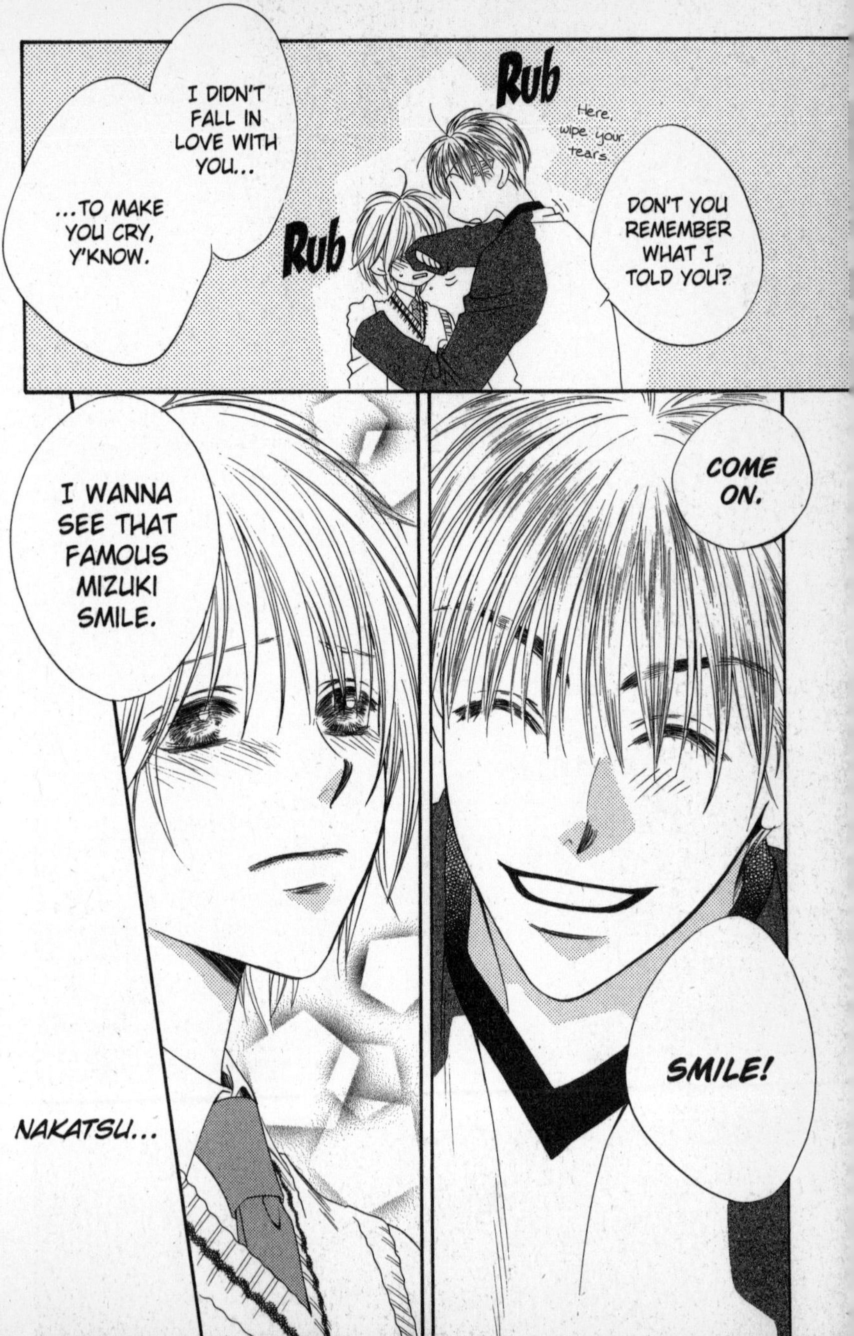
Rub
Here, wipe your tears.
DON'T YOU REMEMBER WHAT I TOLD YOU?
Rub
I DIDN'T FALL IN LOVE WITH YOU...
...TO MAKE YOU CRY, Y'KNOW.
COME ON.
SMILE!
I WANNA SEE THAT FAMOUS MIZUKI SMILE.
NAKATSU...

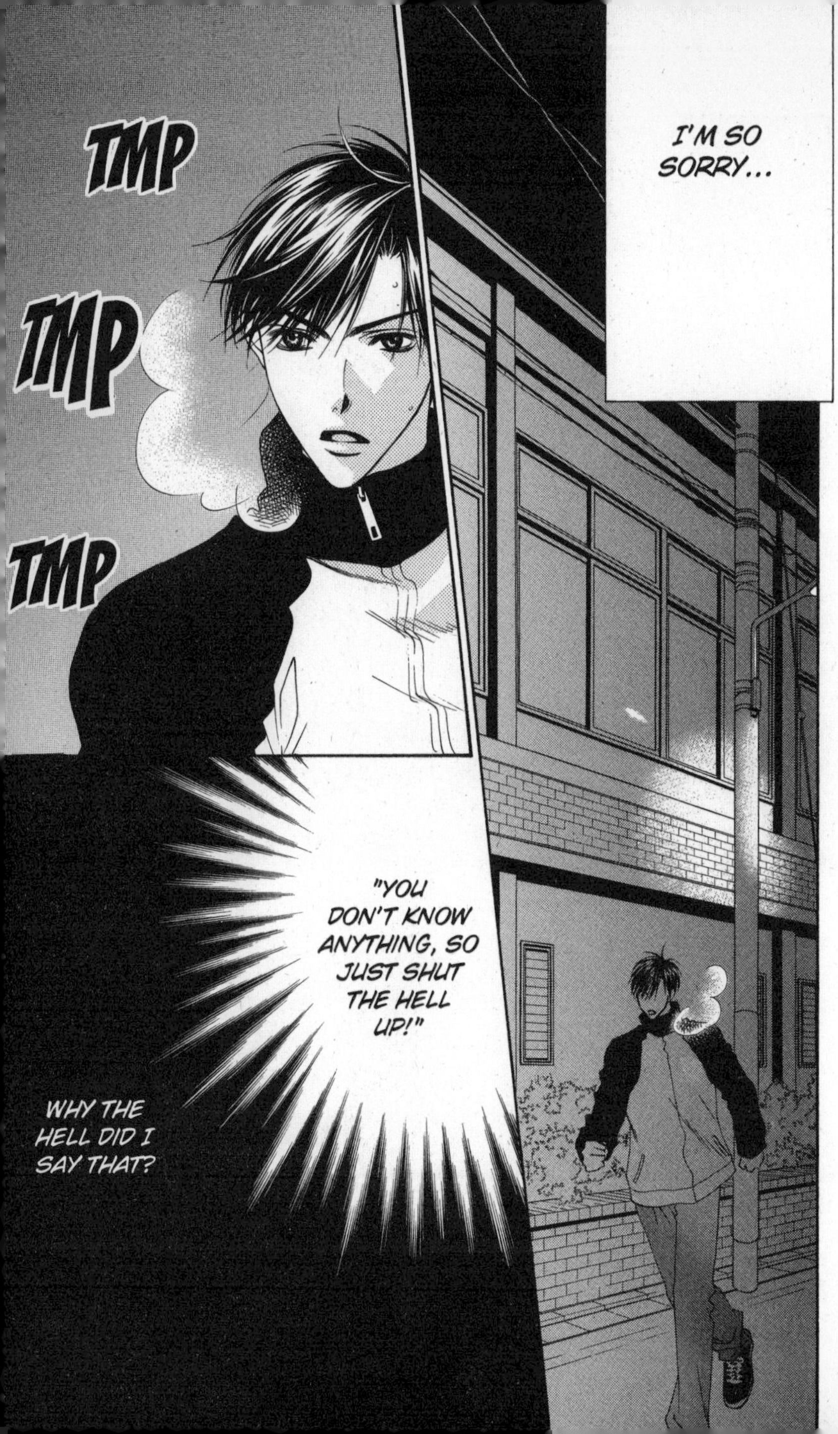
I'M SO SORRY...
TMP
TMP
TMP
"YOU DON'T KNOW ANYTHING, SO JUST SHUT THE HELL UP!"
WHY THE HELL DID I SAY THAT?

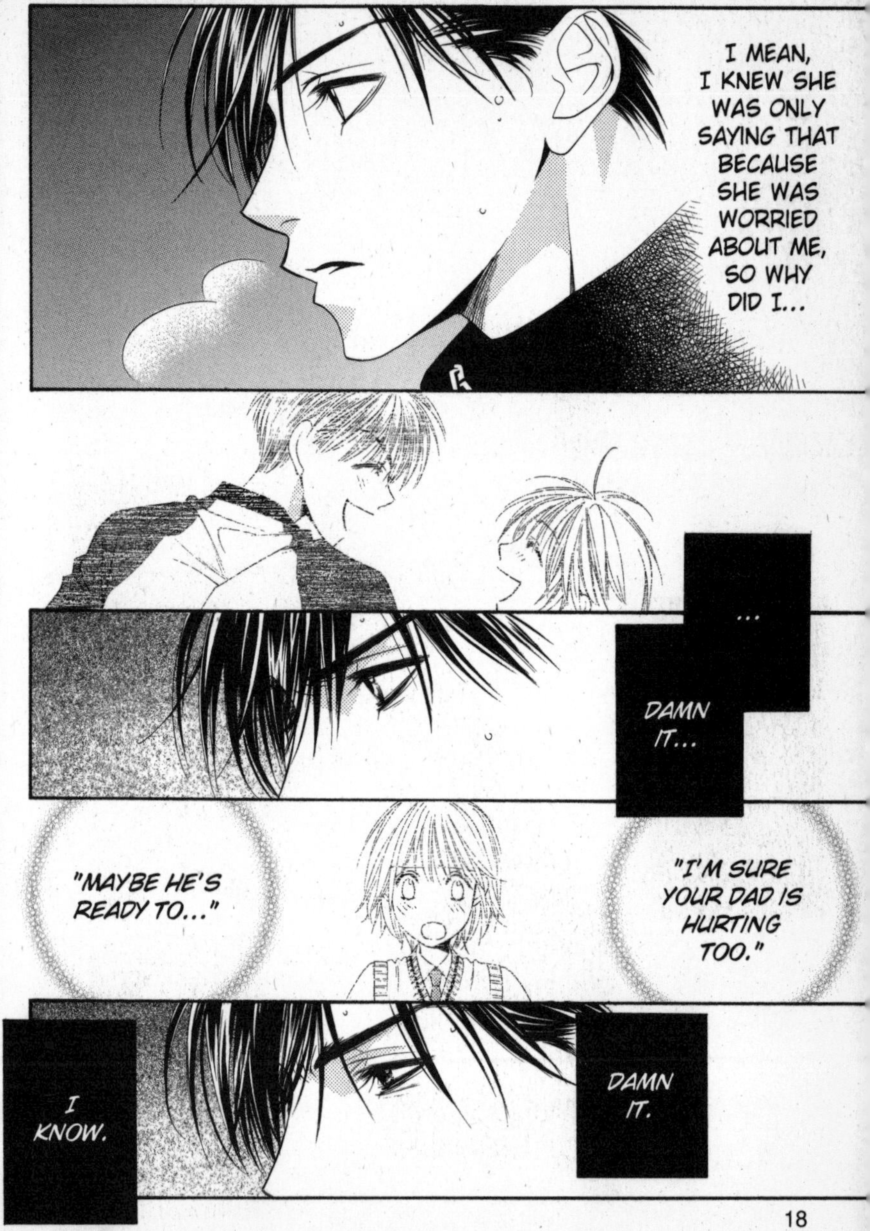
I MEAN, I KNEW SHE WAS ONLY SAYING THAT BECAUSE SHE WAS WORRIED ABOUT ME, SO WHY DID I...
...
DAMN IT...
"I'M SURE YOUR DAD IS HURTING TOO."
"MAYBE HE'S READY TO..."
DAMN IT.
I KNOW.

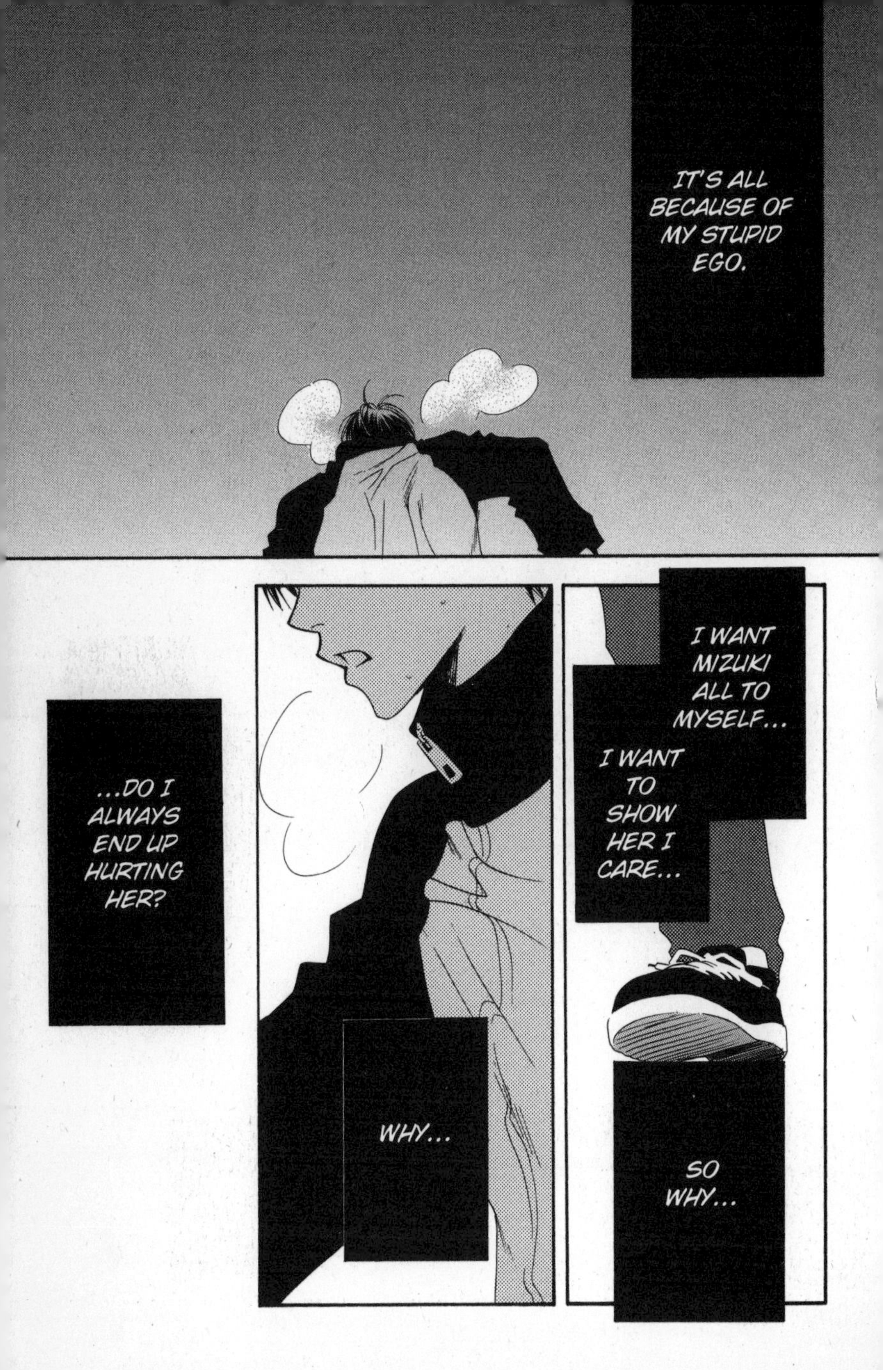
IT'S ALL BECAUSE OF MY STUPID EGO.
I WANT MIZUKI ALL TO MYSELF...
I WANT TO SHOW HER I CARE...
SO WHY...
WHY...
...DO I ALWAYS END UP HURTING HER?

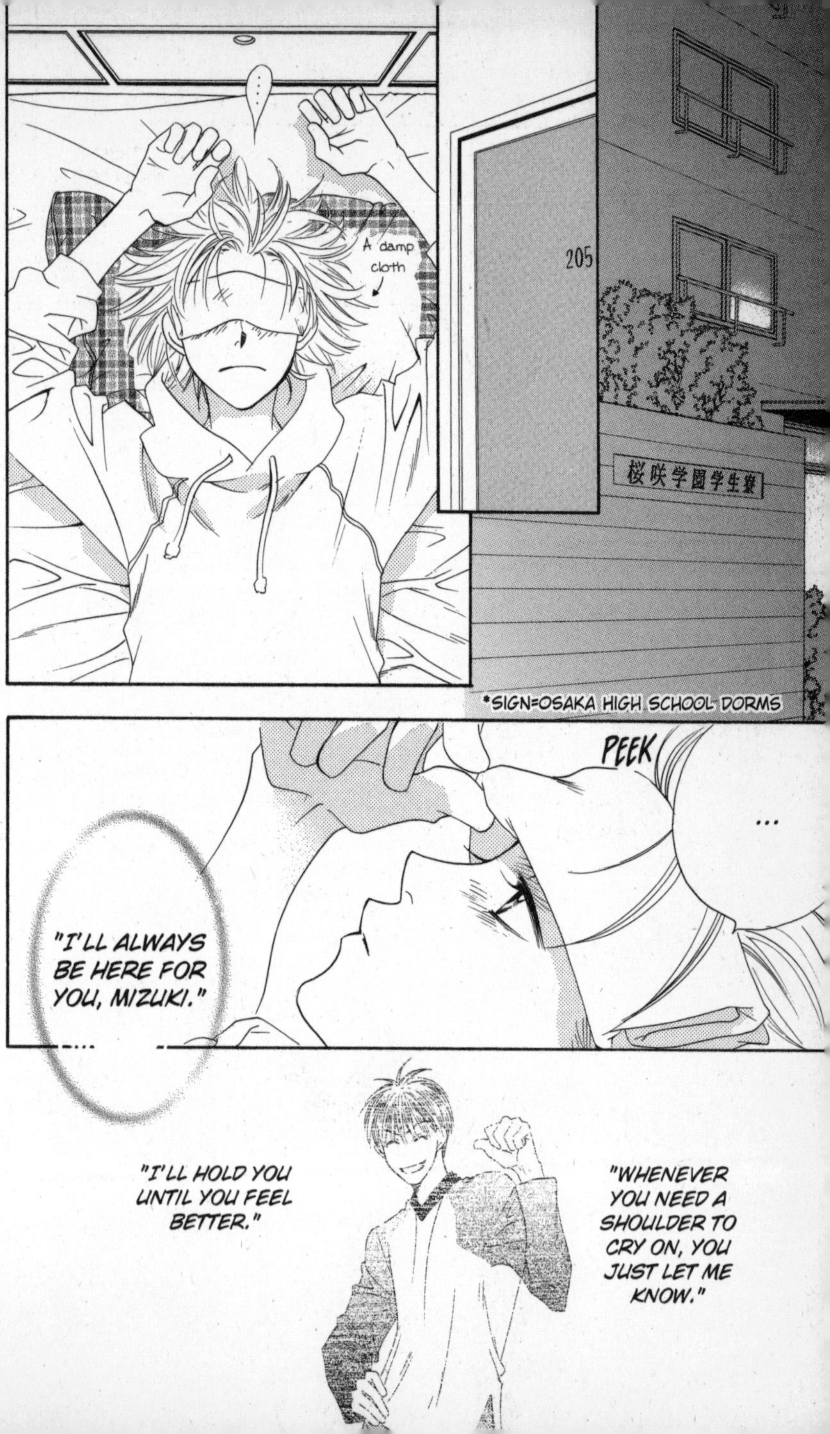
205
桜咲学園学生寮
*SIGN=OSAKA HIGH SCHOOL DORMS
A damp cloth
PEEK
...
"I'LL ALWAYS BE HERE FOR YOU, MIZUKI."
—...
"WHENEVER YOU NEED A SHOULDER TO CRY ON, YOU JUST LET ME KNOW."
"I'LL HOLD YOU UNTIL YOU FEEL BETTER."

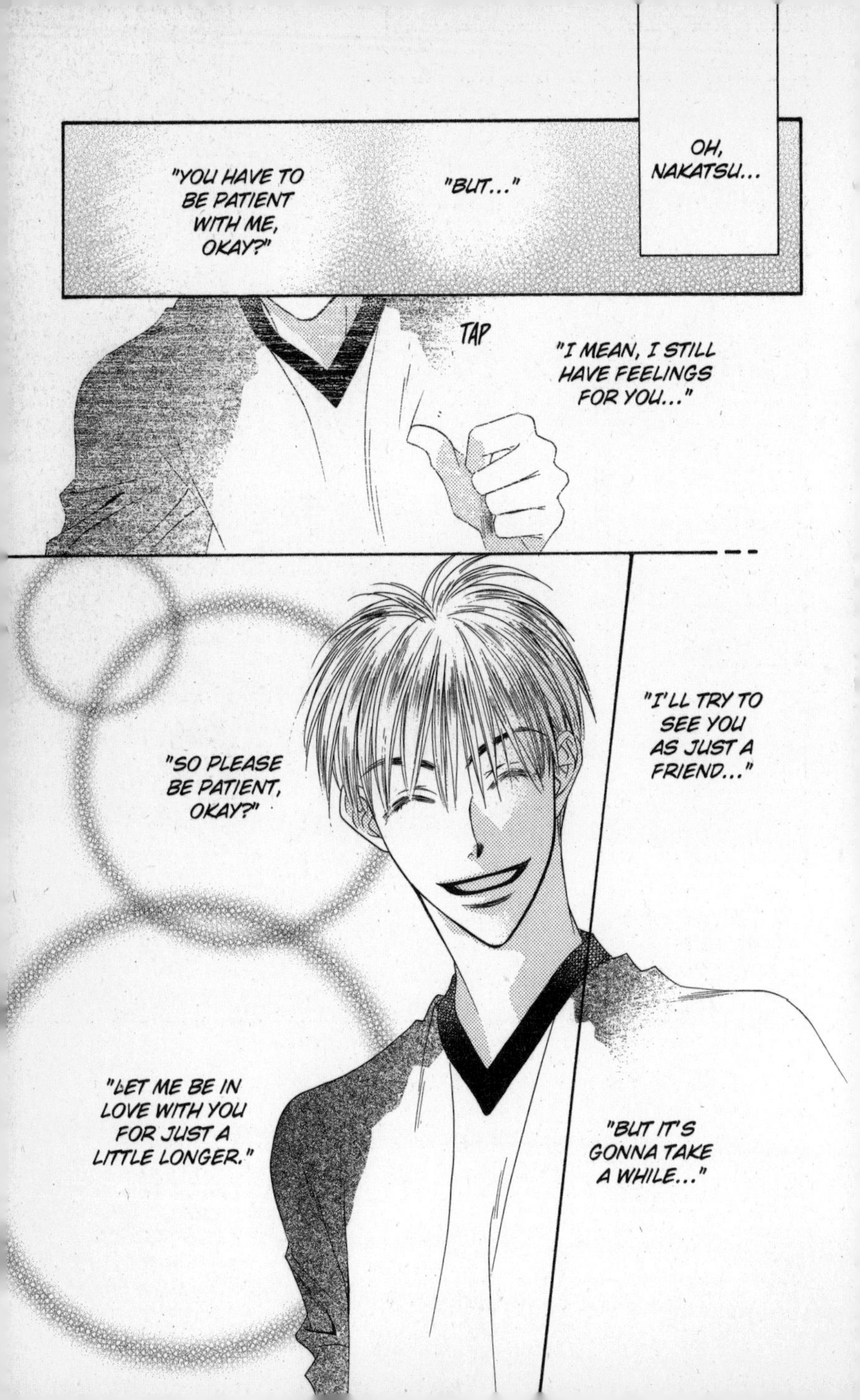
OH, NAKATSU...
"BUT..."
"YOU HAVE TO BE PATIENT WITH ME, OKAY?"
"I MEAN, I STILL HAVE FEELINGS FOR YOU..."
TAP
"I'LL TRY TO SEE YOU AS JUST A FRIEND..."
"BUT IT'S GONNA TAKE A WHILE..."
"SO PLEASE BE PATIENT, OKAY?"
"LET ME BE IN LOVE WITH YOU FOR JUST A LITTLE LONGER."

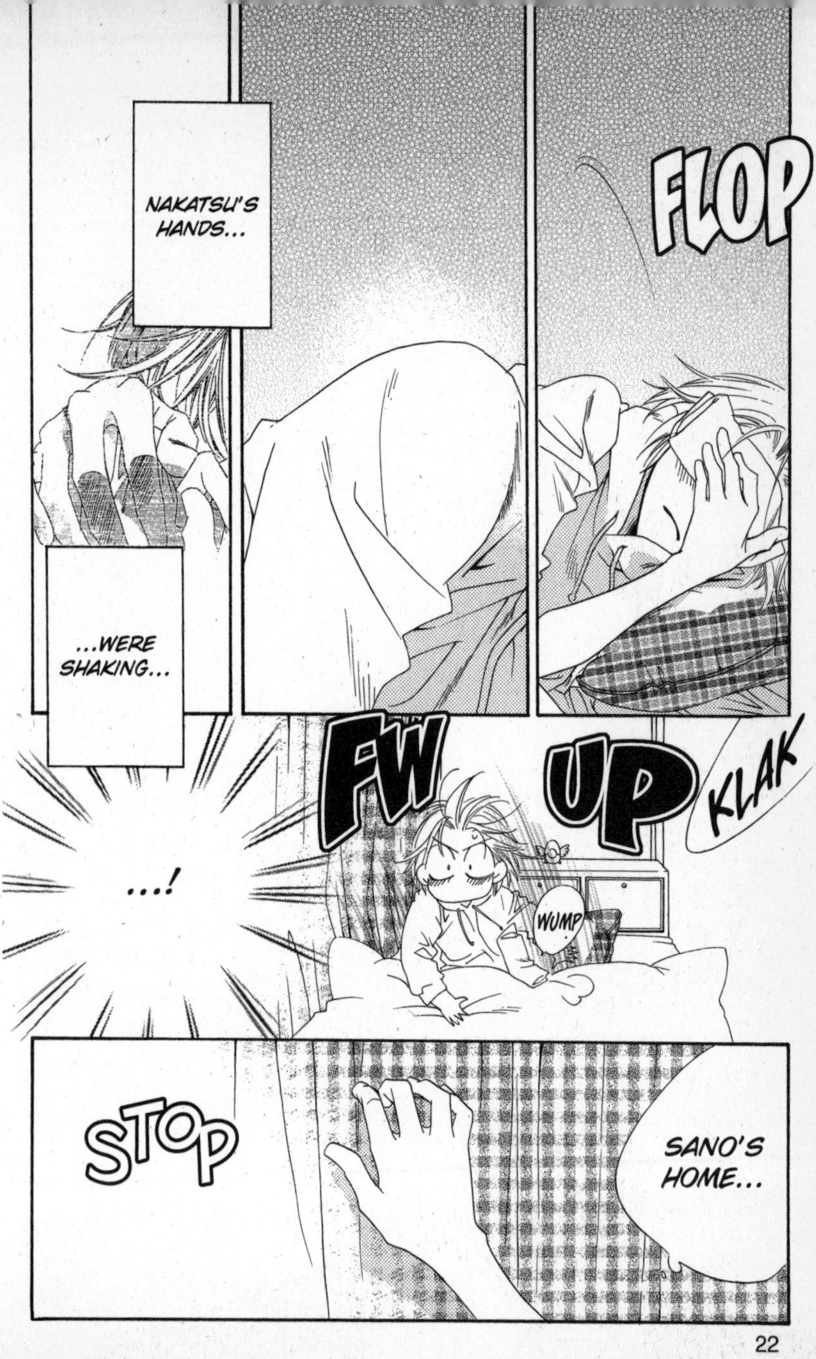
FLOP
NAKATSU'S HANDS...
...WERE SHAKING...
KLAK
FW UP
WUMP
...!
SANO'S HOME...
STOP

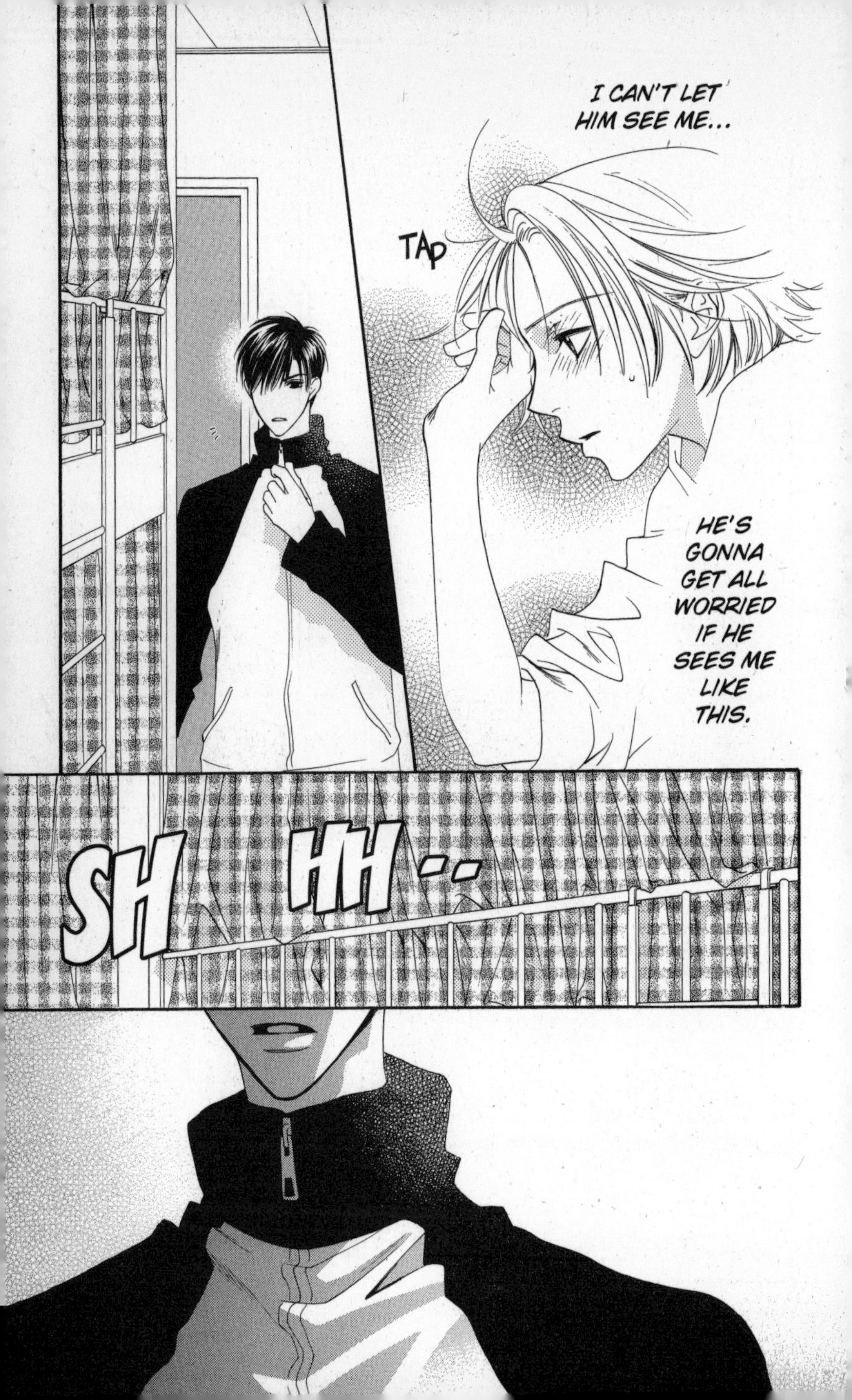
I CAN'T LET HIM SEE ME...
TAP
HE'S GONNA GET ALL WORRIED IF HE SEES ME LIKE THIS.
SH HH ..

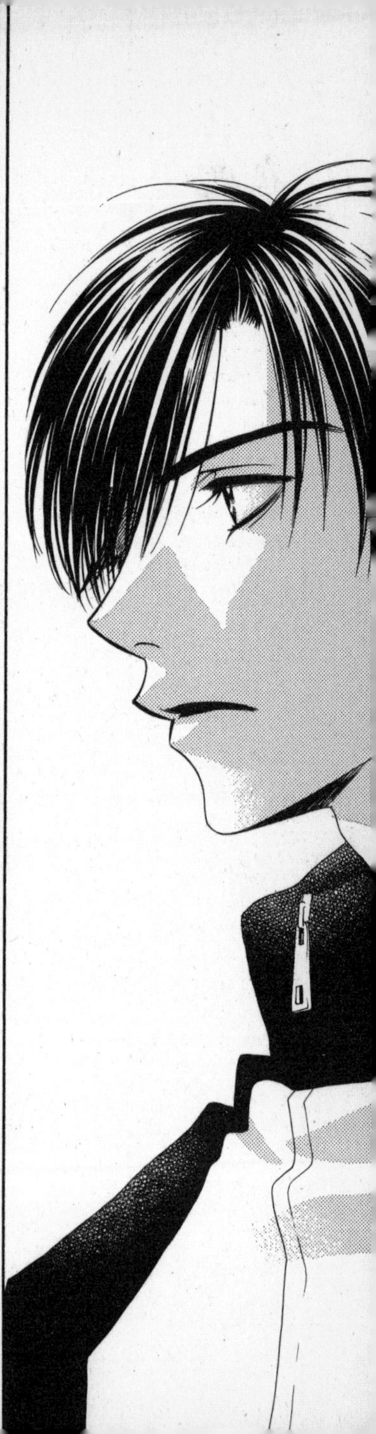

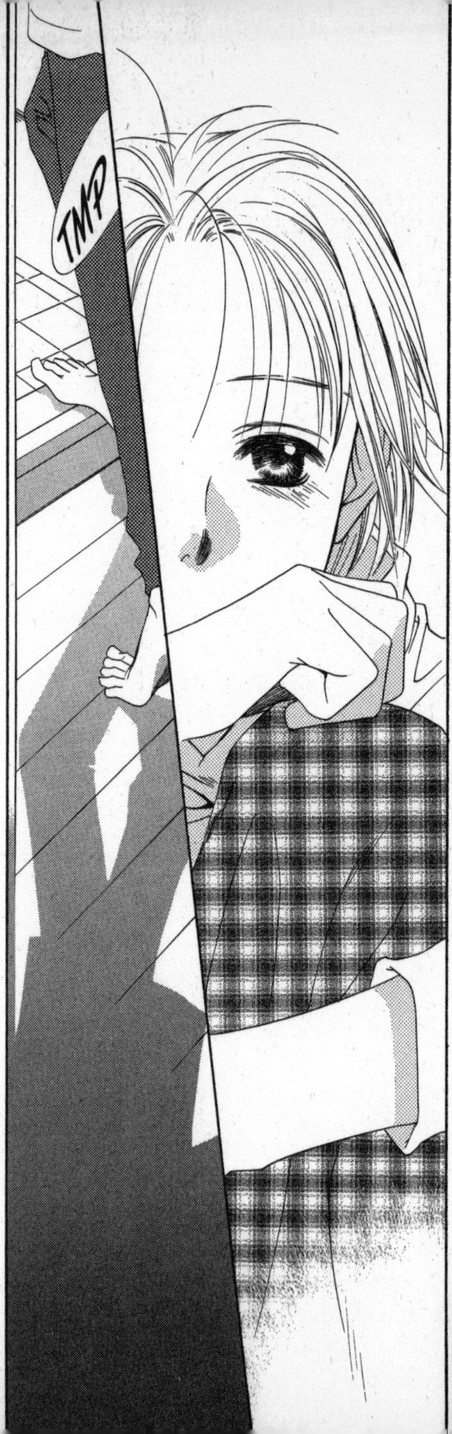
TMP

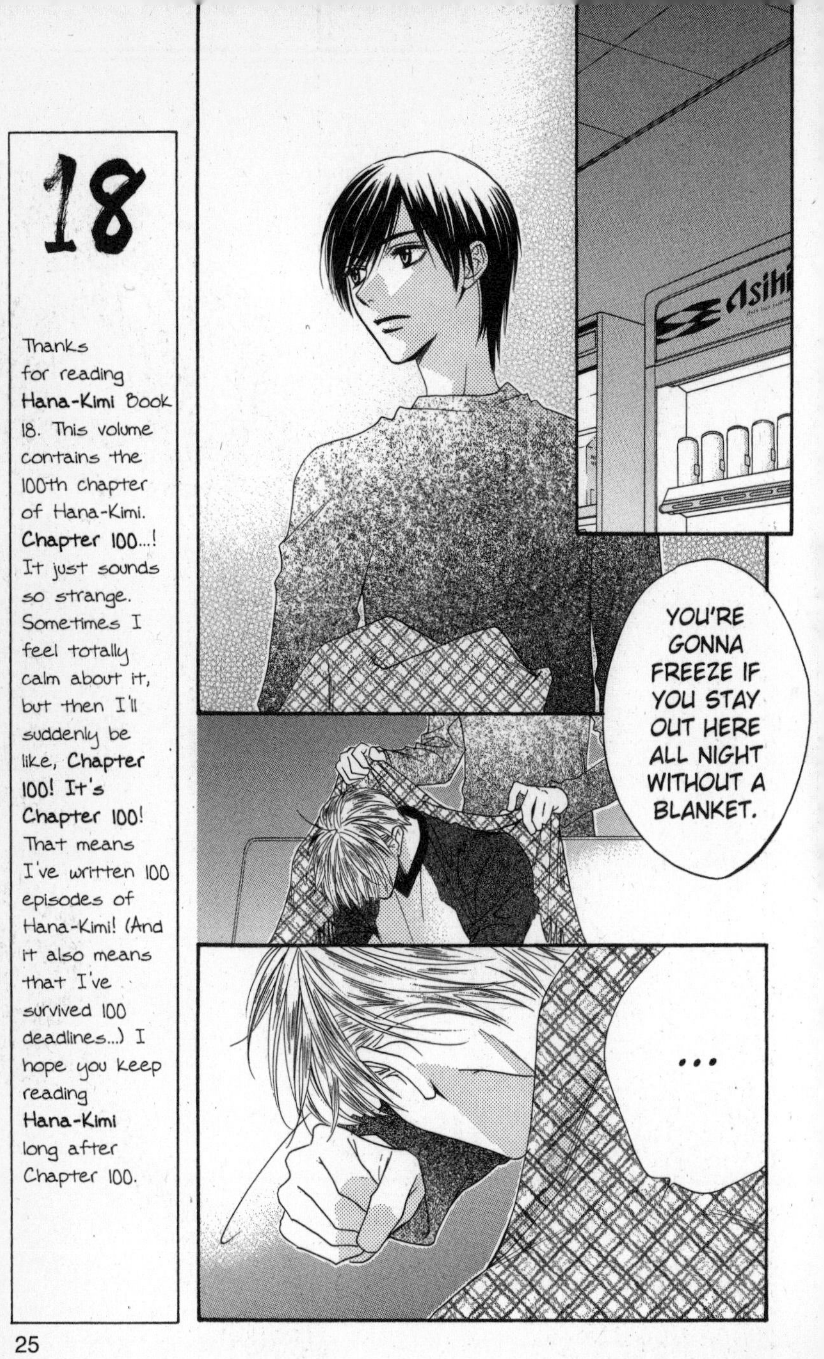
Asihi
YOU'RE GONNA FREEZE IF YOU STAY OUT HERE ALL NIGHT WITHOUT A BLANKET.
...

18

Thanks for reading **Hana-Kimi** Book 18. This volume contains the 100th chapter of Hana-Kimi. **Chapter 100...!** It just sounds so strange. Sometimes I feel totally calm about it, but then I'll suddenly be like, **Chapter 100! It's Chapter 100!** That means I've written 100 episodes of Hana-Kimi! (And it also means that I've survived 100 deadlines...) I hope you keep reading **Hana-Kimi** long after Chapter 100.

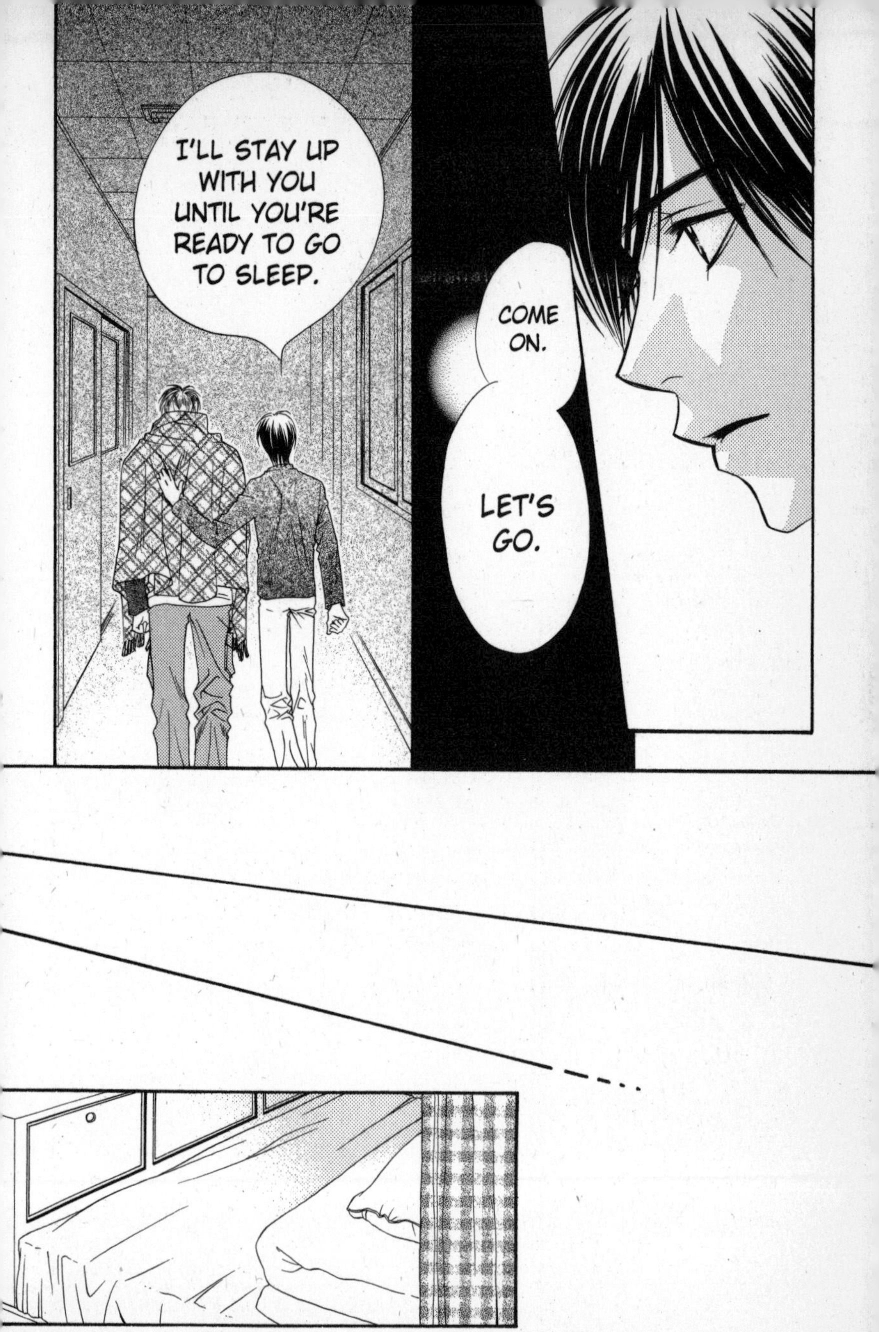
COME ON.
LET'S GO.
I'LL STAY UP WITH YOU UNTIL YOU'RE READY TO GO TO SLEEP.

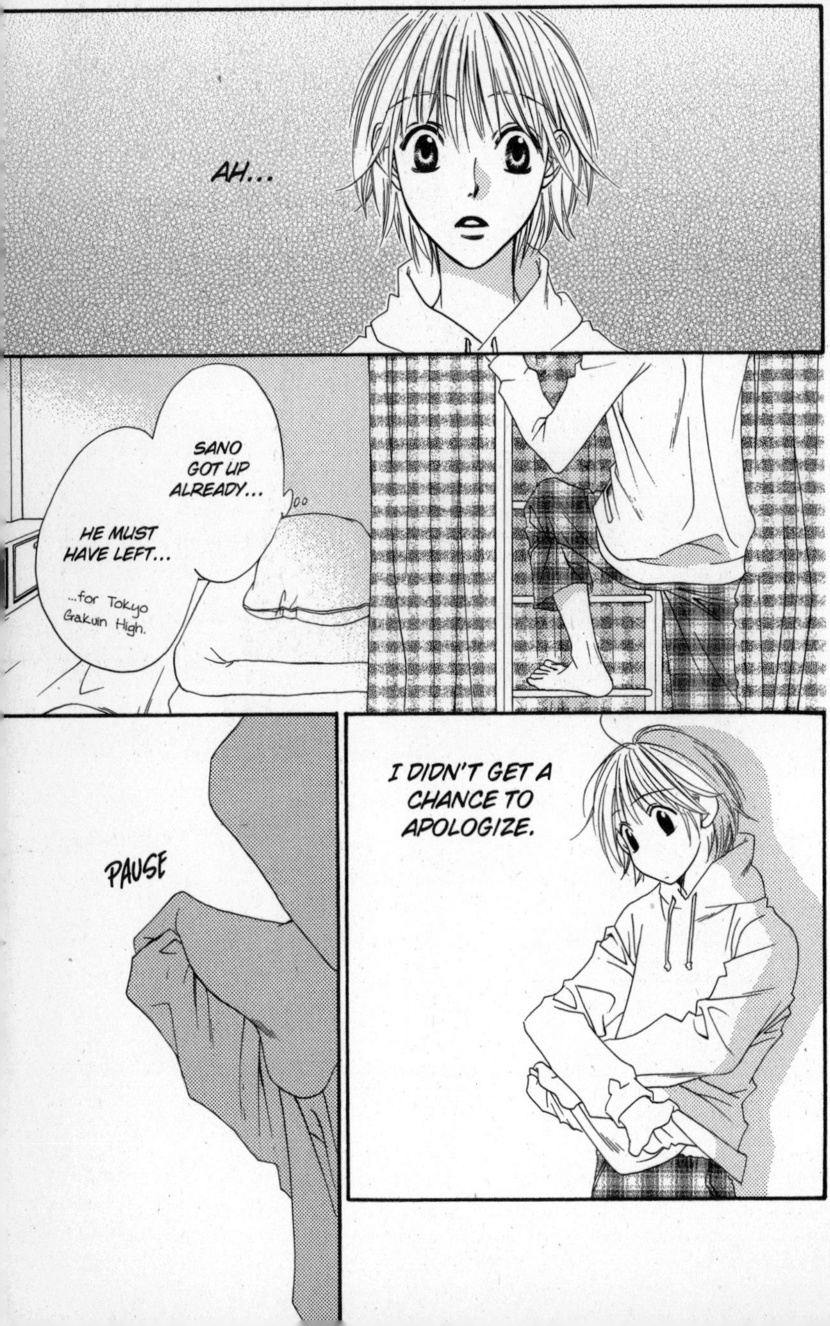
AH...
SANO GOT UP ALREADY...
HE MUST HAVE LEFT...
...for Tokyo Gakuin High.
I DIDN'T GET A CHANCE TO APOLOGIZE.
PAUSE

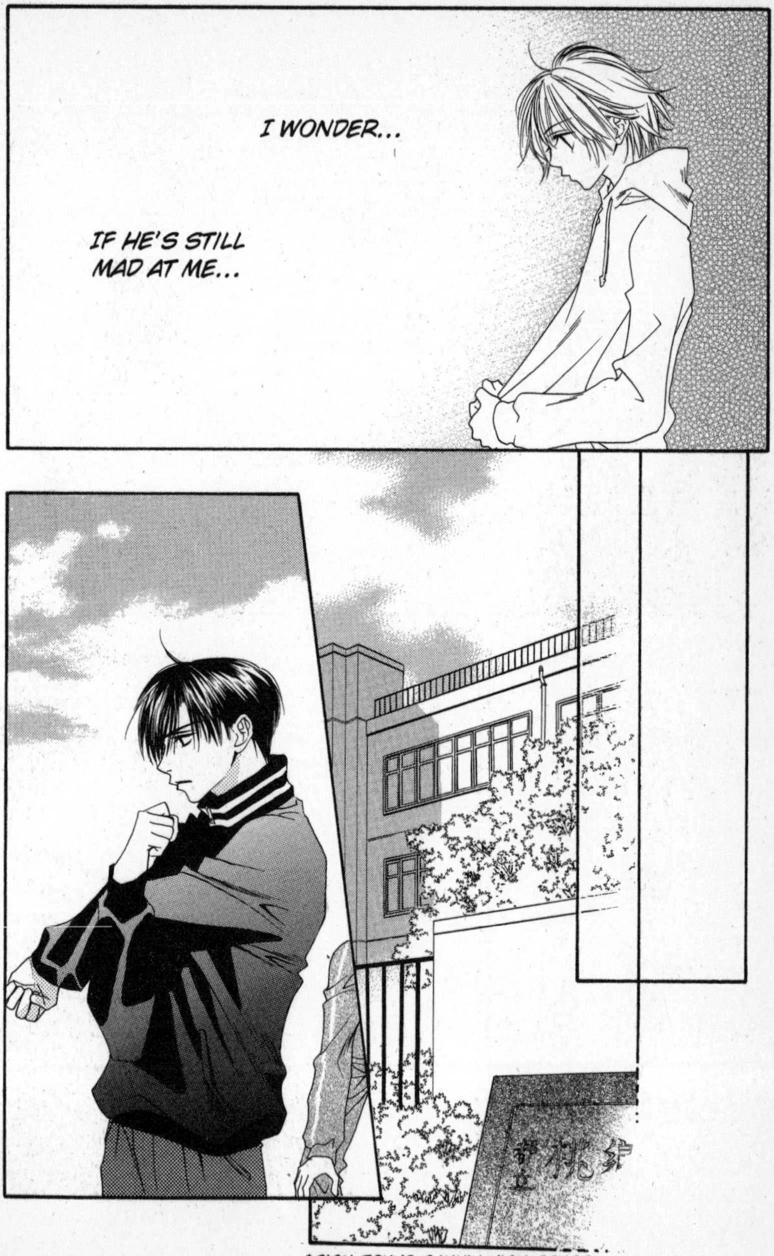
I WONDER...
IF HE'S STILL MAD AT ME...
*SIGN=TOKYO GAKUIN HIGH SCHOOL

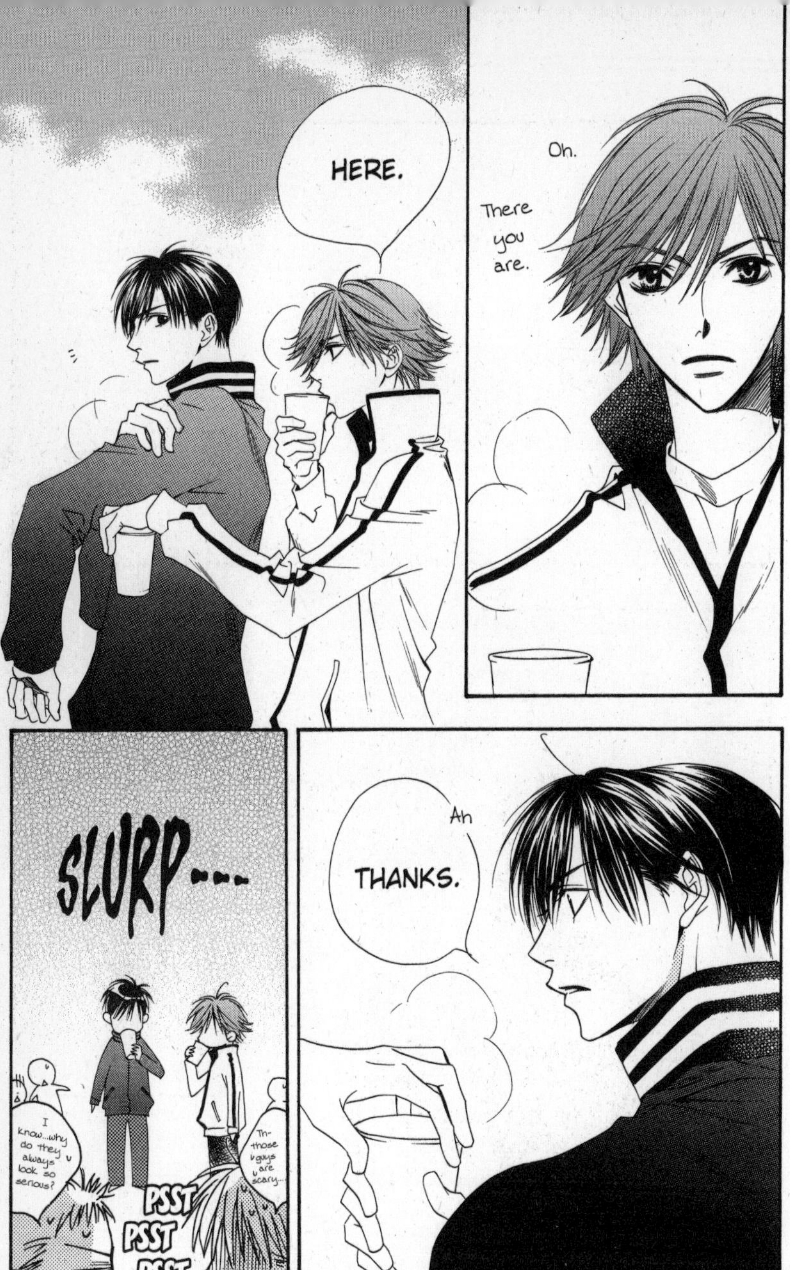
Oh.
There you are.
HERE.
An
THANKS.
SLURP...
Th-those guys are scary...
I know...why do they always look so serious?
PSST PSST PSST

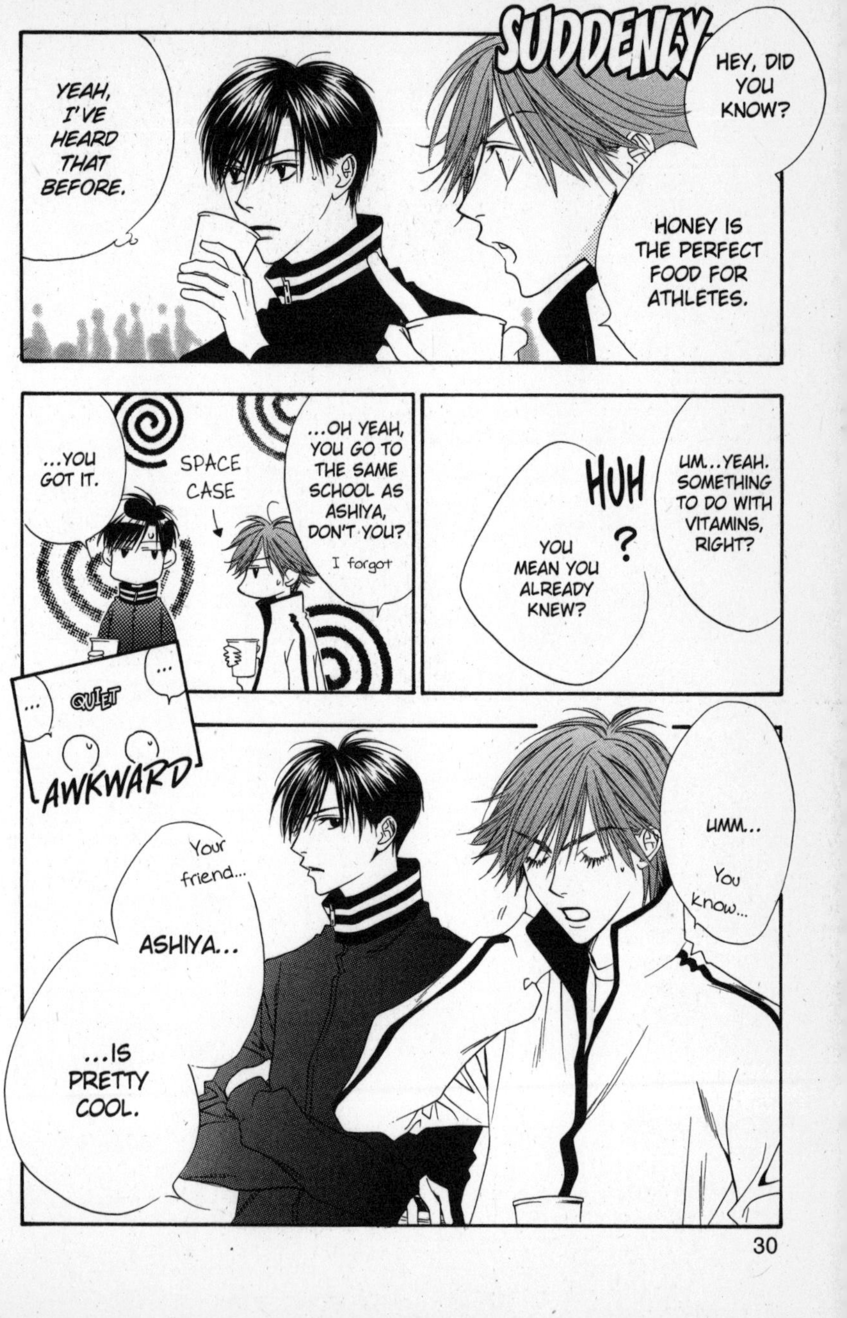
SUDDENLY
HEY, DID YOU KNOW?
HONEY IS THE PERFECT FOOD FOR ATHLETES.
YEAH, I'VE HEARD THAT BEFORE.
UM...YEAH. SOMETHING TO DO WITH VITAMINS, RIGHT?
HUH
?
YOU MEAN YOU ALREADY KNEW?
...OH YEAH, YOU GO TO THE SAME SCHOOL AS ASHIYA, DON'T YOU?
I forgot
SPACE CASE
...YOU GOT IT.
...
...
QUIET
AWKWARD
UMM...
You know...
Your friend...
ASHIYA...
...IS PRETTY COOL.

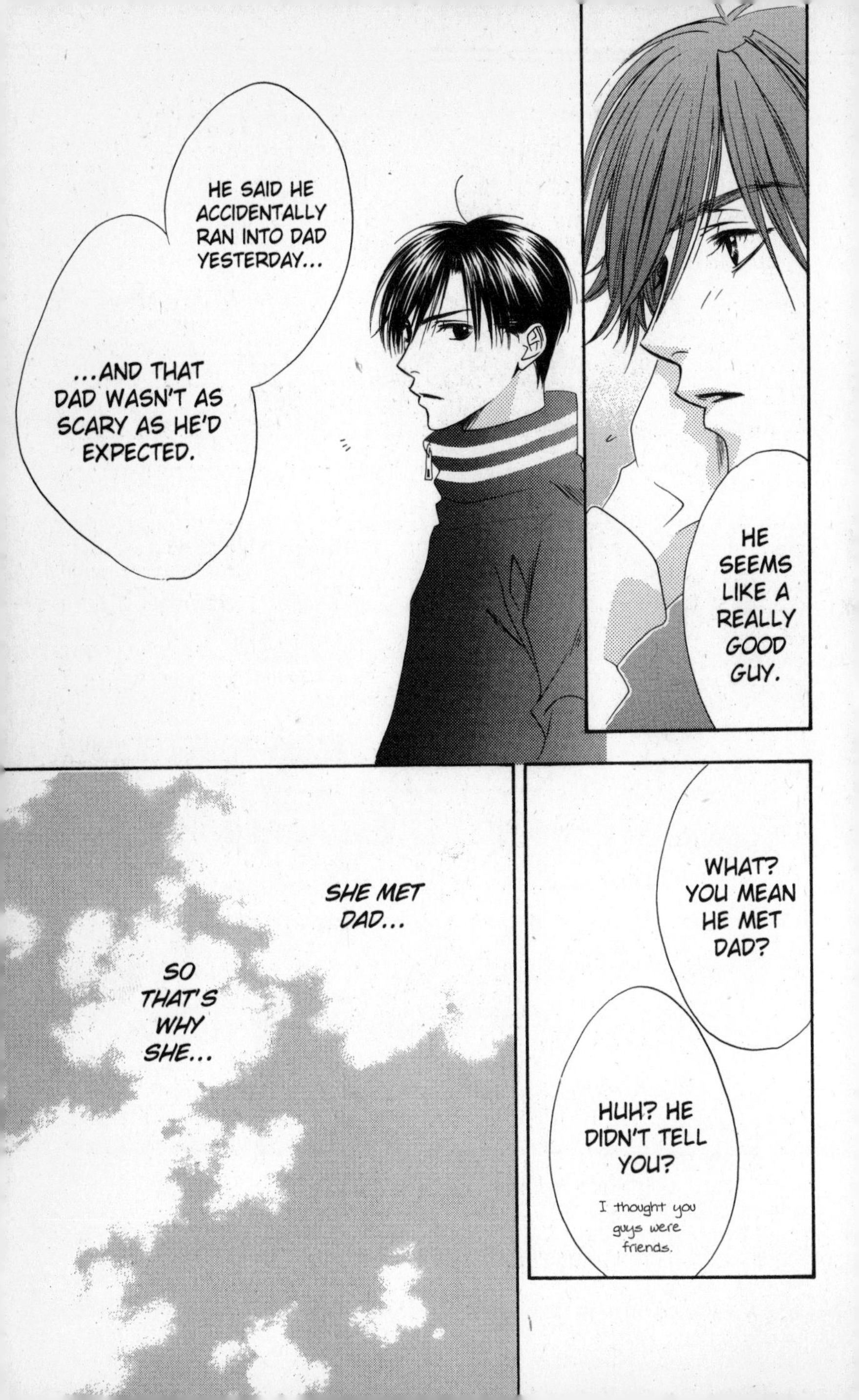
HE SEEMS LIKE A REALLY GOOD GUY.
HE SAID HE ACCIDENTALLY RAN INTO DAD YESTERDAY...
...AND THAT DAD WASN'T AS SCARY AS HE'D EXPECTED.
WHAT? YOU MEAN HE MET DAD?
HUH? HE DIDN'T TELL YOU?
I thought you guys were friends.
SHE MET DAD...
SO THAT'S WHY SHE...

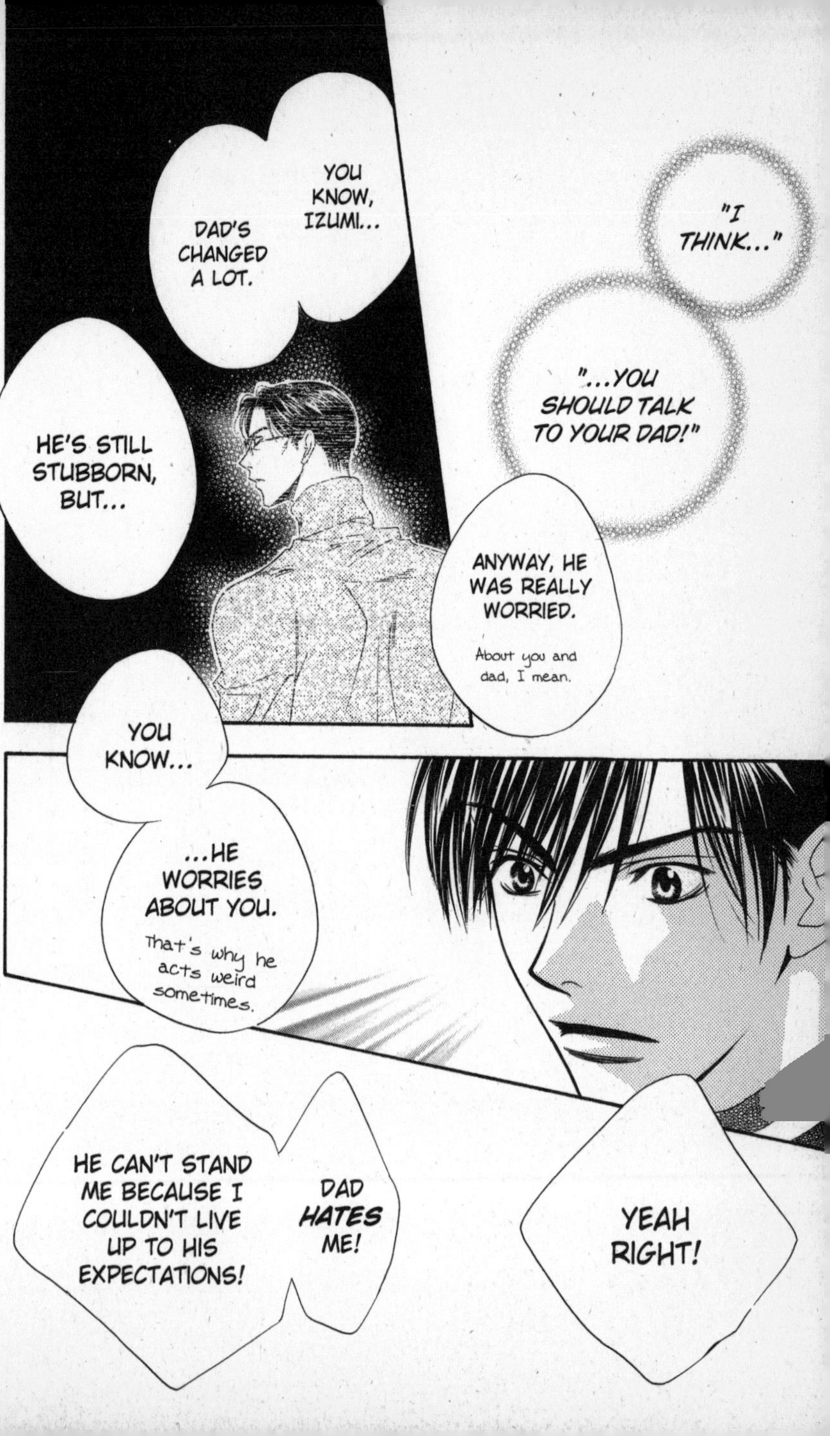
"I THINK..."
"...YOU SHOULD TALK TO YOUR DAD!"
YOU KNOW, IZUMI...
DAD'S CHANGED A LOT.
HE'S STILL STUBBORN, BUT...
ANYWAY, HE WAS REALLY WORRIED.
About you and dad, I mean.
YOU KNOW...
...HE WORRIES ABOUT YOU.
That's why he acts weird sometimes.
YEAH RIGHT!
DAD HATES ME!
HE CAN'T STAND ME BECAUSE I COULDN'T LIVE UP TO HIS EXPECTATIONS!

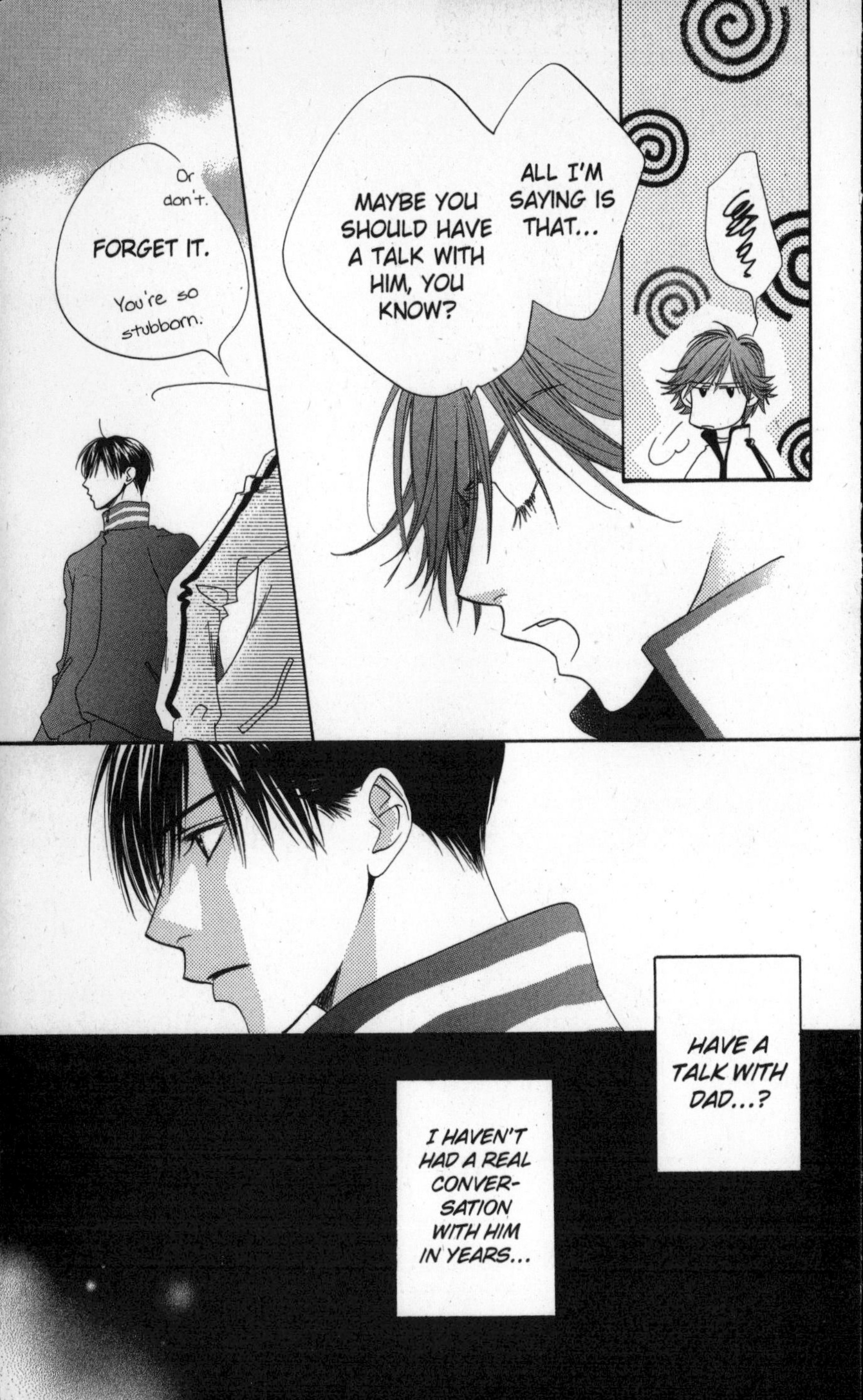
ALL I'M SAYING IS THAT...
MAYBE YOU SHOULD HAVE A TALK WITH HIM, YOU KNOW?
Or don't.
FORGET IT.
You're so stubborn.
HAVE A TALK WITH DAD...?
I HAVEN'T HAD A REAL CONVER-SATION WITH HIM IN YEARS...

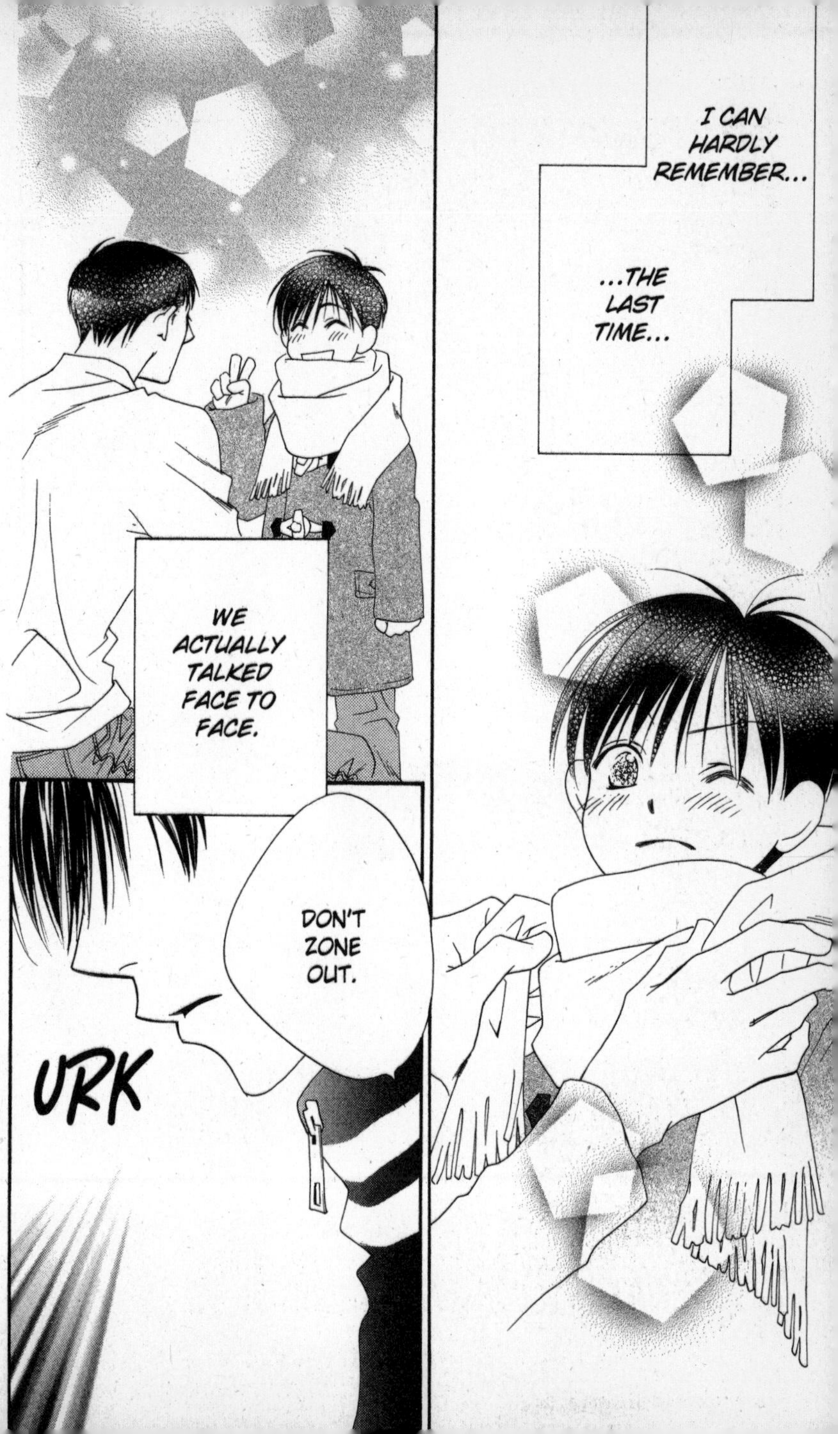
I CAN HARDLY REMEMBER...
...THE LAST TIME...
WE ACTUALLY TALKED FACE TO FACE.
DON'T ZONE OUT.
URK

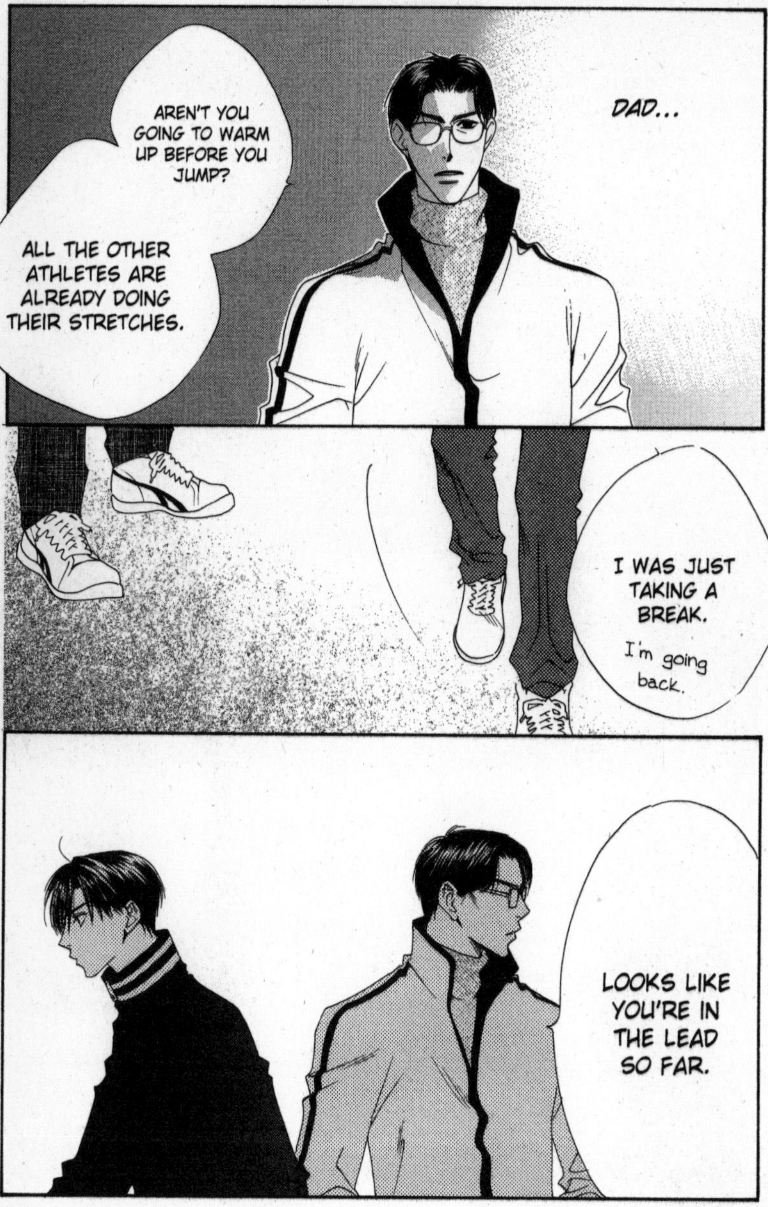
DAD...
AREN'T YOU GOING TO WARM UP BEFORE YOU JUMP?
ALL THE OTHER ATHLETES ARE ALREADY DOING THEIR STRETCHES.
I WAS JUST TAKING A BREAK.
I'm going back.
LOOKS LIKE YOU'RE IN THE LEAD SO FAR.

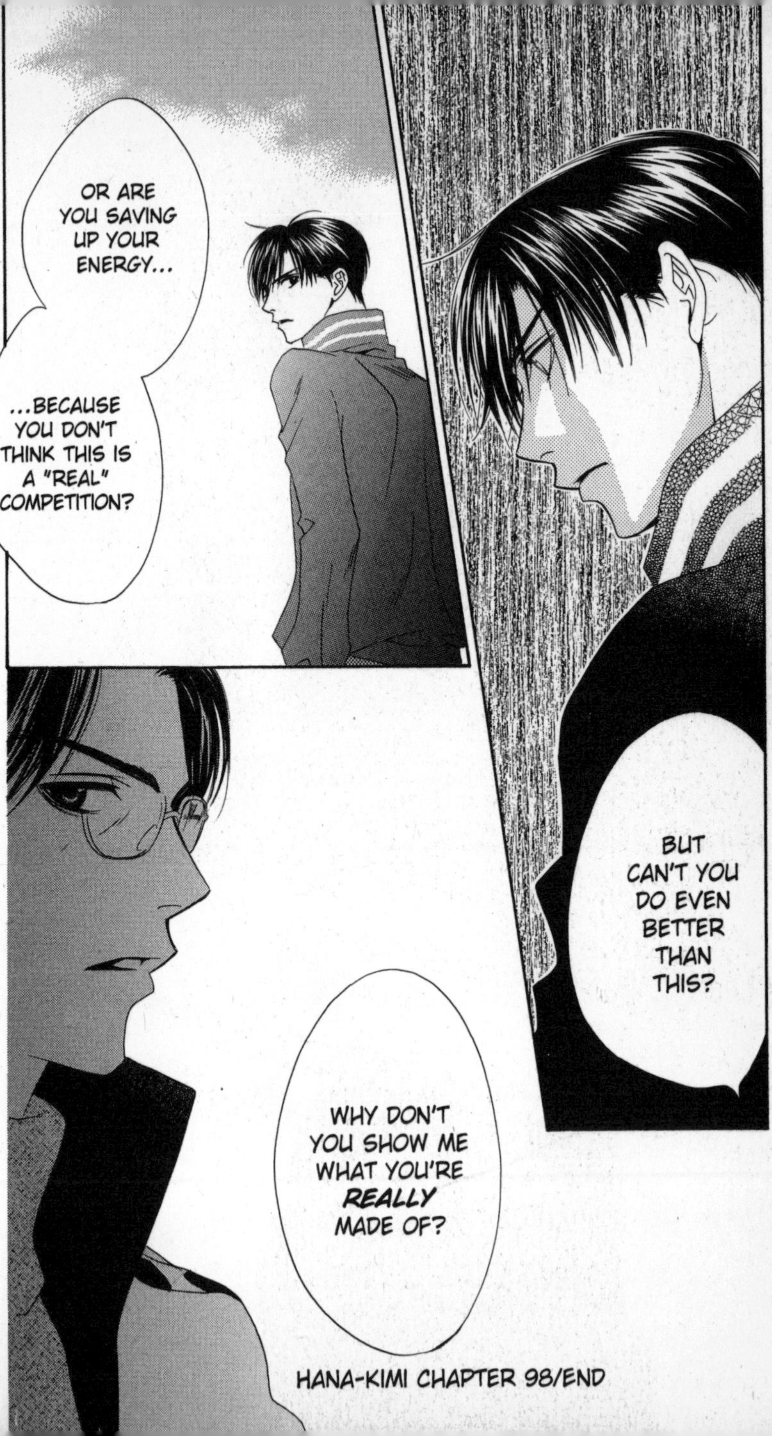
OR ARE YOU SAVING UP YOUR ENERGY...
...BECAUSE YOU DON'T THINK THIS IS A "REAL" COMPETITION?
BUT CAN'T YOU DO EVEN BETTER THAN THIS?
WHY DON'T YOU SHOW ME WHAT YOU'RE *REALLY* MADE OF?
HANA-KIMI CHAPTER 98/END

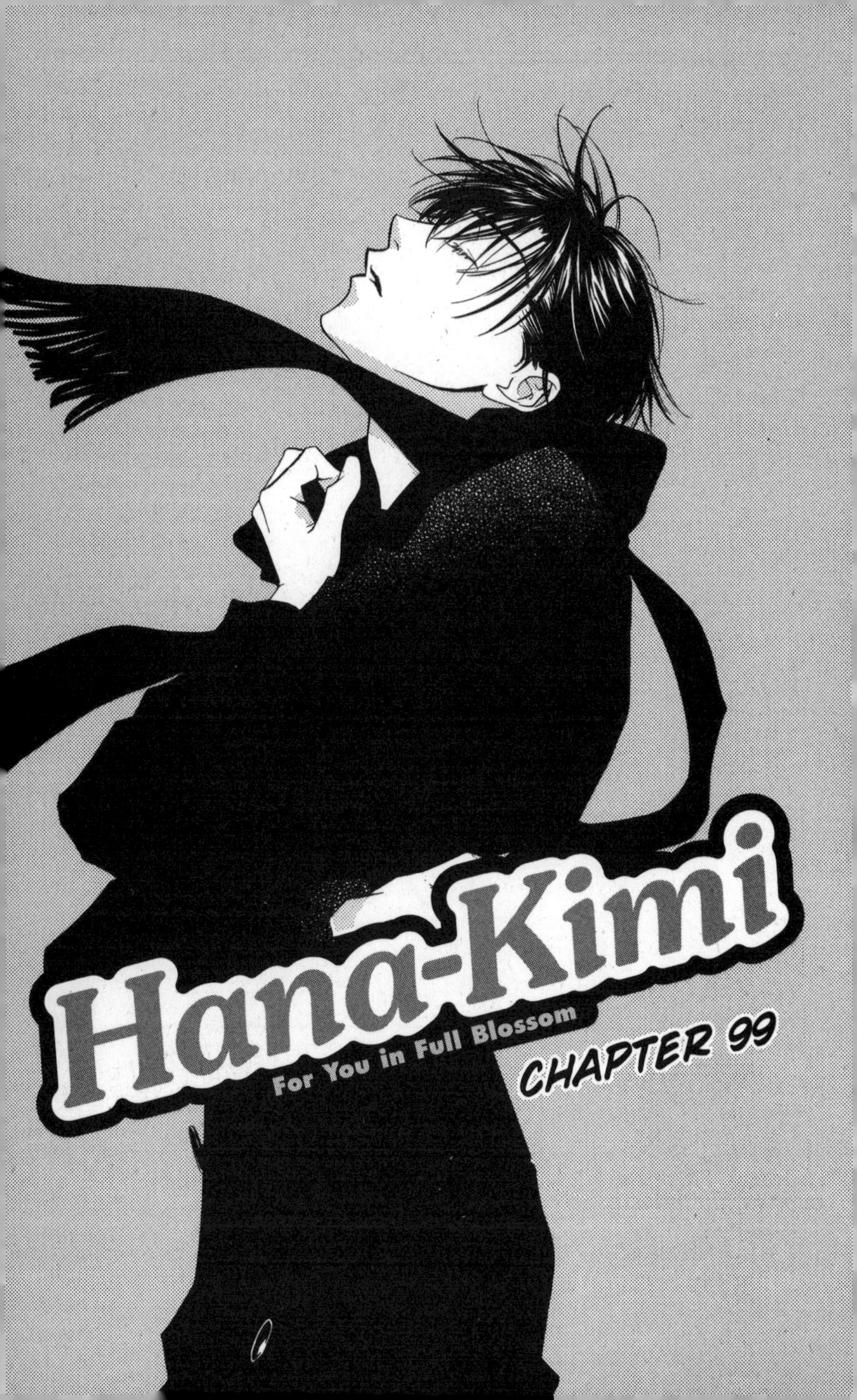
Hana-Kimi
For You in Full Blossom
CHAPTER 99

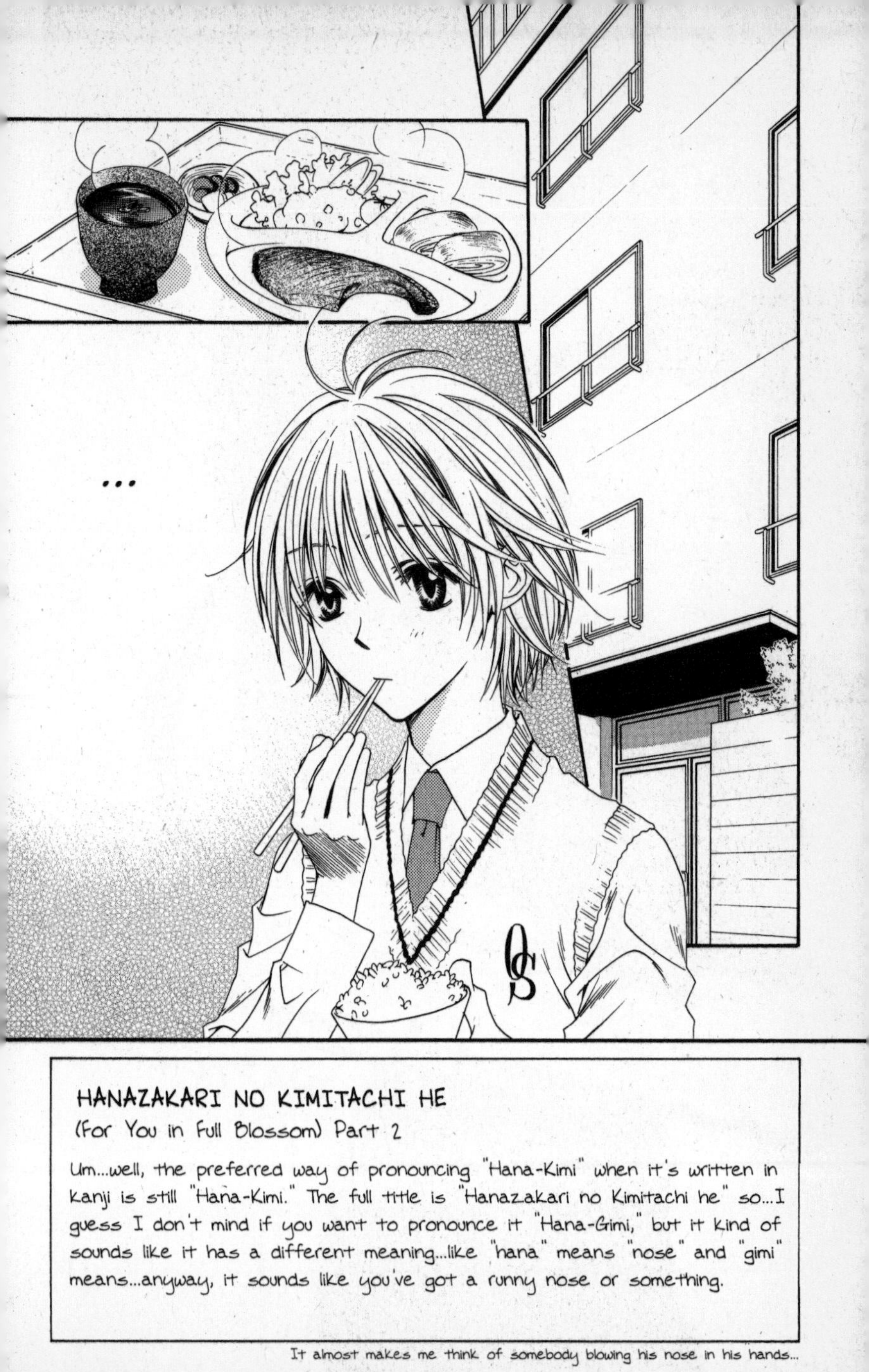
...

HANAZAKARI NO KIMITACHI HE

(For You in Full Blossom) Part 2

Um...well, the preferred way of pronouncing "Hana-Kimi" when it's written in kanji is still "Hana-Kimi." The full title is "Hanazakari no Kimitachi he" so...I guess I don't mind if you want to pronounce it "Hana-Gimi," but it kind of sounds like it has a different meaning...like "hana" means "nose" and "gimi" means...anyway, it sounds like you've got a runny nose or something.

It almost makes me think of somebody blowing his nose in his hands...

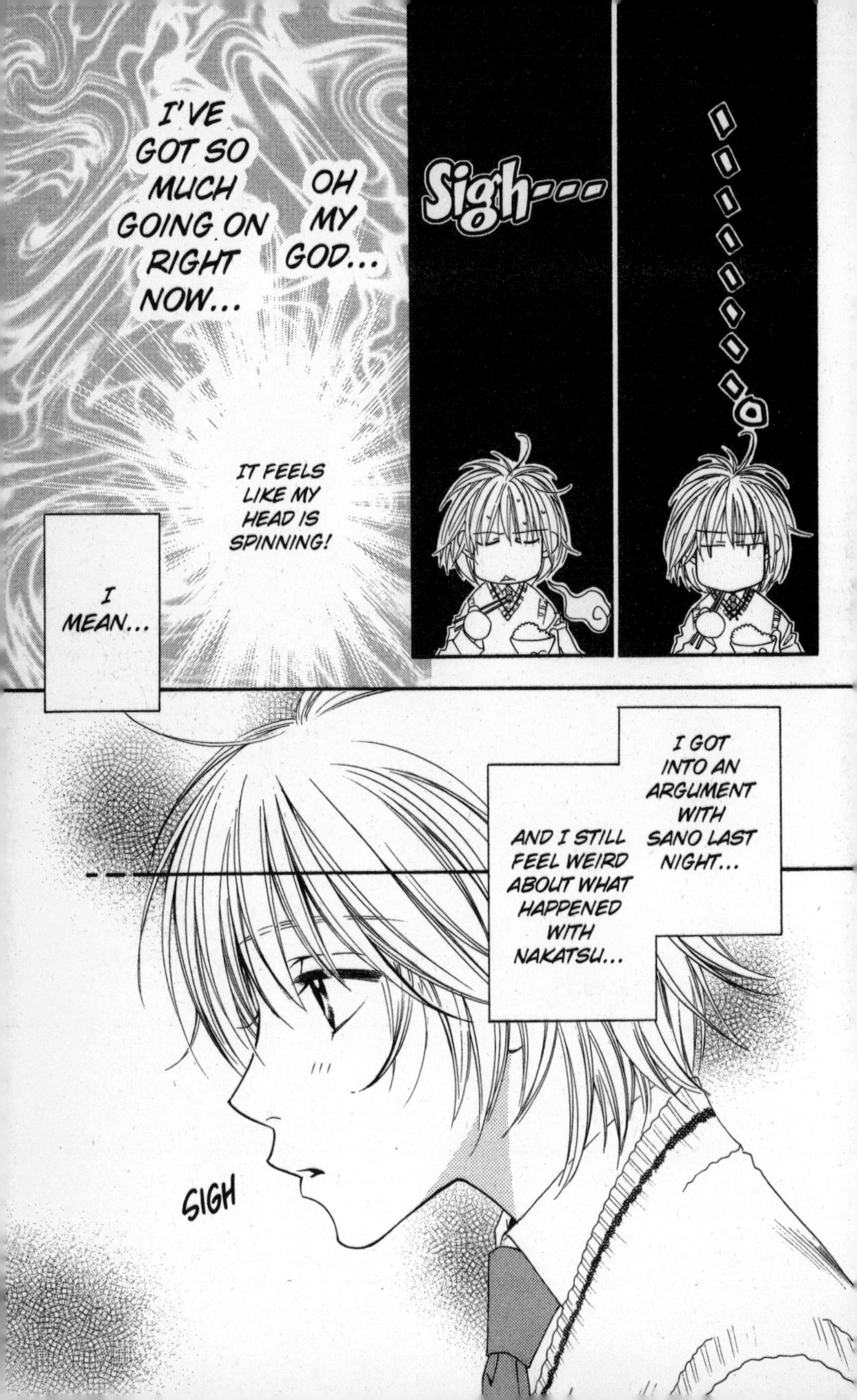

Sigh...
OH MY GOD...
I'VE GOT SO MUCH GOING ON RIGHT NOW...
IT FEELS LIKE MY HEAD IS SPINNING!
I MEAN...
I GOT INTO AN ARGUMENT WITH SANO LAST NIGHT...
AND I STILL FEEL WEIRD ABOUT WHAT HAPPENED WITH NAKATSU...
SIGH

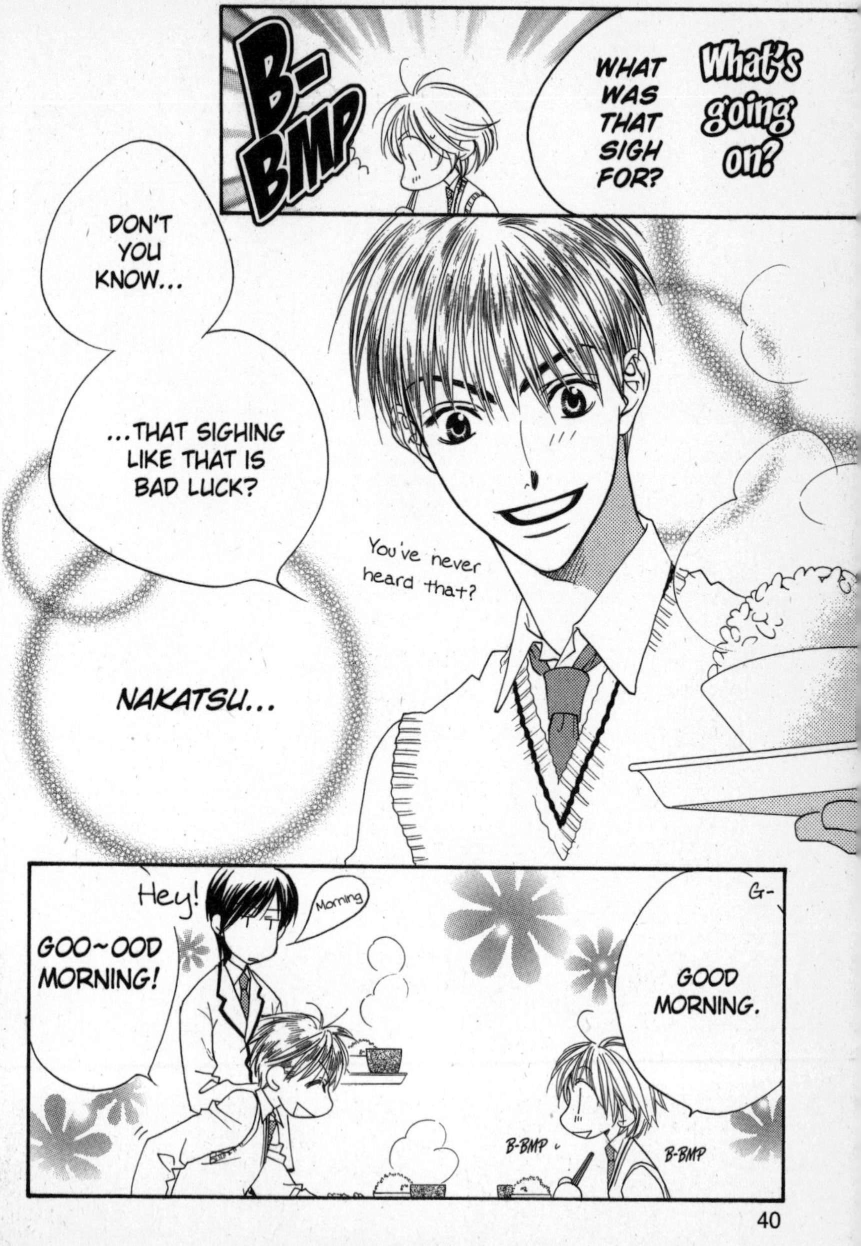

What's going on?
WHAT WAS THAT SIGH FOR?
B-BMP
DON'T YOU KNOW...
...THAT SIGHING LIKE THAT IS BAD LUCK?
You've never heard that?
NAKATSU...
G- GOOD MORNING.
B-BMP
B-BMP
Morning
Hey!
GOO~OOD MORNING!

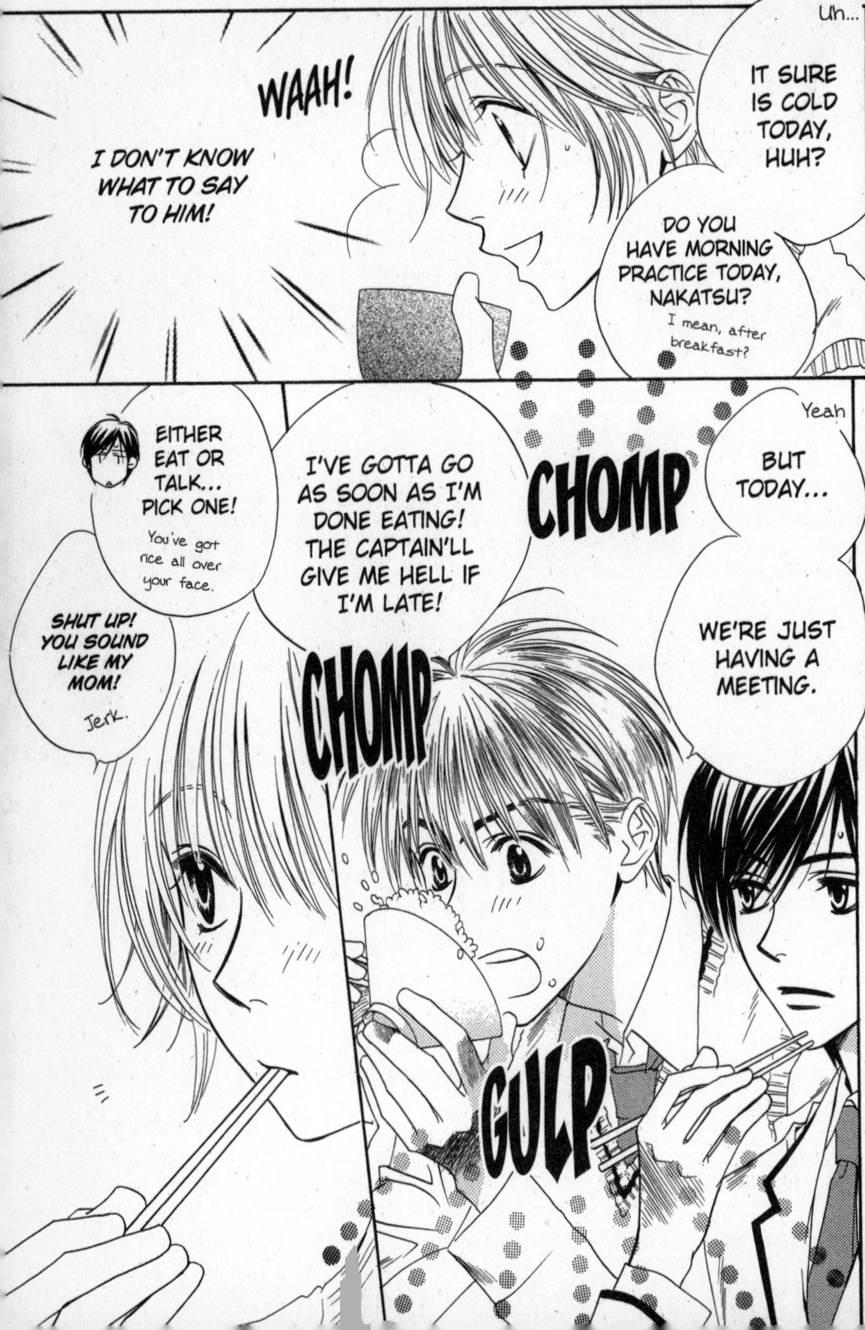
Uh...
IT SURE IS COLD TODAY, HUH?
DO YOU HAVE MORNING PRACTICE TODAY, NAKATSU?
I mean, after breakfast?
WAAH!
I DON'T KNOW WHAT TO SAY TO HIM!
Yeah
BUT TODAY...
WE'RE JUST HAVING A MEETING.
CHOMP
I'VE GOTTA GO AS SOON AS I'M DONE EATING! THE CAPTAIN'LL GIVE ME HELL IF I'M LATE!
CHOMP
GULP
EITHER EAT OR TALK... PICK ONE!
You've got rice all over your face.
SHUT UP! YOU SOUND LIKE MY MOM!
Jerk.

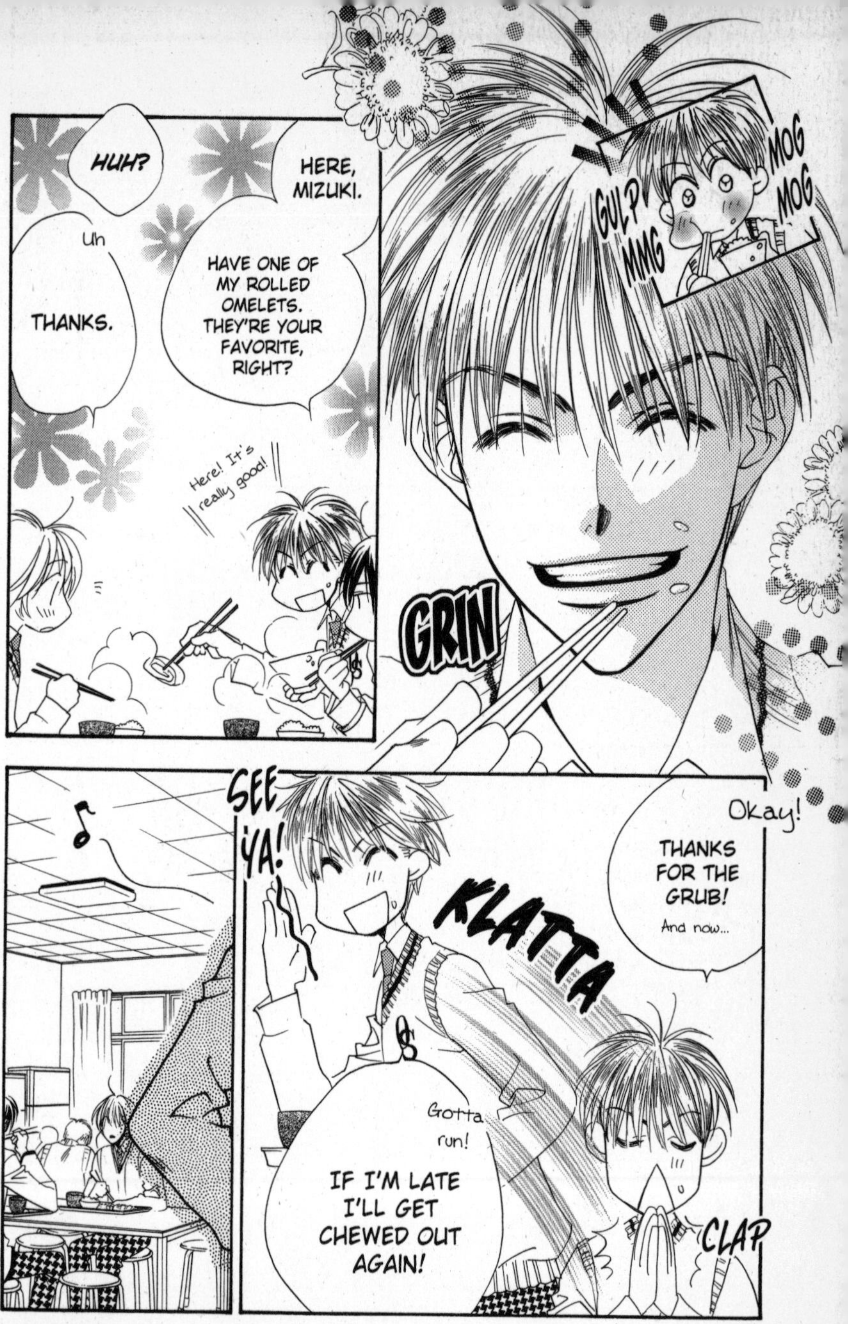
MOG MOG
GULP MMG
GRIN
HERE, MIZUKI.
HAVE ONE OF MY ROLLED OMELETS. THEY'RE YOUR FAVORITE, RIGHT?
HUH?
Uh
THANKS.
Here! It's really good!
Okay!
THANKS FOR THE GRUB!
And now...
KLATTA
CLAP
SEE YA!
Gotta run!
IF I'M LATE I'LL GET CHEWED OUT AGAIN!

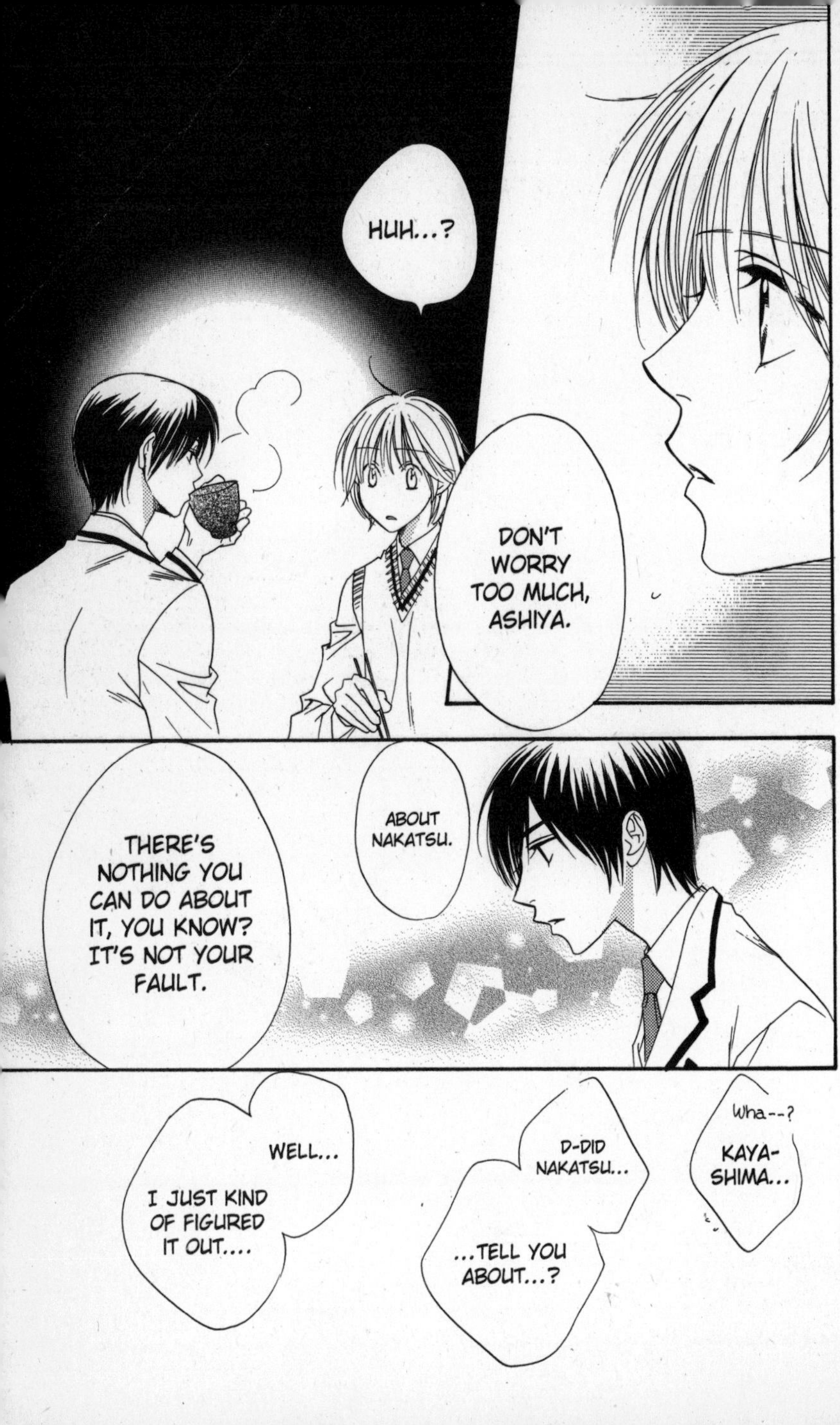
DON'T WORRY TOO MUCH, ASHIYA.
HUH...?
ABOUT NAKATSU.
THERE'S NOTHING YOU CAN DO ABOUT IT, YOU KNOW? IT'S NOT YOUR FAULT.
Wha--?
KAYA-SHIMA...
D-DID NAKATSU...
...TELL YOU ABOUT...?
WELL...
I JUST KIND OF FIGURED IT OUT....

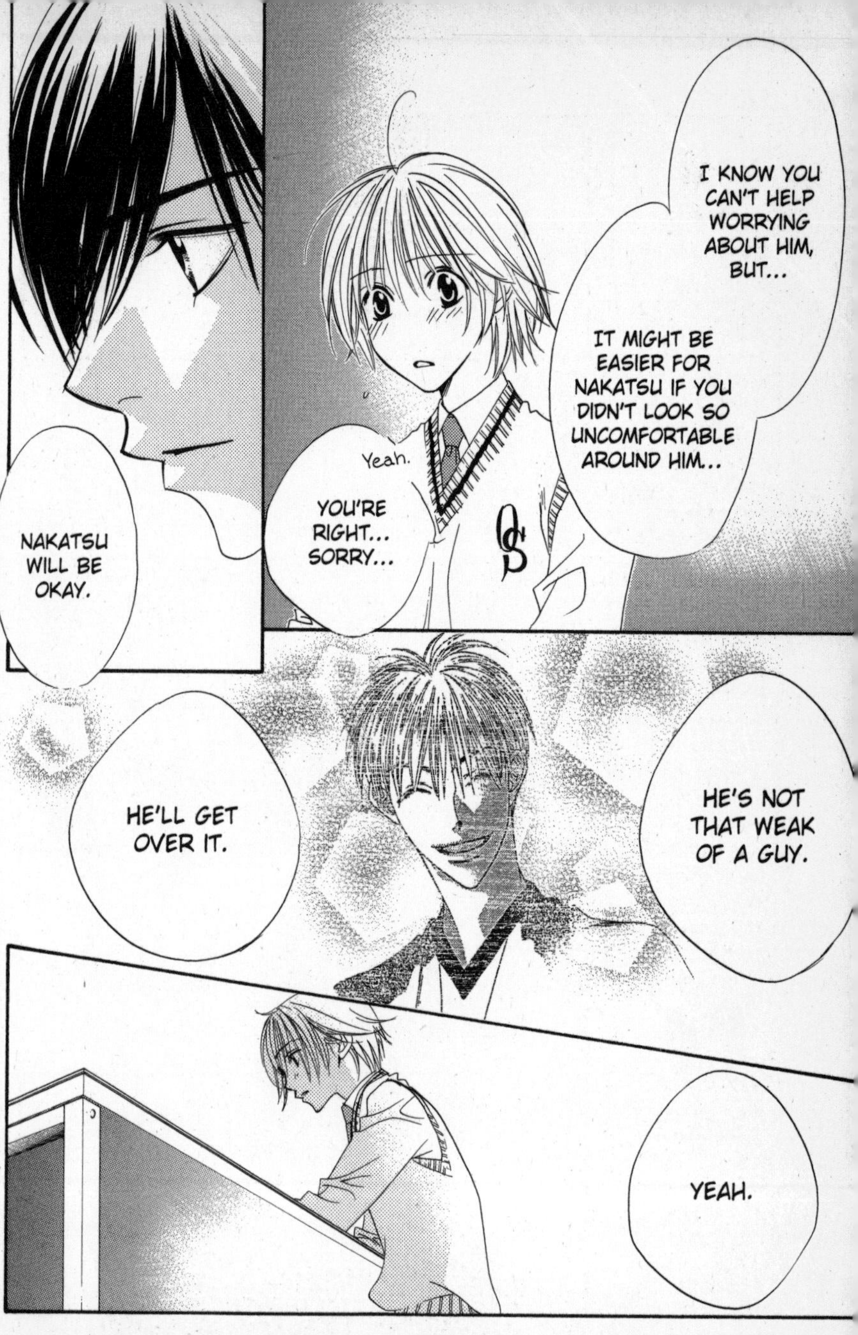
I KNOW YOU CAN'T HELP WORRYING ABOUT HIM, BUT...
IT MIGHT BE EASIER FOR NAKATSU IF YOU DIDN'T LOOK SO UNCOMFORTABLE AROUND HIM...
Yeah.
YOU'RE RIGHT... SORRY...
NAKATSU WILL BE OKAY.
HE'S NOT THAT WEAK OF A GUY.
HE'LL GET OVER IT.
YEAH.

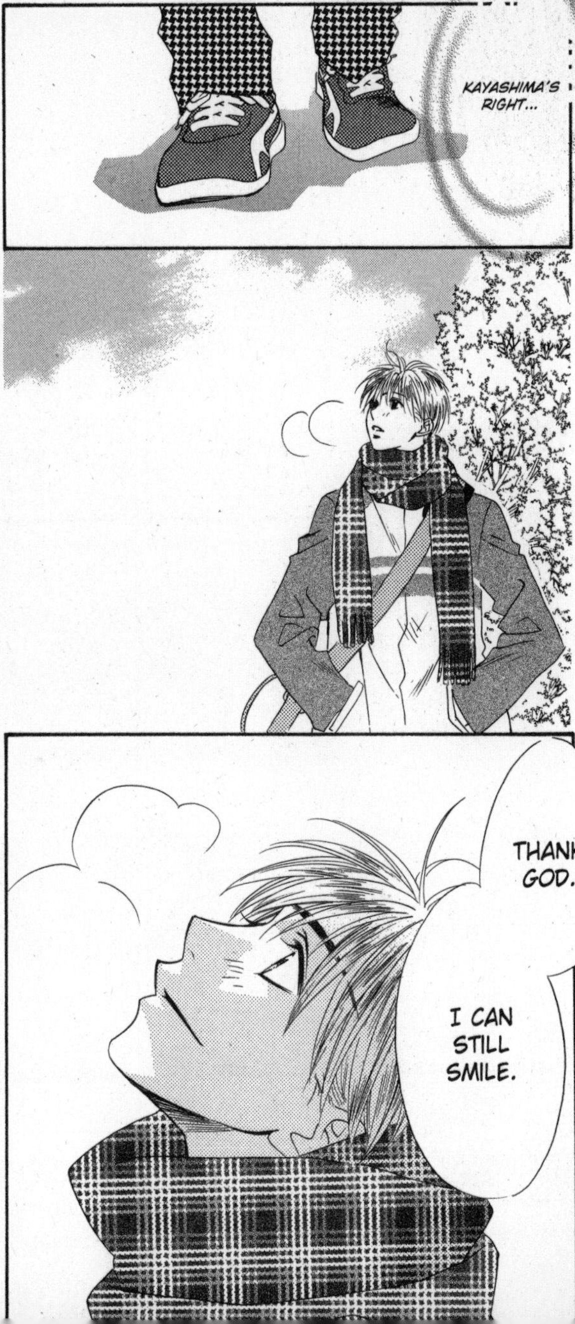
KAYASHIMA'S RIGHT...
THANK GOD.
I CAN STILL SMILE.

Scent

Okay, here it goes...I kind of like smelling cat's paws. While my two cats are sleeping, sometimes I like to touch their paws (they're so soft), and that's when I sniff them! It's not like they stink or anything, but they do have a very distinctive smell, and I'm kind of addicted to it. I wash their paws often so that they won't stink. I saw something on TV about how smelling is part of human nature, and we smell things to protect our bodily functions... so I guess I will follow my instincts and keep smelling their paws.

I only smell my own cats. Not other people's.

I don't want them to stink or anything...

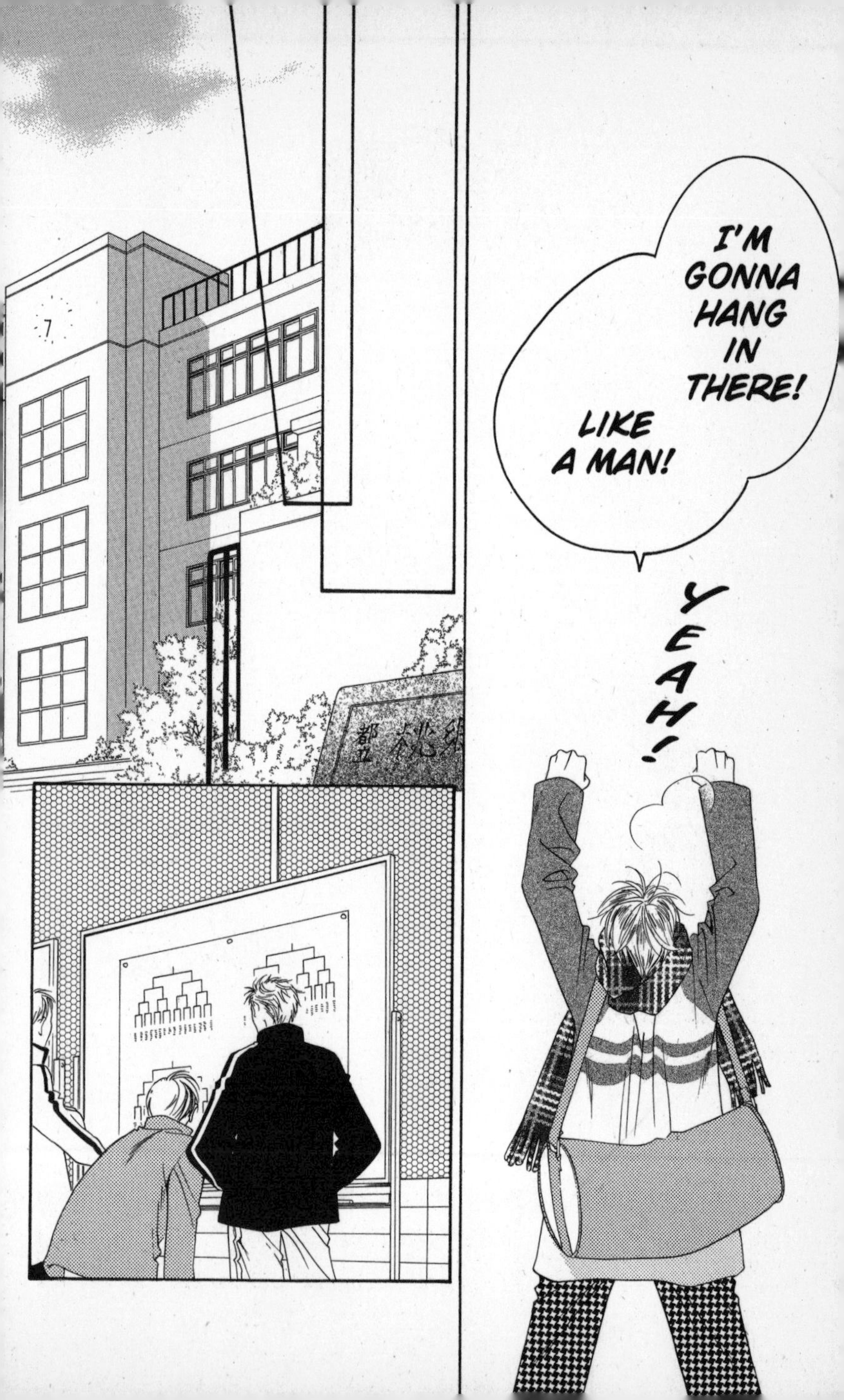
I'M GONNA HANG IN THERE! LIKE A MAN!
YEAH!

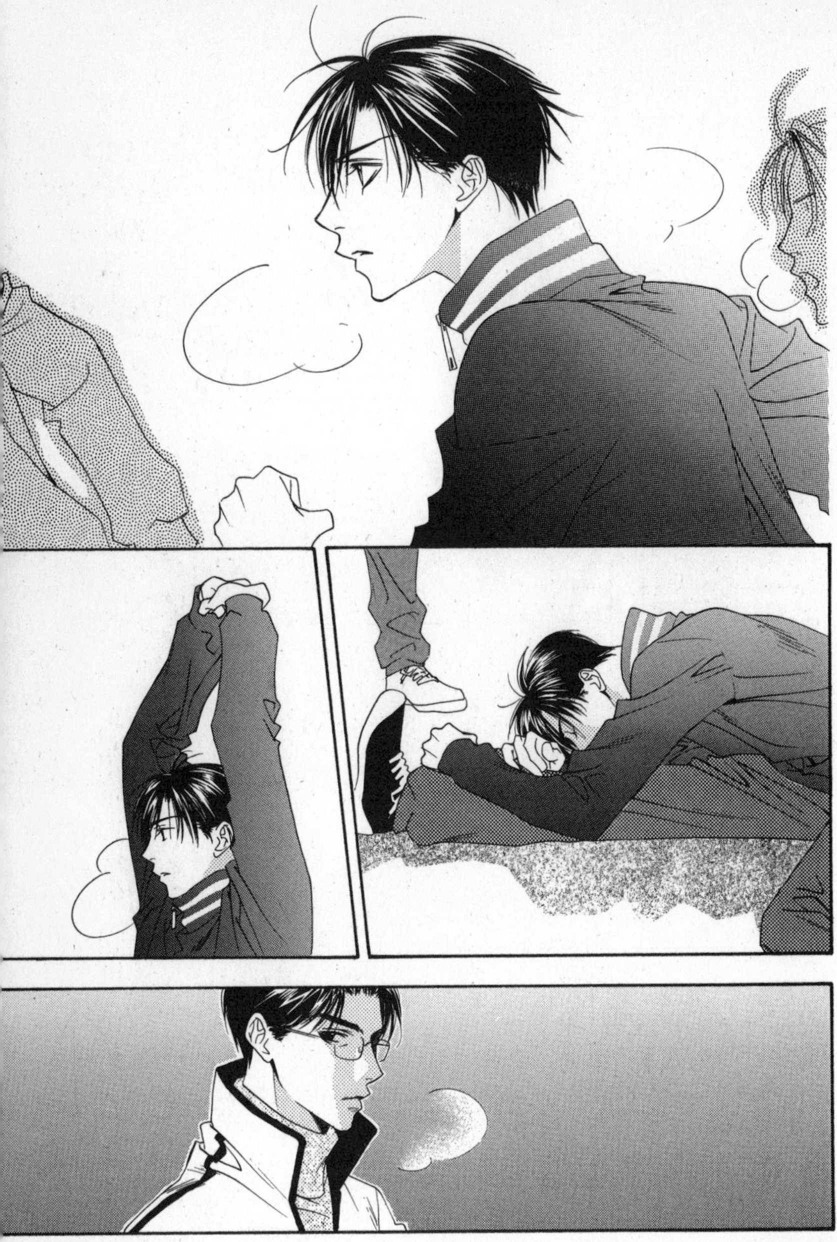

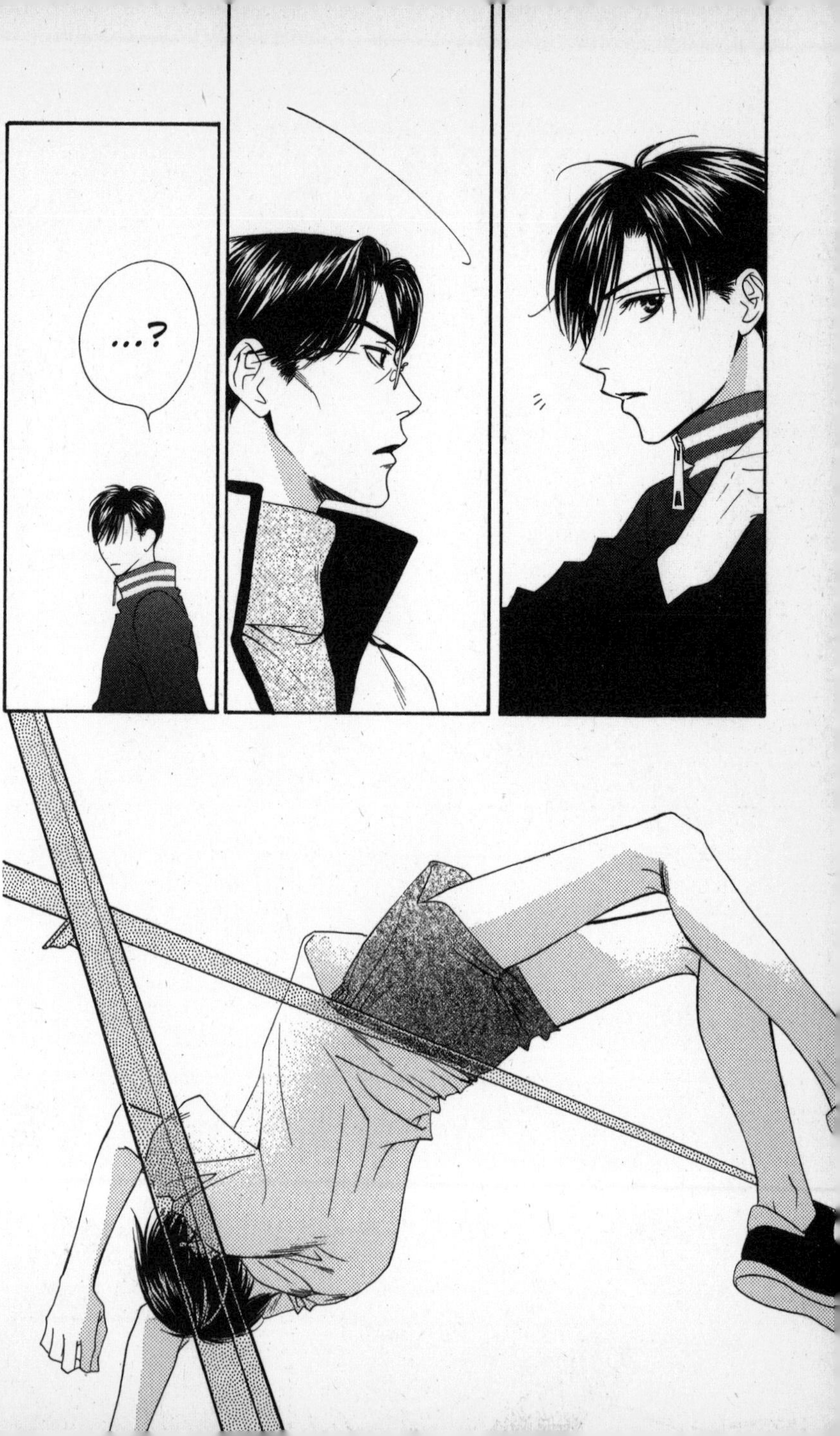
...?

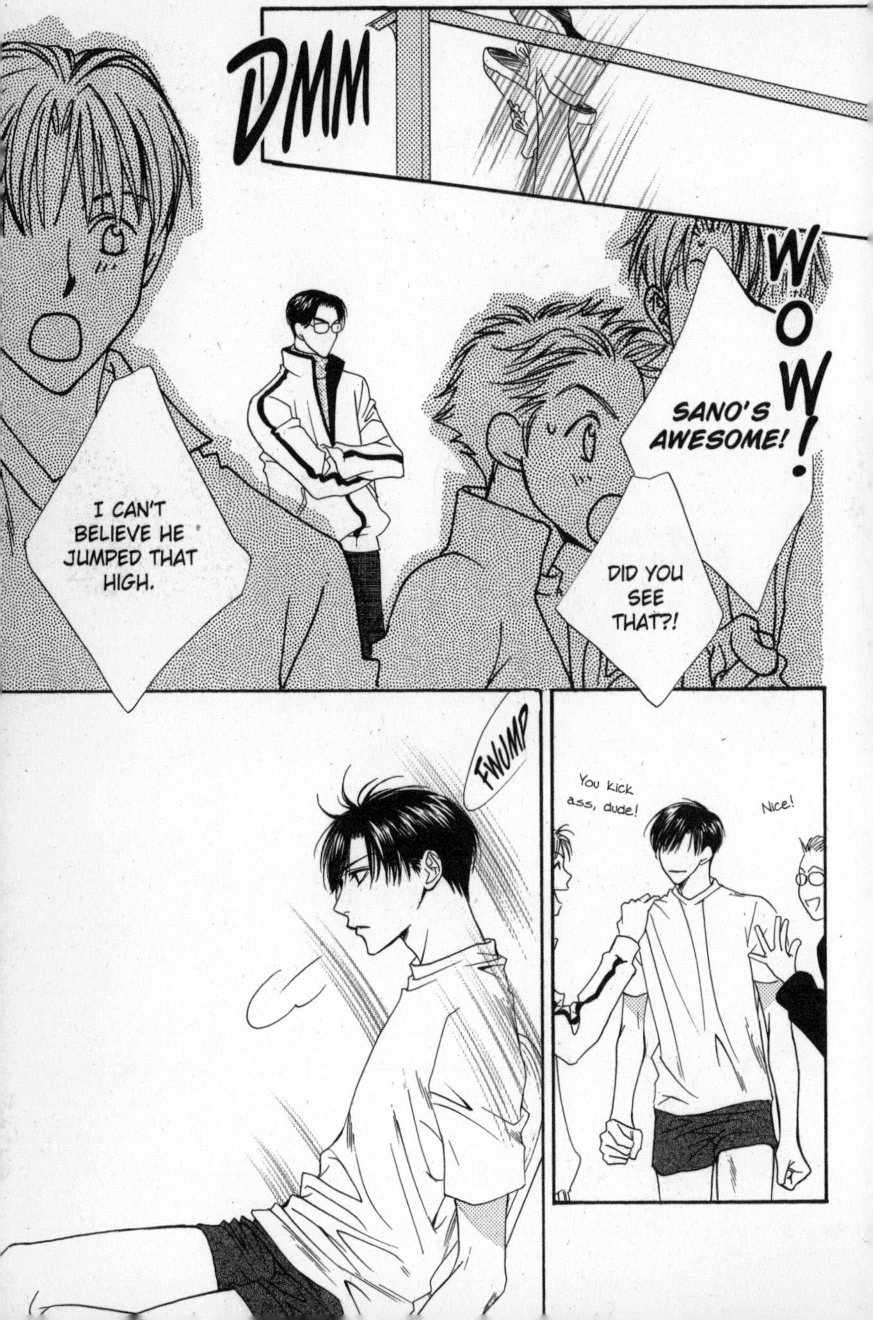
DMM
WOW!
SANO'S AWESOME!
DID YOU SEE THAT?!
I CAN'T BELIEVE HE JUMPED THAT HIGH.
Nice!
You kick ass, dude!
FWUMP

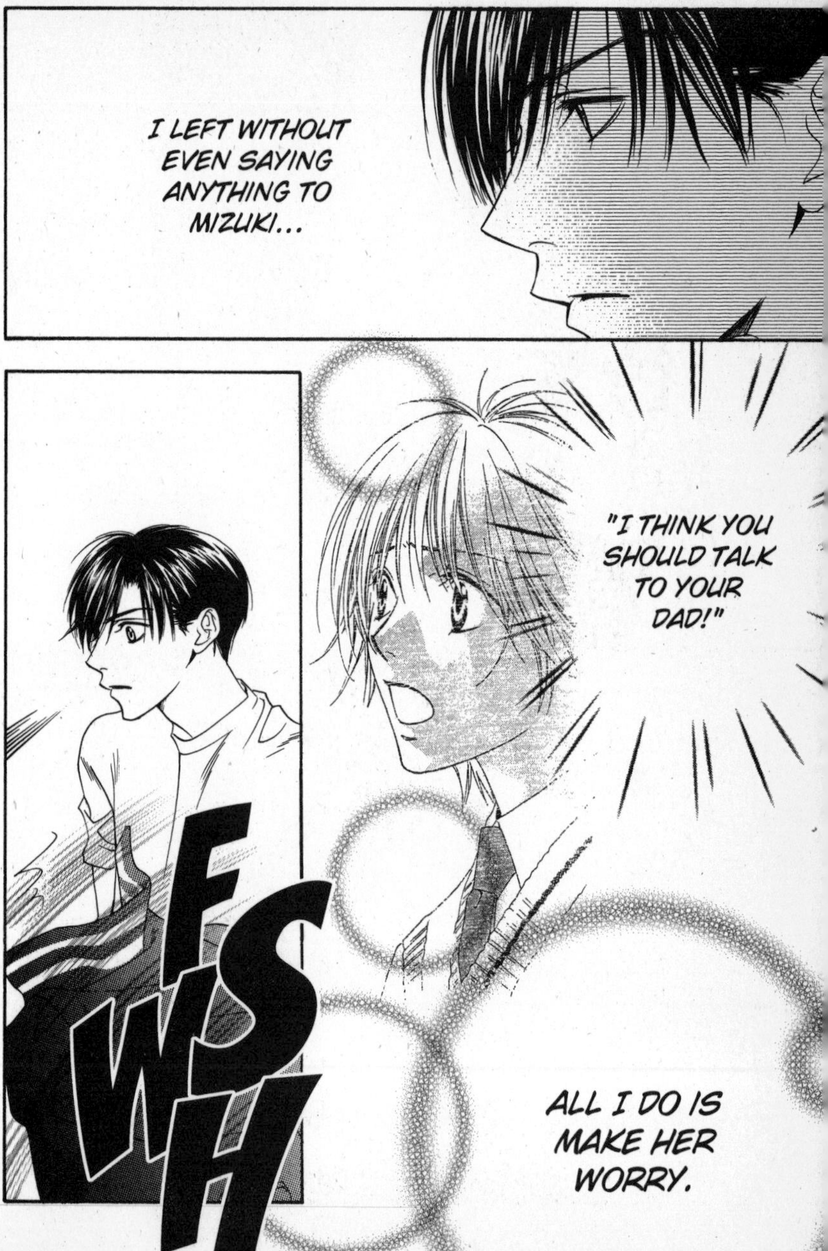
I LEFT WITHOUT EVEN SAYING ANYTHING TO MIZUKI...
"I THINK YOU SHOULD TALK TO YOUR DAD!"
ALL I DO IS MAKE HER WORRY.
FWSH

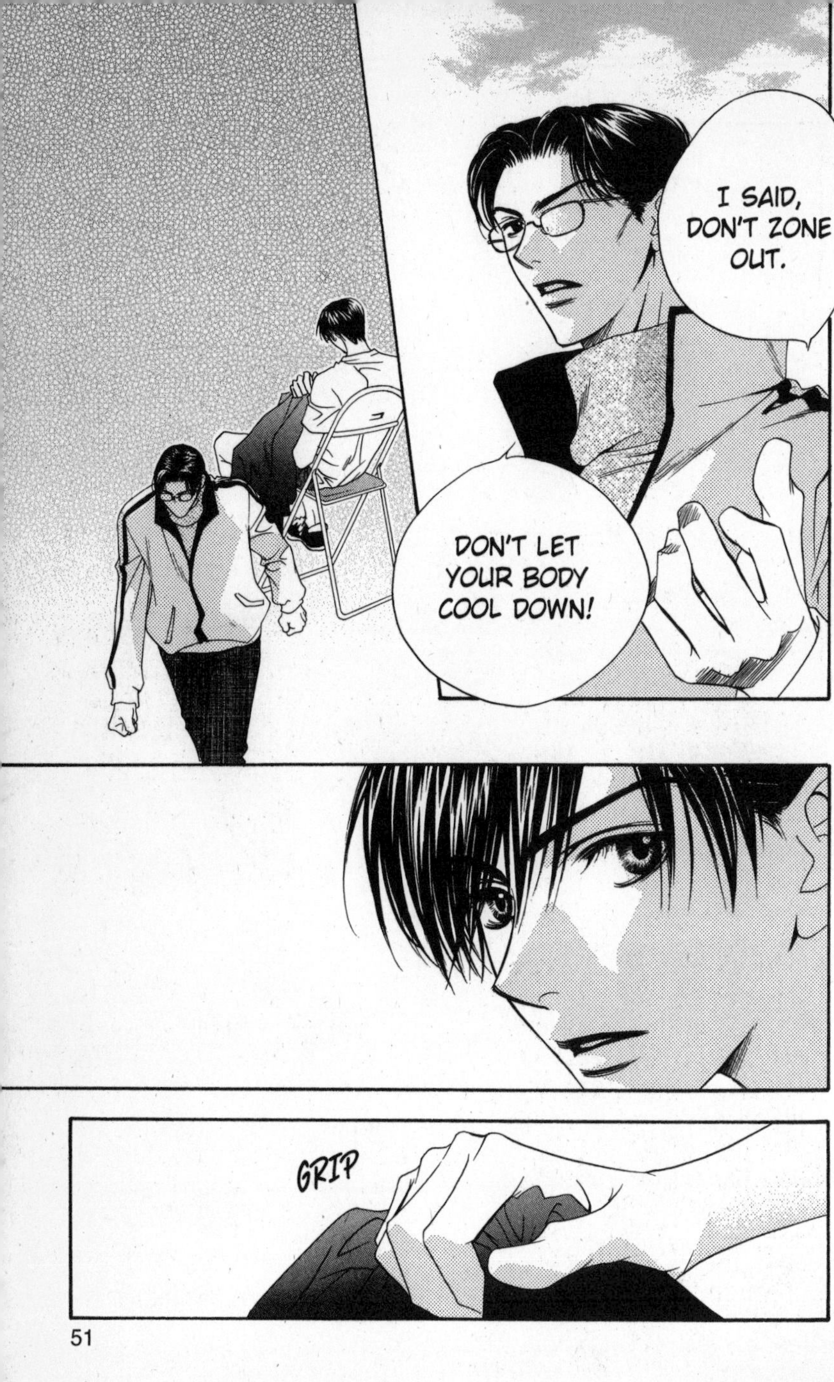
I SAID, DON'T ZONE OUT.
DON'T LET YOUR BODY COOL DOWN!
GRIP

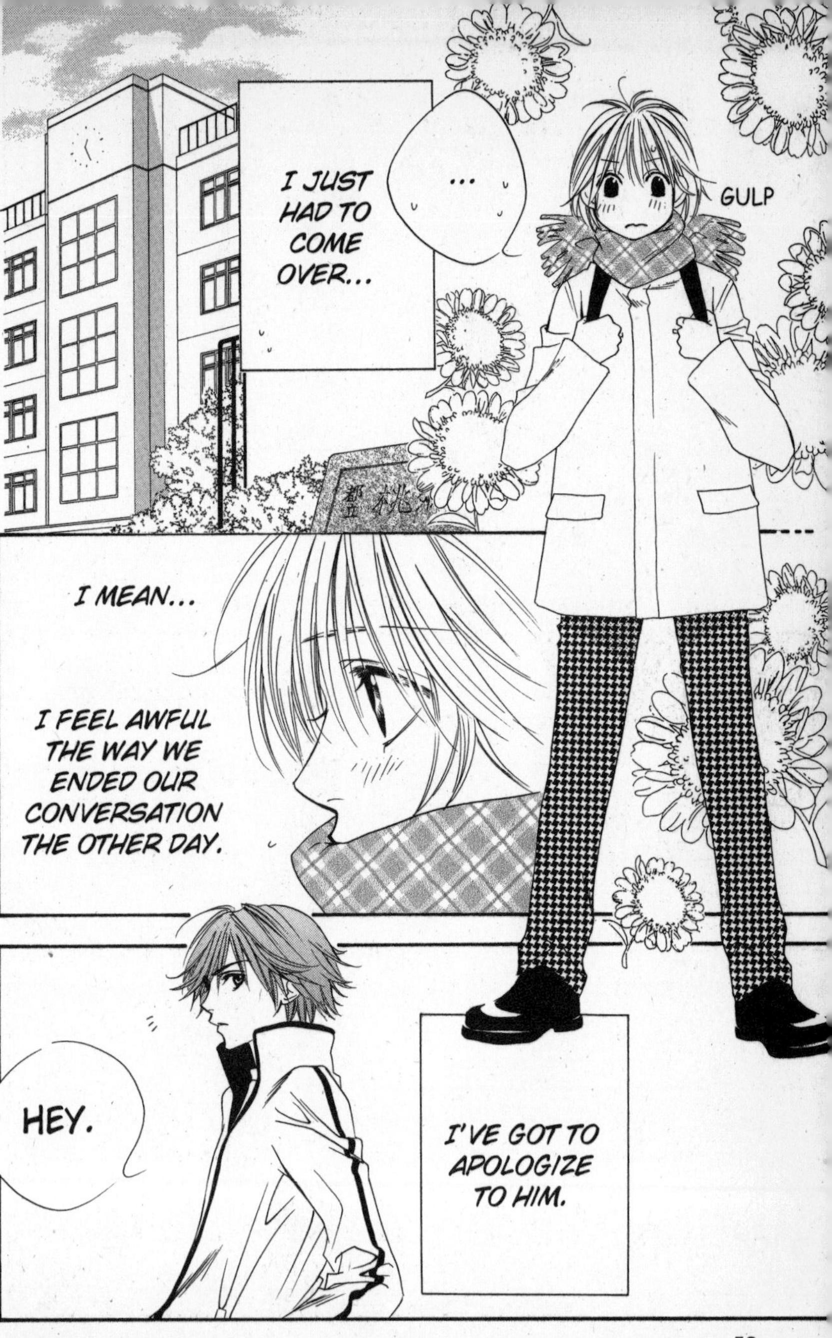
GULP
...
I JUST HAD TO COME OVER...
I MEAN...
I FEEL AWFUL THE WAY WE ENDED OUR CONVERSATION THE OTHER DAY.
I'VE GOT TO APOLOGIZE TO HIM.
HEY.

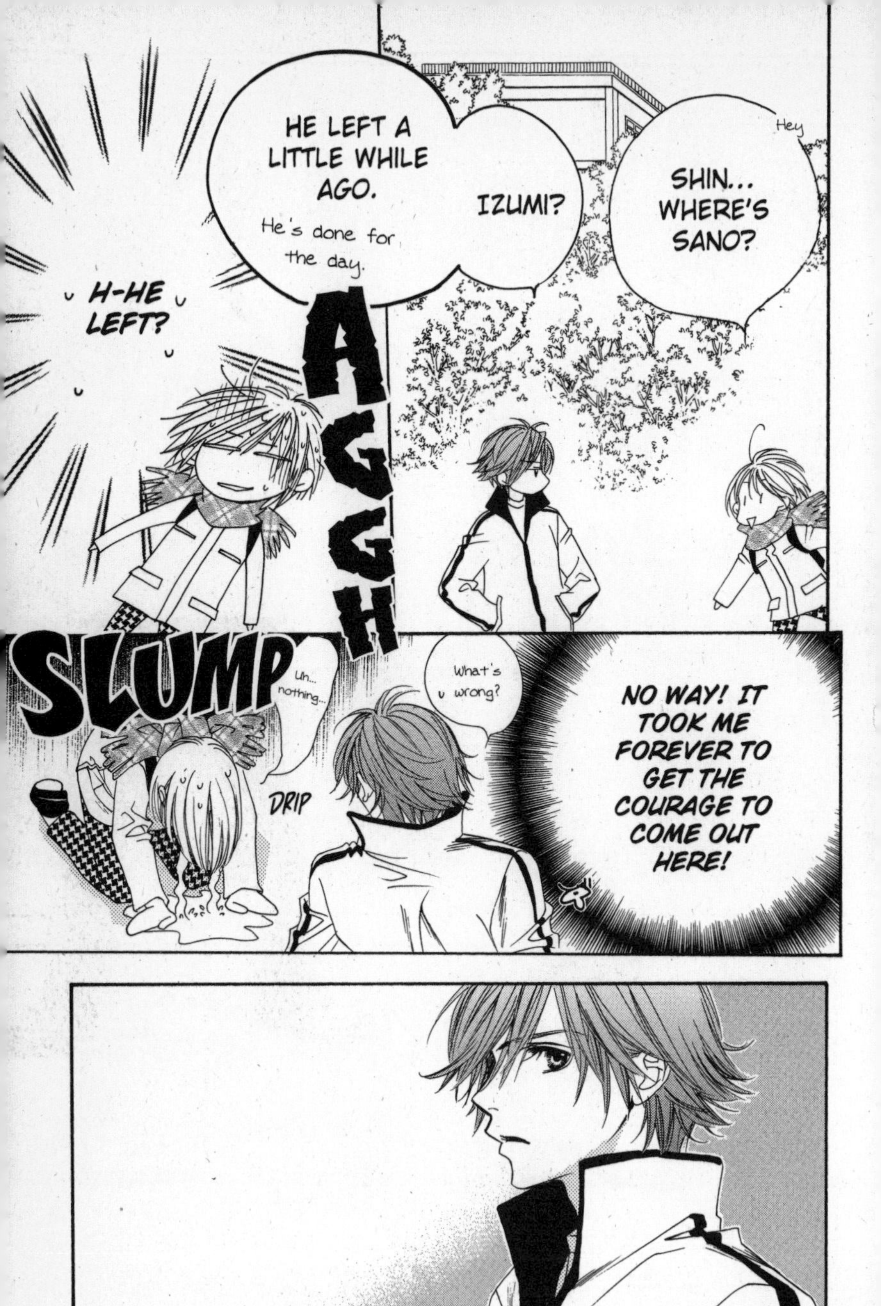
Hey
SHIN... WHERE'S SANO?
IZUMI?
HE LEFT A LITTLE WHILE AGO.
He's done for the day.
AGGH
H-HE LEFT?
NO WAY! IT TOOK ME FOREVER TO GET THE COURAGE TO COME OUT HERE!
What's wrong?
Uh... nothing...
SLUMP
DRIP

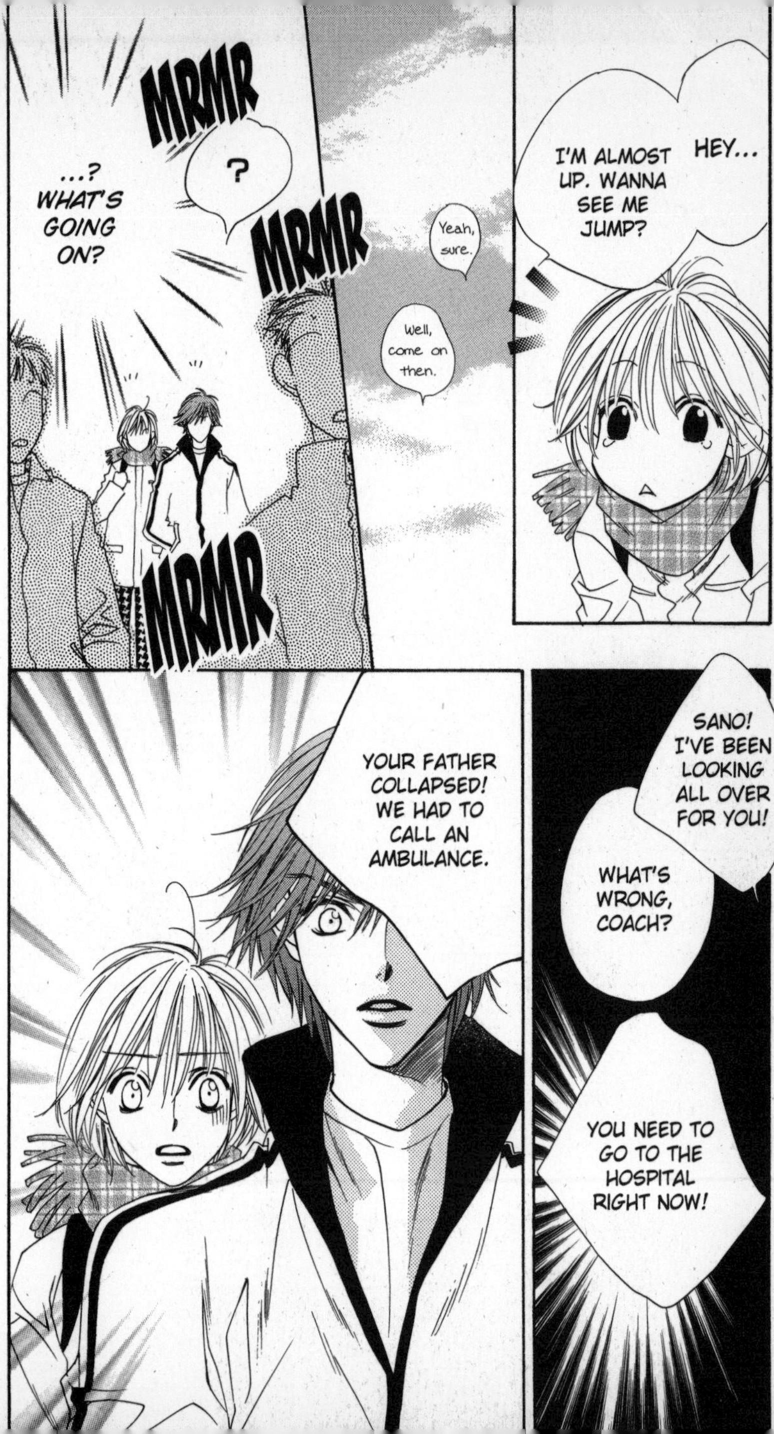
HEY...
I'M ALMOST UP. WANNA SEE ME JUMP?
Yeah, sure.
Well, come on then.
MRMR
?
MRMR
...? WHAT'S GOING ON?
MRMR
SANO! I'VE BEEN LOOKING ALL OVER FOR YOU!
WHAT'S WRONG, COACH?
YOU NEED TO GO TO THE HOSPITAL RIGHT NOW!
YOUR FATHER COLLAPSED! WE HAD TO CALL AN AMBULANCE.

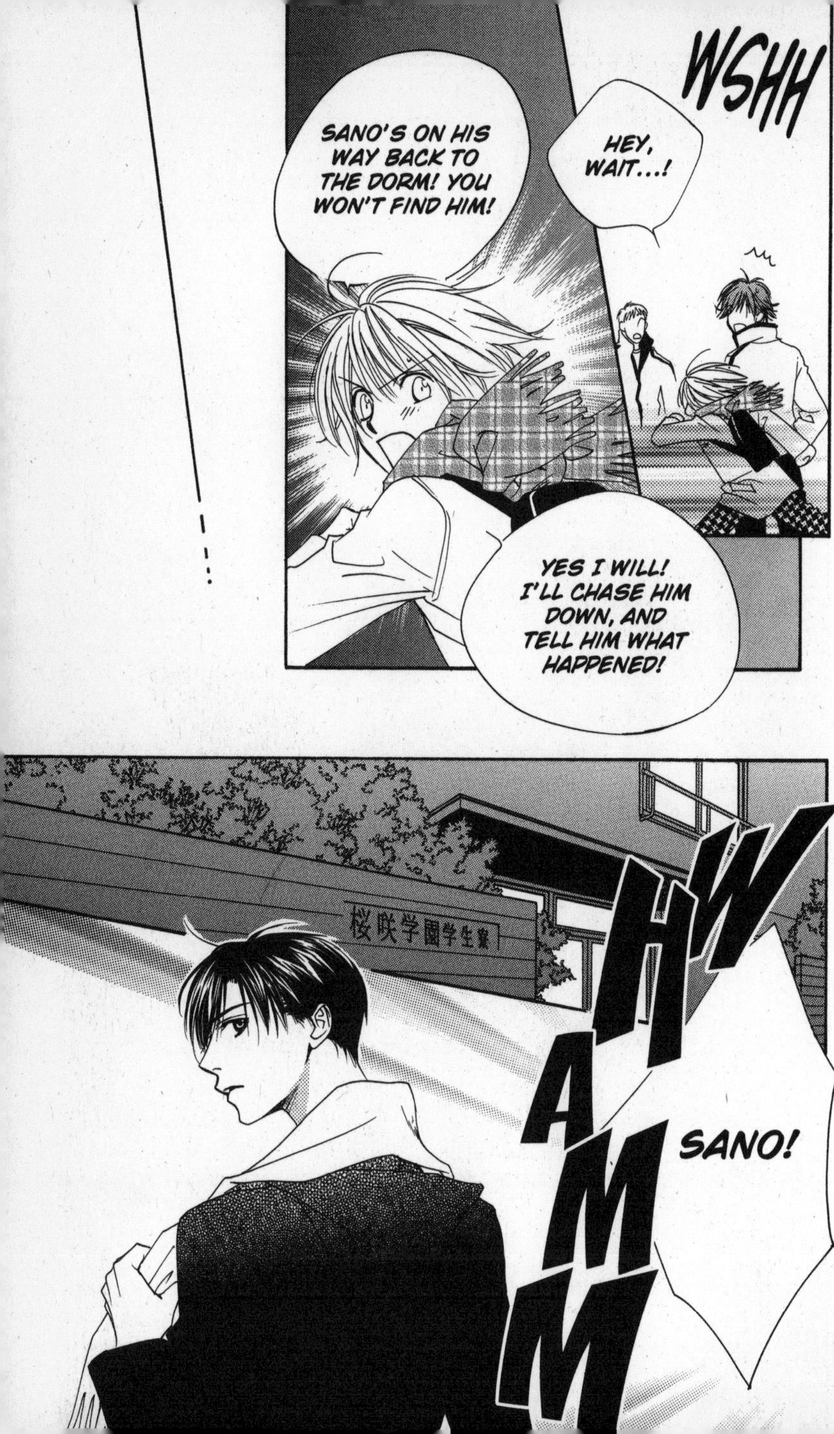
WSHH
HEY, WAIT...!
SANO'S ON HIS WAY BACK TO THE DORM! YOU WON'T FIND HIM!
YES I WILL! I'LL CHASE HIM DOWN, AND TELL HIM WHAT HAPPENED!
桜咲学園学生寮
WHAMM
SANO!

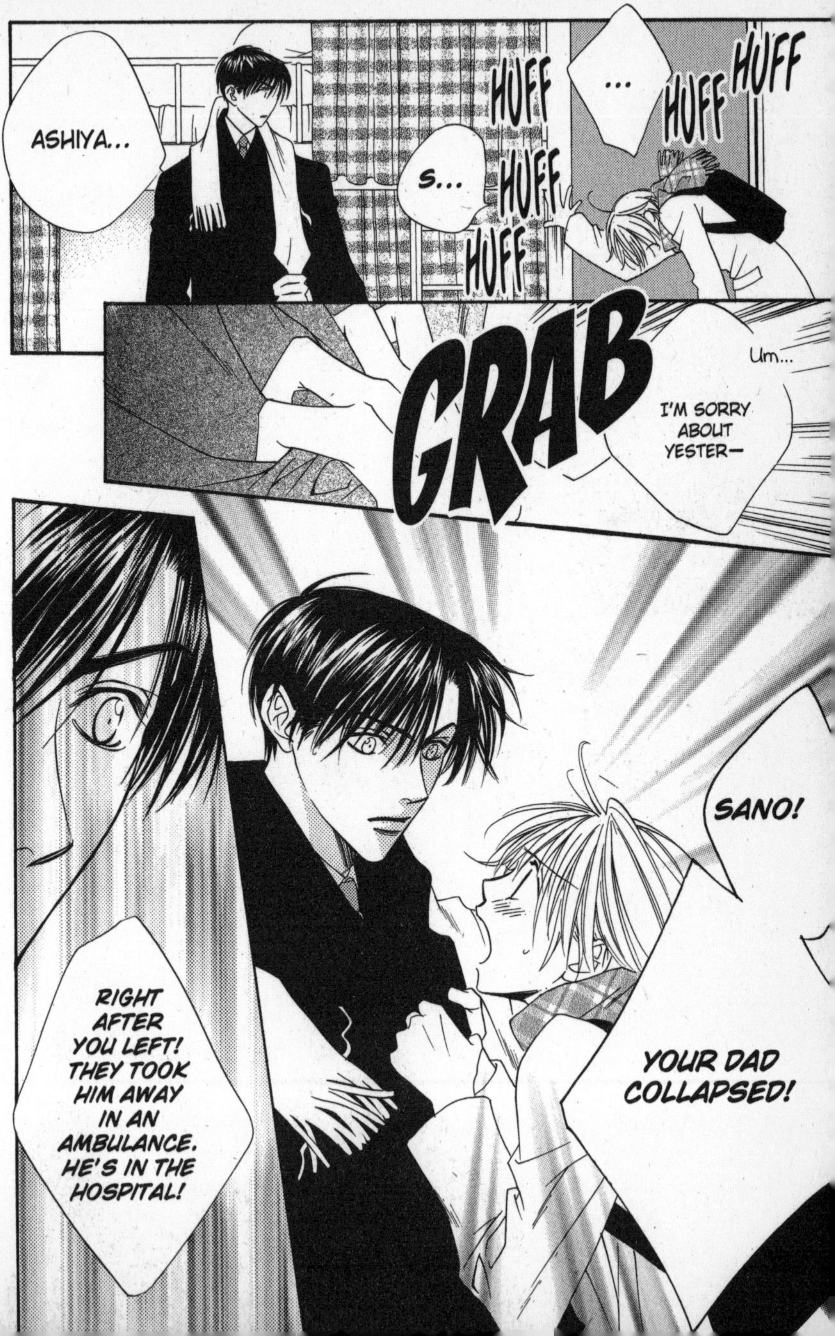
HUFF HUFF
...
HUFF
HUFF HUFF
HUFF
S...
ASHIYA...
Um...
I'M SORRY ABOUT YESTER—
GRAB
SANO!
YOUR DAD COLLAPSED!
RIGHT AFTER YOU LEFT! THEY TOOK HIM AWAY IN AN AMBULANCE. HE'S IN THE HOSPITAL!

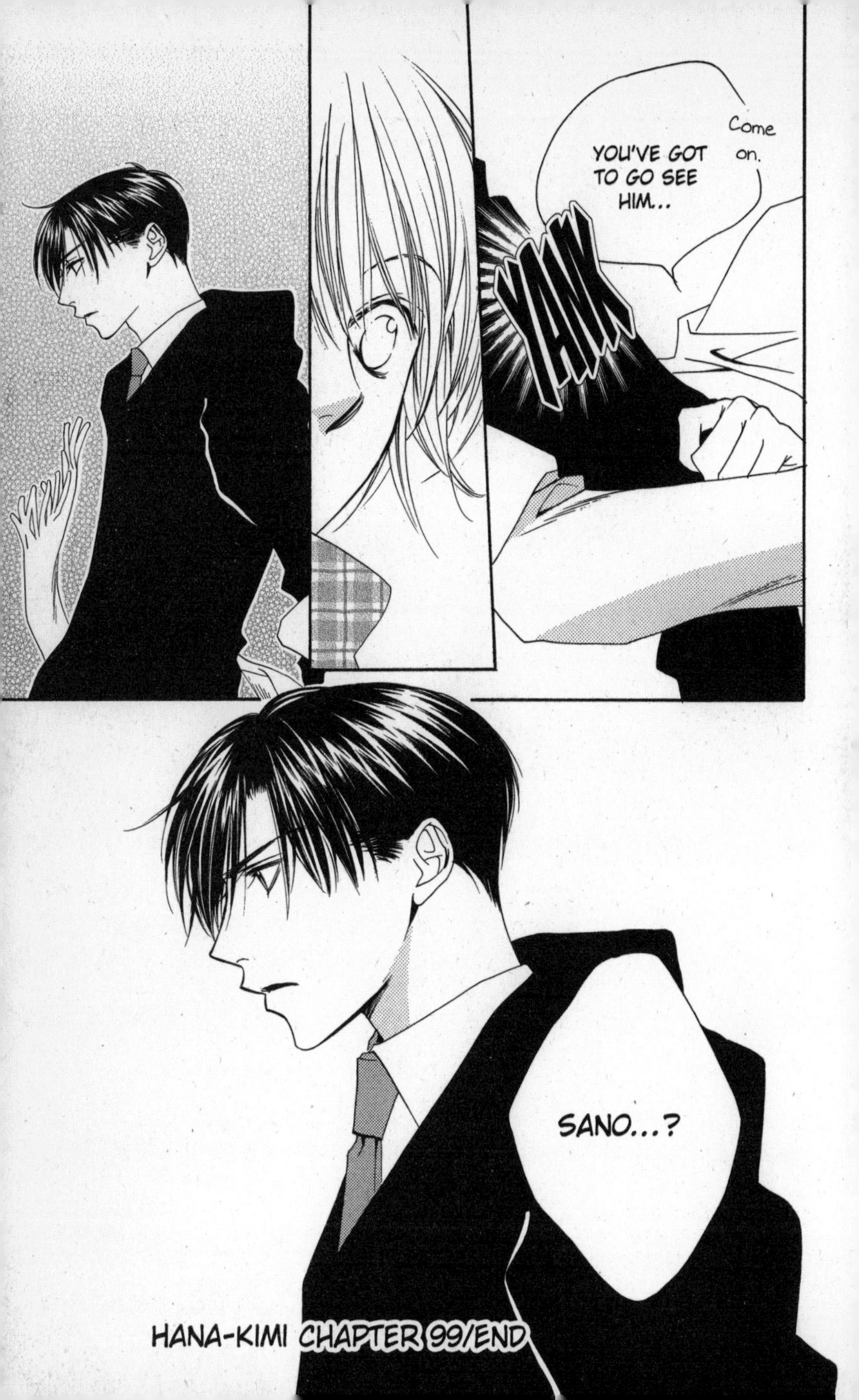
Come on.
YOU'VE GOT TO GO SEE HIM...
YANK
SANO...?
HANA-KIMI CHAPTER 99/END

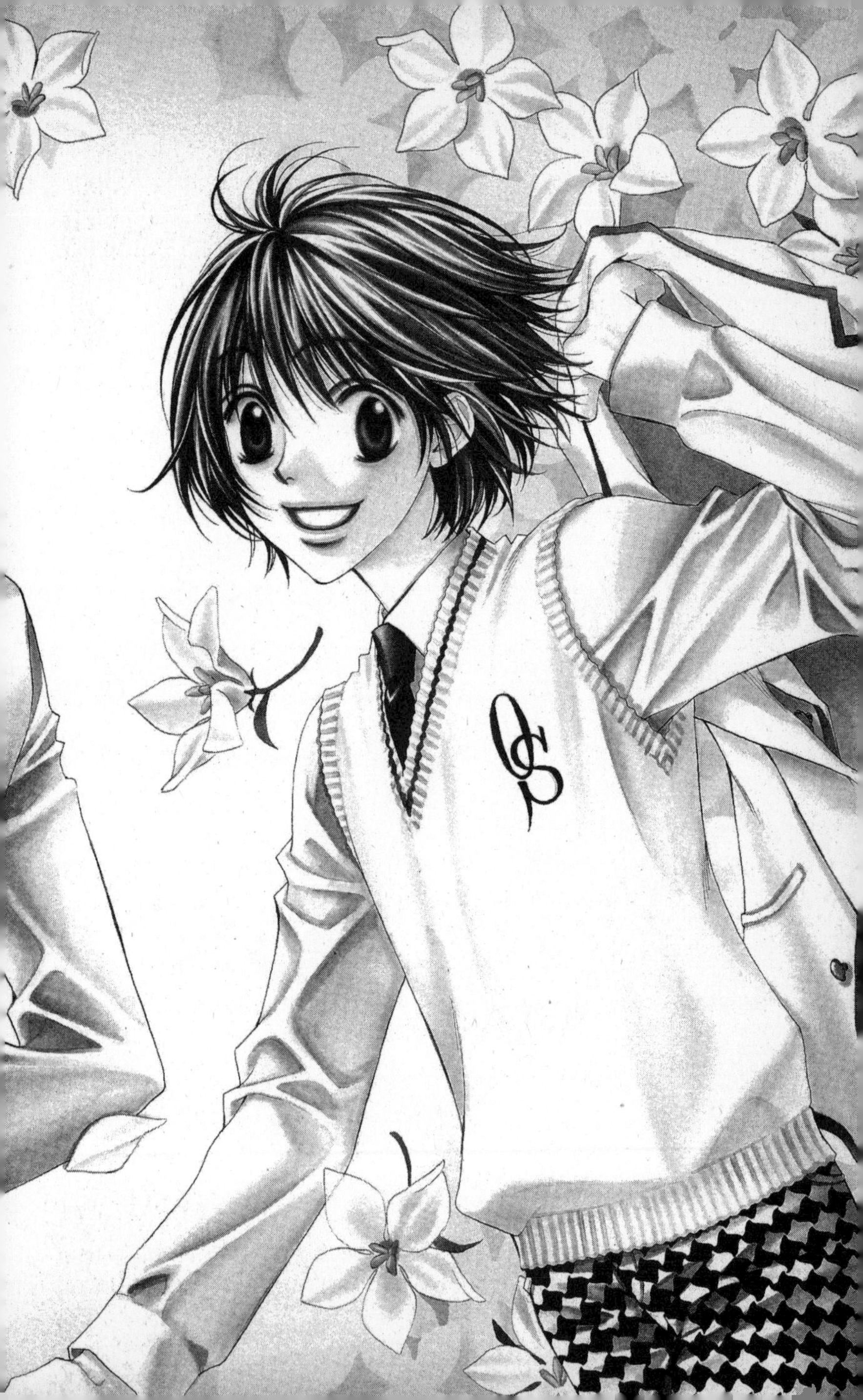

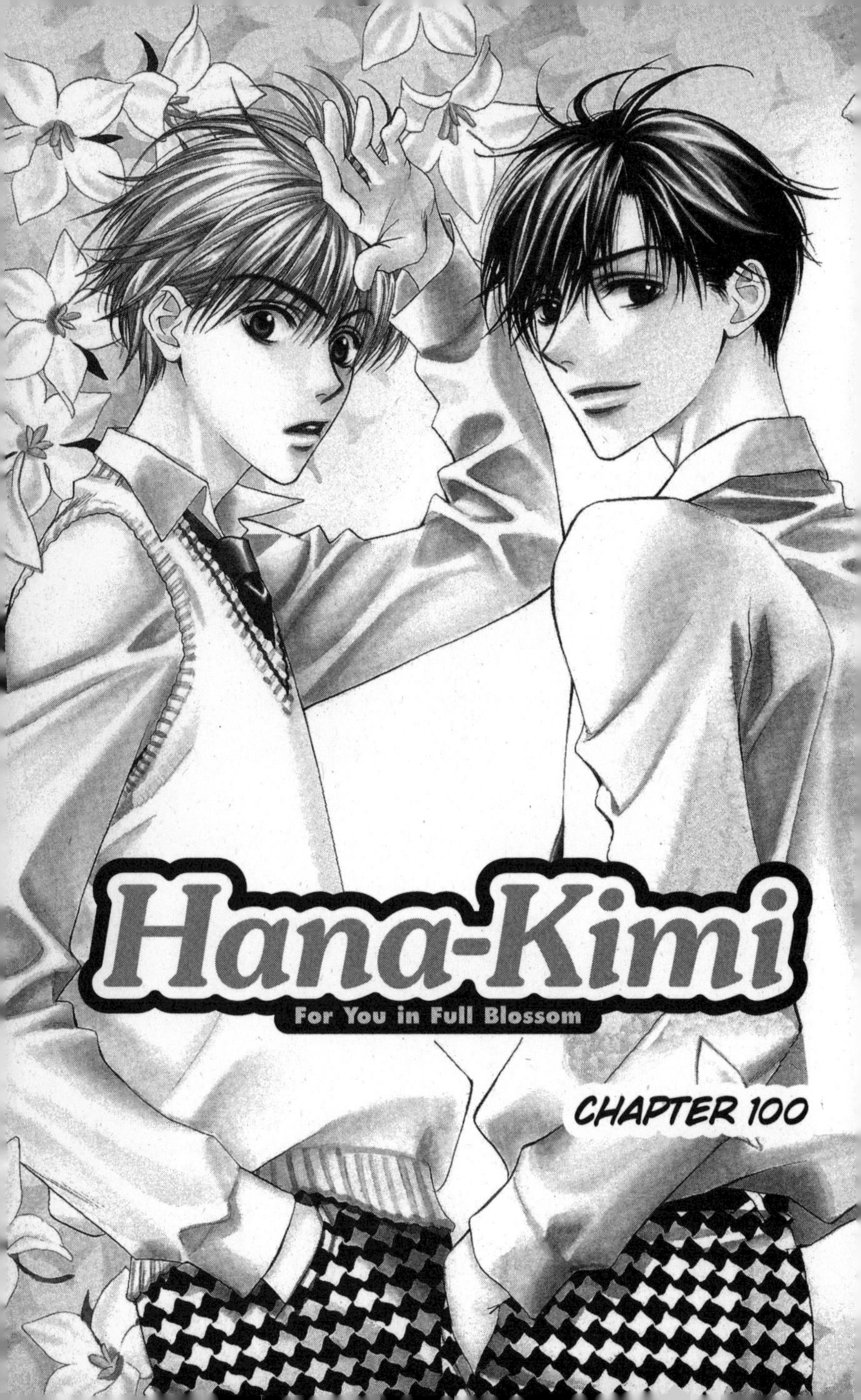
Hana-Kimi
For You in Full Blossom
CHAPTER 100

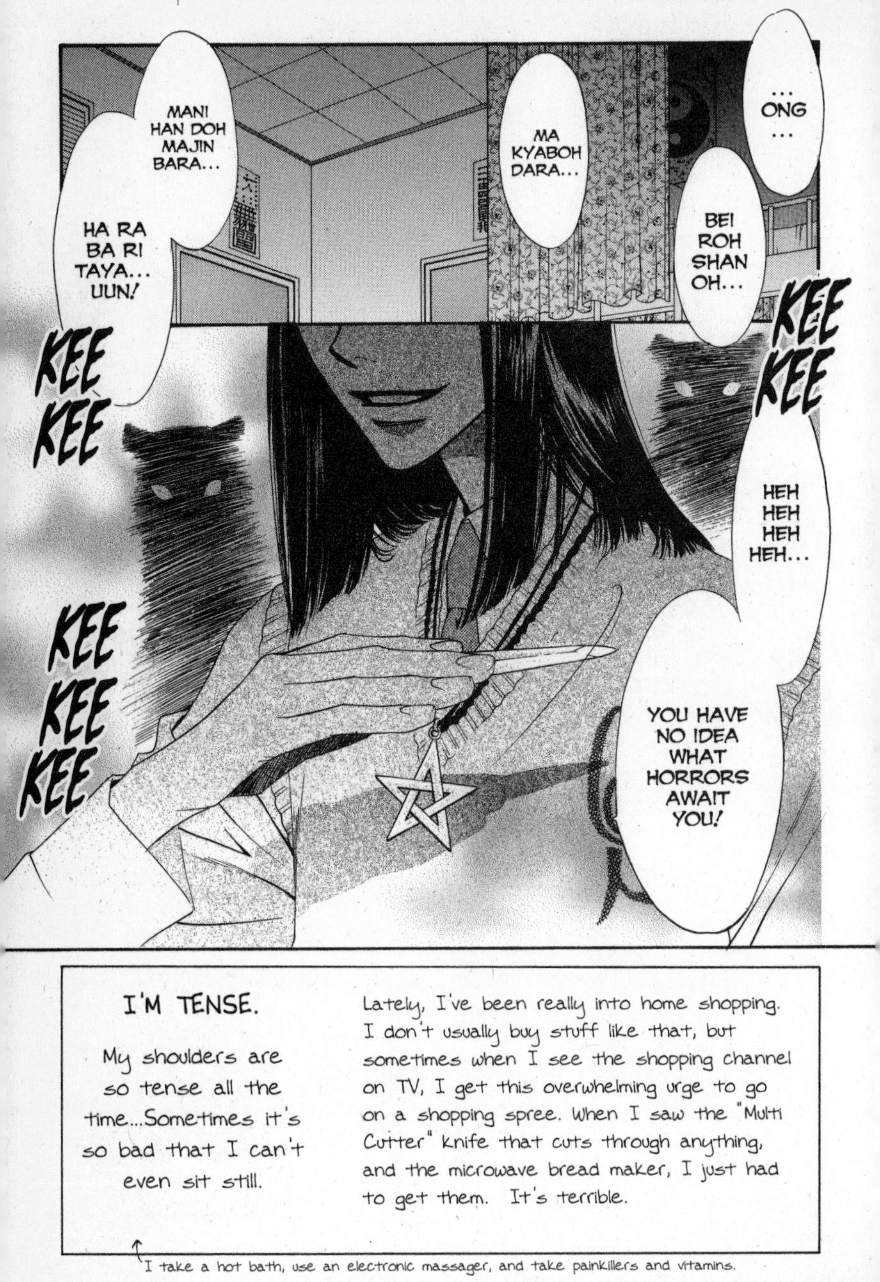
... ONG ...
BEI ROH SHAN OH...
MA KYABOH DARA...
MANI HAN DOH MAJIN BARA...
HA RA BA RI TAYA... UUN!
KEE KEE
HEH HEH HEH HEH...
YOU HAVE NO IDEA WHAT HORRORS AWAIT YOU!
KEE KEE
KEE KEE KEE

I'M TENSE.

My shoulders are so tense all the time...Sometimes it's so bad that I can't even sit still.

Lately, I've been really into home shopping. I don't usually buy stuff like that, but sometimes when I see the shopping channel on TV, I get this overwhelming urge to go on a shopping spree. When I saw the "Multi Cutter" knife that cuts through anything, and the microwave bread maker, I just had to get them. It's terrible.

↑I take a hot bath, use an electronic massager, and take painkillers and vitamins.

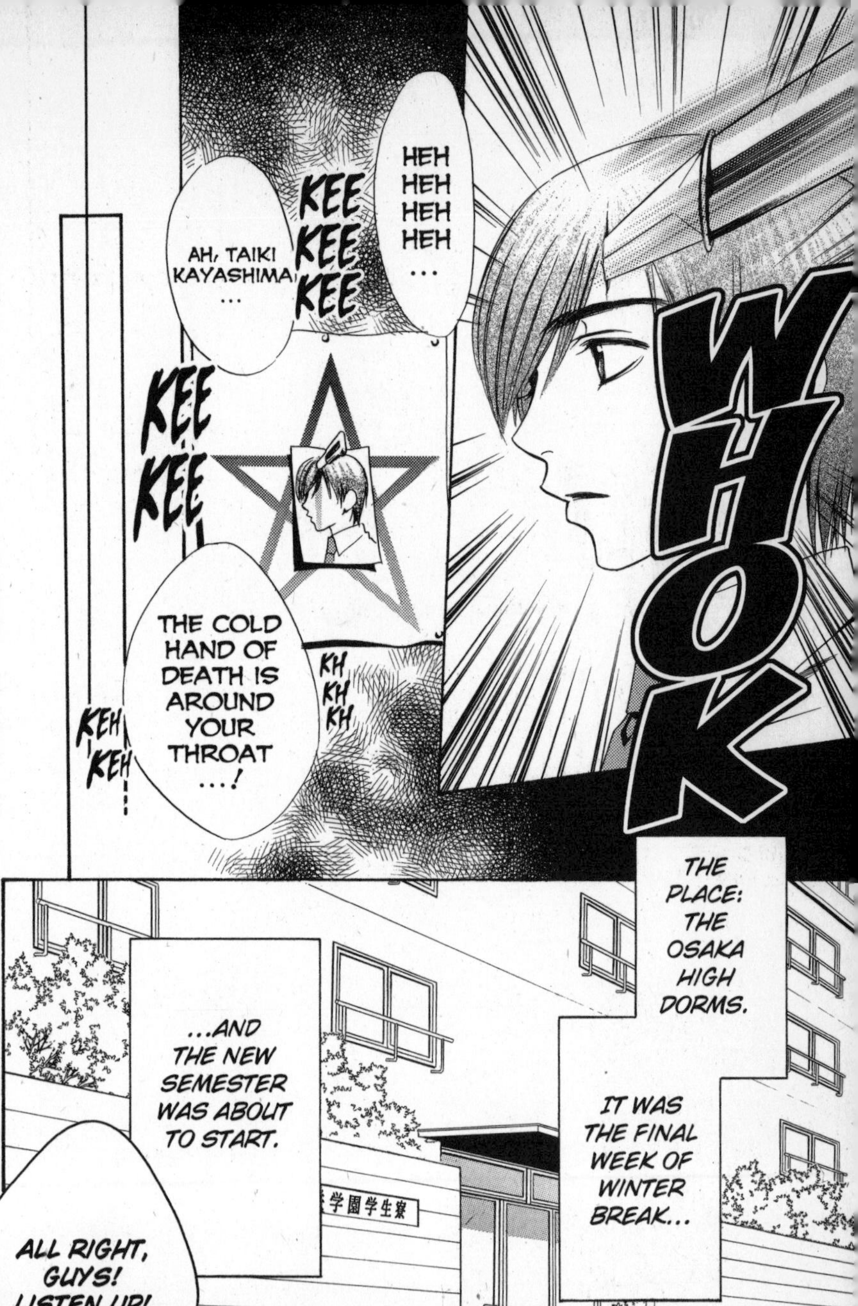

WHOK
HEH HEH HEH HEH ...
KEE KEE KEE
AH, TAIKI KAYASHIMA ...
KEE KEE
THE COLD HAND OF DEATH IS AROUND YOUR THROAT ...!
KH KH KH
KEH KEH
THE PLACE: THE OSAKA HIGH DORMS.
IT WAS THE FINAL WEEK OF WINTER BREAK...
...AND THE NEW SEMESTER WAS ABOUT TO START.
ALL RIGHT, GUYS! LISTEN UP!

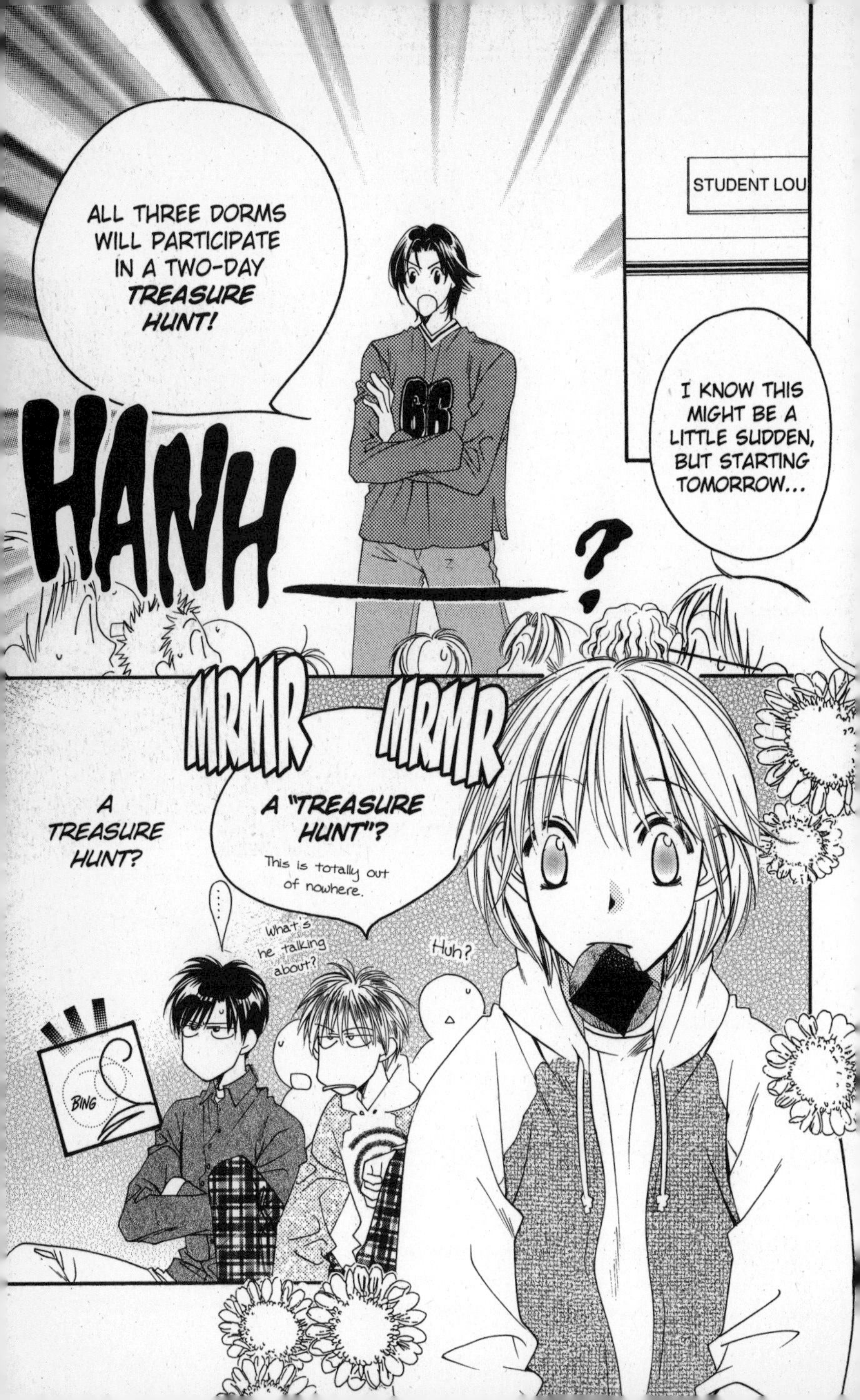
STUDENT LOU
I KNOW THIS MIGHT BE A LITTLE SUDDEN, BUT STARTING TOMORROW...
ALL THREE DORMS WILL PARTICIPATE IN A TWO-DAY *TREASURE HUNT!*
HANH
?
MRMR MRMR
A "TREASURE HUNT"?
This is totally out of nowhere.
A TREASURE HUNT?
Huh?
What's he talking about?
...
BING

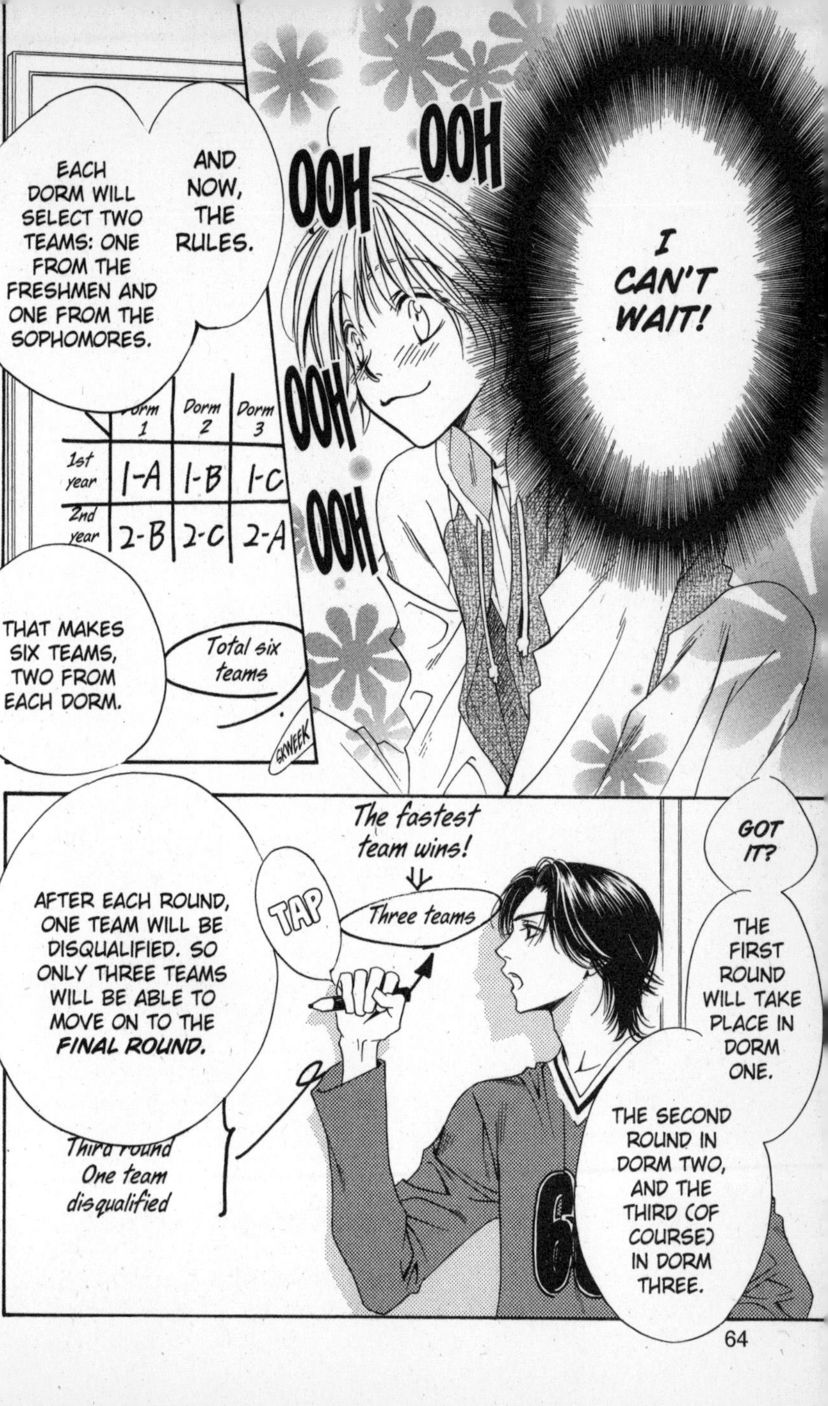
I CAN'T WAIT!
OOH OOH
OOH
OOH
AND NOW, THE RULES.
EACH DORM WILL SELECT TWO TEAMS: ONE FROM THE FRESHMEN AND ONE FROM THE SOPHOMORES.
Dorm 1 Dorm 2 Dorm 3
1st year 1-A 1-B 1-C
2nd year 2-B 2-C 2-A
THAT MAKES SIX TEAMS, TWO FROM EACH DORM.
Total six teams
SKWEEK
GOT IT?
THE FIRST ROUND WILL TAKE PLACE IN DORM ONE.
THE SECOND ROUND IN DORM TWO, AND THE THIRD (OF COURSE) IN DORM THREE.
The fastest team wins!
Three teams
TAP
AFTER EACH ROUND, ONE TEAM WILL BE DISQUALIFIED. SO ONLY THREE TEAMS WILL BE ABLE TO MOVE ON TO THE ***FINAL ROUND.***
One team disqualified

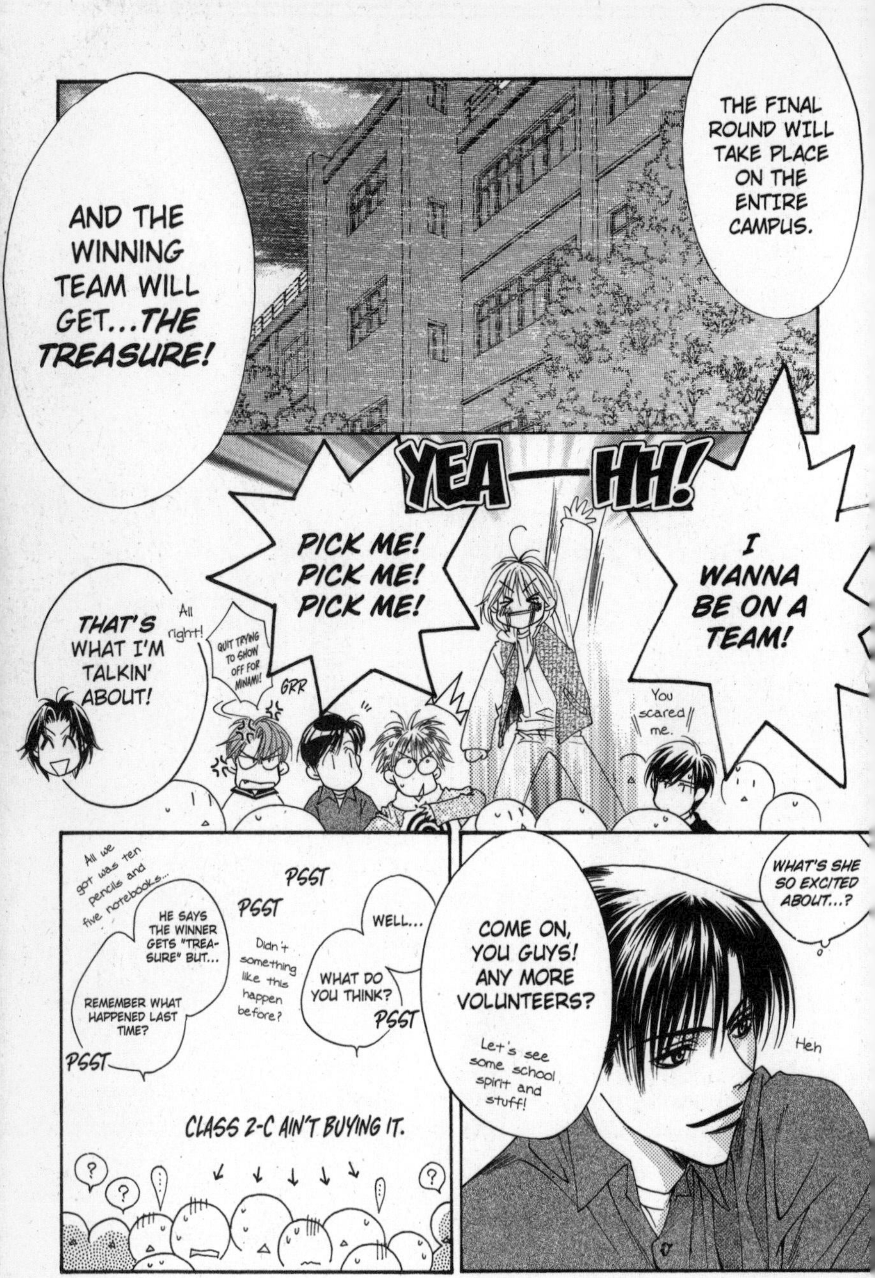
THE FINAL ROUND WILL TAKE PLACE ON THE ENTIRE CAMPUS.
AND THE WINNING TEAM WILL GET...THE TREASURE!
YEA—HH!
I WANNA BE ON A TEAM!
PICK ME! PICK ME! PICK ME!
You scared me.
GRR
QUIT TRYING TO SHOW OFF FOR MINAMI!
All right!
THAT'S WHAT I'M TALKIN' ABOUT!
WHAT'S SHE SO EXCITED ABOUT...?
Heh
COME ON, YOU GUYS! ANY MORE VOLUNTEERS?
Let's see some school spirit and stuff!
PSST
WELL...
WHAT DO YOU THINK?
PSST
PSST
Didn't something like this happen before?
All we got was ten pencils and five notebooks...
HE SAYS THE WINNER GETS "TREA-SURE" BUT...
REMEMBER WHAT HAPPENED LAST TIME?
PSST
CLASS 2-C AIN'T BUYING IT.

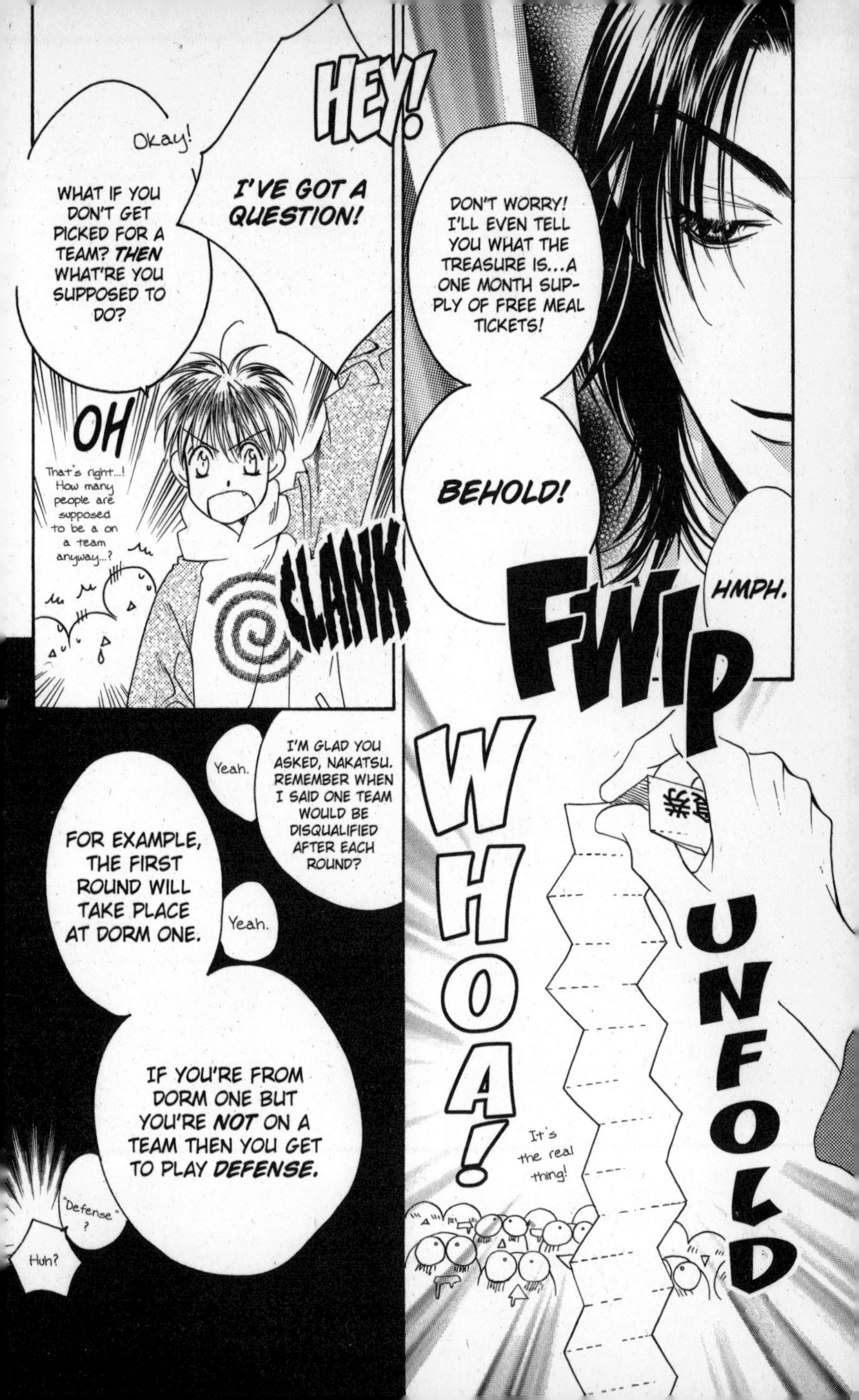
DON'T WORRY! I'LL EVEN TELL YOU WHAT THE TREASURE IS...A ONE MONTH SUP-PLY OF FREE MEAL TICKETS!
BEHOLD!
HMPH.
FWIP
UNFOLD
WHOA!
It's the real thing!
HEY!
I'VE GOT A QUESTION!
Okay!
WHAT IF YOU DON'T GET PICKED FOR A TEAM? THEN WHAT'RE YOU SUPPOSED TO DO?
OH
That's right...! How many people are supposed to be a on a team anyway...?
CLANK
I'M GLAD YOU ASKED, NAKATSU. REMEMBER WHEN I SAID ONE TEAM WOULD BE DISQUALIFIED AFTER EACH ROUND?
Yeah.
FOR EXAMPLE, THE FIRST ROUND WILL TAKE PLACE AT DORM ONE.
Yeah.
IF YOU'RE FROM DORM ONE BUT YOU'RE NOT ON A TEAM THEN YOU GET TO PLAY DEFENSE.
"Defense"?
Huh?

HANA-KIMI CHAPTER 100! VIVA!

I don't get to see the number 100 often, so it feels kind of strange.

Oh, except on 100 yen coins.

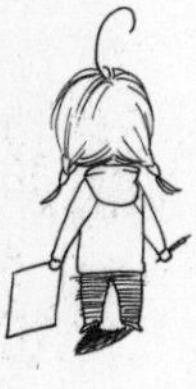

It's thanks to all of you readers that I've managed to make it this far. Thank you so much!

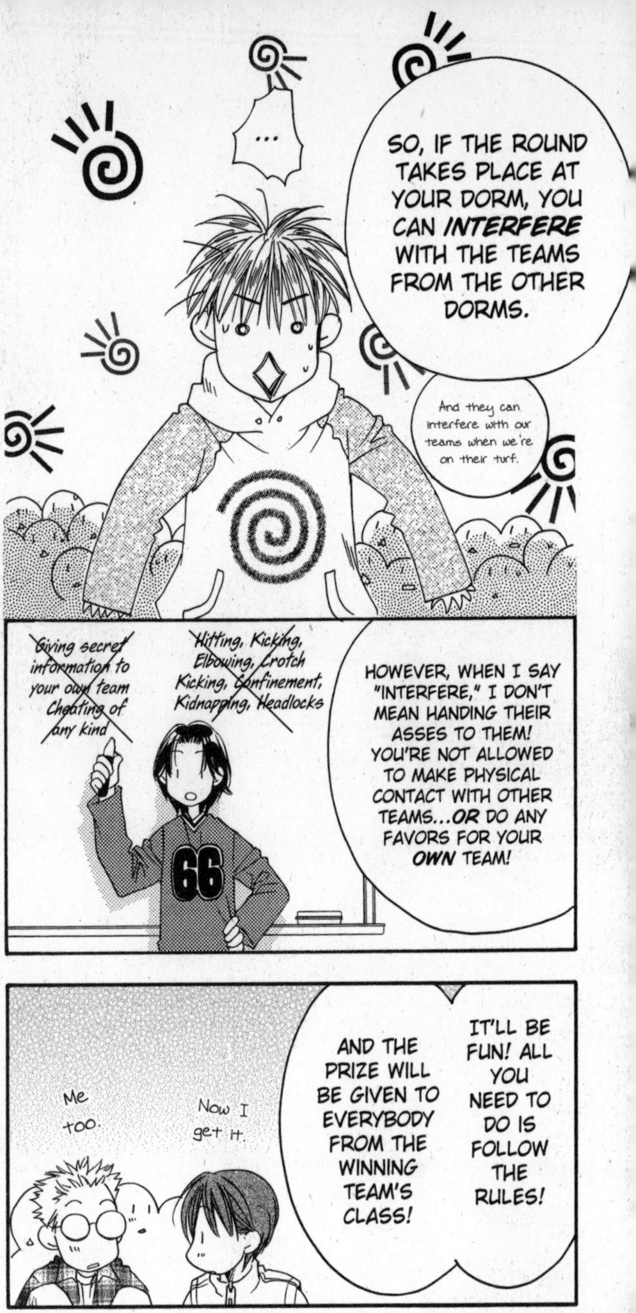

SO, IF THE ROUND TAKES PLACE AT YOUR DORM, YOU CAN *INTERFERE* WITH THE TEAMS FROM THE OTHER DORMS.
And they can interfere with our teams when we're on their turf.
...
HOWEVER, WHEN I SAY "INTERFERE," I DON'T MEAN HANDING THEIR ASSES TO THEM! YOU'RE NOT ALLOWED TO MAKE PHYSICAL CONTACT WITH OTHER TEAMS...*OR* DO ANY FAVORS FOR YOUR *OWN* TEAM!
Hitting, Kicking, Elbowing, Crotch Kicking, Confinement, Kidnapping, Headlocks
Giving secret information to your own team
Cheating of any kind
IT'LL BE FUN! ALL YOU NEED TO DO IS FOLLOW THE RULES!
AND THE PRIZE WILL BE GIVEN TO EVERYBODY FROM THE WINNING TEAM'S CLASS!
Now I get it.
Me too.

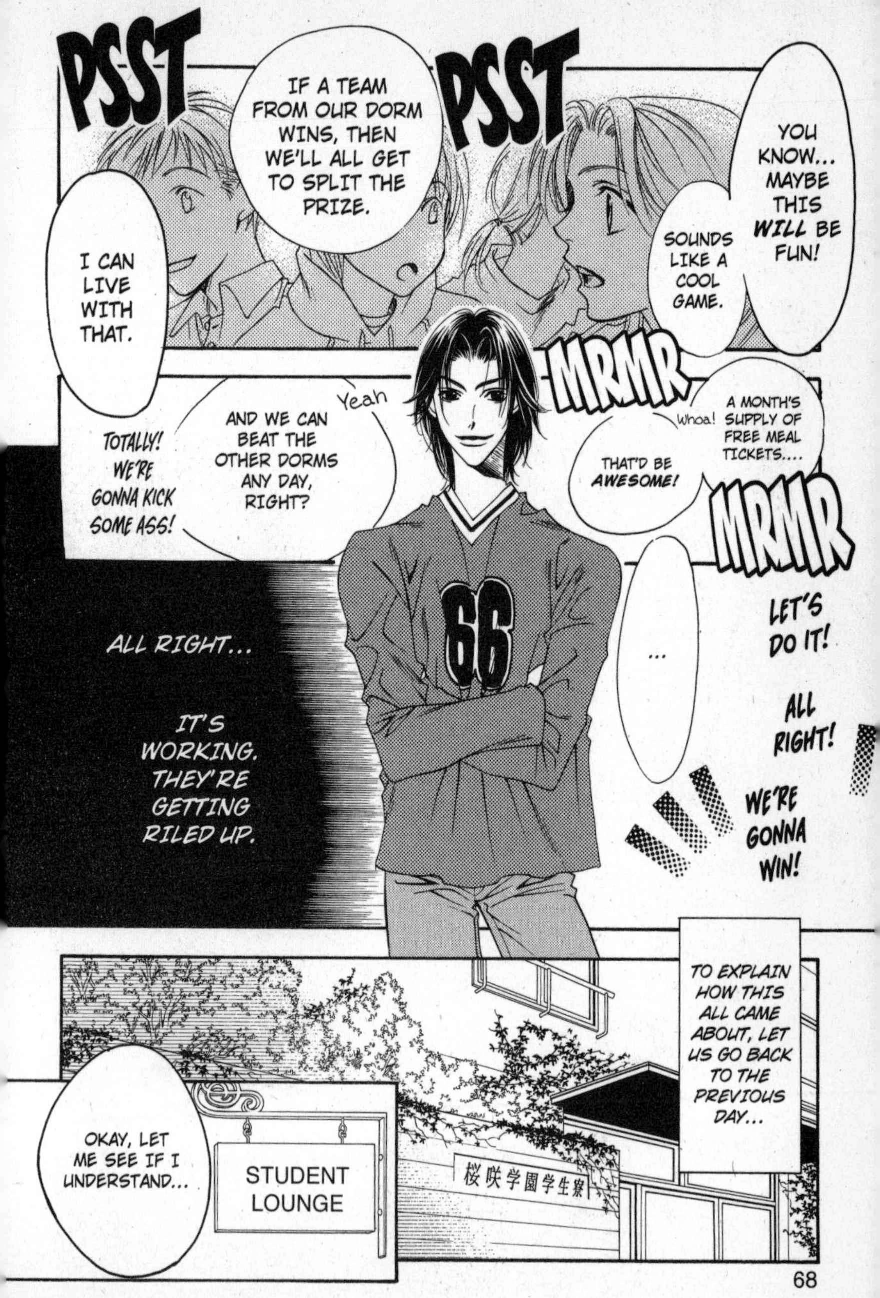
YOU KNOW... MAYBE THIS WILL BE FUN!
SOUNDS LIKE A COOL GAME.
PSST
IF A TEAM FROM OUR DORM WINS, THEN WE'LL ALL GET TO SPLIT THE PRIZE.
PSST
I CAN LIVE WITH THAT.
MRMR
A MONTH'S SUPPLY OF FREE MEAL TICKETS....
Whoa!
THAT'D BE AWESOME!
MRMR
Yeah
AND WE CAN BEAT THE OTHER DORMS ANY DAY, RIGHT?
TOTALLY! WE'RE GONNA KICK SOME ASS!
...
LET'S DO IT!
ALL RIGHT!
WE'RE GONNA WIN!
ALL RIGHT...
IT'S WORKING. THEY'RE GETTING RILED UP.
TO EXPLAIN HOW THIS ALL CAME ABOUT, LET US GO BACK TO THE PREVIOUS DAY...
桜咲学園学生寮
STUDENT LOUNGE
OKAY, LET ME SEE IF I UNDERSTAND...

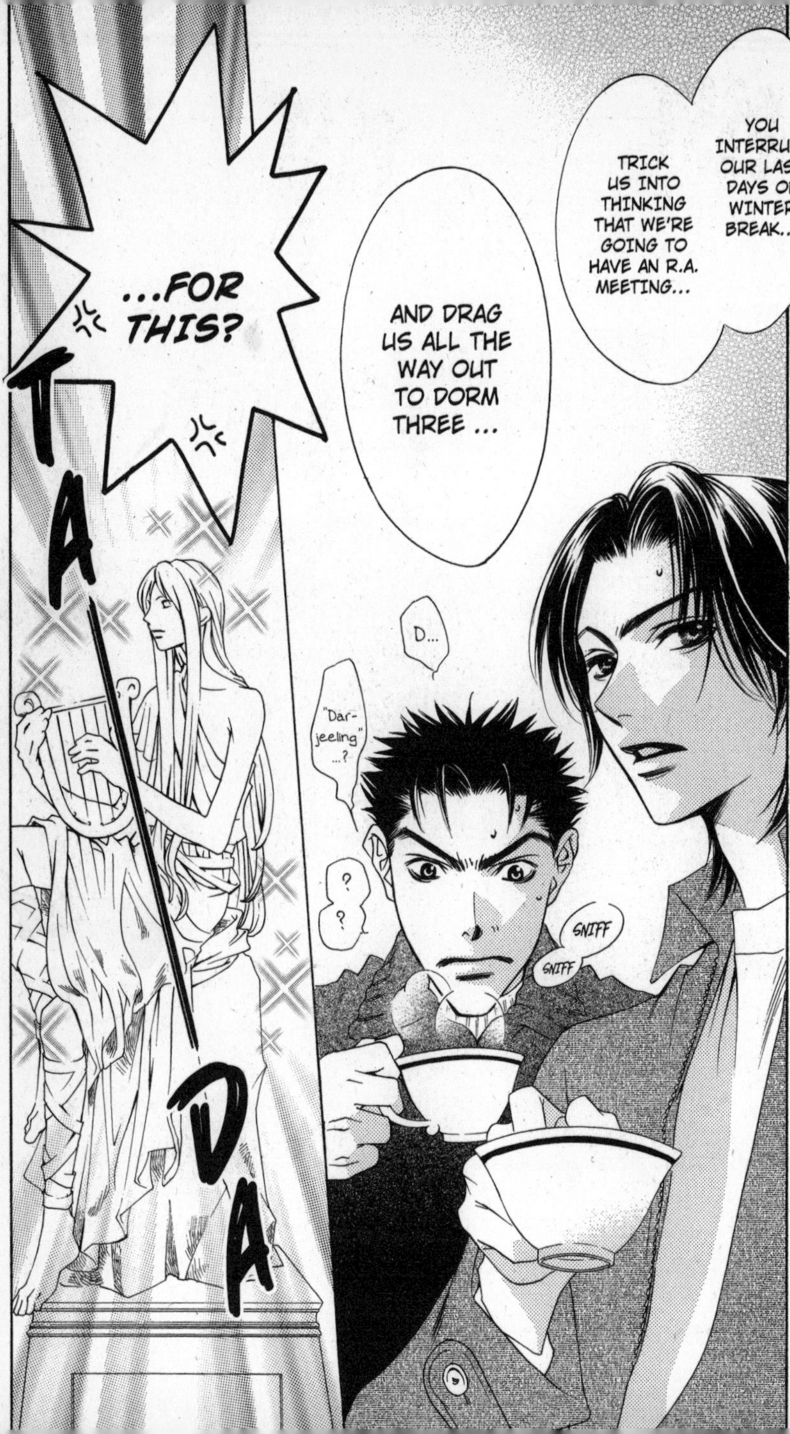
YOU INTERRUPT OUR LAST DAYS OF WINTER BREAK...
TRICK US INTO THINKING THAT WE'RE GOING TO HAVE AN R.A. MEETING...
AND DRAG US ALL THE WAY OUT TO DORM THREE ...
D...
"Dar-jeeling" ...?
? ?
SNIFF
SNIFF
...FOR THIS?
TA
DA

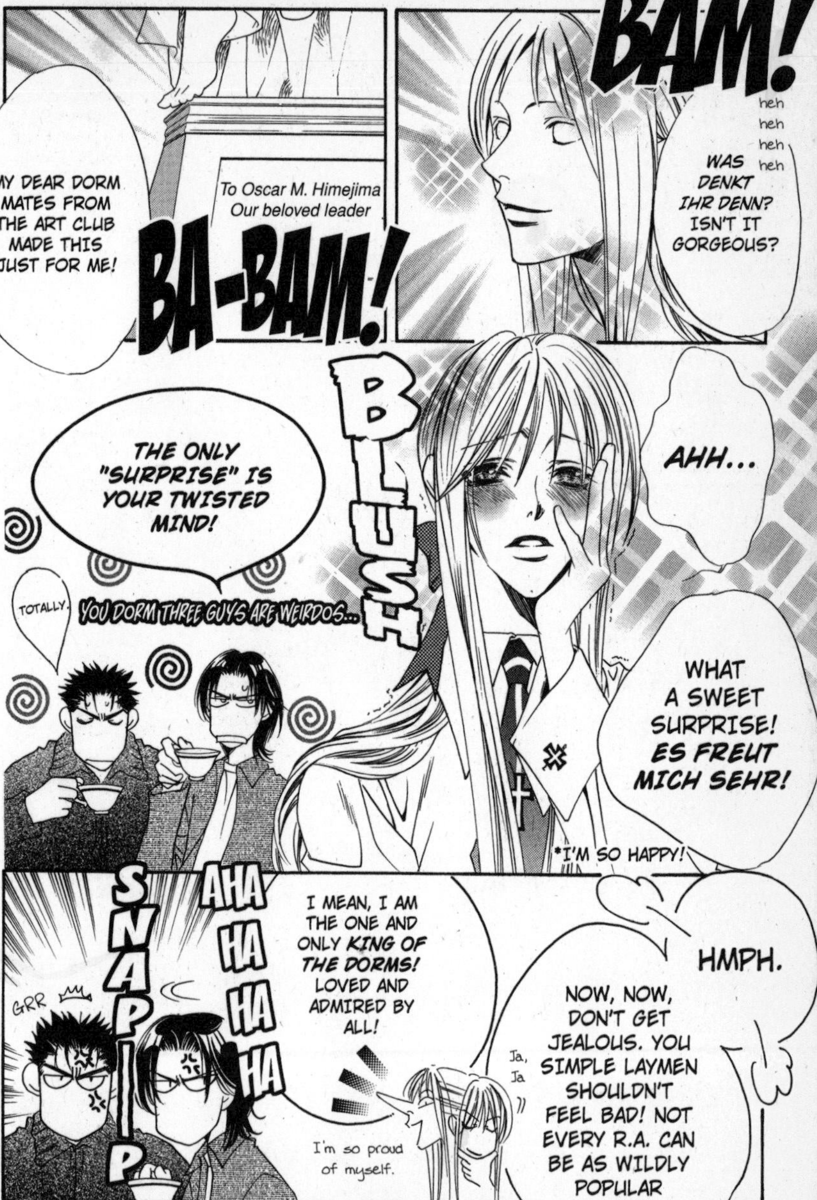
BAM!
heh heh heh heh
WAS DENKT IHR DENN? ISN'T IT GORGEOUS?
MY DEAR DORM MATES FROM THE ART CLUB MADE THIS JUST FOR ME!
To Oscar M. Himejima Our beloved leader
BA-BAM!
AHH...
WHAT A SWEET SURPRISE! ES FREUT MICH SEHR!
*I'M SO HAPPY!
BLUSH
THE ONLY "SURPRISE" IS YOUR TWISTED MIND!
YOU DORM THREE GUYS ARE WEIRDOS...
TOTALLY.
HMPH.
NOW, NOW, DON'T GET JEALOUS. YOU SIMPLE LAYMEN SHOULDN'T FEEL BAD! NOT EVERY R.A. CAN BE AS WILDLY POPULAR AS ME.
Ja, Ja
I MEAN, I AM THE ONE AND ONLY KING OF THE DORMS! LOVED AND ADMIRED BY ALL!
I'm so proud of myself.
AHAHAHAHA
SNAP!
GRR

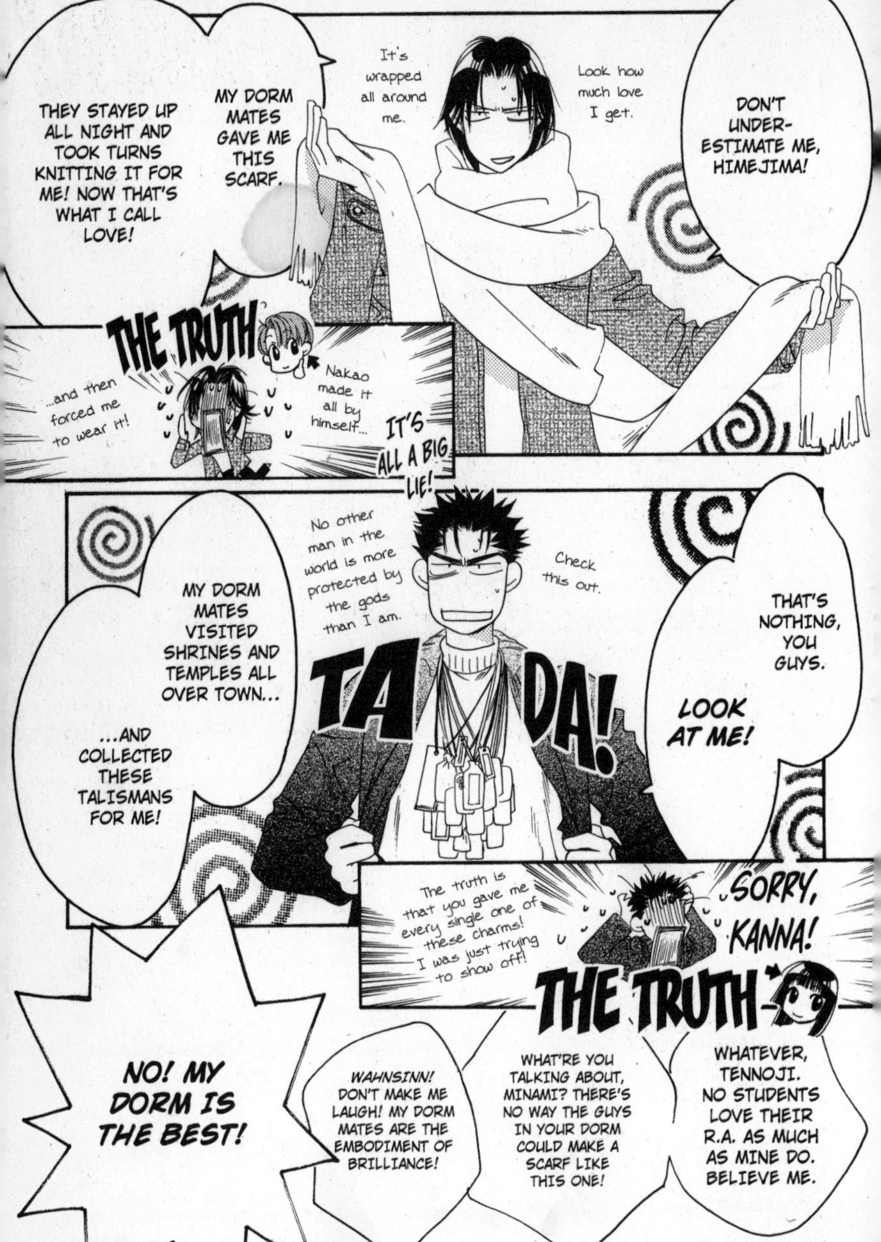
DON'T UNDER-ESTIMATE ME, HIMEJIMA!
Look how much love I get.
It's wrapped all around me.
MY DORM MATES GAVE ME THIS SCARF.
THEY STAYED UP ALL NIGHT AND TOOK TURNS KNITTING IT FOR ME! NOW THAT'S WHAT I CALL LOVE!
THE TRUTH
Nakao made it all by himself...
...and then forced me to wear it!
IT'S ALL A BIG LIE!
THAT'S NOTHING, YOU GUYS.
LOOK AT ME!
Check this out.
No other man in the world is more protected by the gods than I am.
TA DA!
MY DORM MATES VISITED SHRINES AND TEMPLES ALL OVER TOWN...
...AND COLLECTED THESE TALISMANS FOR ME!
SORRY, KANNA!
The truth is that you gave me every single one of these charms! I was just trying to show off!
THE TRUTH
WHATEVER, TENNOJI. NO STUDENTS LOVE THEIR R.A. AS MUCH AS MINE DO. BELIEVE ME.
WHAT'RE YOU TALKING ABOUT, MINAMI? THERE'S NO WAY THE GUYS IN YOUR DORM COULD MAKE A SCARF LIKE THIS ONE!
WAHNSINN! DON'T MAKE ME LAUGH! MY DORM MATES ARE THE EMBODIMENT OF BRILLIANCE!
NO! MY DORM IS THE BEST!

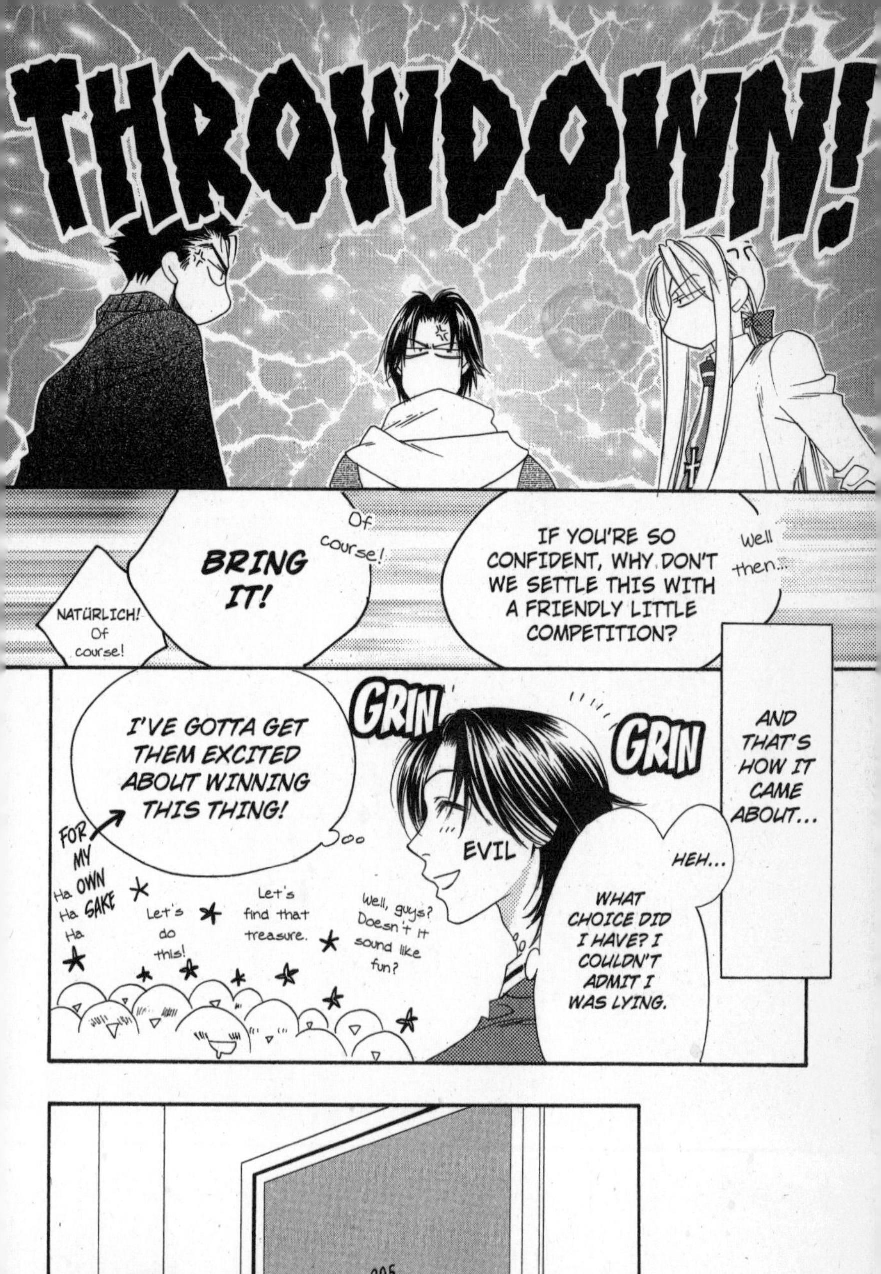
THROWDOWN!
Well then...
IF YOU'RE SO CONFIDENT, WHY DON'T WE SETTLE THIS WITH A FRIENDLY LITTLE COMPETITION?
Of course!
BRING IT!
NATÜRLICH! Of course!
AND THAT'S HOW IT CAME ABOUT...
HEH...
WHAT CHOICE DID I HAVE? I COULDN'T ADMIT I WAS LYING.
GRIN
GRIN
EVIL
I'VE GOTTA GET THEM EXCITED ABOUT WINNING THIS THING!
FOR MY OWN SAKE
Well, guys? Doesn't it sound like fun?
Let's find that treasure.
Let's do this!
Ha Ha Ha

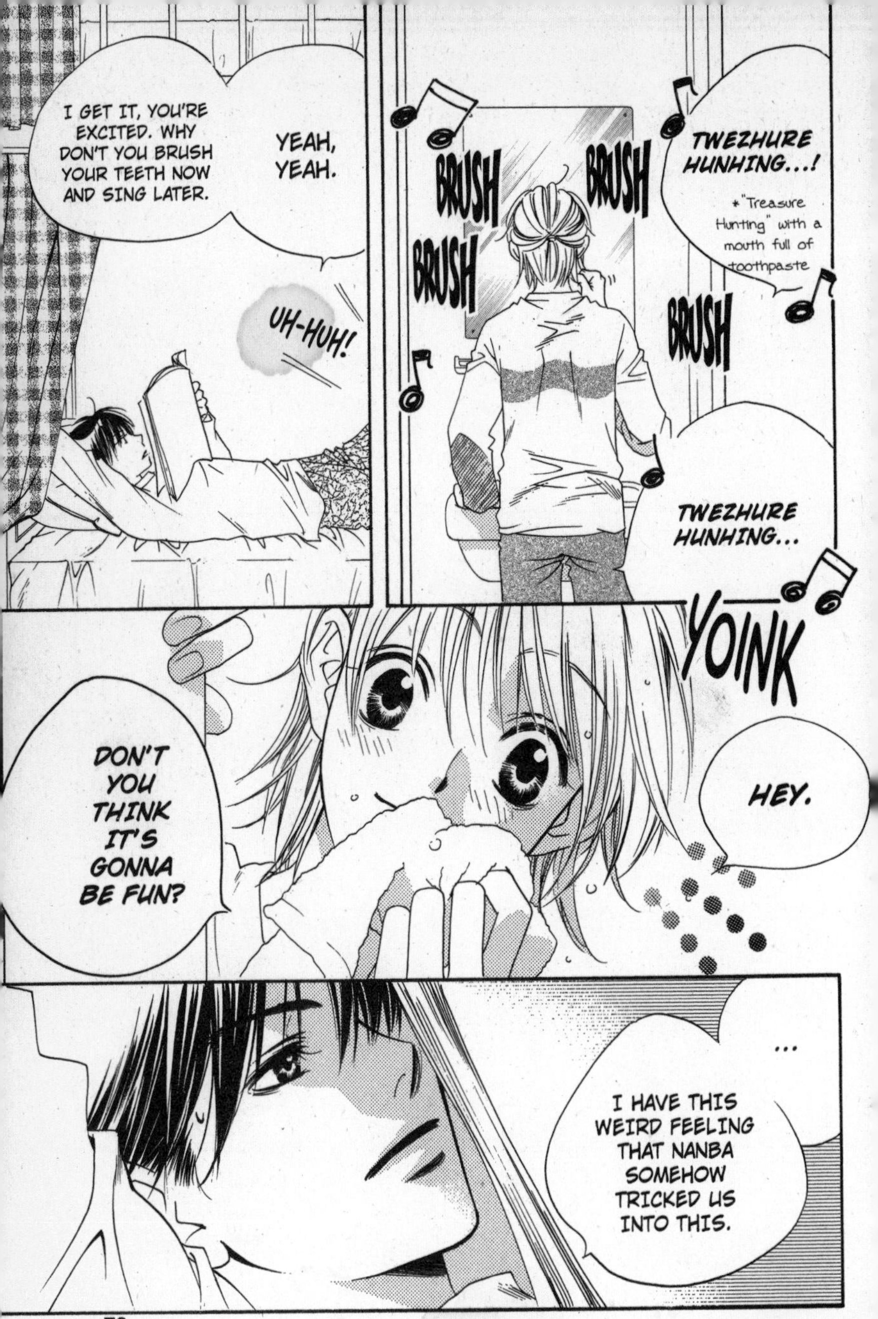
BRUSH
BRUSH
BRUSH
TWEZHURE HUNHING...!
*"Treasure Hunting" with a mouth full of toothpaste
BRUSH
TWEZHURE HUNHING...
I GET IT, YOU'RE EXCITED. WHY DON'T YOU BRUSH YOUR TEETH NOW AND SING LATER.
YEAH, YEAH.
UH-HUH!
YOINK
HEY.
DON'T YOU THINK IT'S GONNA BE FUN?
...
I HAVE THIS WEIRD FEELING THAT NANBA SOMEHOW TRICKED US INTO THIS.

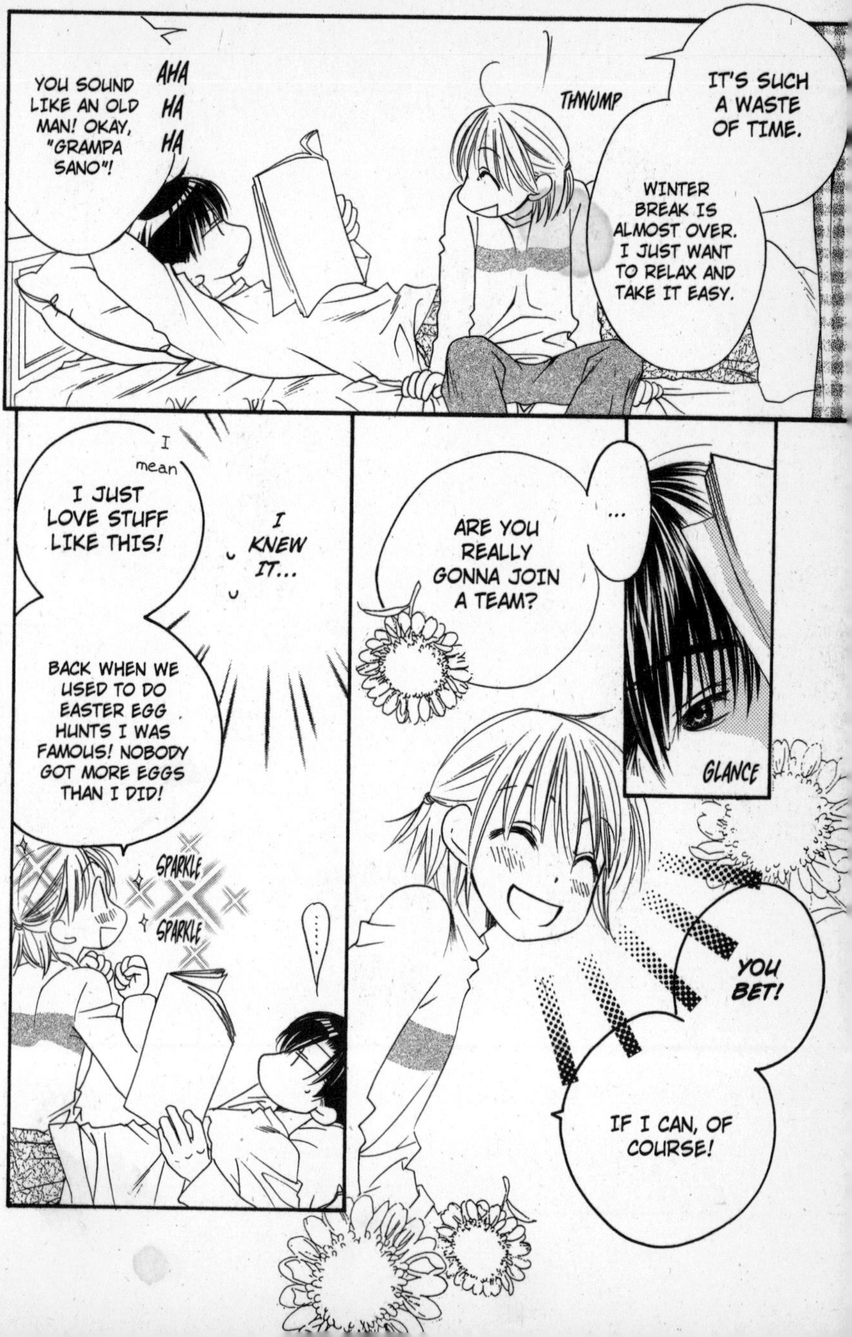
IT'S SUCH A WASTE OF TIME.
WINTER BREAK IS ALMOST OVER. I JUST WANT TO RELAX AND TAKE IT EASY.
THWUMP
YOU SOUND LIKE AN OLD MAN! OKAY, "GRAMPA SANO"!
AHA HA HA
...
GLANCE
ARE YOU REALLY GONNA JOIN A TEAM?
YOU BET!
IF I CAN, OF COURSE!
I mean
I JUST LOVE STUFF LIKE THIS!
I KNEW IT...
BACK WHEN WE USED TO DO EASTER EGG HUNTS I WAS FAMOUS! NOBODY GOT MORE EGGS THAN I DID!
SPARKLE
SPARKLE
......!

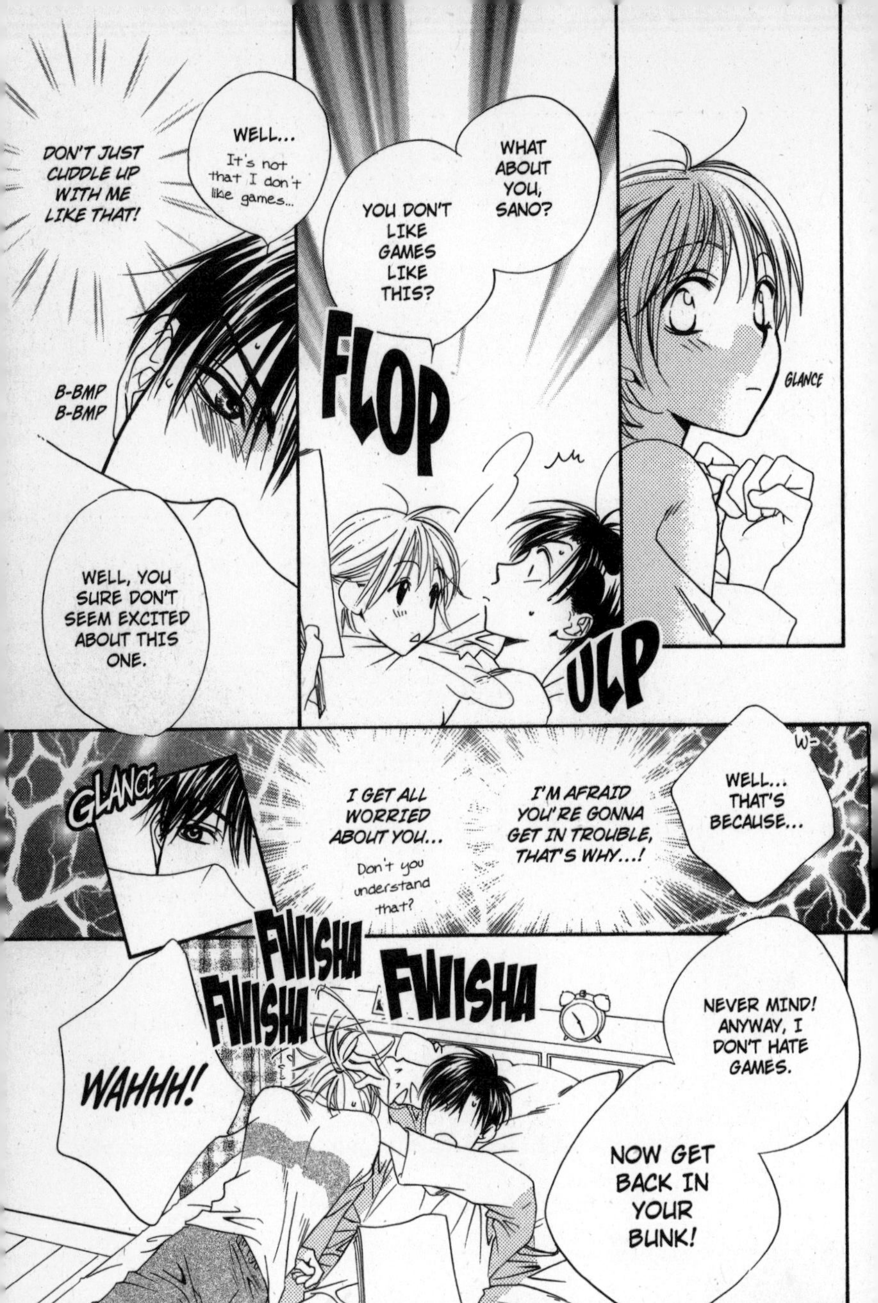
GLANCE
WHAT ABOUT YOU, SANO?
YOU DON'T LIKE GAMES LIKE THIS?
FLOP
ULP
WELL... It's not that I don't like games...
DON'T JUST CUDDLE UP WITH ME LIKE THAT!
B-BMP B-BMP
WELL, YOU SURE DON'T SEEM EXCITED ABOUT THIS ONE.
W-
WELL... THAT'S BECAUSE...
I'M AFRAID YOU'RE GONNA GET IN TROUBLE, THAT'S WHY...!
I GET ALL WORRIED ABOUT YOU...
Don't you understand that?
GLANCE
NEVER MIND! ANYWAY, I DON'T HATE GAMES.
NOW GET BACK IN YOUR BUNK!
FWISHA
FWISHA
FWISHA
WAHHH!

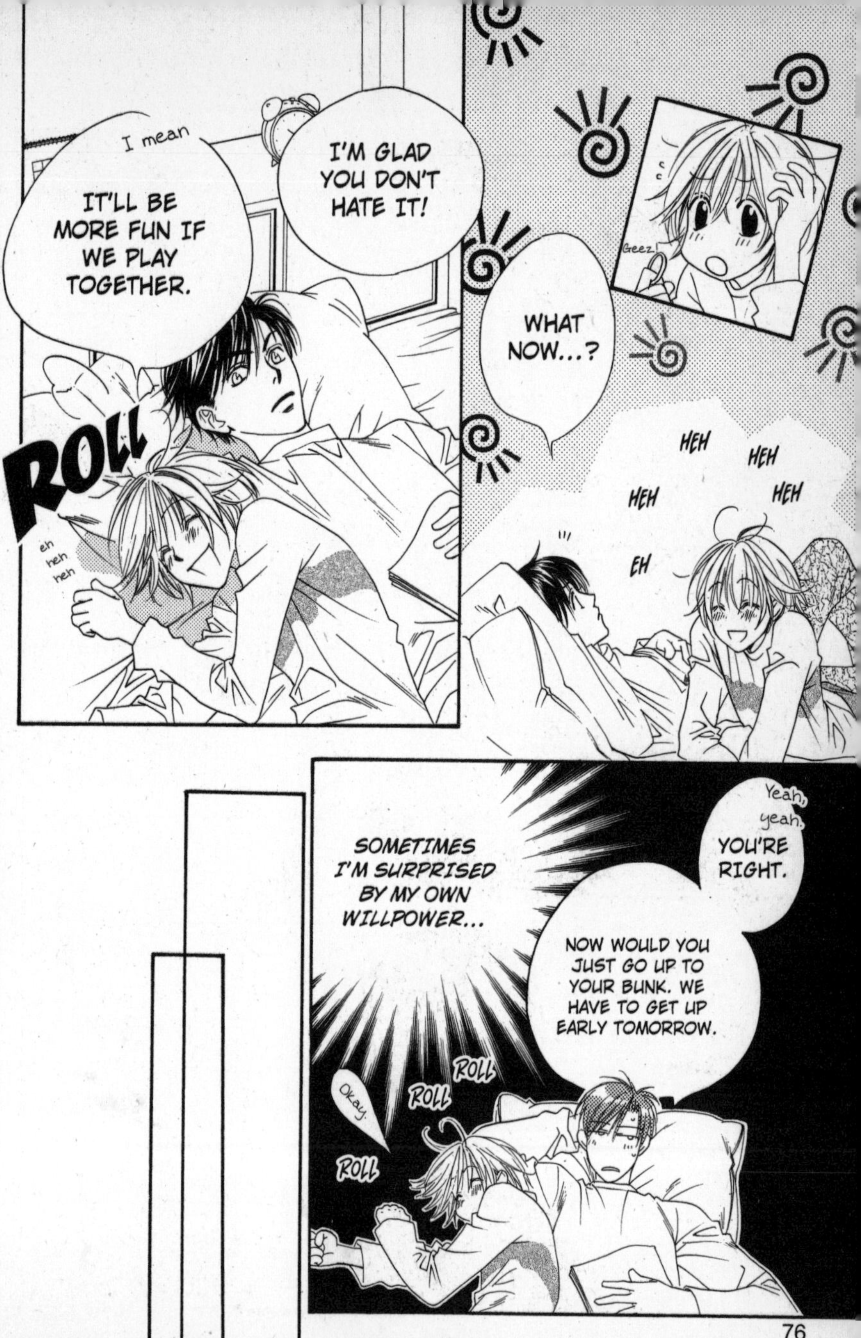
Geez
WHAT NOW...?
HEH HEH HEH HEH EH
I'M GLAD YOU DON'T HATE IT!
I mean
IT'LL BE MORE FUN IF WE PLAY TOGETHER.
ROLL
eh heh heh
Yeah, yeah. YOU'RE RIGHT.
NOW WOULD YOU JUST GO UP TO YOUR BUNK. WE HAVE TO GET UP EARLY TOMORROW.
SOMETIMES I'M SURPRISED BY MY OWN WILLPOWER...
ROLL
ROLL
Okay.
ROLL

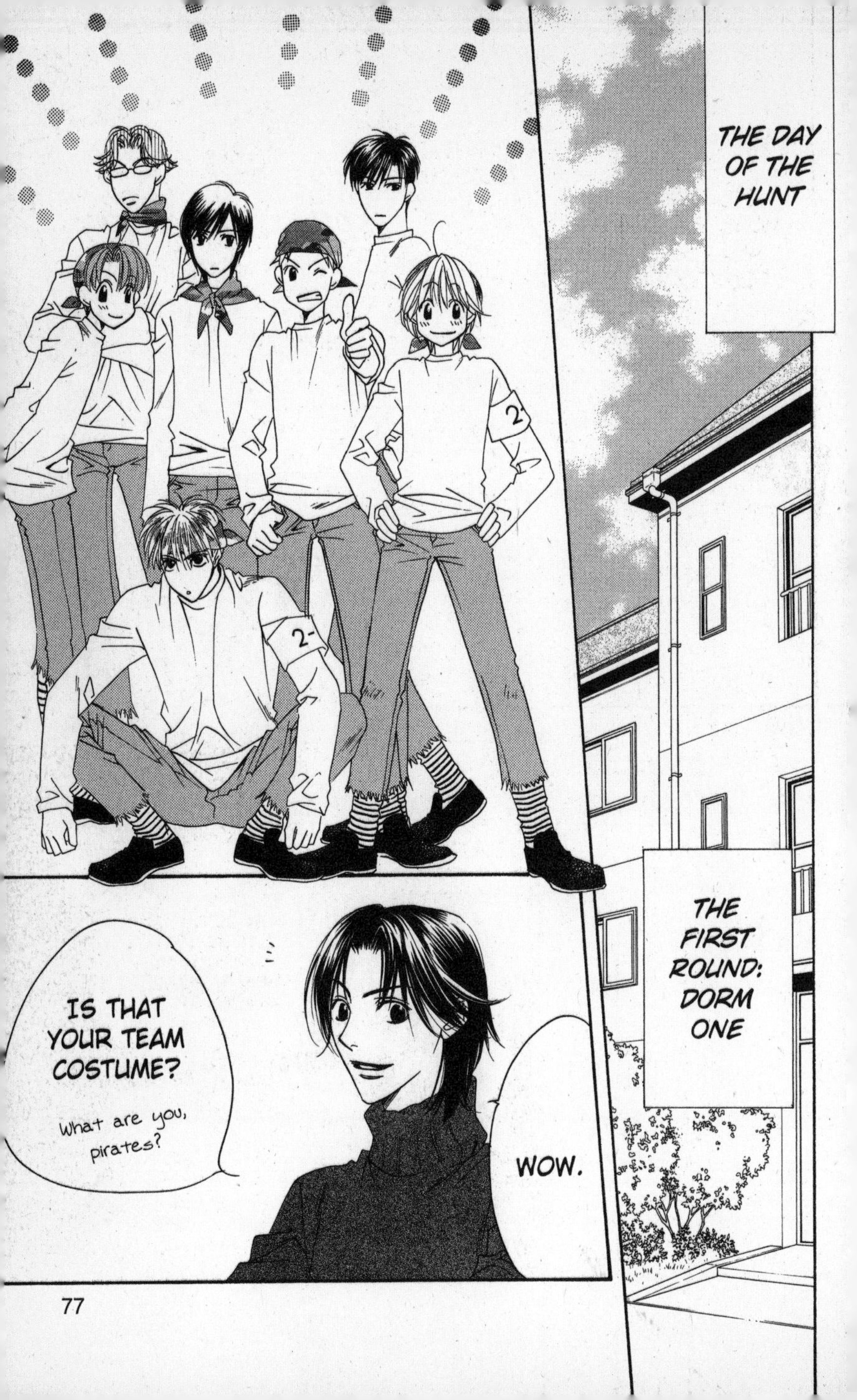
THE DAY OF THE HUNT
THE FIRST ROUND: DORM ONE
WOW.
IS THAT YOUR TEAM COSTUME?
What are you, pirates?

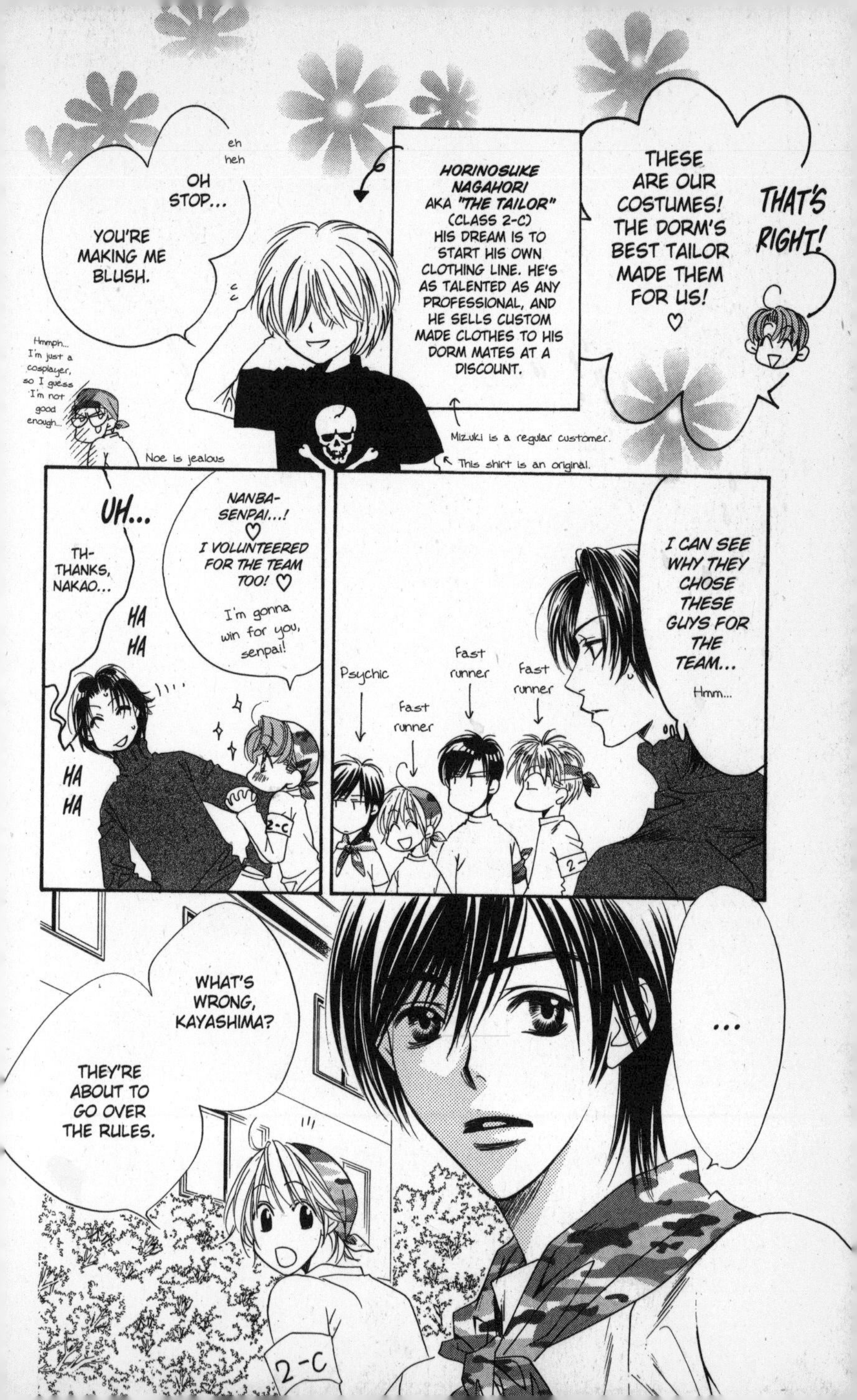
THAT'S RIGHT!
THESE ARE OUR COSTUMES! THE DORM'S BEST TAILOR MADE THEM FOR US! ♡
HORINOSUKE NAGAHORI AKA "THE TAILOR" (CLASS 2-C) HIS DREAM IS TO START HIS OWN CLOTHING LINE. HE'S AS TALENTED AS ANY PROFESSIONAL, AND HE SELLS CUSTOM MADE CLOTHES TO HIS DORM MATES AT A DISCOUNT.
Mizuki is a regular customer.
This shirt is an original.
eh heh
OH STOP...
YOU'RE MAKING ME BLUSH.
Hmmph... I'm just a cosplayer, so I guess I'm not good enough...
Noe is jealous
I CAN SEE WHY THEY CHOSE THESE GUYS FOR THE TEAM...
Hmm...
Fast runner
Fast runner
Fast runner
Psychic
NANBA-SENPAI...! ♡ I VOLUNTEERED FOR THE TEAM TOO! ♡
I'm gonna win for you, senpai!
UH...
TH-THANKS, NAKAO...
HA HA
HA HA
...
WHAT'S WRONG, KAYASHIMA?
THEY'RE ABOUT TO GO OVER THE RULES.

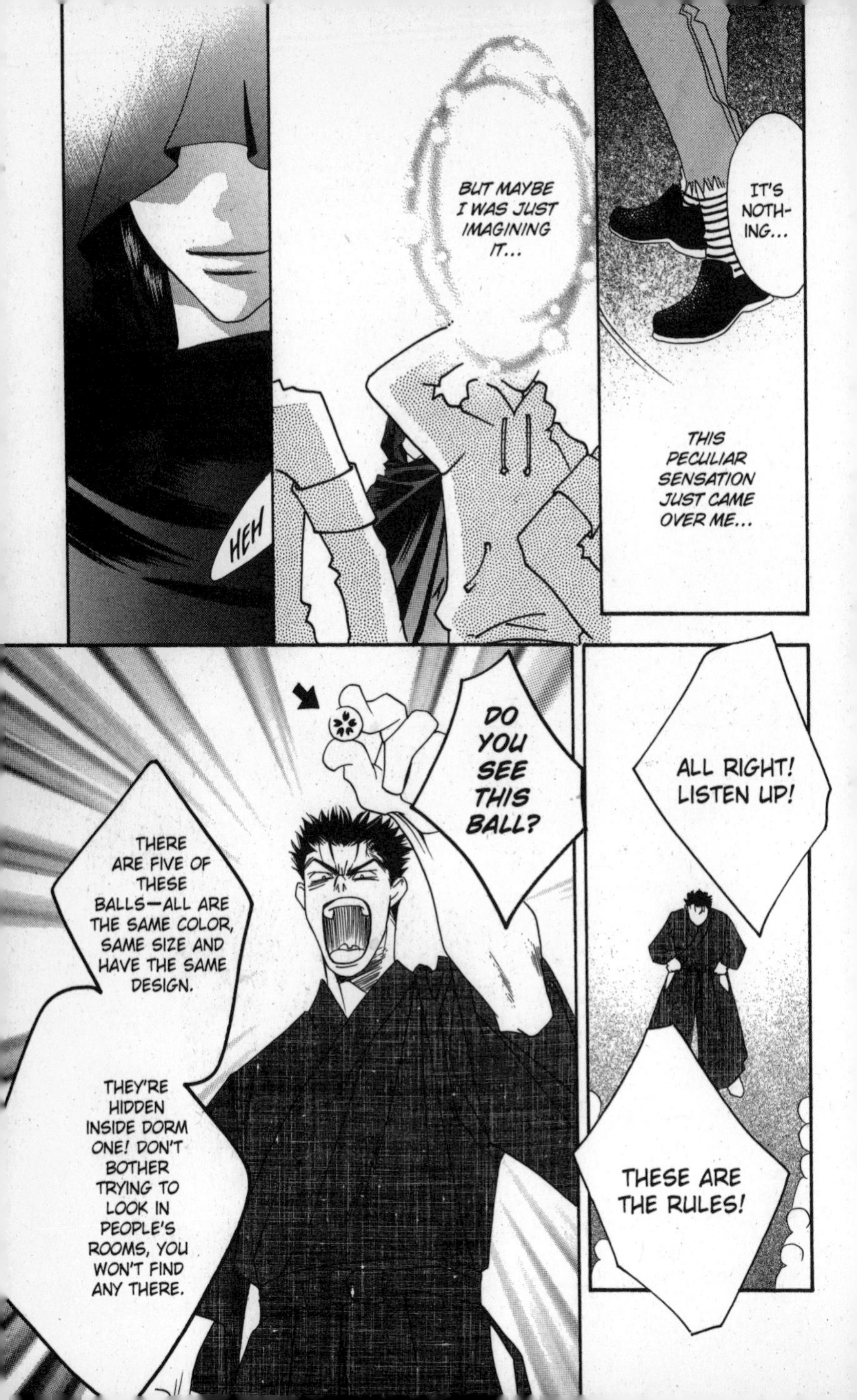
IT'S NOTHING...
THIS PECULIAR SENSATION JUST CAME OVER ME...
BUT MAYBE I WAS JUST IMAGINING IT...
HEH
ALL RIGHT! LISTEN UP!
THESE ARE THE RULES!
DO YOU SEE THIS BALL?
THERE ARE FIVE OF THESE BALLS—ALL ARE THE SAME COLOR, SAME SIZE AND HAVE THE SAME DESIGN.
THEY'RE HIDDEN INSIDE DORM ONE! DON'T BOTHER TRYING TO LOOK IN PEOPLE'S ROOMS, YOU WON'T FIND ANY THERE.

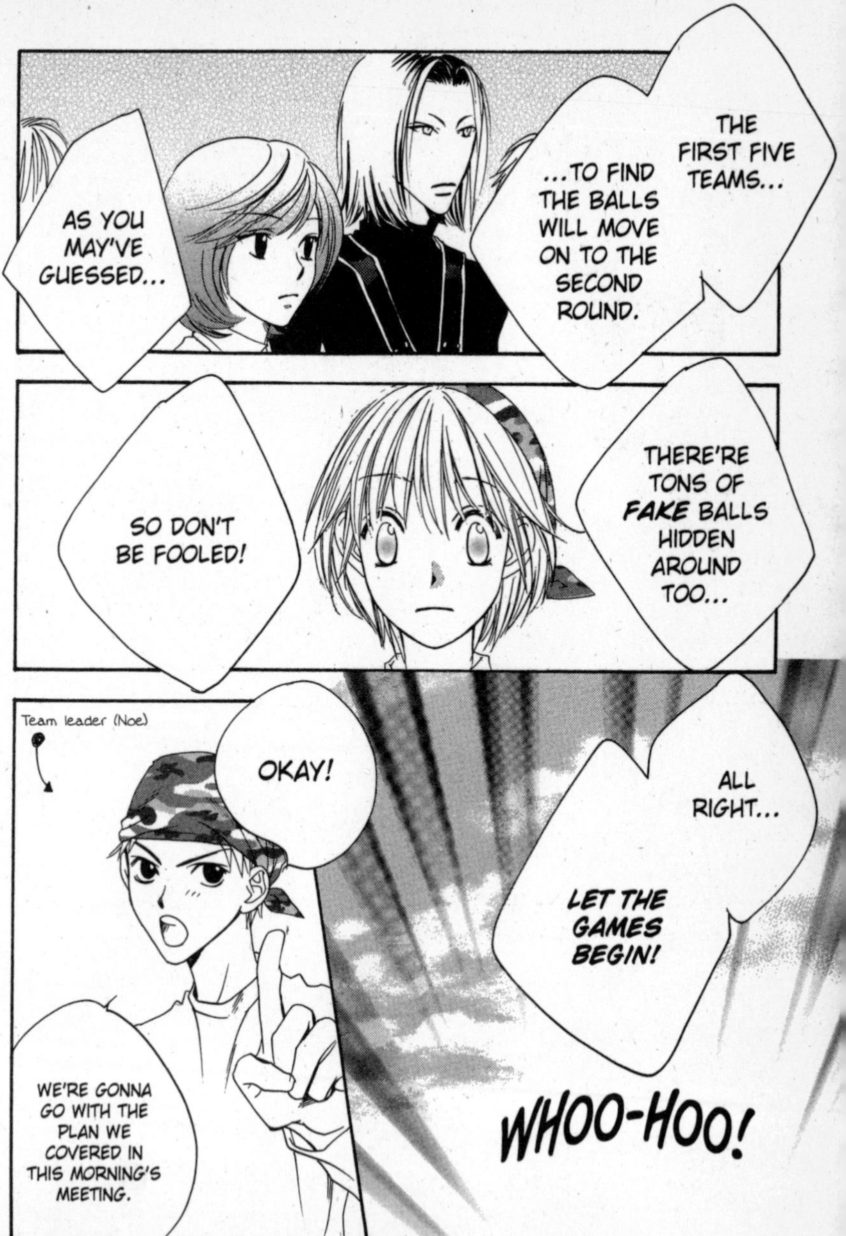
THE FIRST FIVE TEAMS...
...TO FIND THE BALLS WILL MOVE ON TO THE SECOND ROUND.
AS YOU MAY'VE GUESSED...
THERE'RE TONS OF *FAKE* BALLS HIDDEN AROUND TOO...
SO DON'T BE FOOLED!
ALL RIGHT...
LET THE GAMES BEGIN!
WHOO-HOO!
OKAY!
Team leader (Noe)
WE'RE GONNA GO WITH THE PLAN WE COVERED IN THIS MORNING'S MEETING.

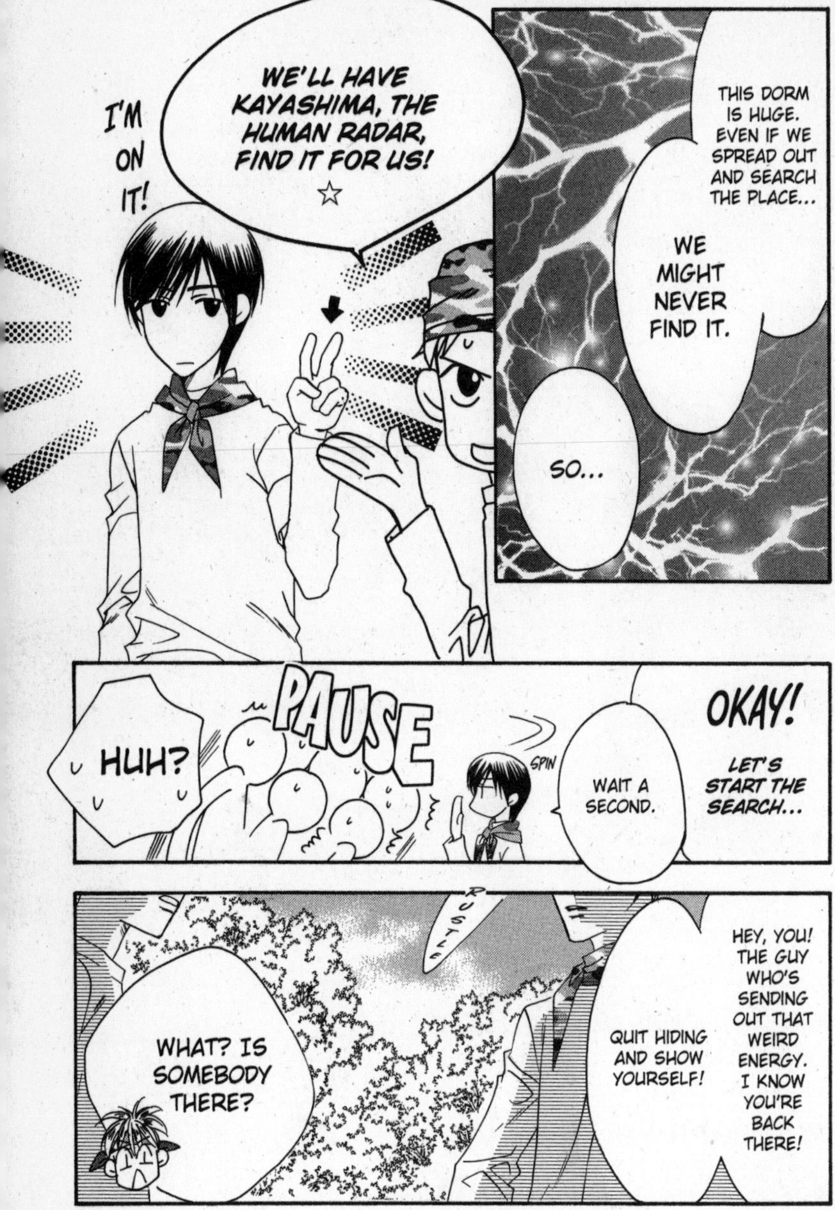
THIS DORM IS HUGE. EVEN IF WE SPREAD OUT AND SEARCH THE PLACE...
WE MIGHT NEVER FIND IT.
SO...
WE'LL HAVE KAYASHIMA, THE HUMAN RADAR, FIND IT FOR US! ☆
I'M ON IT!
OKAY!
LET'S START THE SEARCH...
WAIT A SECOND.
SPIN
PAUSE
HUH?
RUSTLE
HEY, YOU! THE GUY WHO'S SENDING OUT THAT WEIRD ENERGY. I KNOW YOU'RE BACK THERE!
QUIT HIDING AND SHOW YOURSELF!
WHAT? IS SOMEBODY THERE?

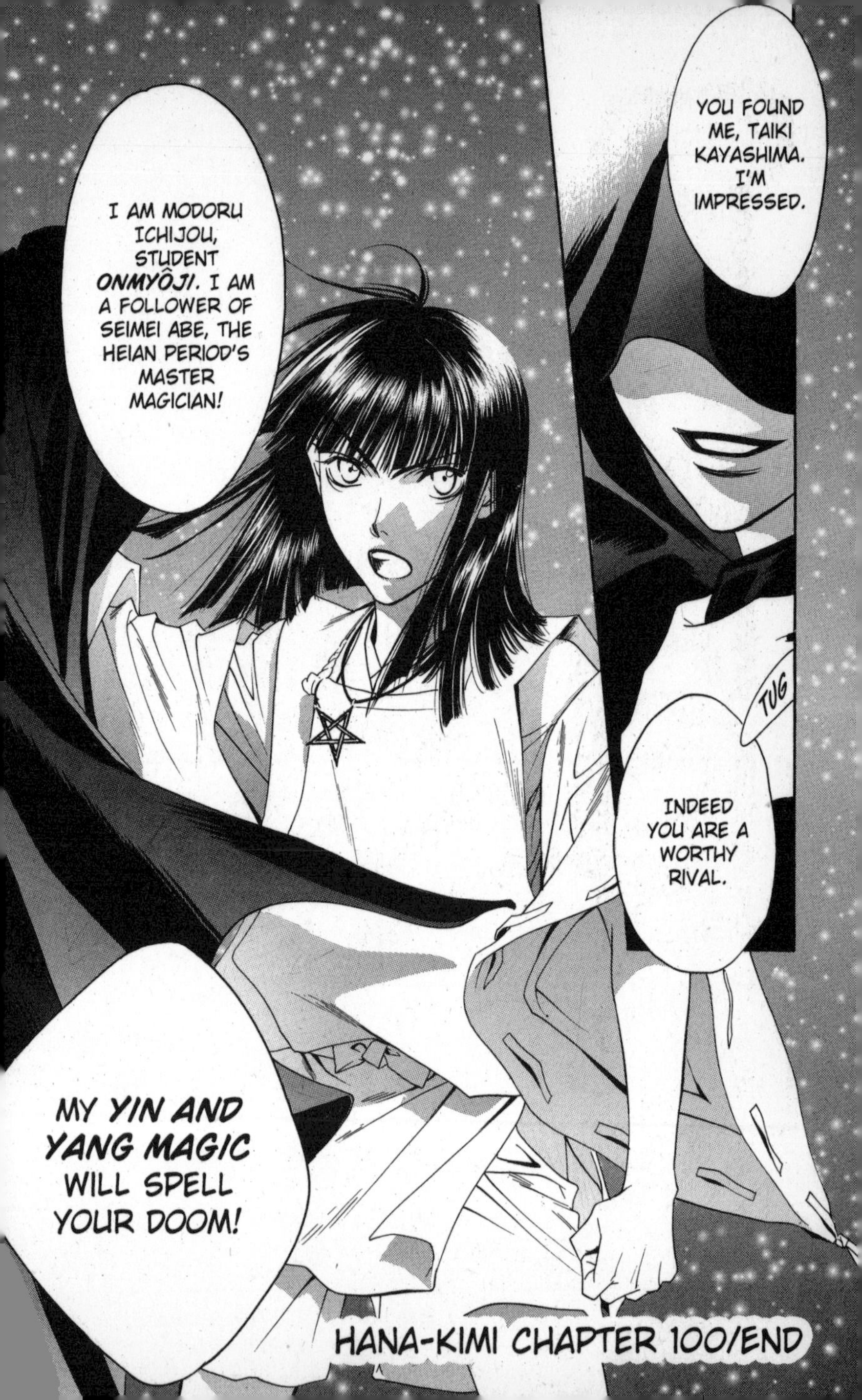

HANA-KIMI CHAPTER 100/END

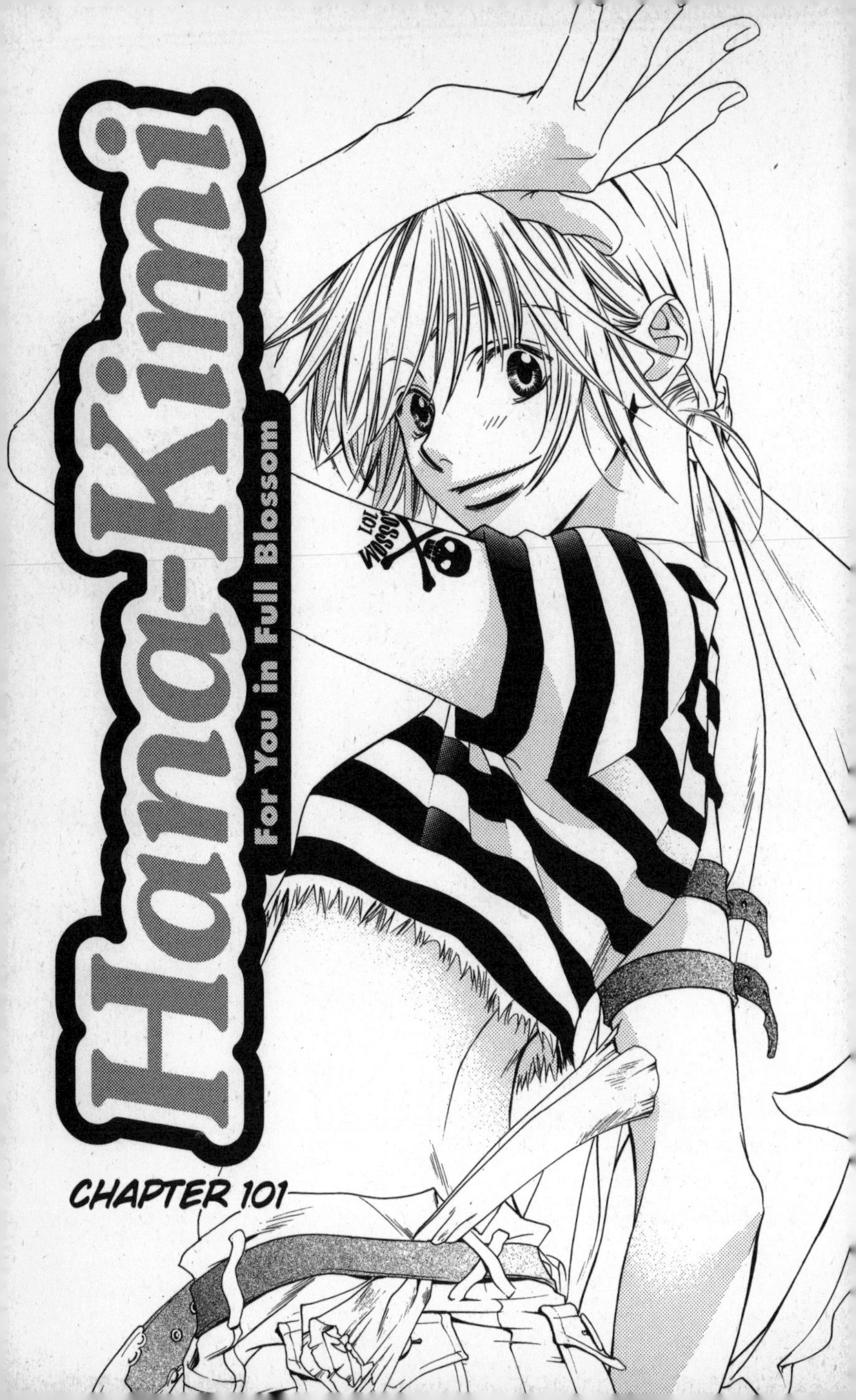
Hana-Kimi
For You in Full Blossom
CHAPTER 101

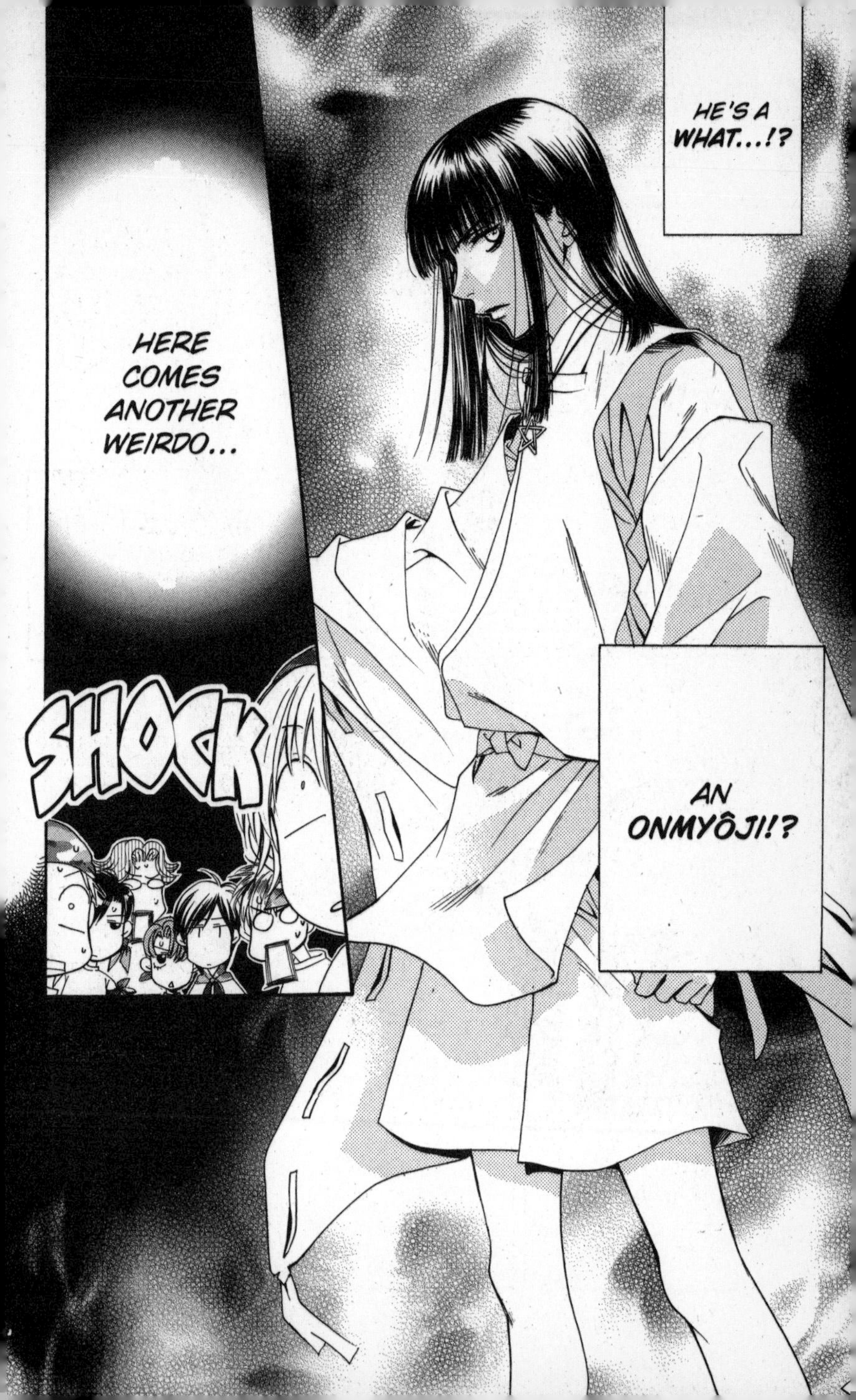
HE'S A WHAT...!?
AN ONMYÔJI!?
HERE COMES ANOTHER WEIRDO...
SHOCK

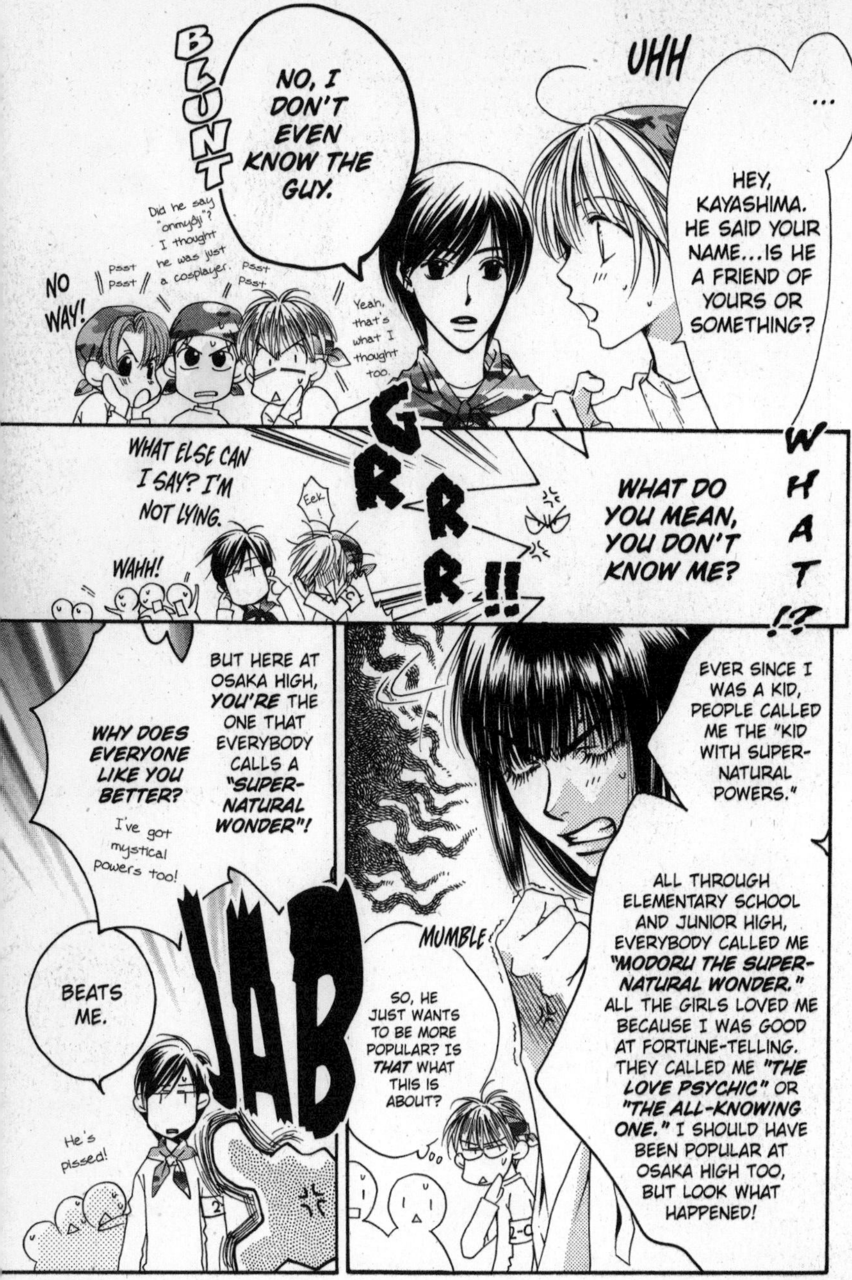
UHH
...
HEY, KAYASHIMA. HE SAID YOUR NAME...IS HE A FRIEND OF YOURS OR SOMETHING?
NO, I DON'T EVEN KNOW THE GUY.
BLUNT
Yeah, that's what I thought too.
Did he say "onmyôji"? I thought he was just a cosplayer.
Psst Psst
Psst Psst
NO WAY!
WHAT!?
WHAT DO YOU MEAN, YOU DON'T KNOW ME?
GRRR!!
Eek!
WHAT ELSE CAN I SAY? I'M NOT LYING.
WAHH!
EVER SINCE I WAS A KID, PEOPLE CALLED ME THE "KID WITH SUPER-NATURAL POWERS."
ALL THROUGH ELEMENTARY SCHOOL AND JUNIOR HIGH, EVERYBODY CALLED ME "MODORU THE SUPER-NATURAL WONDER." ALL THE GIRLS LOVED ME BECAUSE I WAS GOOD AT FORTUNE-TELLING. THEY CALLED ME "THE LOVE PSYCHIC" OR "THE ALL-KNOWING ONE." I SHOULD HAVE BEEN POPULAR AT OSAKA HIGH TOO, BUT LOOK WHAT HAPPENED!
MUMBLE
SO, HE JUST WANTS TO BE MORE POPULAR? IS THAT WHAT THIS IS ABOUT?
BUT HERE AT OSAKA HIGH, YOU'RE THE ONE THAT EVERYBODY CALLS A "SUPER-NATURAL WONDER"!
WHY DOES EVERYONE LIKE YOU BETTER?
I've got mystical powers too!
JAB
BEATS ME.
He's pissed!

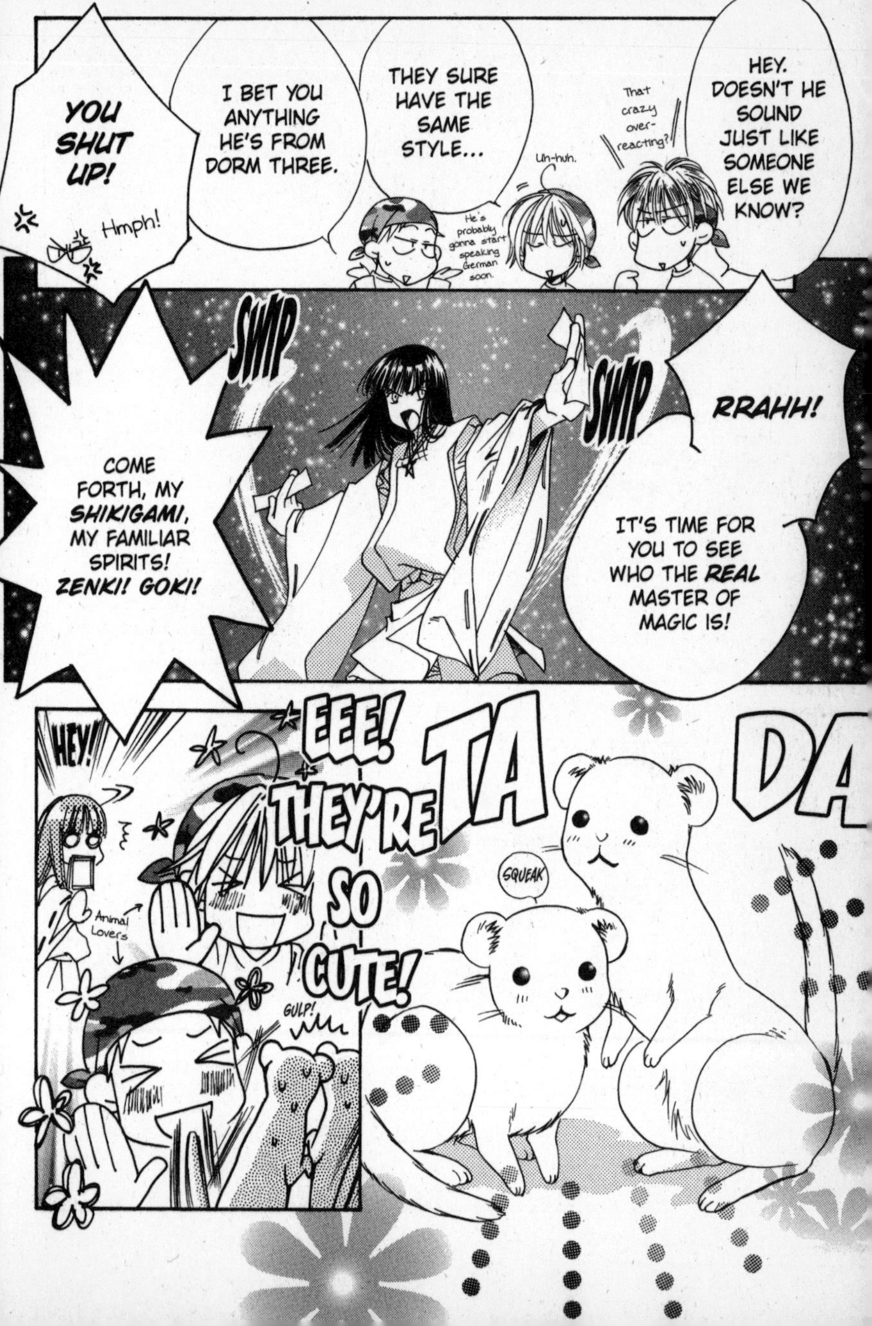
HEY. DOESN'T HE SOUND JUST LIKE SOMEONE ELSE WE KNOW?
That crazy over-reacting?
Uh-huh.
THEY SURE HAVE THE SAME STYLE...
He's probably gonna start speaking German soon.
I BET YOU ANYTHING HE'S FROM DORM THREE.
YOU SHUT UP!
Hmph!
RRAHH!
IT'S TIME FOR YOU TO SEE WHO THE REAL MASTER OF MAGIC IS!
SWIP
SWIP
COME FORTH, MY SHIKIGAMI, MY FAMILIAR SPIRITS! ZENKI! GOKI!
TA DA
SQUEAK
EEE! THEY'RE SO CUTE!
HEY!
Animal Lovers
GULP!

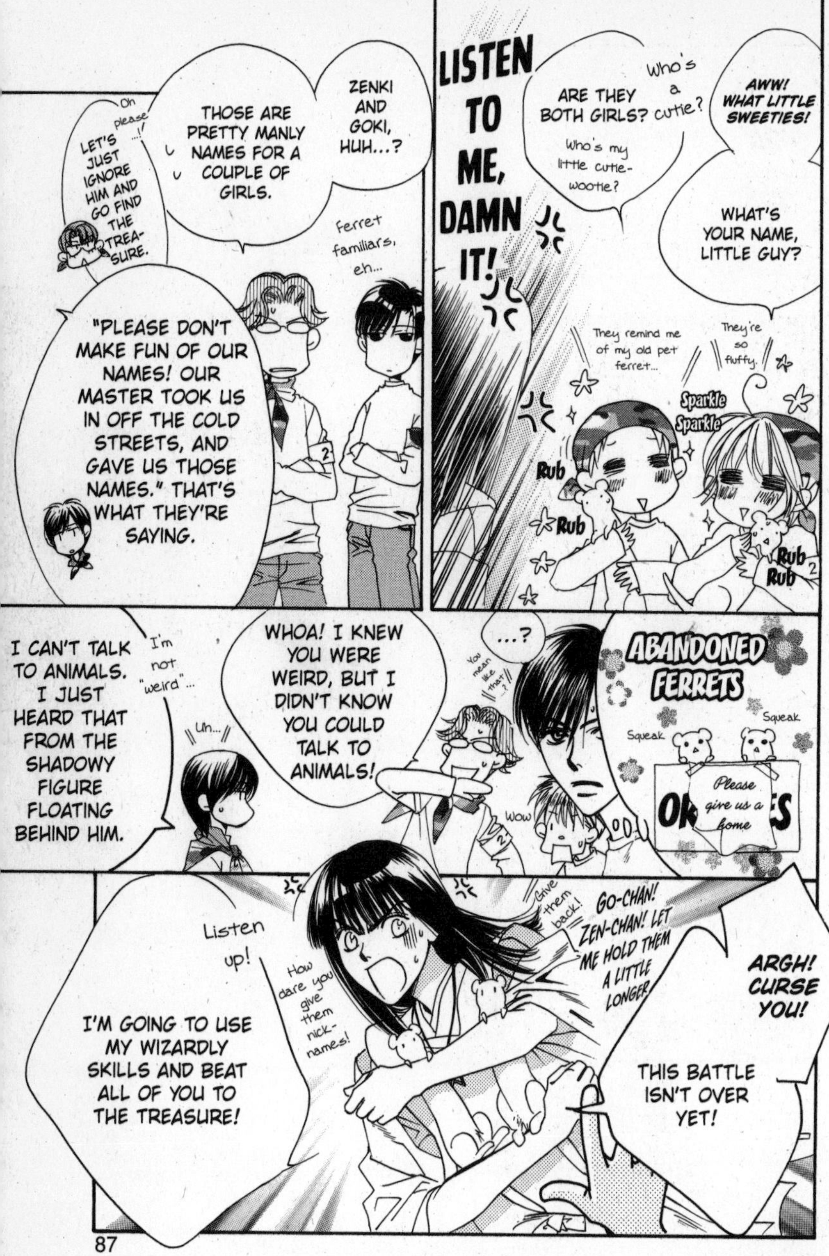
AWW! WHAT LITTLE SWEETIES!
WHAT'S YOUR NAME, LITTLE GUY?
Who's a cutie?
ARE THEY BOTH GIRLS?
Who's my little cutie-wootie?
LISTEN TO ME, DAMN IT!
They're so fluffy.
Sparkle Sparkle
They remind me of my old pet ferret...
Rub Rub
Rub
Rub
ZENKI AND GOKI, HUH...?
THOSE ARE PRETTY MANLY NAMES FOR A COUPLE OF GIRLS.
Oh please...!
LET'S JUST IGNORE HIM AND GO FIND THE TREASURE.
Ferret familiars, eh...
"PLEASE DON'T MAKE FUN OF OUR NAMES! OUR MASTER TOOK US IN OFF THE COLD STREETS, AND GAVE US THOSE NAMES." THAT'S WHAT THEY'RE SAYING.
ABANDONED FERRETS
Squeak
Squeak
Please give us a home
...?
You mean like that...?
Wow
WHOA! I KNEW YOU WERE WEIRD, BUT I DIDN'T KNOW YOU COULD TALK TO ANIMALS!
I'm not "weird"...
I CAN'T TALK TO ANIMALS. I JUST HEARD THAT FROM THE SHADOWY FIGURE FLOATING BEHIND HIM.
Uh...
ARGH! CURSE YOU!
THIS BATTLE ISN'T OVER YET!
GO-CHAN! ZEN-CHAN! LET ME HOLD THEM A LITTLE LONGER
Give them back!
How dare you give them nick-names!
Listen up!
I'M GOING TO USE MY WIZARDLY SKILLS AND BEAT ALL OF YOU TO THE TREASURE!

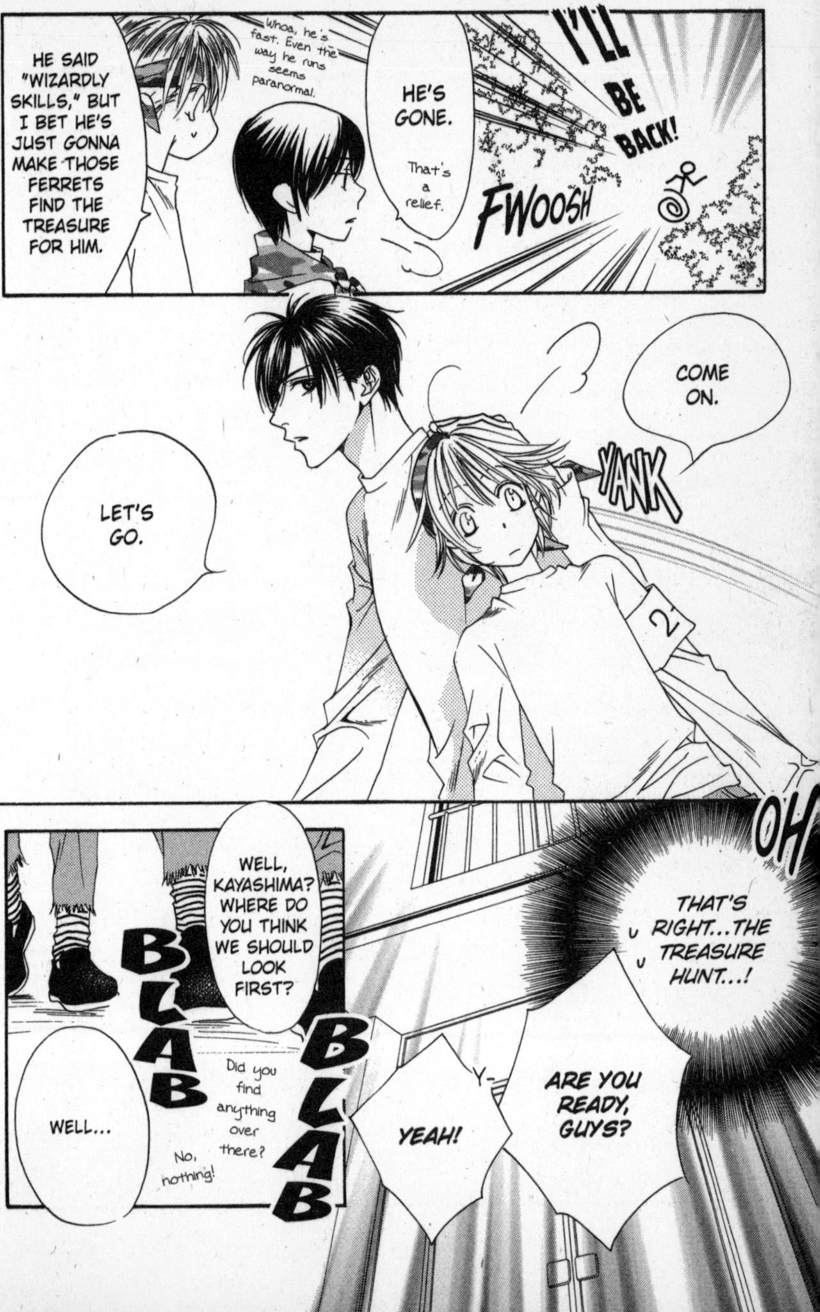
I'LL BE BACK!
FWOOSH
HE'S GONE.
That's a relief.
Whoa, he's fast. Even the way he runs seems paranormal.
HE SAID "WIZARDLY SKILLS," BUT I BET HE'S JUST GONNA MAKE THOSE FERRETS FIND THE TREASURE FOR HIM.
COME ON.
YANK
LET'S GO.
OH
THAT'S RIGHT...THE TREASURE HUNT...!
ARE YOU READY, GUYS?
Y-
YEAH!
WELL, KAYASHIMA? WHERE DO YOU THINK WE SHOULD LOOK FIRST?
BLAB BLAB
Did you find anything over there?
No, nothing!
BLAB BLAB
WELL...

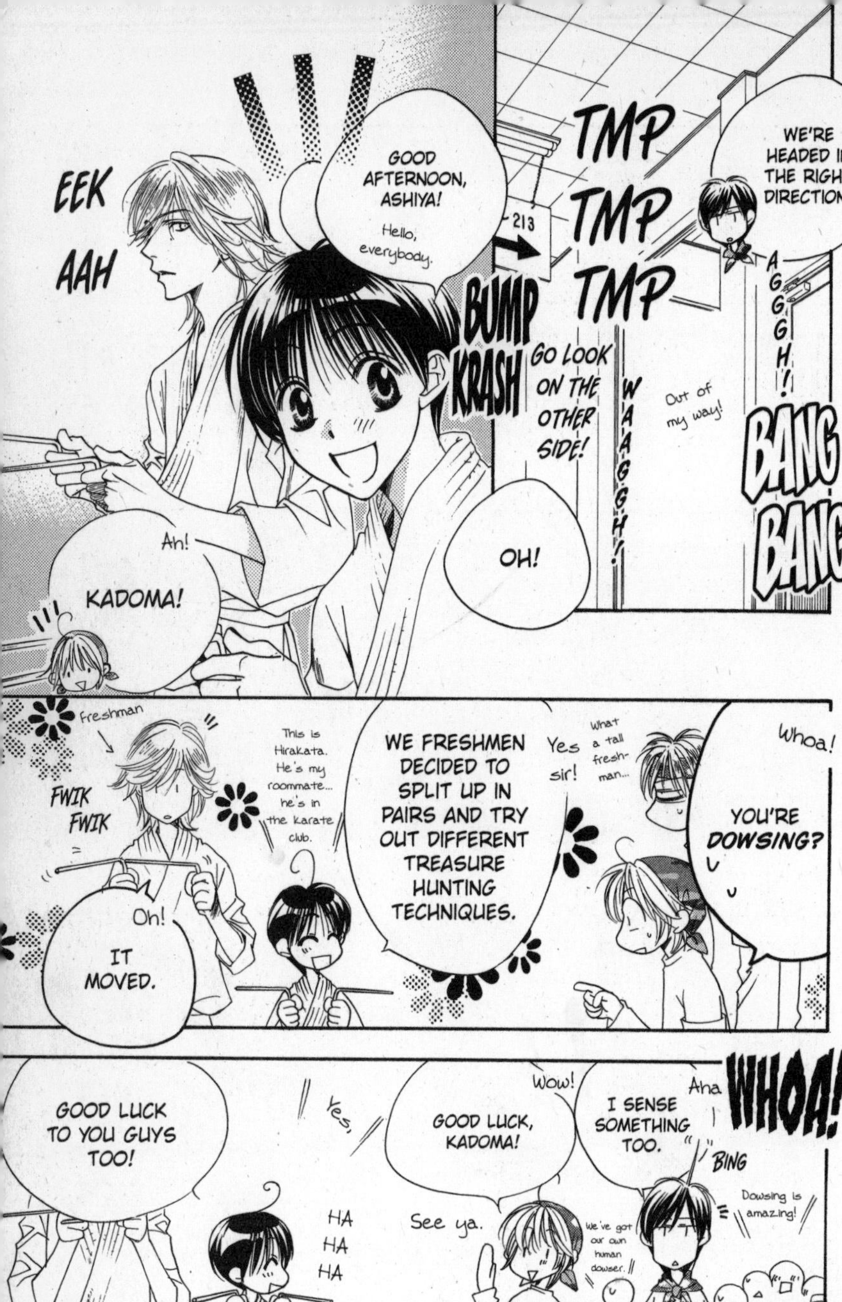
WE'RE HEADED IN THE RIGHT DIRECTION.
TMP TMP TMP
213
AGGGH!
BANG BANG
Out of my way!
WAAAGGGH!
GO LOOK ON THE OTHER SIDE!
BUMP KRASH
GOOD AFTERNOON, ASHIYA!
Hello, everybody.
OH!
EEK AAH
Ah!
KADOMA!
Whoa!
YOU'RE DOWSING?
What a tall freshman...
Yes sir!
WE FRESHMEN DECIDED TO SPLIT UP IN PAIRS AND TRY OUT DIFFERENT TREASURE HUNTING TECHNIQUES.
This is Hirakata. He's my roommate... he's in the karate club.
Freshman
FWIK FWIK
Oh!
IT MOVED.
WHOA!
Aha
I SENSE SOMETHING TOO.
BING
Dowsing is amazing!
We've got our own human dowser.
Wow!
GOOD LUCK, KADOMA!
See ya.
Yes,
GOOD LUCK TO YOU GUYS TOO!
HA HA HA

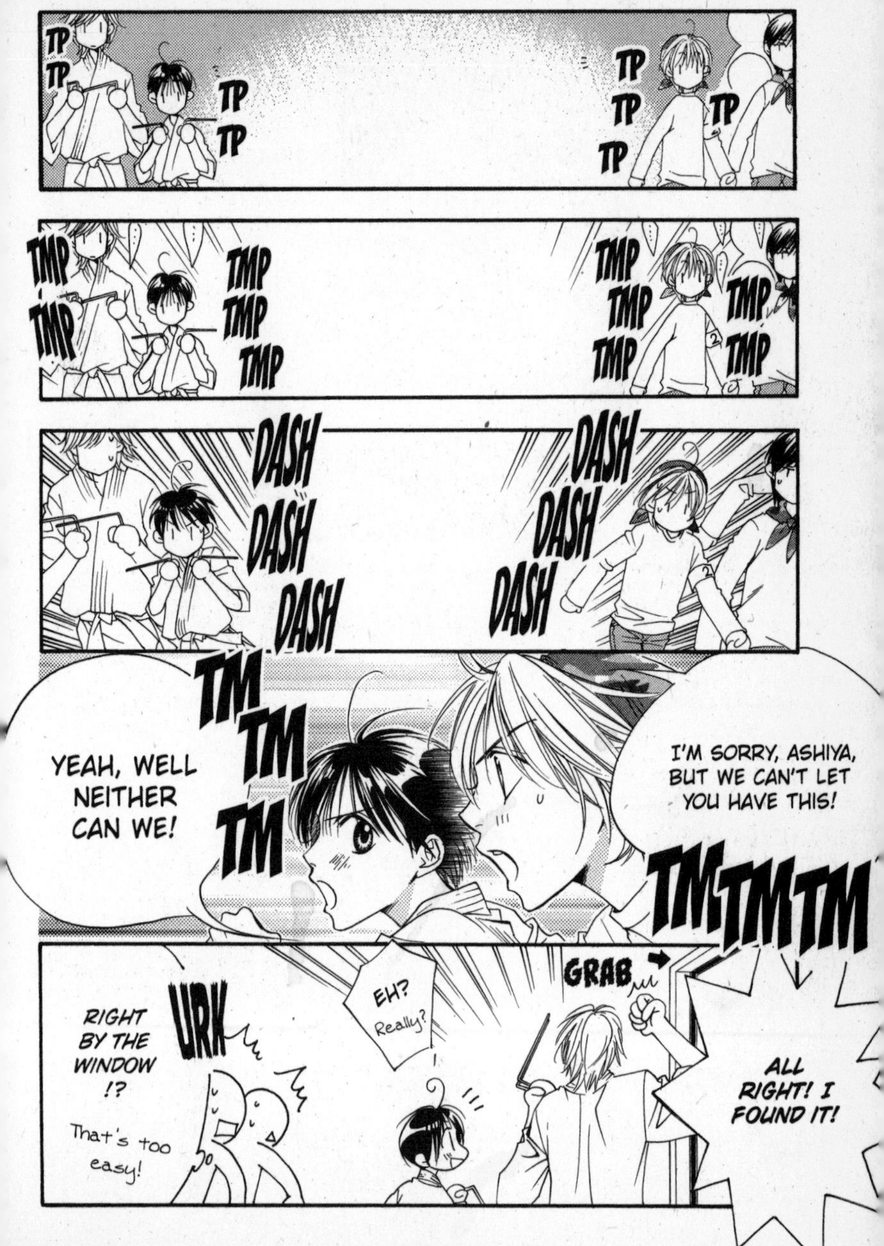
TP TP TP TP
TP TP TP TP
TMP TMP TMP TMP TMP
TMP TMP TMP TMP TMP
DASH DASH DASH
DASH DASH DASH
I'M SORRY, ASHIYA, BUT WE CAN'T LET YOU HAVE THIS!
TM TM TM
TM TM TM
YEAH, WELL NEITHER CAN WE!
ALL RIGHT! I FOUND IT!
GRAB
EH? Really?
URK
RIGHT BY THE WINDOW !?
That's too easy!

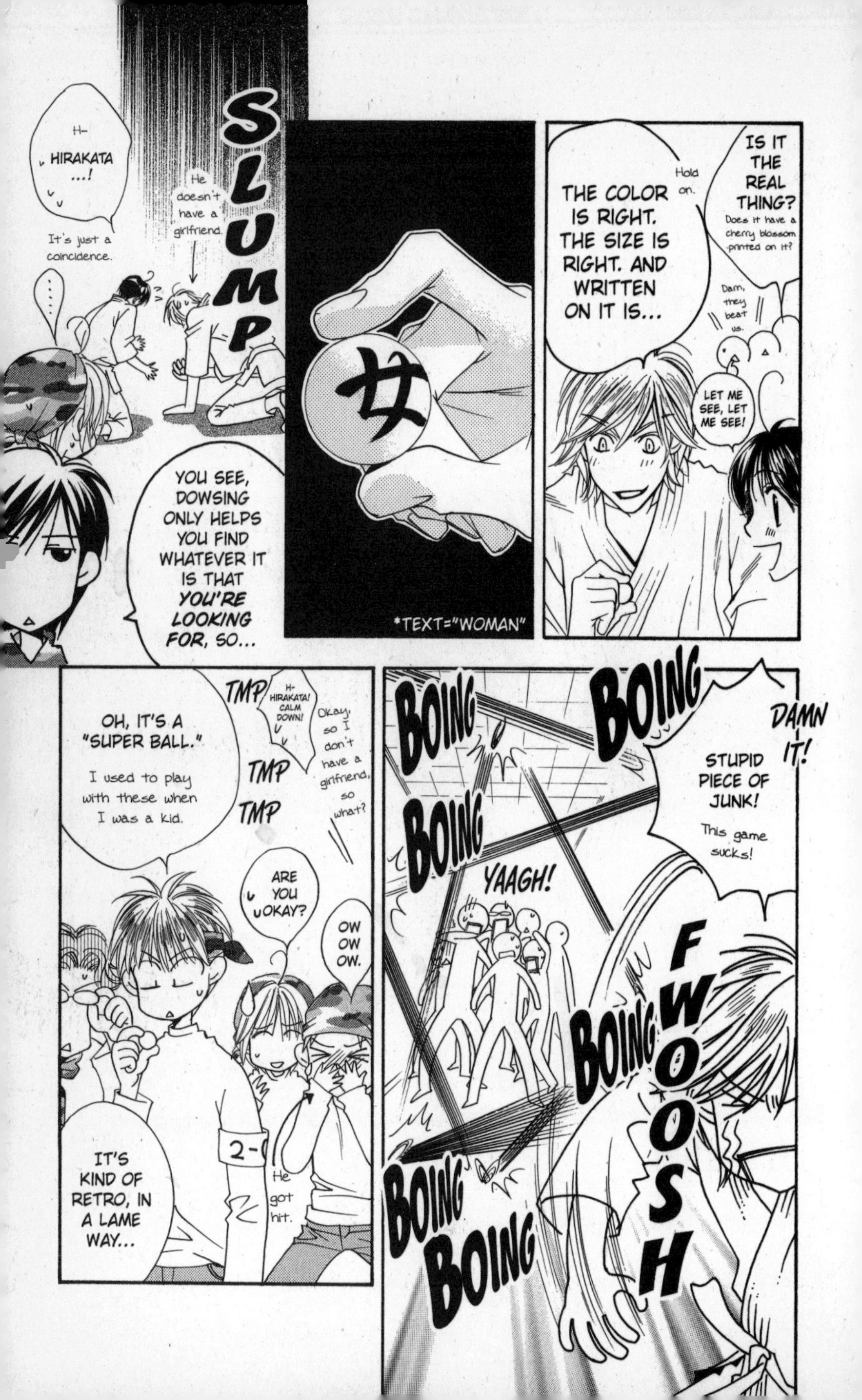
IS IT THE REAL THING?
Does it have a cherry blossom printed on it?
Hold on.
THE COLOR IS RIGHT. THE SIZE IS RIGHT. AND WRITTEN ON IT IS...
Dam, they beat us.
LET ME SEE, LET ME SEE!
女
*TEXT="WOMAN"
SLUMP
He doesn't have a girlfriend.
H- HIRAKATA...!
It's just a coincidence.
...
YOU SEE, DOWSING ONLY HELPS YOU FIND WHATEVER IT IS THAT YOU'RE LOOKING FOR, SO...
DAMN IT!
STUPID PIECE OF JUNK!
This game sucks!
BOING
BOING
BOING
YAAGH!
BOING
FWOOSH
BOING
BOING
BOING
Okay, so I don't have a girlfriend, so what?
H-HIRAKATA! CALM DOWN!
TMP
TMP
TMP
OH, IT'S A "SUPER BALL."
I used to play with these when I was a kid.
OW OW OW.
ARE YOU OKAY?
He got hit.
2-
IT'S KIND OF RETRO, IN A LAME WAY...

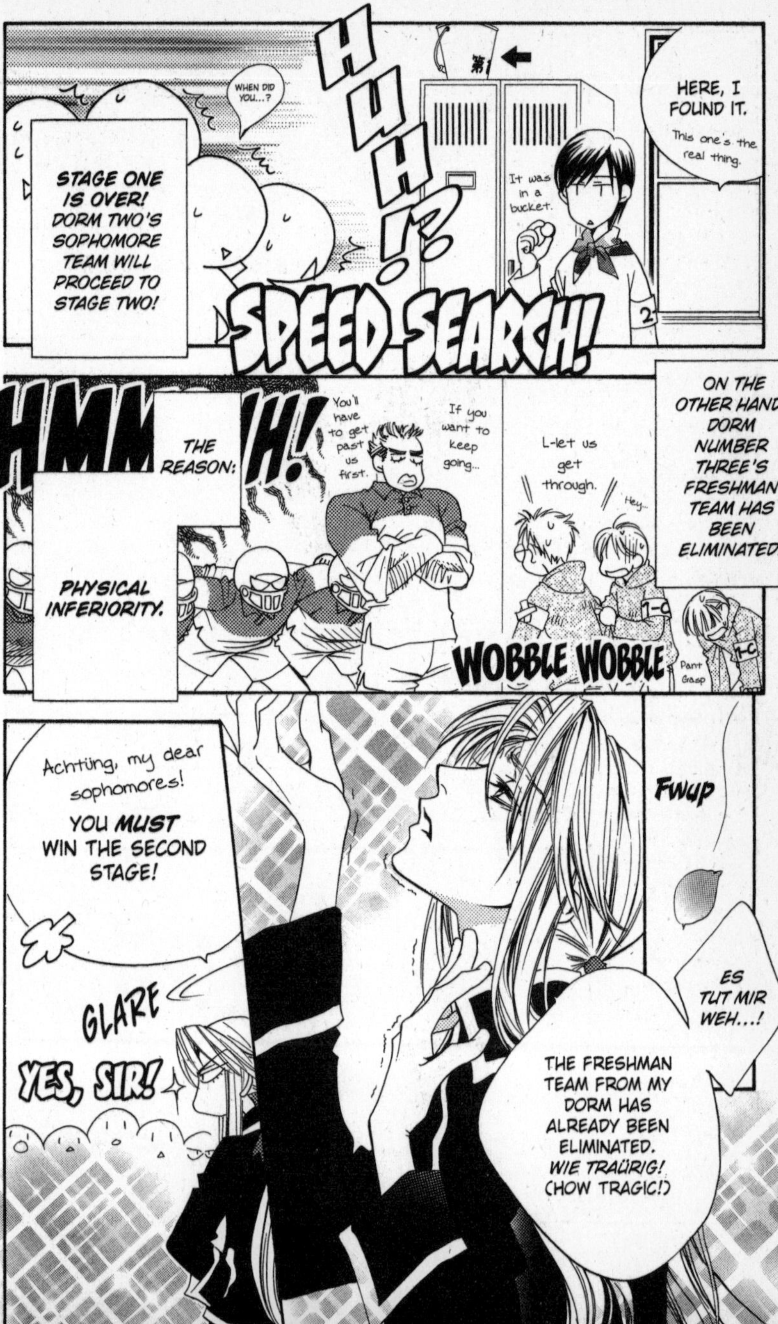
HERE, I FOUND IT.
This one's the real thing.
It was in a bucket.
HUH!?
WHEN DID YOU...?
STAGE ONE IS OVER! DORM TWO'S SOPHOMORE TEAM WILL PROCEED TO STAGE TWO!
SPEED SEARCH!
ON THE OTHER HAND, DORM NUMBER THREE'S FRESHMAN TEAM HAS BEEN ELIMINATED.
L-let us get through.
Hey...
WOBBLE WOBBLE
Pant Grasp
If you want to keep going...
You'll have to get past us first.
THE REASON:
HMM
H!
PHYSICAL INFERIORITY.
Fwup
ES TUT MIR WEH...!
THE FRESHMAN TEAM FROM MY DORM HAS ALREADY BEEN ELIMINATED. WIE TRAÜRIG! (HOW TRAGIC!)
Achtüng, my dear sophomores!
YOU MUST WIN THE SECOND STAGE!
GLARE
YES, SIR!

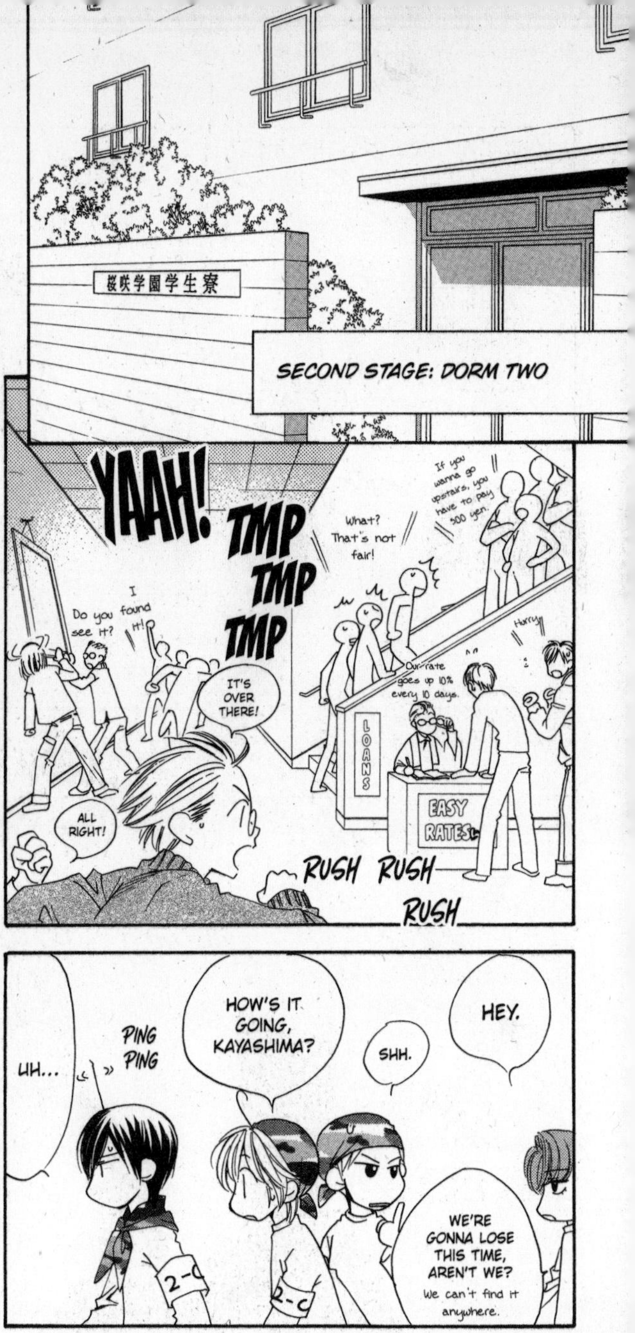
桜咲学園学生寮
SECOND STAGE: DORM TWO
If you wanna go upstairs, you have to pay 500 yen.
Hurry
What? That's not fair!
Our rate goes up 10% every 10 days.
LOANS
EASY RATES
YAAH!
TMP TMP TMP
I found it!
Do you see it?
IT'S OVER THERE!
ALL RIGHT!
RUSH RUSH RUSH
HEY.
SHH.
HOW'S IT GOING, KAYASHIMA?
PING PING
UH...
WE'RE GONNA LOSE THIS TIME, AREN'T WE?
We can't find it anywhere.

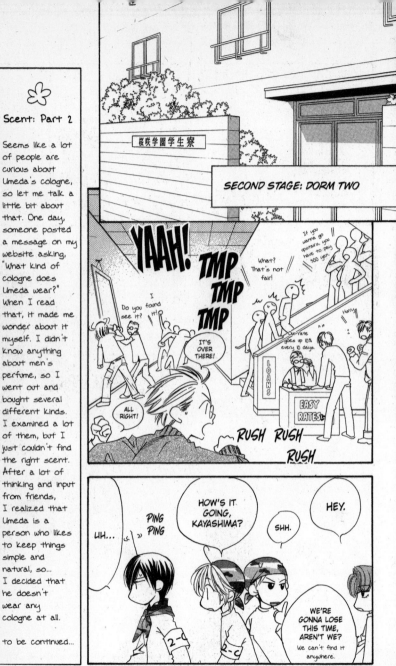

Scent: Part 2

Seems like a lot of people are curious about Umeda's cologne, so let me talk a little bit about that. One day, someone posted a message on my website asking, "What kind of cologne does Umeda wear?" When I read that, it made me wonder about it myself. I didn't know anything about men's perfume, so I went out and bought several different kinds. I examined a lot of them, but I just couldn't find the right scent. After a lot of thinking and input from friends, I realized that Umeda is a person who likes to keep things simple and natural, so... I decided that he doesn't wear any cologne at all.

to be continued...

But he does wear Jean Paul Gaultier clothes...

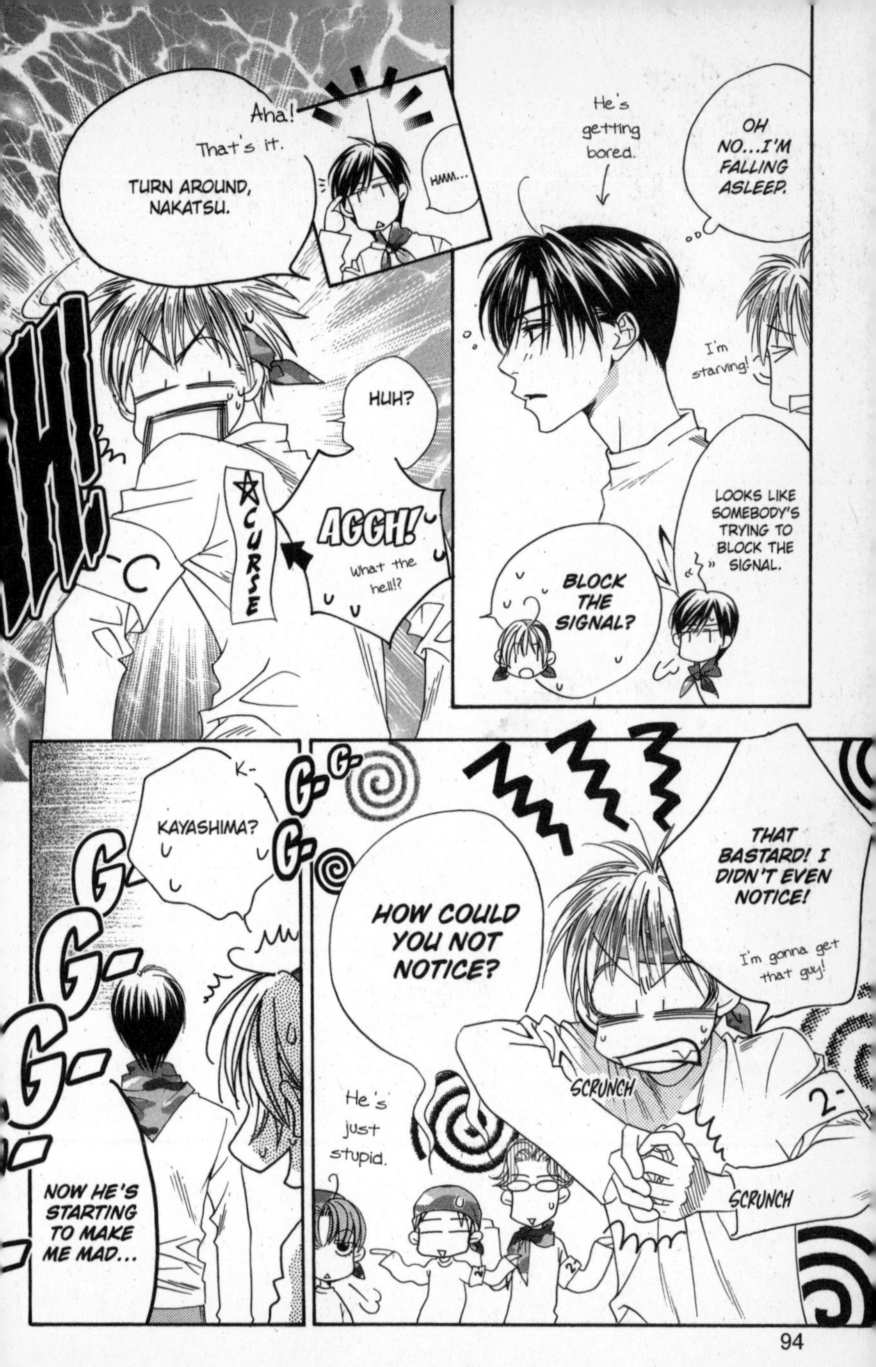
OH NO...I'M FALLING ASLEEP.
He's getting bored.
I'm starving!
LOOKS LIKE SOMEBODY'S TRYING TO BLOCK THE SIGNAL.
BLOCK THE SIGNAL?
HMM...
Aha! That's it.
TURN AROUND, NAKATSU.
HUH?
AGGH!
What the hell!?
CURSE
H!
THAT BASTARD! I DIDN'T EVEN NOTICE!
I'm gonna get that guy!
HOW COULD YOU NOT NOTICE?
SCRUNCH
SCRUNCH
He's just stupid.
K-
KAYASHIMA?
G-G-
G-
G-
G-
G-
NOW HE'S STARTING TO MAKE ME MAD...

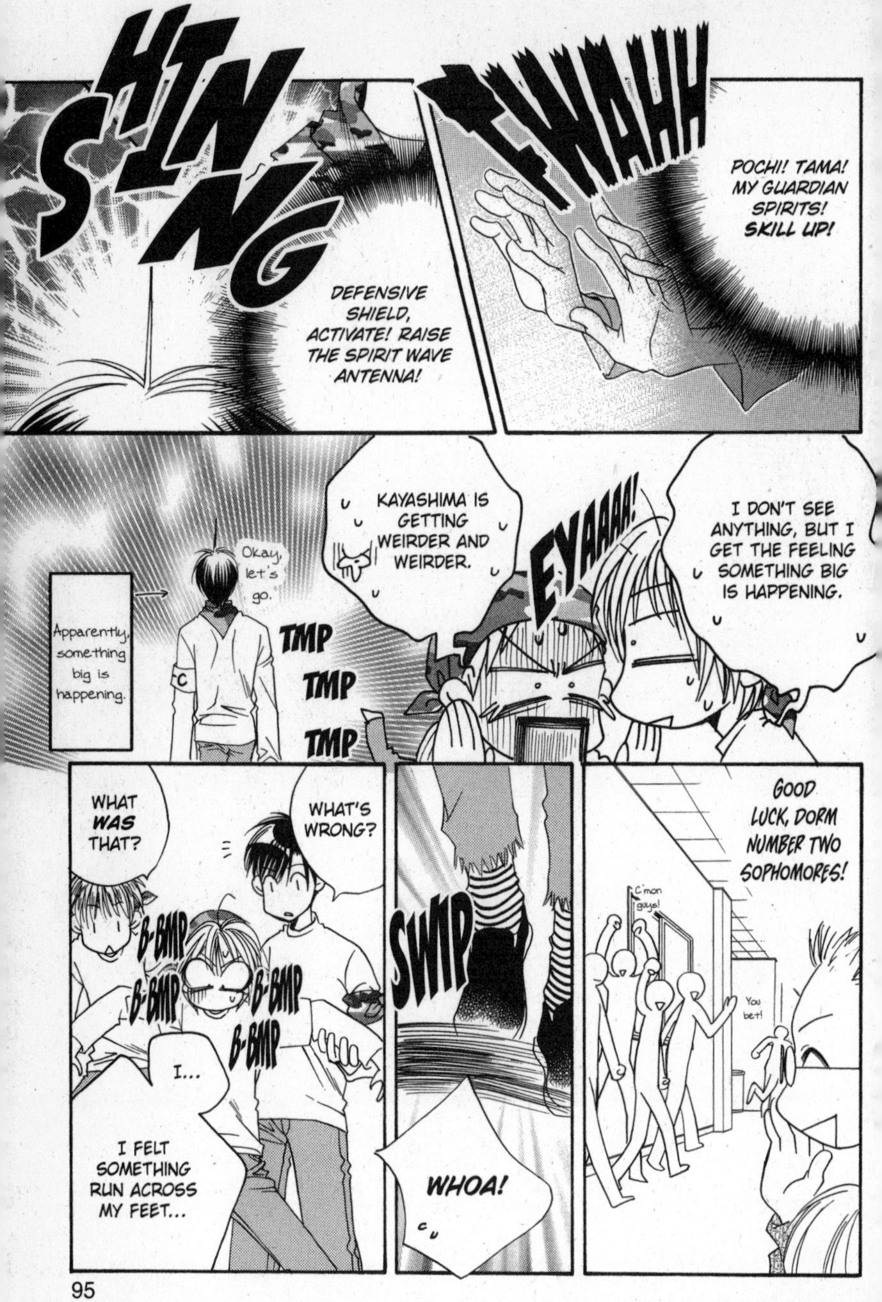
POCHI! TAMA! MY GUARDIAN SPIRITS! SKILL UP!
DEFENSIVE SHIELD, ACTIVATE! RAISE THE SPIRIT WAVE ANTENNA!
I DON'T SEE ANYTHING, BUT I GET THE FEELING SOMETHING BIG IS HAPPENING.
EYAAAA!
KAYASHIMA IS GETTING WEIRDER AND WEIRDER.
Okay, let's go.
TMP
TMP
TMP
Apparently, something big is happening.
GOOD LUCK, DORM NUMBER TWO SOPHOMORES!
C'mon guys!
You bet!
SWIP
WHOA!
WHAT'S WRONG?
WHAT WAS THAT?
B-BMP
B-BMP
B-BMP
B-BMP
B-BMP
I...
I FELT SOMETHING RUN ACROSS MY FEET...

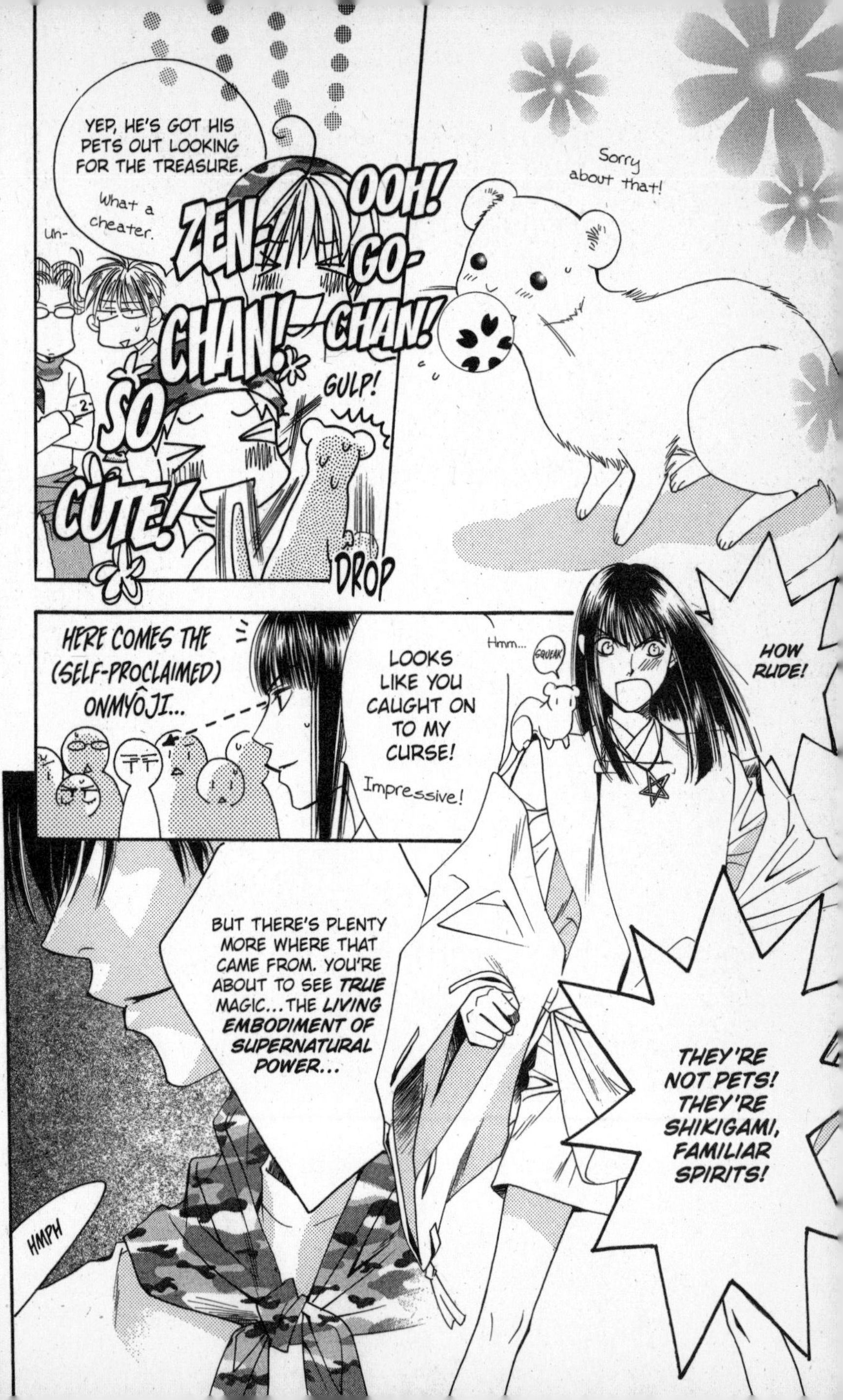
Sorry about that!
YEP, HE'S GOT HIS PETS OUT LOOKING FOR THE TREASURE.
What a cheater.
Un-
OOH! GO-CHAN!
ZEN-CHAN!
SO CUTE!
GULP!
DROP
HOW RUDE!
THEY'RE NOT PETS! THEY'RE SHIKIGAMI, FAMILIAR SPIRITS!
Hmm...
SQUEAK
LOOKS LIKE YOU CAUGHT ON TO MY CURSE!
Impressive!
HERE COMES THE (SELF-PROCLAIMED) ONMYÔJI...
BUT THERE'S PLENTY MORE WHERE THAT CAME FROM. YOU'RE ABOUT TO SEE *TRUE* MAGIC...THE *LIVING EMBODIMENT OF SUPERNATURAL POWER...*
HMPH

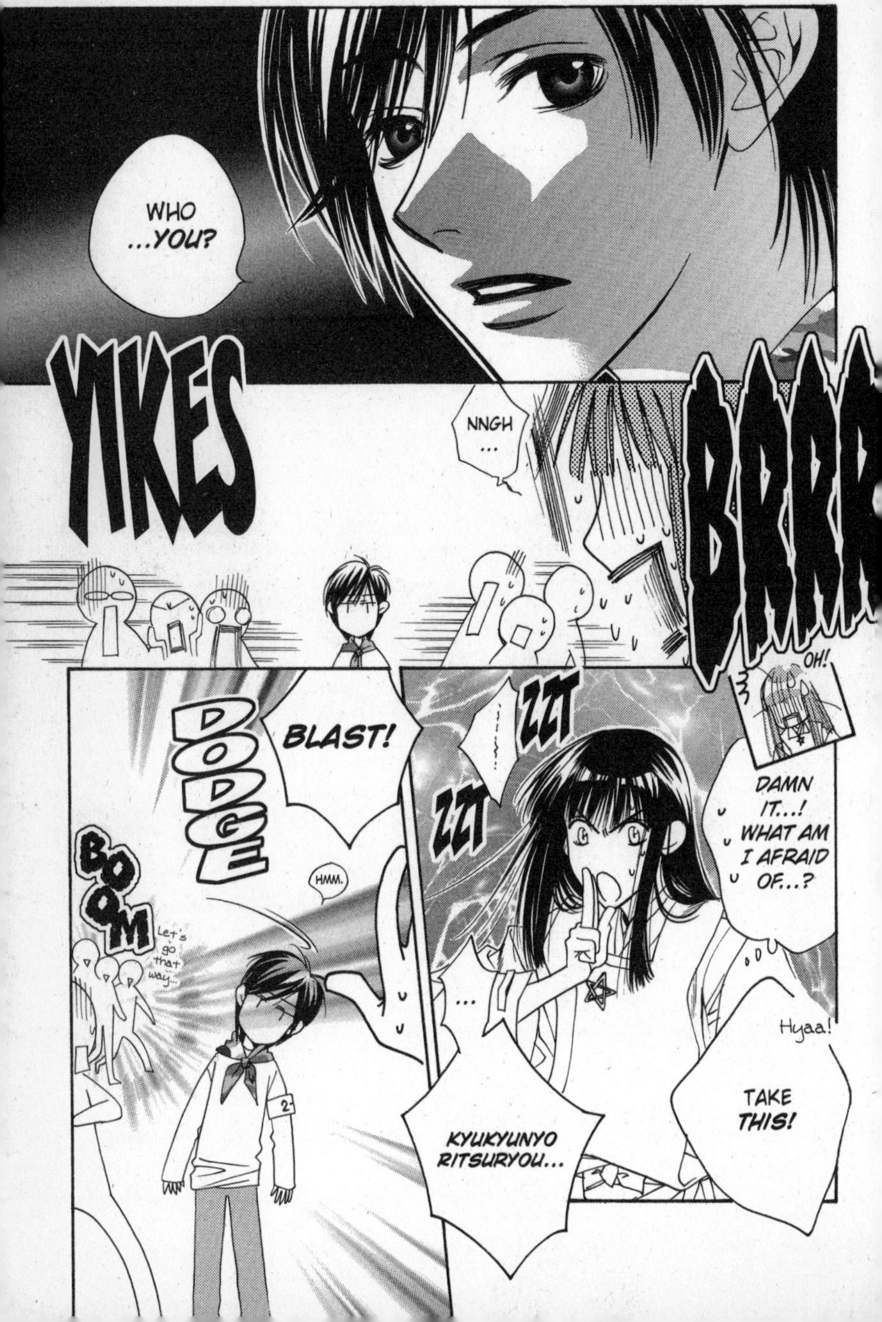
WHO ...YOU?
BRRR
NNGH ...
YIKES
OH!
DAMN IT...! WHAT AM I AFRAID OF...?
ZZT
ZZT
...
Hyaa!
TAKE THIS!
KYUKYUNYO RITSURYOU...
BLAST!
DODGE
HMM.
BOOM
Let's go that way...
...

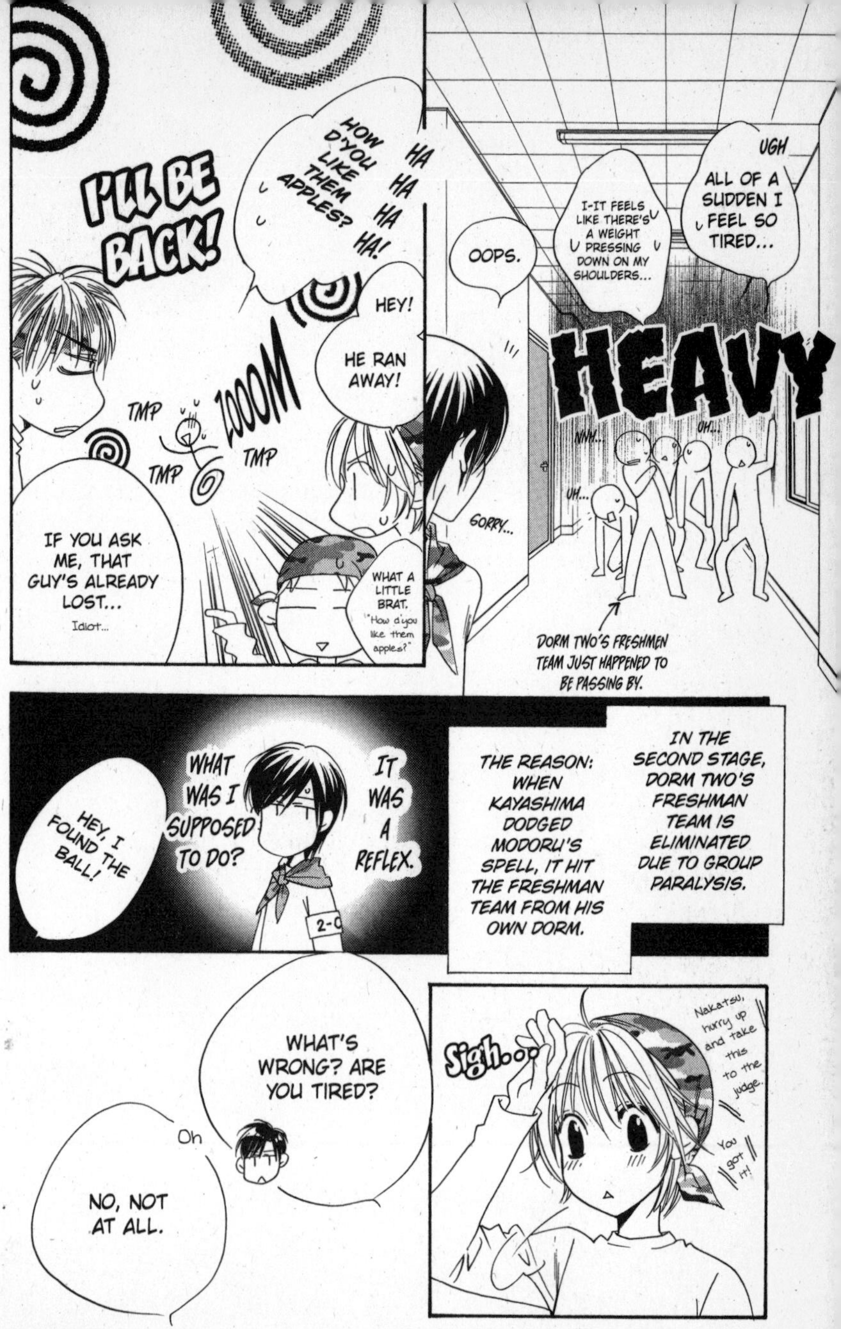
UGH
ALL OF A SUDDEN I FEEL SO TIRED...
I-IT FEELS LIKE THERE'S A WEIGHT PRESSING DOWN ON MY SHOULDERS...
OOPS.
HEAVY
UH...
NNN...
UH...
SORRY...
DORM TWO'S FRESHMEN TEAM JUST HAPPENED TO BE PASSING BY.
HA HA HA HA!
HOW D'YOU LIKE THEM APPLES?
I'LL BE BACK!
HEY!
HE RAN AWAY!
ZOOOM
TMP
TMP
TMP
WHAT A LITTLE BRAT.
"How d'you like them apples?"
IF YOU ASK ME, THAT GUY'S ALREADY LOST...
Idiot...
IN THE SECOND STAGE, DORM TWO'S FRESHMAN TEAM IS ELIMINATED DUE TO GROUP PARALYSIS.
THE REASON: WHEN KAYASHIMA DODGED MODORU'S SPELL, IT HIT THE FRESHMAN TEAM FROM HIS OWN DORM.
IT WAS A REFLEX.
WHAT WAS I SUPPOSED TO DO?
2-C
HEY, I FOUND THE BALL!
Nakatsu, hurry up and take this to the judge.
You got it!
Sigh...
WHAT'S WRONG? ARE YOU TIRED?
Oh
NO, NOT AT ALL.

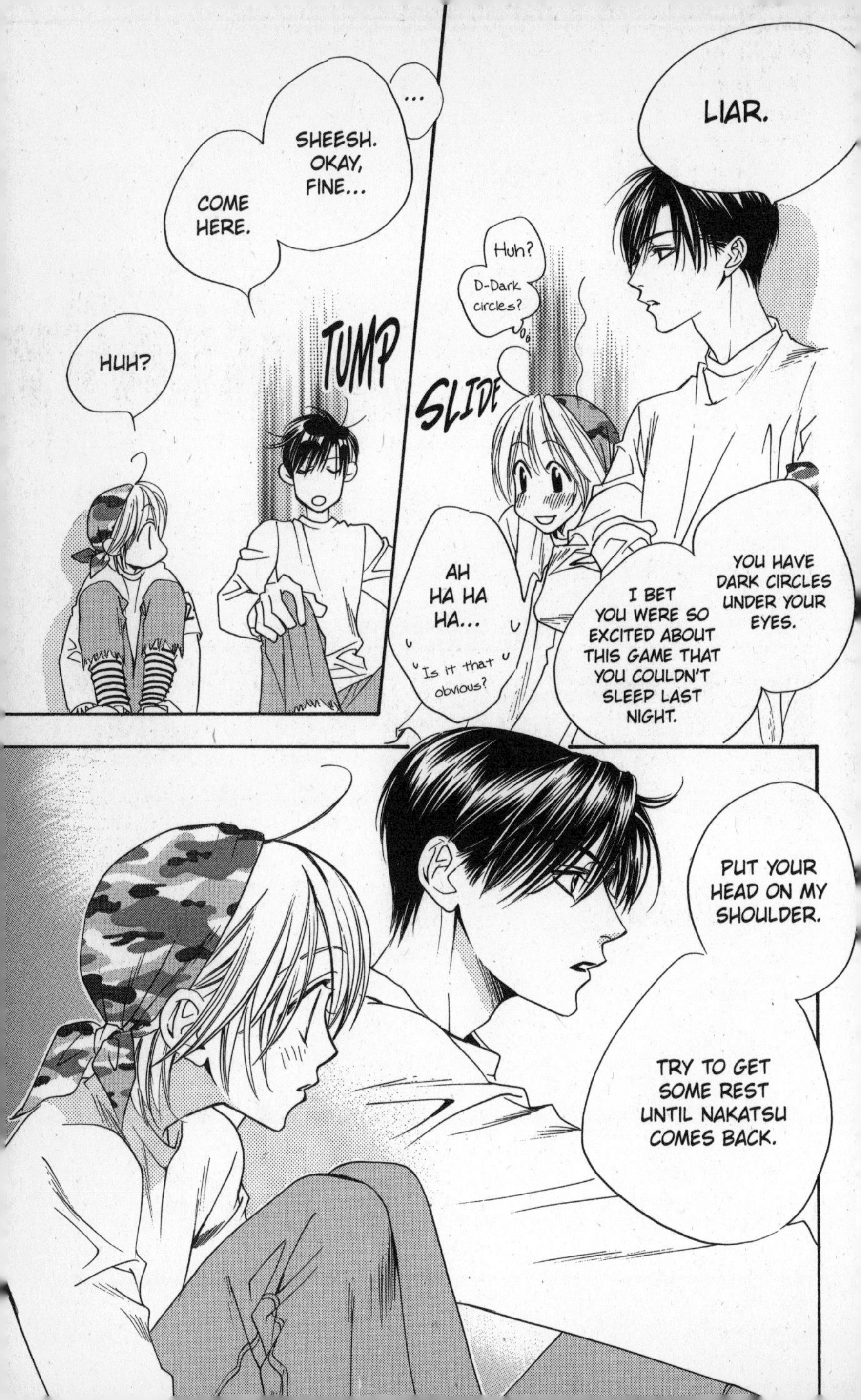
LIAR.
YOU HAVE DARK CIRCLES UNDER YOUR EYES.
I BET YOU WERE SO EXCITED ABOUT THIS GAME THAT YOU COULDN'T SLEEP LAST NIGHT.
Huh?
D-Dark circles?
SLIDE
AH HA HA HA...
Is it that obvious?
...
SHEESH. OKAY, FINE...
COME HERE.
TUMP
HUH?
PUT YOUR HEAD ON MY SHOULDER.
TRY TO GET SOME REST UNTIL NAKATSU COMES BACK.

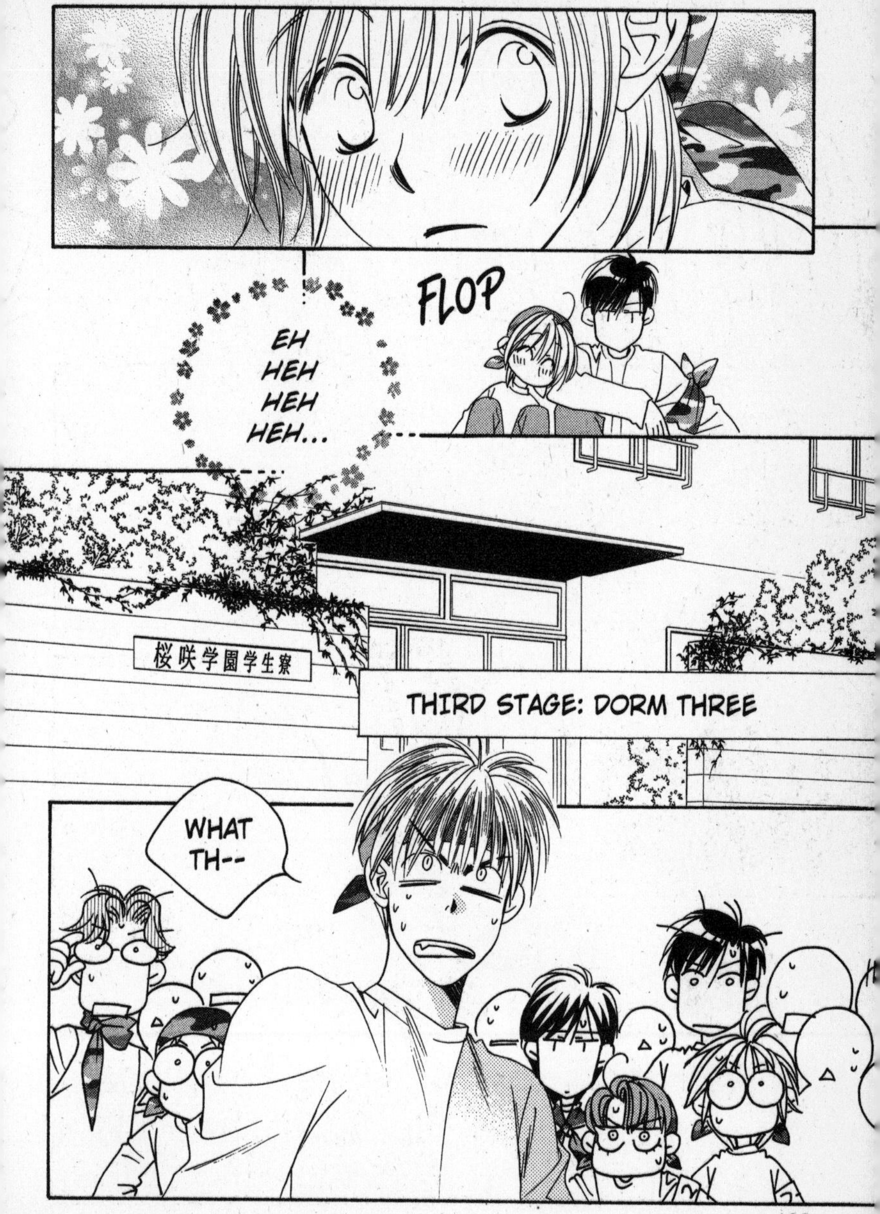
FLOP
EH HEH HEH HEH...
THIRD STAGE: DORM THREE
桜咲学園学生寮
WHAT TH--

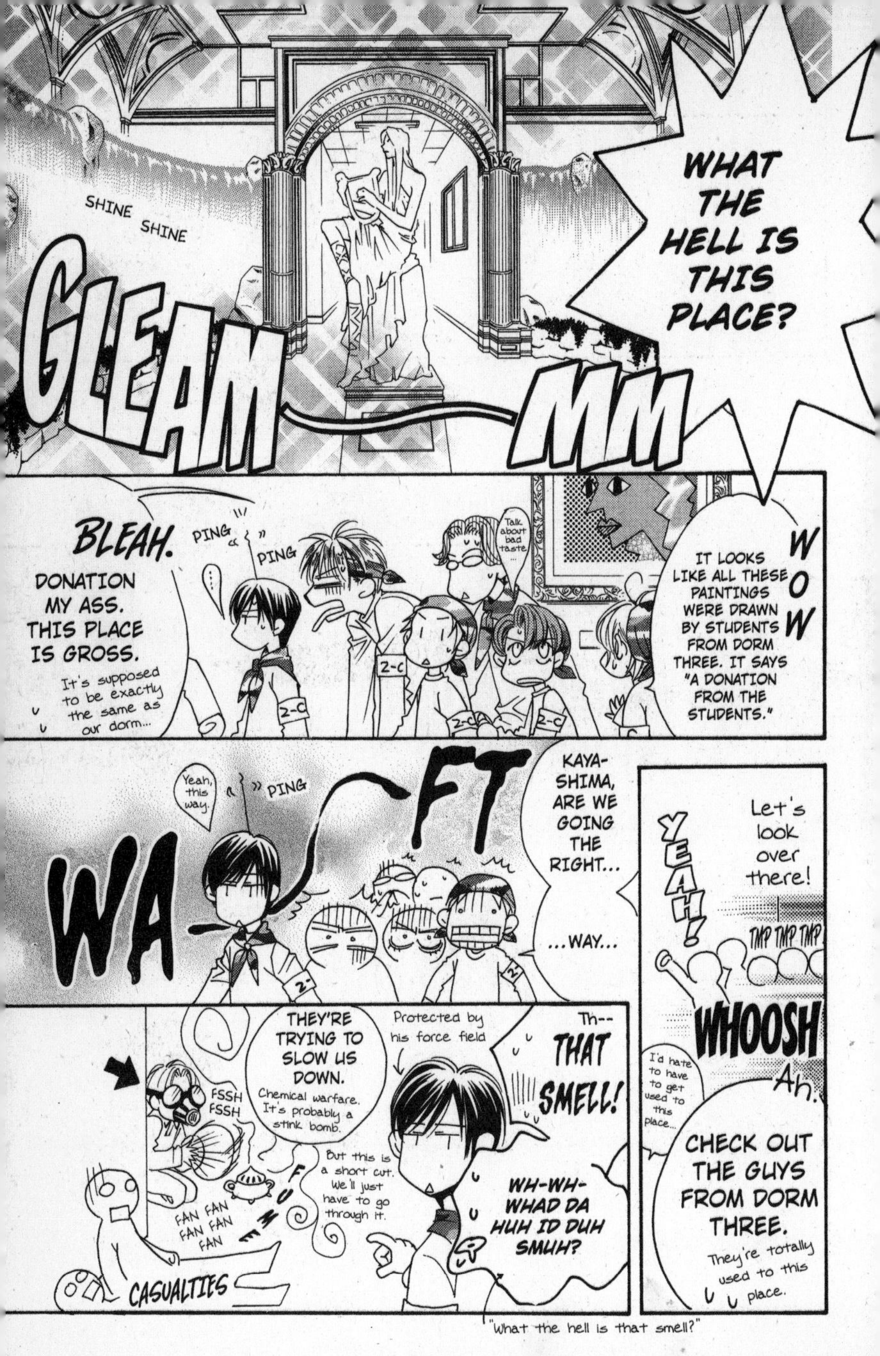
WHAT THE HELL IS THIS PLACE?
SHINE SHINE
GLEAM—MM
WOW
IT LOOKS LIKE ALL THESE PAINTINGS WERE DRAWN BY STUDENTS FROM DORM THREE. IT SAYS "A DONATION FROM THE STUDENTS."
Talk about bad taste...
PING PING
BLEAH.
DONATION MY ASS. THIS PLACE IS GROSS.
It's supposed to be exactly the same as our dorm...
2-C
Let's look over there!
YEAH!
TMP TMP TMP
WHOOSH
Ah.
I'd hate to have to get used to this place...
CHECK OUT THE GUYS FROM DORM THREE.
They're totally used to this place.
KAYA-SHIMA, ARE WE GOING THE RIGHT...
...WAY...
Yeah, this way.
PING
WA-FT
Th-- THAT SMELL!
Protected by his force field
THEY'RE TRYING TO SLOW US DOWN.
Chemical warfare. It's probably a stink bomb.
But this is a short cut. We'll just have to go through it.
WH-WH-WHAD DA HUH ID DUH SMUH?
FUME
FSSH FSSH
FAN FAN FAN FAN FAN
CASUALTIES
"What the hell is that smell?"

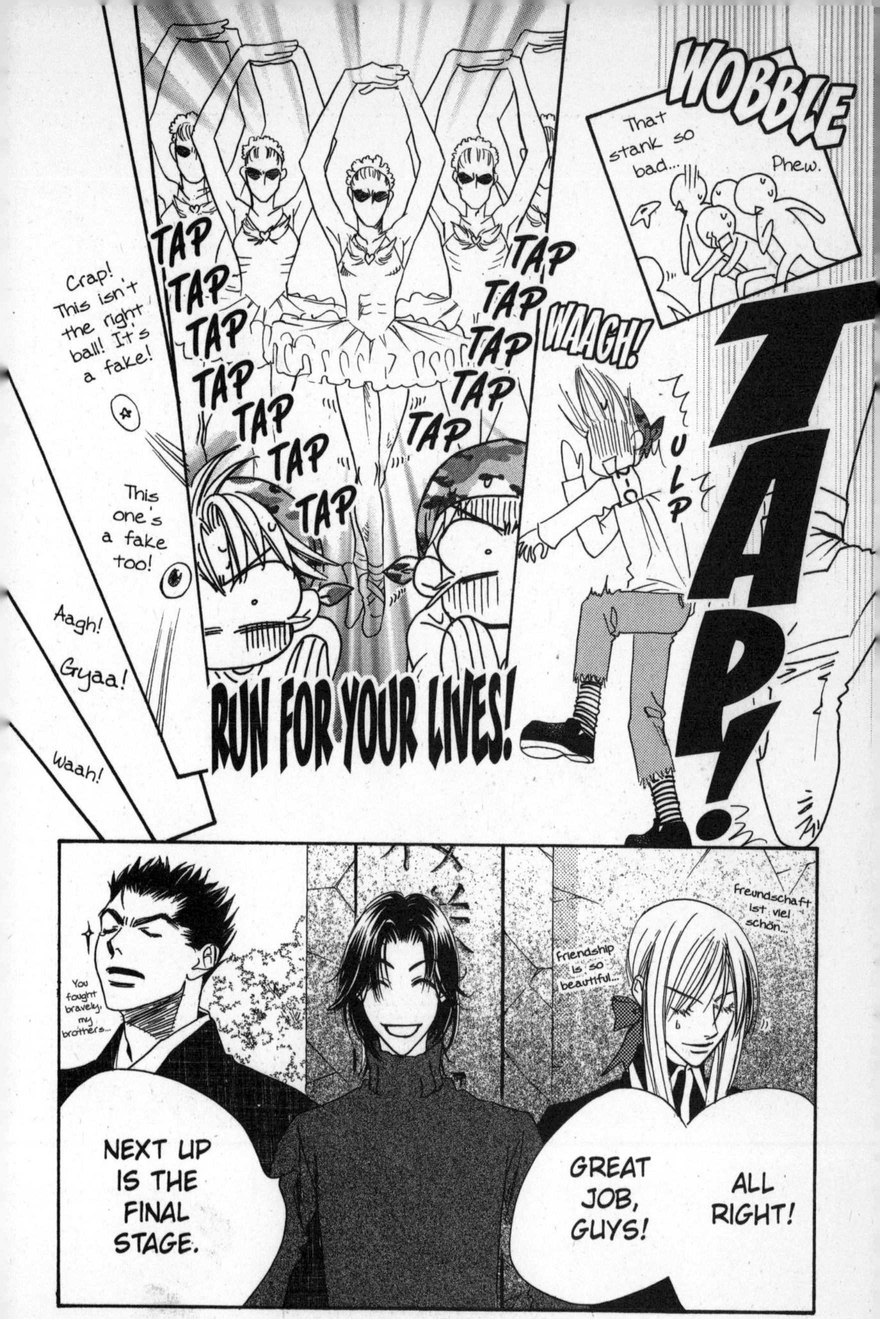
WOBBLE
That stank so bad...
Phew.
TAP!
WAAGH!
ULP
TAP TAP TAP TAP TAP
TAP TAP TAP TAP TAP TAP TAP
RUN FOR YOUR LIVES!
Crap! This isn't the right ball! It's a fake!
This one's a fake too!
Aagh!
Gyaa!
Waah!
Freundschaft ist viel schön...
Friendship is so beautiful...
ALL RIGHT!
GREAT JOB, GUYS!
You fought bravely, my brothers...
NEXT UP IS THE FINAL STAGE.

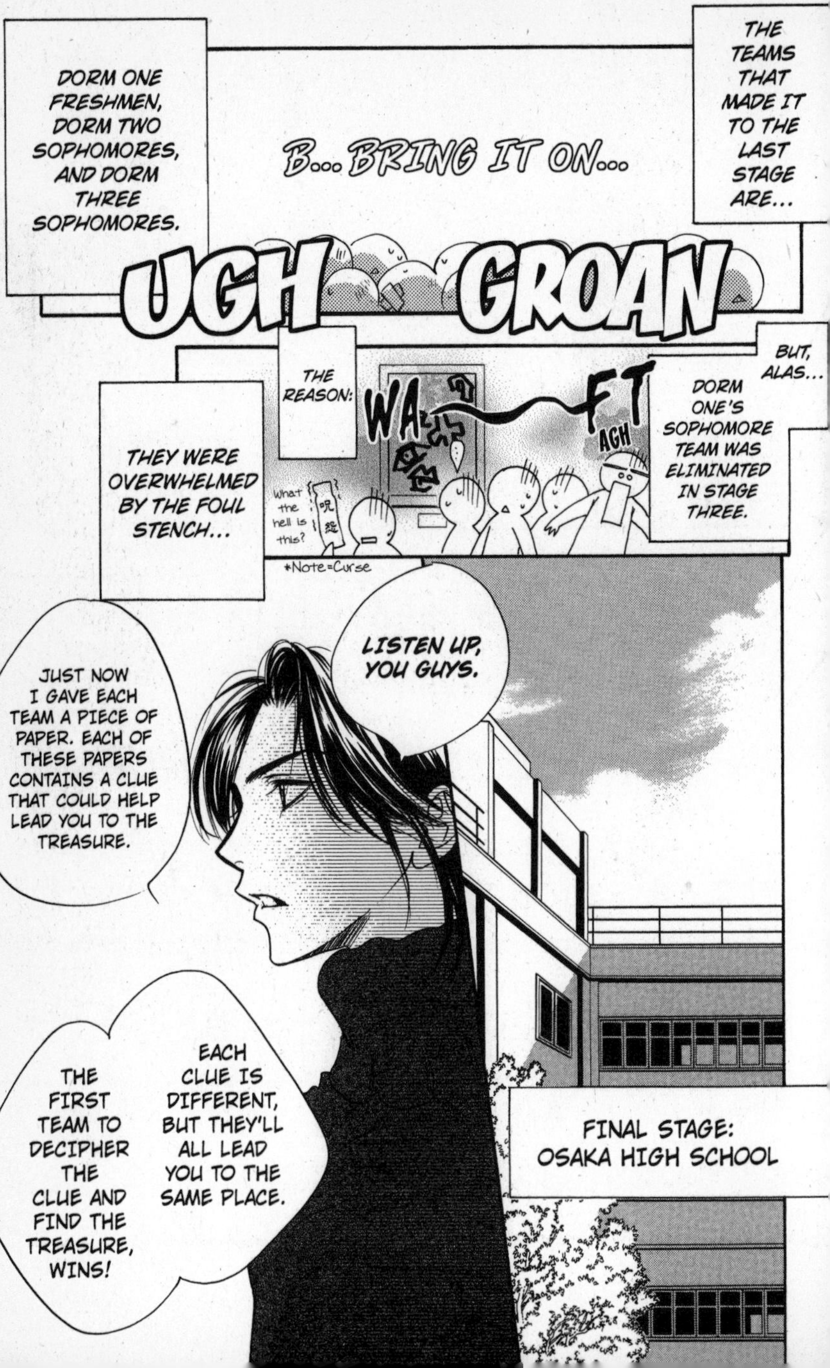

THE TEAMS THAT MADE IT TO THE LAST STAGE ARE...
DORM ONE FRESHMEN, DORM TWO SOPHOMORES, AND DORM THREE SOPHOMORES.
B... BRING IT ON...
GROAN
UGH
BUT, ALAS...
DORM ONE'S SOPHOMORE TEAM WAS ELIMINATED IN STAGE THREE.
AGH
WA-FT
THE REASON:
呪怨
What the hell is this?
THEY WERE OVERWHELMED BY THE FOUL STENCH...
*Note=Curse
LISTEN UP, YOU GUYS.
JUST NOW I GAVE EACH TEAM A PIECE OF PAPER. EACH OF THESE PAPERS CONTAINS A CLUE THAT COULD HELP LEAD YOU TO THE TREASURE.
FINAL STAGE: OSAKA HIGH SCHOOL
EACH CLUE IS DIFFERENT, BUT THEY'LL ALL LEAD YOU TO THE SAME PLACE.
THE FIRST TEAM TO DECIPHER THE CLUE AND FIND THE TREASURE, WINS!

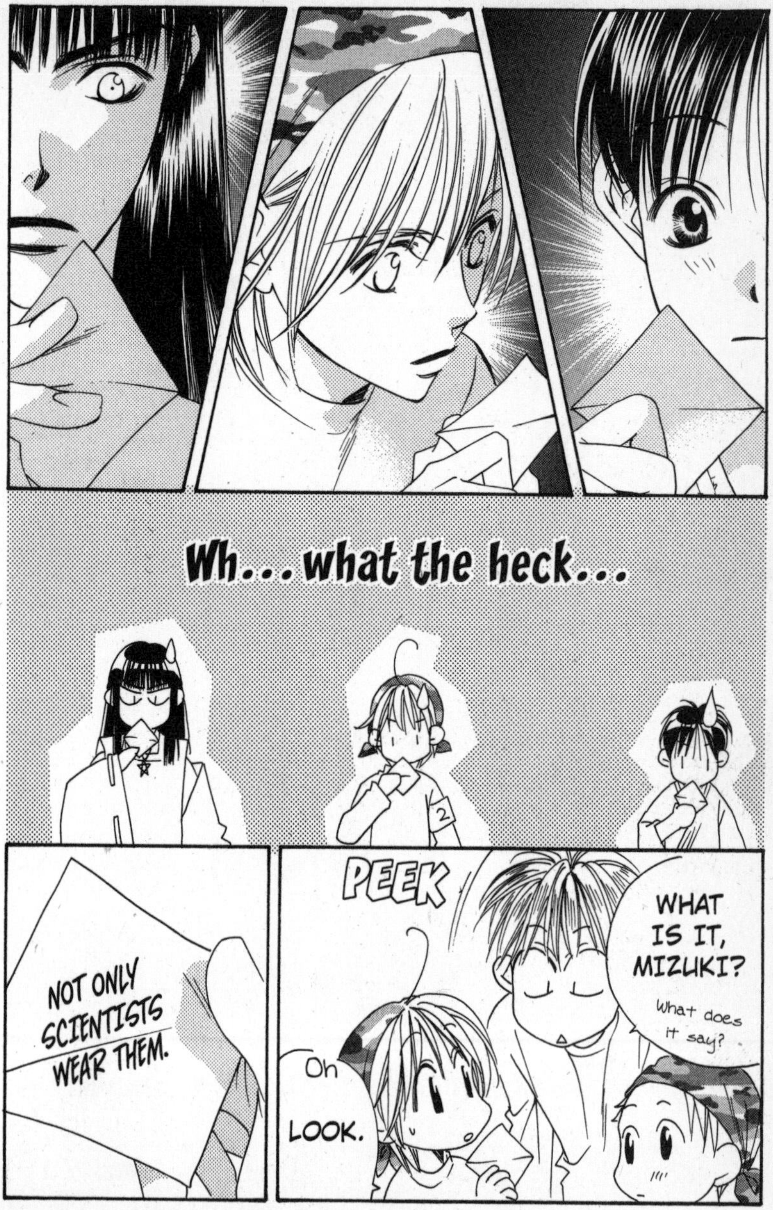
Wh...what the heck...
PEEK
WHAT IS IT, MIZUKI?
What does it say?
Oh
LOOK.
NOT ONLY SCIENTISTS WEAR THEM.

*THE ANSWER TO THE PUZZLE IS "HAKUI" (LAB COAT). THE MISSING LETTERS SPELL OUT "HANA" (#1: FLOWER), "KUDAMONO" (#2: FRUIT), AND "IMO" (#3: POTATO).

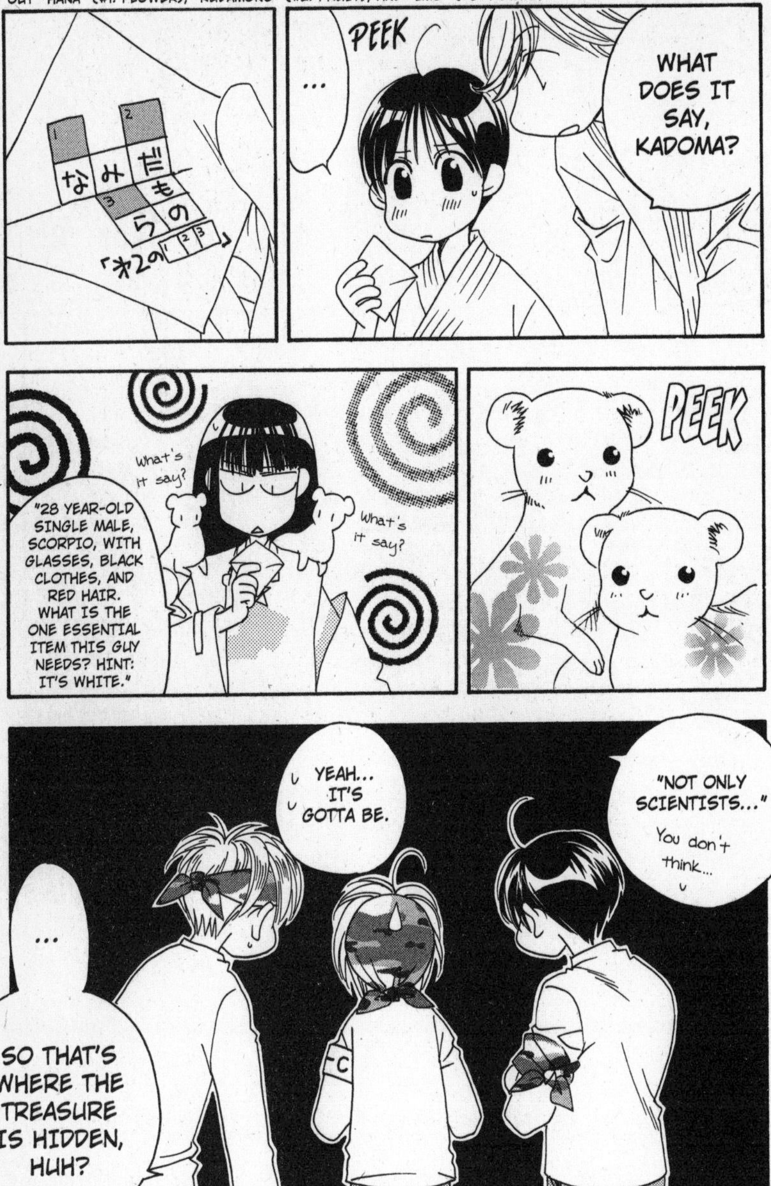
WHAT DOES IT SAY, KADOMA?
PEEK
...
なみだ
も
らの
「※2の 1 2 3」
PEEK
What's it say?
What's it say?
"28 YEAR-OLD SINGLE MALE, SCORPIO, WITH GLASSES, BLACK CLOTHES, AND RED HAIR. WHAT IS THE ONE ESSENTIAL ITEM THIS GUY NEEDS? HINT: IT'S WHITE."
"NOT ONLY SCIENTISTS..."
You don't think...
YEAH... IT'S GOTTA BE.
...
SO THAT'S WHERE THE TREASURE IS HIDDEN, HUH?

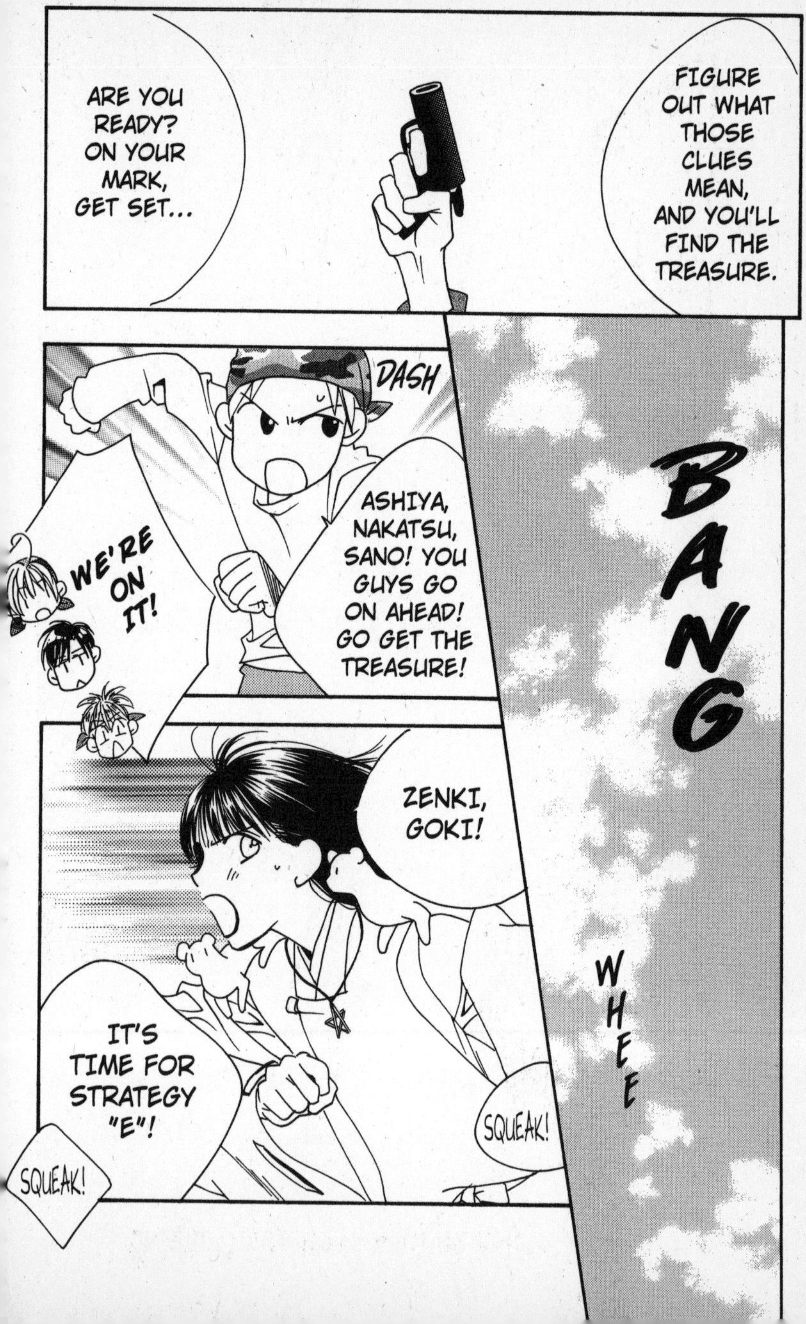
FIGURE OUT WHAT THOSE CLUES MEAN, AND YOU'LL FIND THE TREASURE.
ARE YOU READY? ON YOUR MARK, GET SET...
BANG
WHEE
DASH
ASHIYA, NAKATSU, SANO! YOU GUYS GO ON AHEAD! GO GET THE TREASURE!
WE'RE ON IT!
ZENKI, GOKI!
IT'S TIME FOR STRATEGY "E"!
SQUEAK!
SQUEAK!

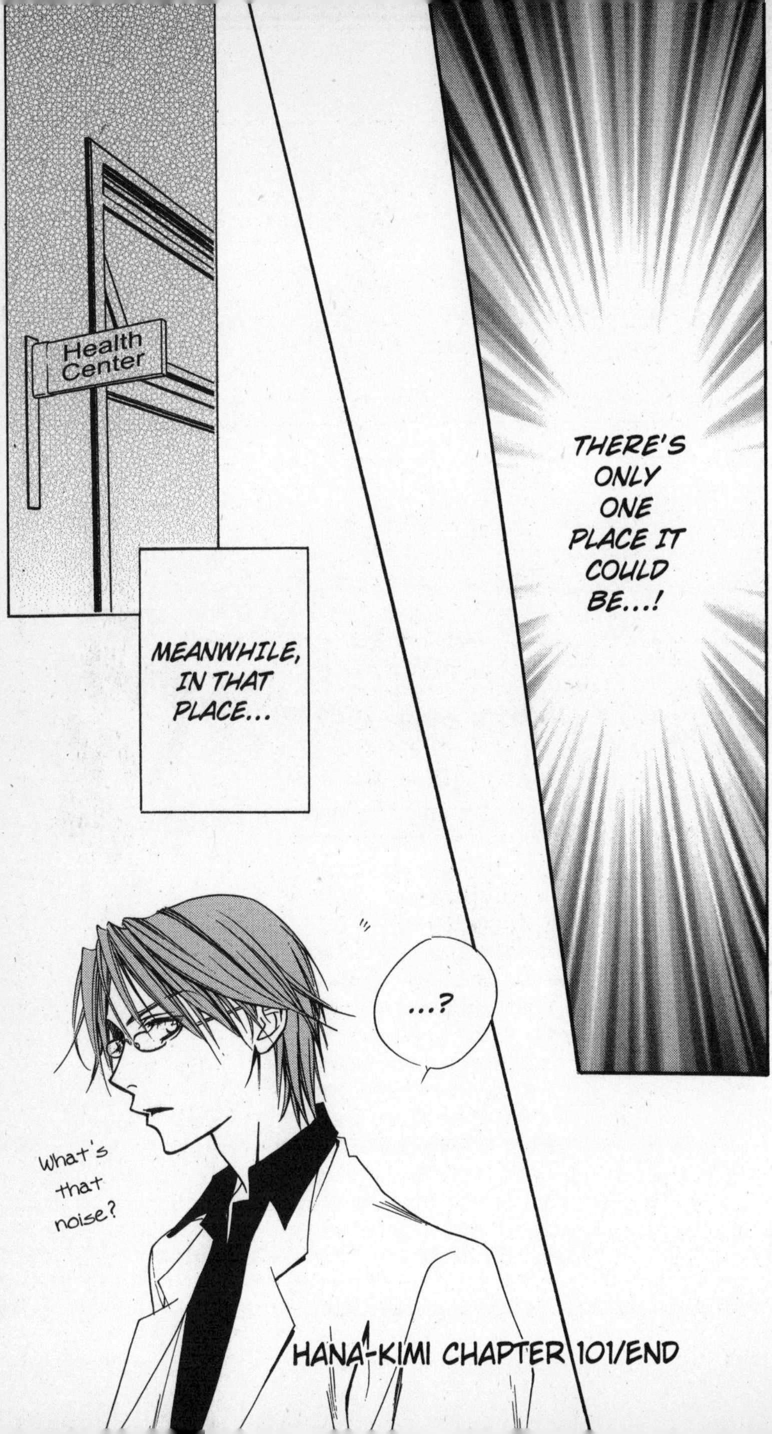
THERE'S ONLY ONE PLACE IT COULD BE...!
Health Center
MEANWHILE, IN THAT PLACE...
...?
What's that noise?

HANA-KIMI CHAPTER 101/END

一条 戻 (17)

Modoru Ichijou (Age 17)

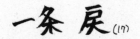

Yep, he's an *onmyôji* all right (*ha ha!*). He was supposed to appear in my manga "Missing Piece" as a character who's possessed by a dog spirit. He originally had a different haircut which went well with his wild personality, but since I changed his occupation to *onmyôji* (?), I decided to make him look a little nicer (heh). I named him after the Ichijou Modoribashi Bridge where the great historical *onmyôji* Seimei Abe used to keep his *shikigami*. Zenki and Goki were the names of the demons that worked for Enno Ozunu, another legendary sorcerer.

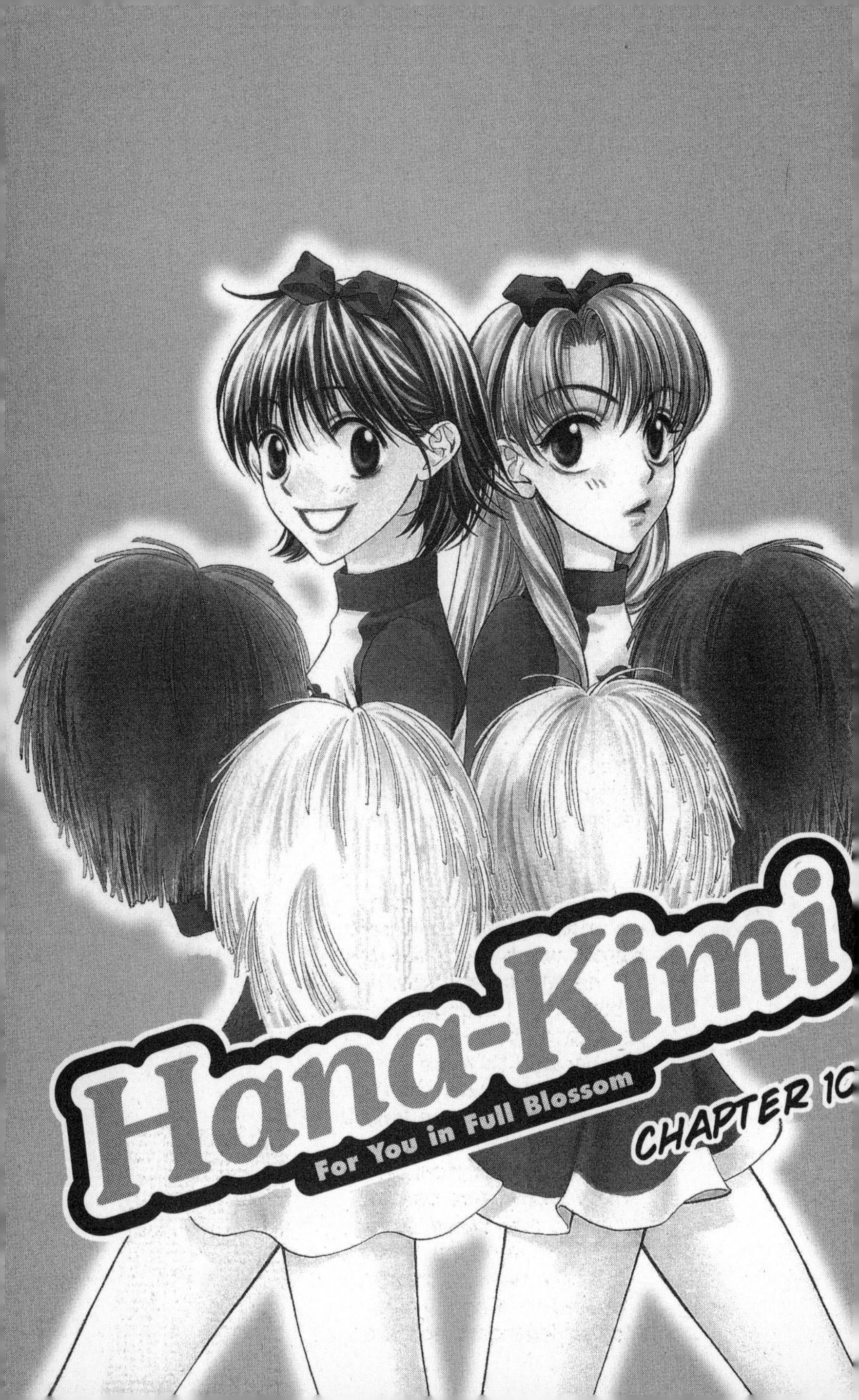
Hana-Kimi
For You in Full Blossom
CHAPTER 10

枚方菊之助 (15)

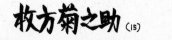

Kikunosuke Hirakata (Age 15)

He's Kadoma's roommate and lives in dorm one. He joined the karate club at the same time Kadoma did. I created this character a long time ago, and I finally decided to include him in a story. He hasn't had too many scenes, but it looks like he's already getting popular. Thank goodness. His grandfather is supposed to be a doll maker, and his mother is Swedish. I came up with the name "Hirakata" because it reminds me of "Hirapaa!" and "Hirapaa" reminds me of the chrysanthemum dolls called "Kiku-ningyo." And "Kikuningyo" made me think of "Kikunosuke"! So that's where his name comes from.

There're lots of characters that never even make it into the manga.

*Hirapaa=short for Hirakata Park (an amusement park)

*Kikuningyo=Chrysanthemum dolls, Hirapaa's main attraction

なみだもの
らの
「※2の123」
THESE CLUES WILL LEAD US TO THE TREASURE!
28 YEAR-OLD SINGLE MALE, SCORPIO, WITH GLASSES, BLACK CLOTHES, AND RED HAIR.
WHAT IS THE ONE ESSENTIAL ITEM THIS GUY NEEDS? HINT: IT'S WHITE.
NOT ONLY SCIENTISTS WEAR THEM.

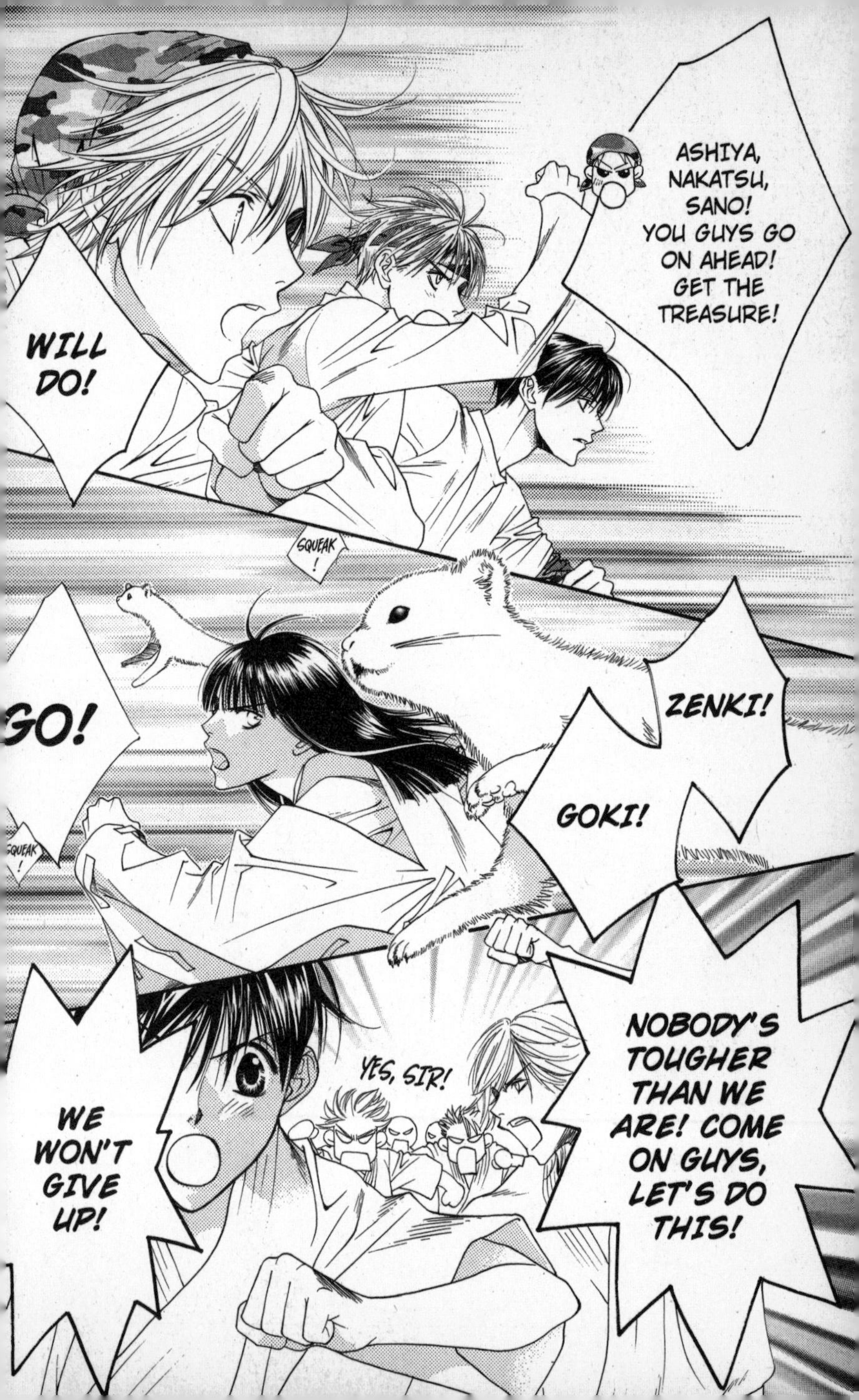
ASHIYA, NAKATSU, SANO! YOU GUYS GO ON AHEAD! GET THE TREASURE!
WILL DO!
ZENKI!
GOKI!
SQUEAK!
GO!
SQUEAK!
NOBODY'S TOUGHER THAN WE ARE! COME ON GUYS, LET'S DO THIS!
YES, SIR!
WE WON'T GIVE UP!

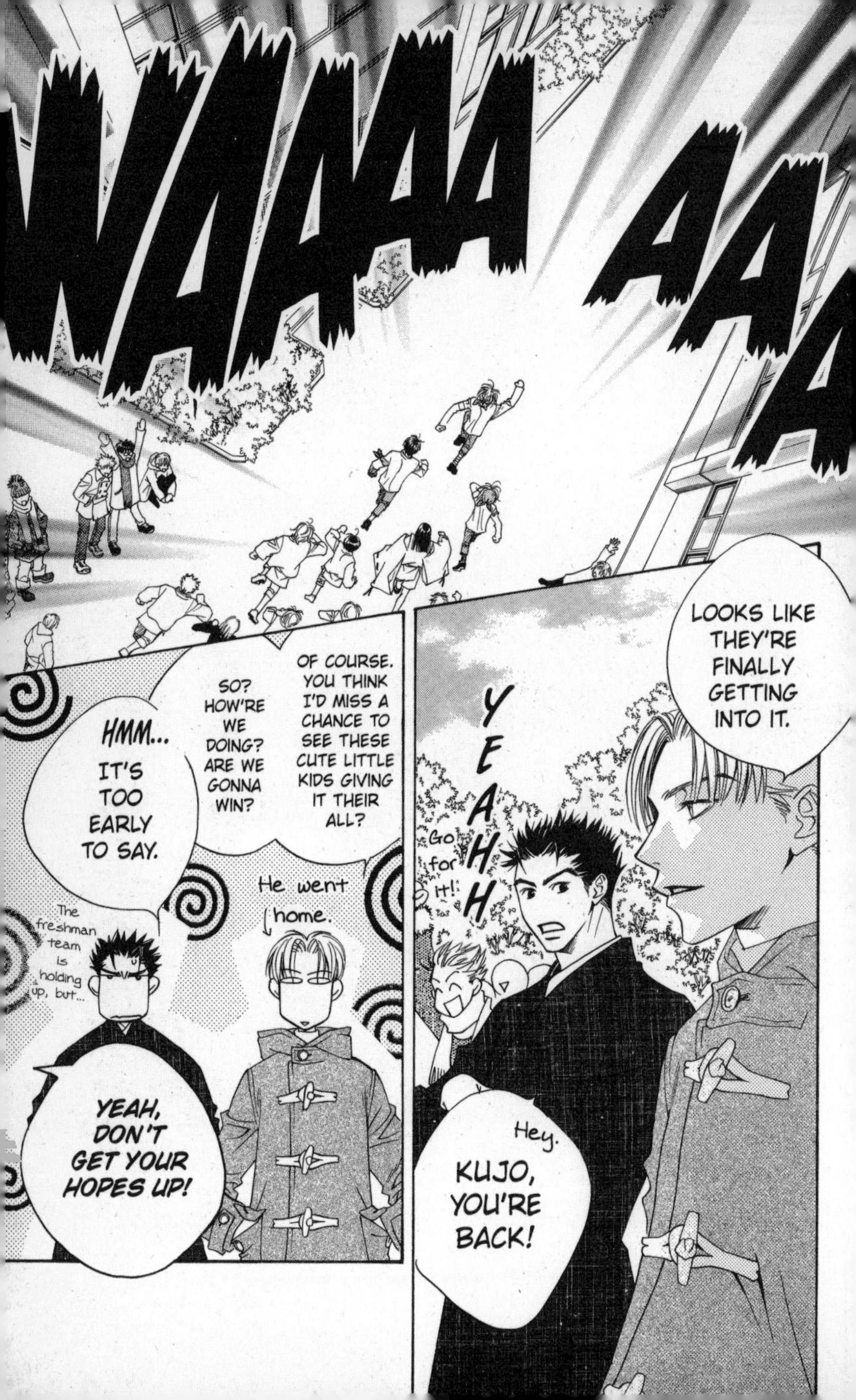
WAAAA AAA
LOOKS LIKE THEY'RE FINALLY GETTING INTO IT.
YEAHH
Go for it!
Hey.
KUJO, YOU'RE BACK!
OF COURSE. YOU THINK I'D MISS A CHANCE TO SEE THESE CUTE LITTLE KIDS GIVING IT THEIR ALL?
SO? HOW'RE WE DOING? ARE WE GONNA WIN?
HMM... IT'S TOO EARLY TO SAY.
He went home.
The freshman team is holding up, but...
YEAH, DON'T GET YOUR HOPES UP!

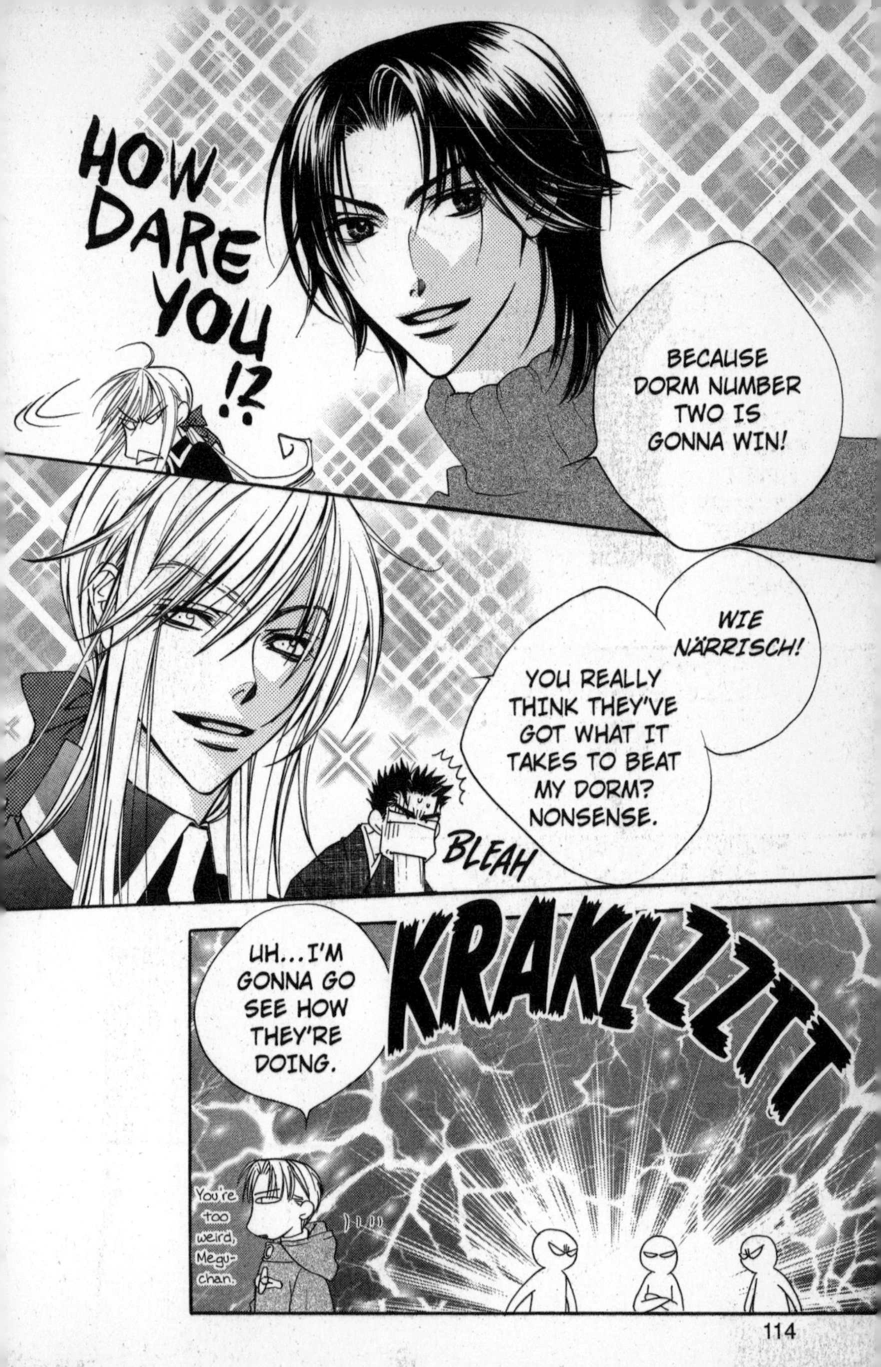
BECAUSE DORM NUMBER TWO IS GONNA WIN!
HOW DARE YOU!?
WIE NÄRRISCH!
YOU REALLY THINK THEY'VE GOT WHAT IT TAKES TO BEAT MY DORM? NONSENSE.
BLEAH
KRAKLZZTT
UH...I'M GONNA GO SEE HOW THEY'RE DOING.
You're too weird, Megu-chan.

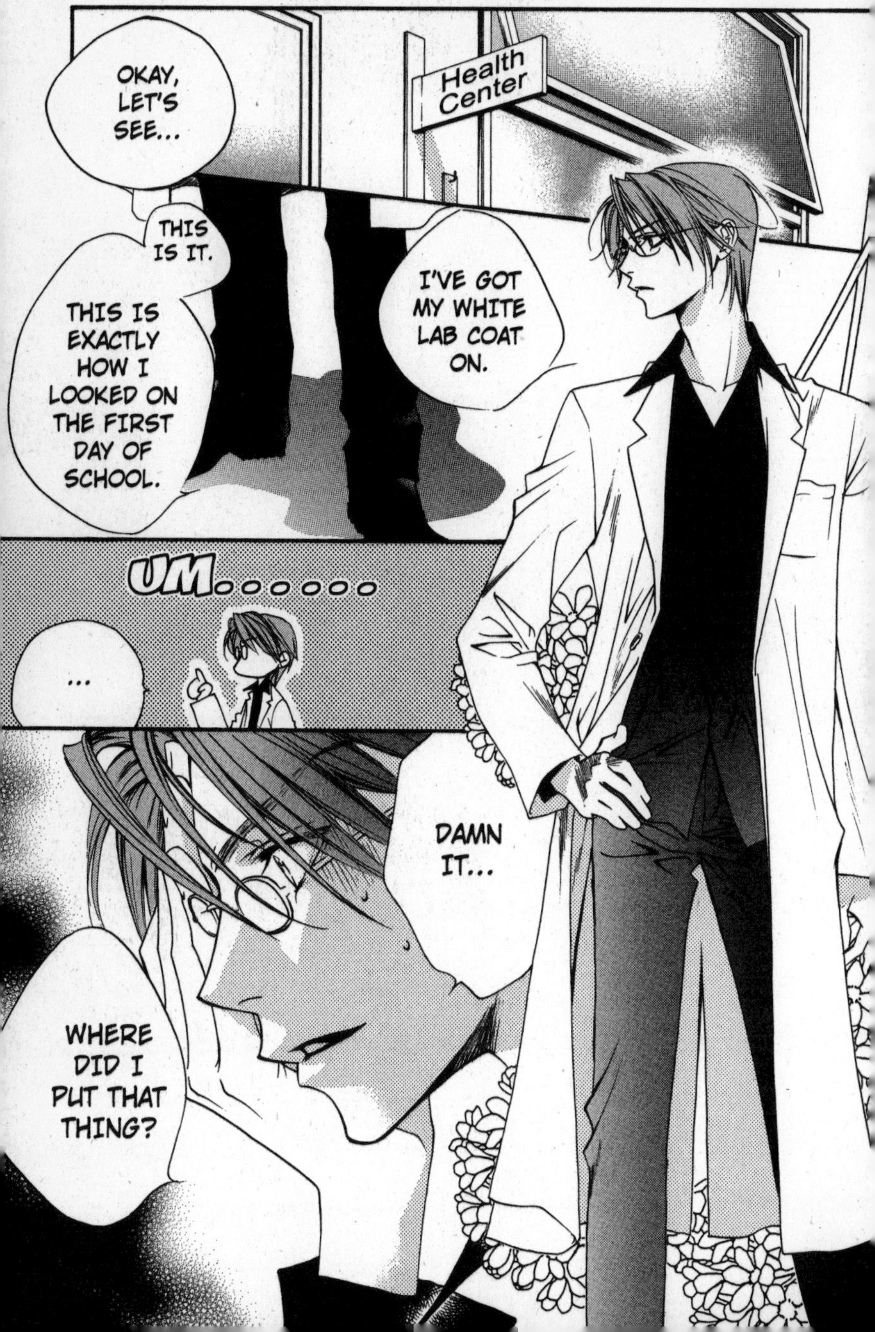
OKAY, LET'S SEE...
THIS IS IT.
I'VE GOT MY WHITE LAB COAT ON.
THIS IS EXACTLY HOW I LOOKED ON THE FIRST DAY OF SCHOOL.
Health Center
UM.......
...
DAMN IT...
WHERE DID I PUT THAT THING?

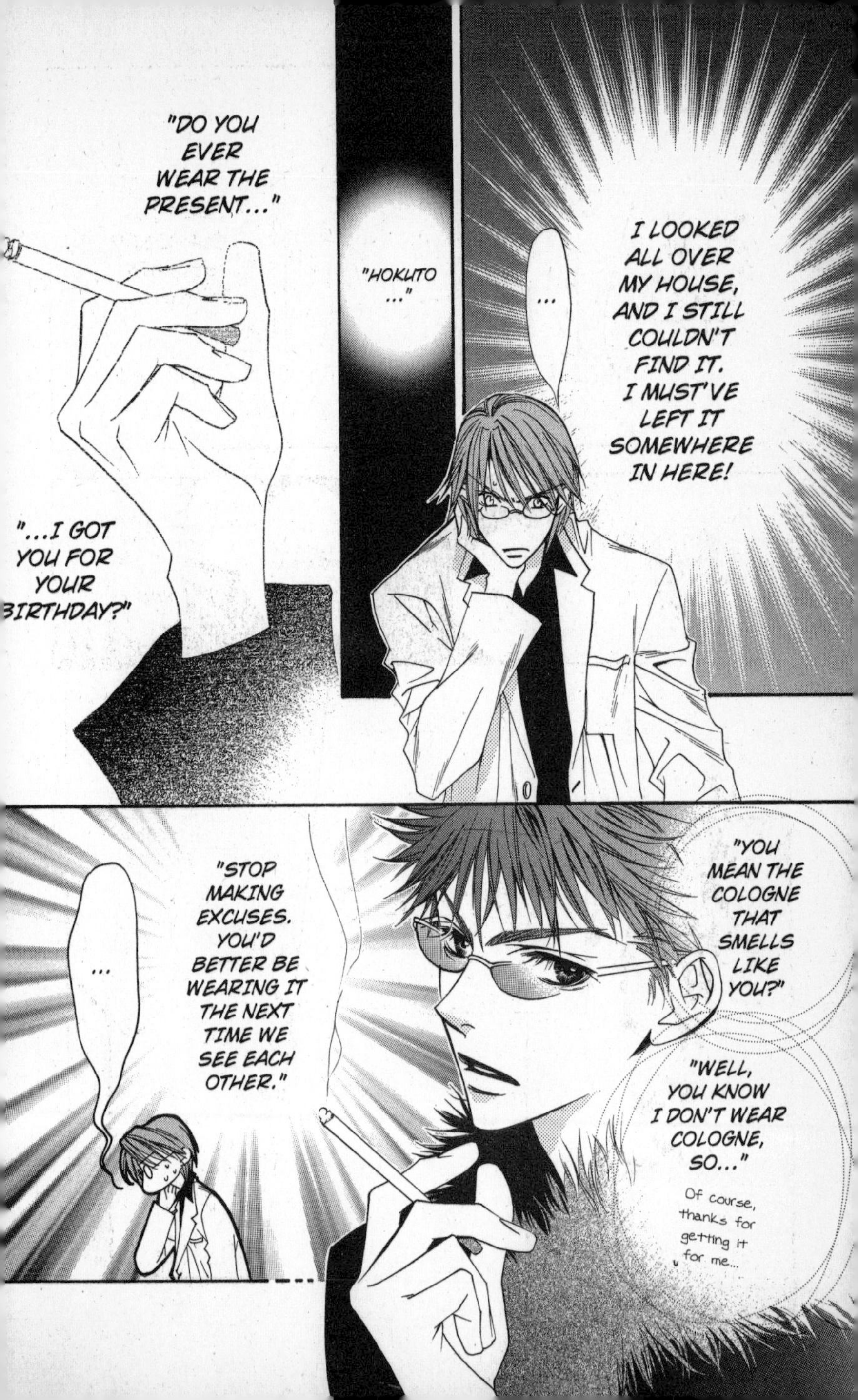
I LOOKED ALL OVER MY HOUSE, AND I STILL COULDN'T FIND IT. I MUST'VE LEFT IT SOMEWHERE IN HERE!
...
"HOKUTO ..."
"DO YOU EVER WEAR THE PRESENT..."
"...I GOT YOU FOR YOUR BIRTHDAY?"
"YOU MEAN THE COLOGNE THAT SMELLS LIKE YOU?"
"WELL, YOU KNOW I DON'T WEAR COLOGNE, SO..."
Of course, thanks for getting it for me...
"STOP MAKING EXCUSES. YOU'D BETTER BE WEARING IT THE NEXT TIME WE SEE EACH OTHER."
...

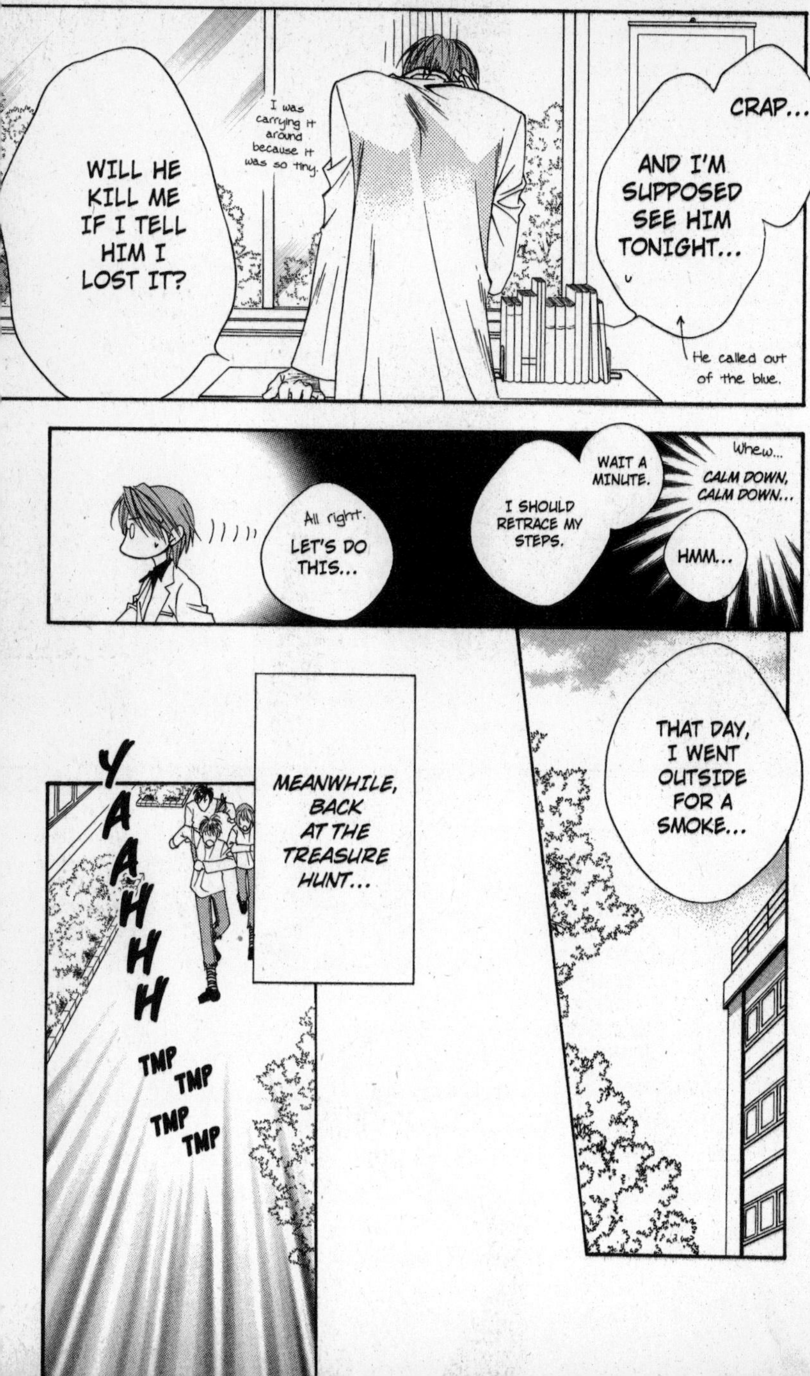
CRAP...
AND I'M SUPPOSED SEE HIM TONIGHT...
He called out of the blue.
I was carrying it around because it was so tiny.
WILL HE KILL ME IF I TELL HIM I LOST IT?
Whew...
CALM DOWN, CALM DOWN...
HMM...
WAIT A MINUTE.
I SHOULD RETRACE MY STEPS.
All right.
LET'S DO THIS...
THAT DAY, I WENT OUTSIDE FOR A SMOKE...
MEANWHILE, BACK AT THE TREASURE HUNT...
YAAAHHHH
TMP TMP TMP TMP

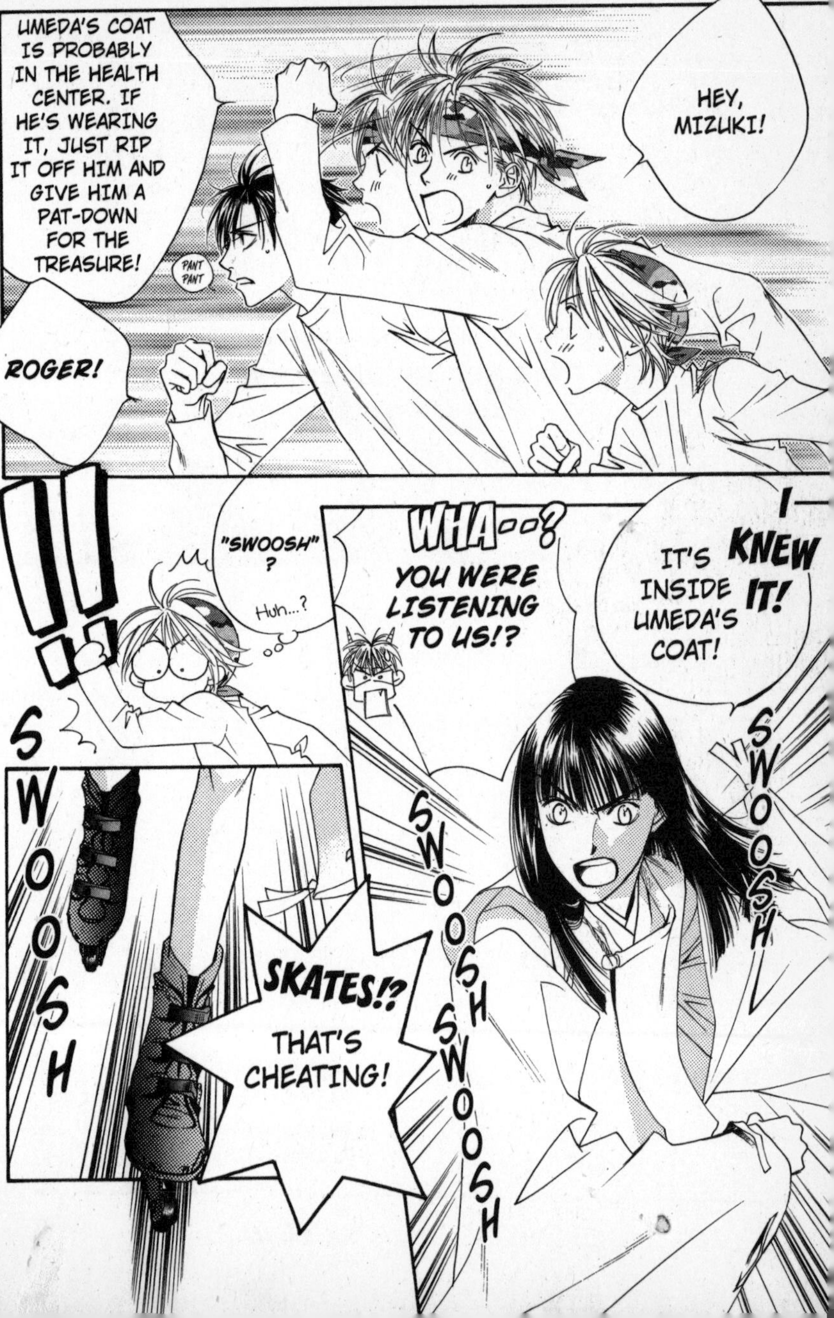
HEY, MIZUKI!
UMEDA'S COAT IS PROBABLY IN THE HEALTH CENTER. IF HE'S WEARING IT, JUST RIP IT OFF HIM AND GIVE HIM A PAT-DOWN FOR THE TREASURE!
PANT PANT
ROGER!
I— KNEW IT!
IT'S INSIDE UMEDA'S COAT!
WHA--?
YOU WERE LISTENING TO US!?
SWOOSH
SWOOSH
SWOOSH
"SWOOSH"?
Huh...?
!!
SWOOSH
SKATES!?
THAT'S CHEATING!

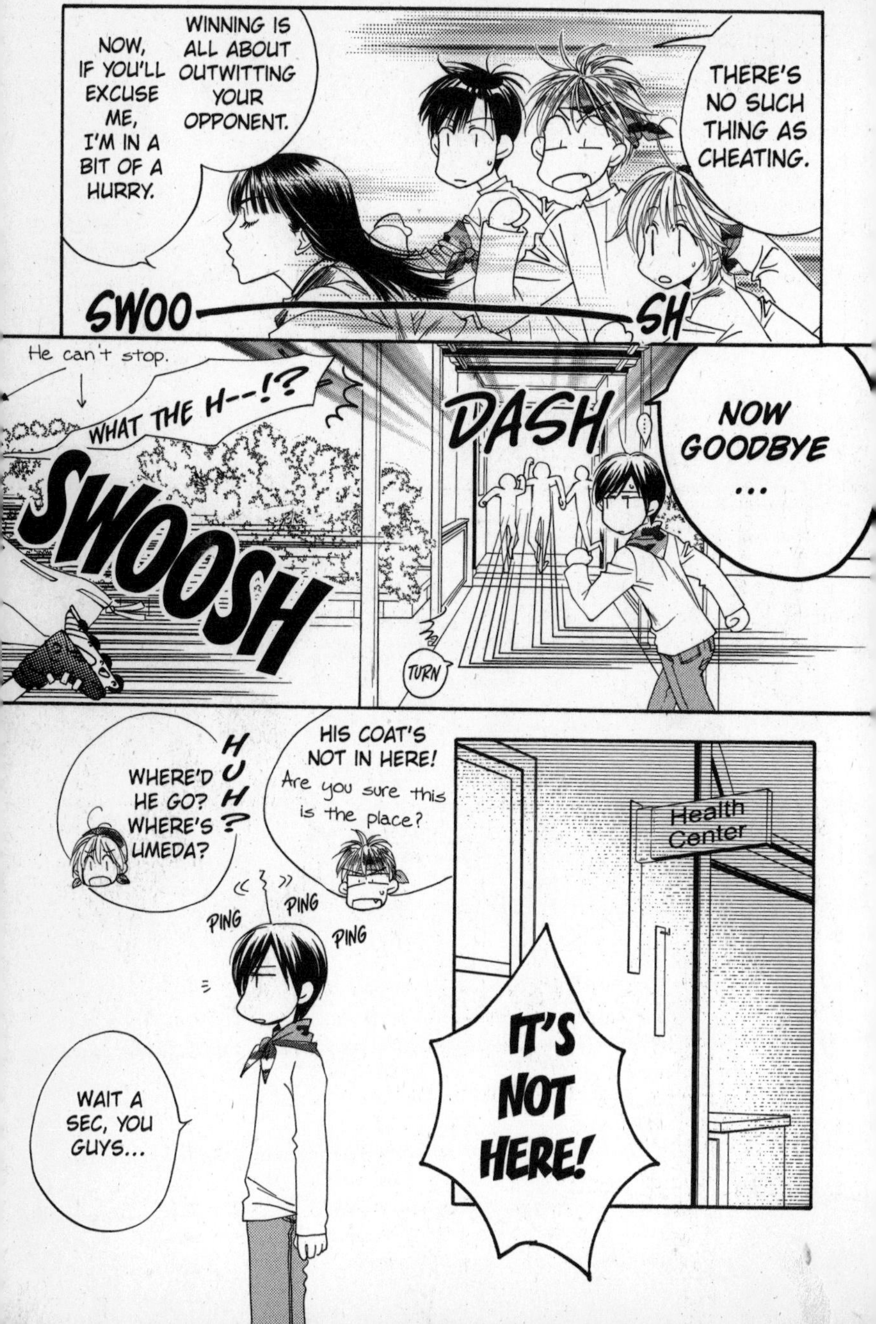
THERE'S NO SUCH THING AS CHEATING.
WINNING IS ALL ABOUT OUTWITTING YOUR OPPONENT.
NOW, IF YOU'LL EXCUSE ME, I'M IN A BIT OF A HURRY.
SWOO—SH
NOW GOODBYE ...
DASH
TURN
WHAT THE H--!?
SWOOSH
He can't stop.
Health Center
IT'S NOT HERE!
HIS COAT'S NOT IN HERE!
Are you sure this is the place?
HUH?
WHERE'D HE GO? WHERE'S UMEDA?
PING
PING
PING
WAIT A SEC, YOU GUYS...

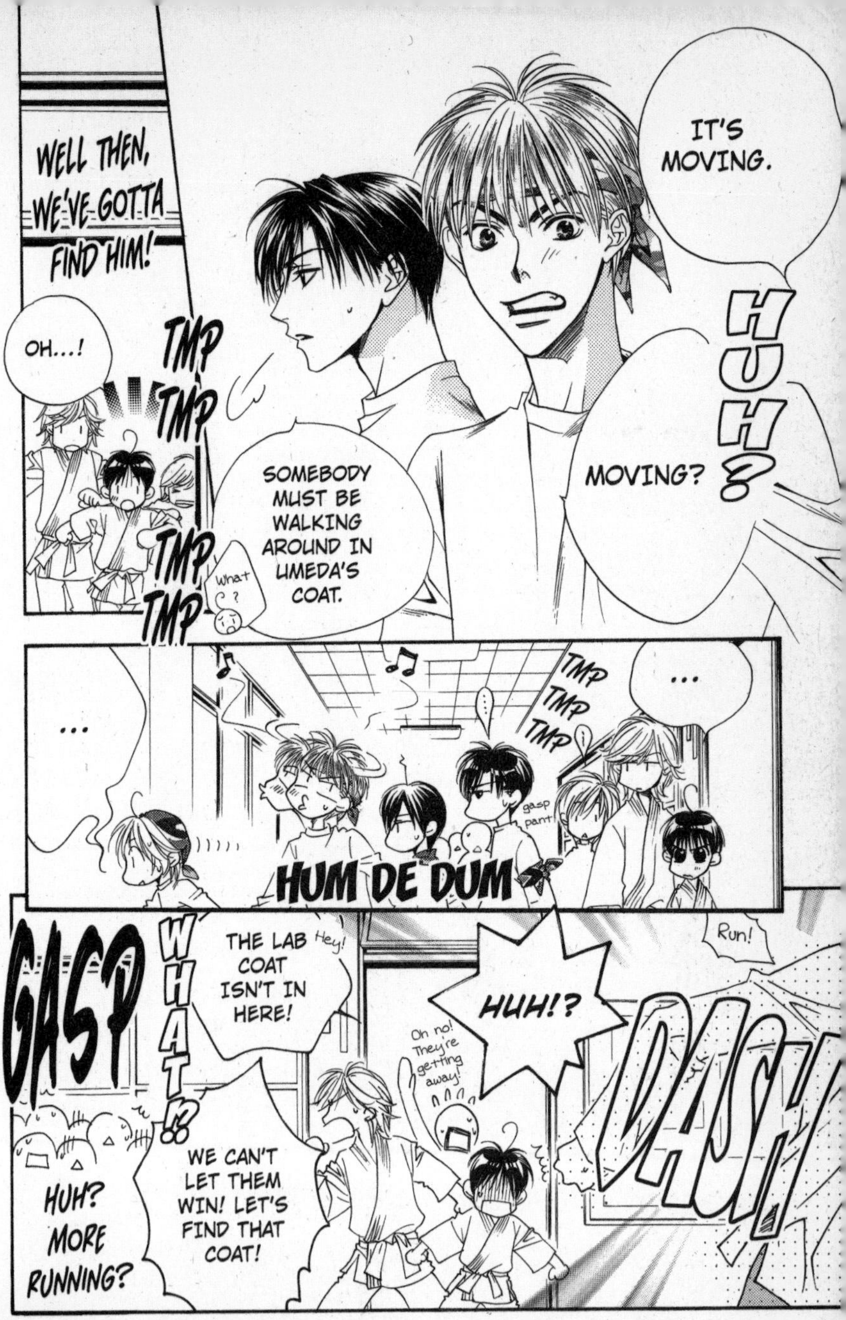
IT'S MOVING.
HUH?
MOVING?
SOMEBODY MUST BE WALKING AROUND IN UMEDA'S COAT.
What?
WELL THEN, WE'VE GOTTA FIND HIM!
OH...!
TMP TMP TMP TMP
...
TMP TMP TMP
gasp pant
HUM DE DUM
...
Run!
DASH
HUH!?
Oh no! They're getting away!
THE LAB COAT ISN'T IN HERE!
Hey!
WHAT!?
WE CAN'T LET THEM WIN! LET'S FIND THAT COAT!
GASP
HUH? MORE RUNNING?

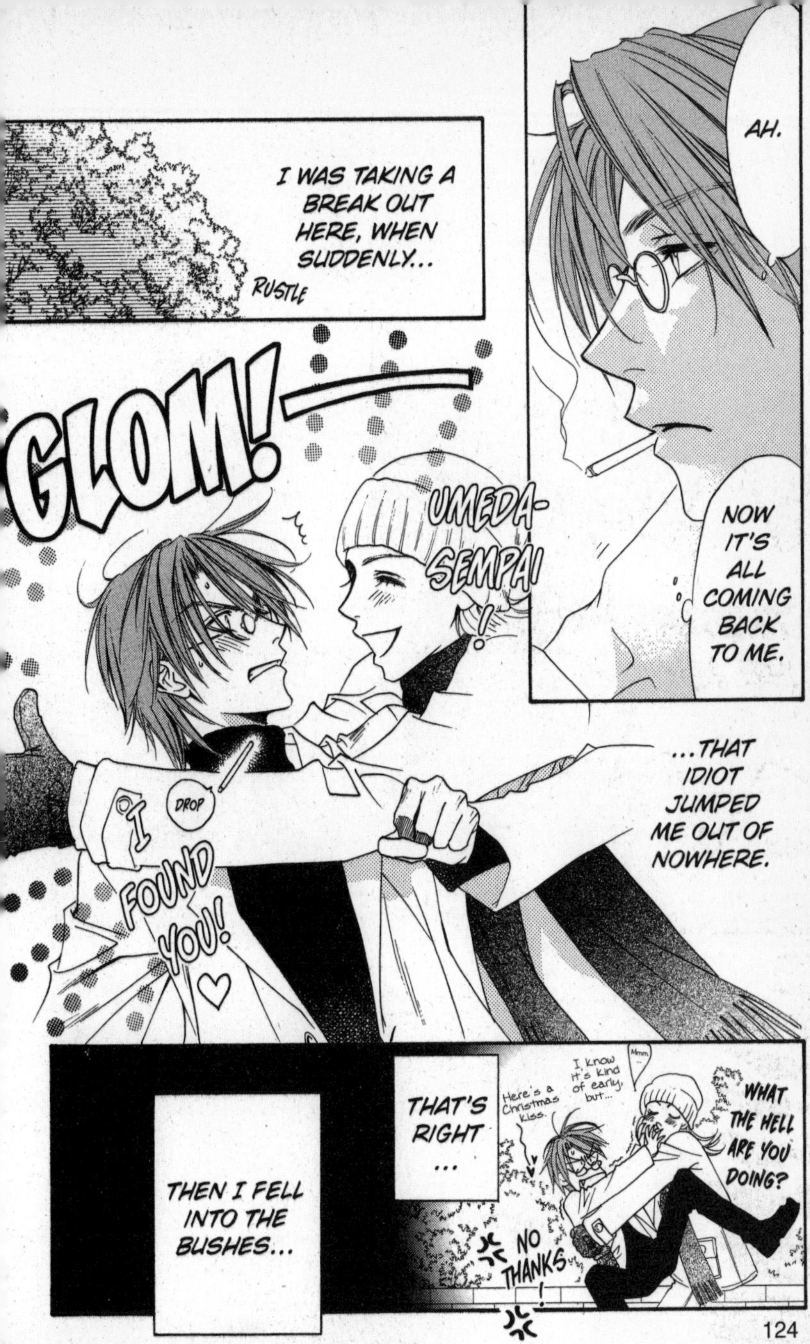
AH.
NOW IT'S ALL COMING BACK TO ME.
I WAS TAKING A BREAK OUT HERE, WHEN SUDDENLY...
RUSTLE
GLOM!
UMEDA-SEMPAI!
...THAT IDIOT JUMPED ME OUT OF NOWHERE.
DROP
I FOUND YOU! ♥
WHAT THE HELL ARE YOU DOING?
Mmm...
I know it's kind of early, but...
Here's a Christmas kiss.
THAT'S RIGHT...
NO THANKS!
THEN I FELL INTO THE BUSHES...

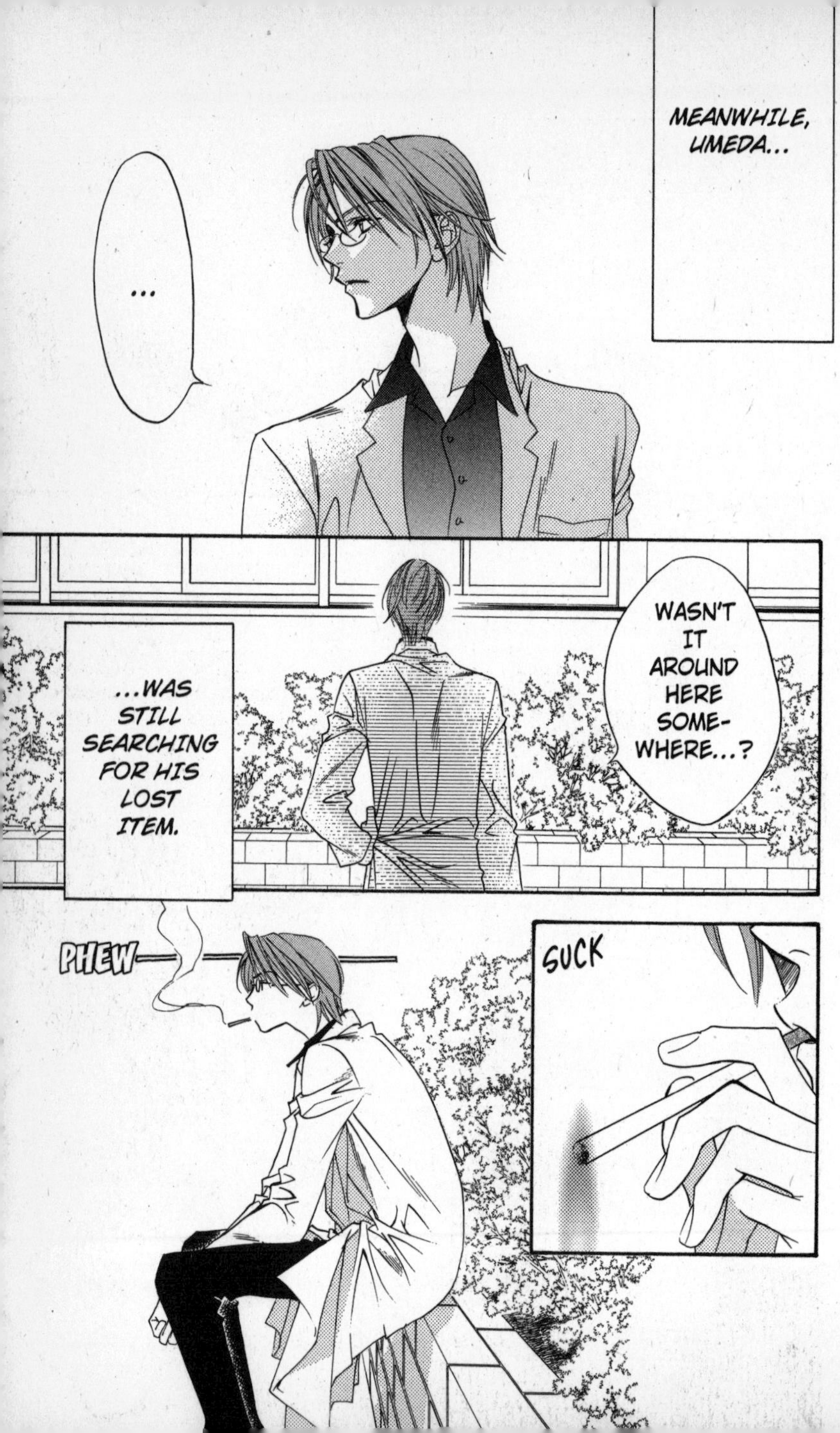
MEANWHILE, UMEDA...
...
WASN'T IT AROUND HERE SOME-WHERE...?
...WAS STILL SEARCHING FOR HIS LOST ITEM.
SUCK
PHEW

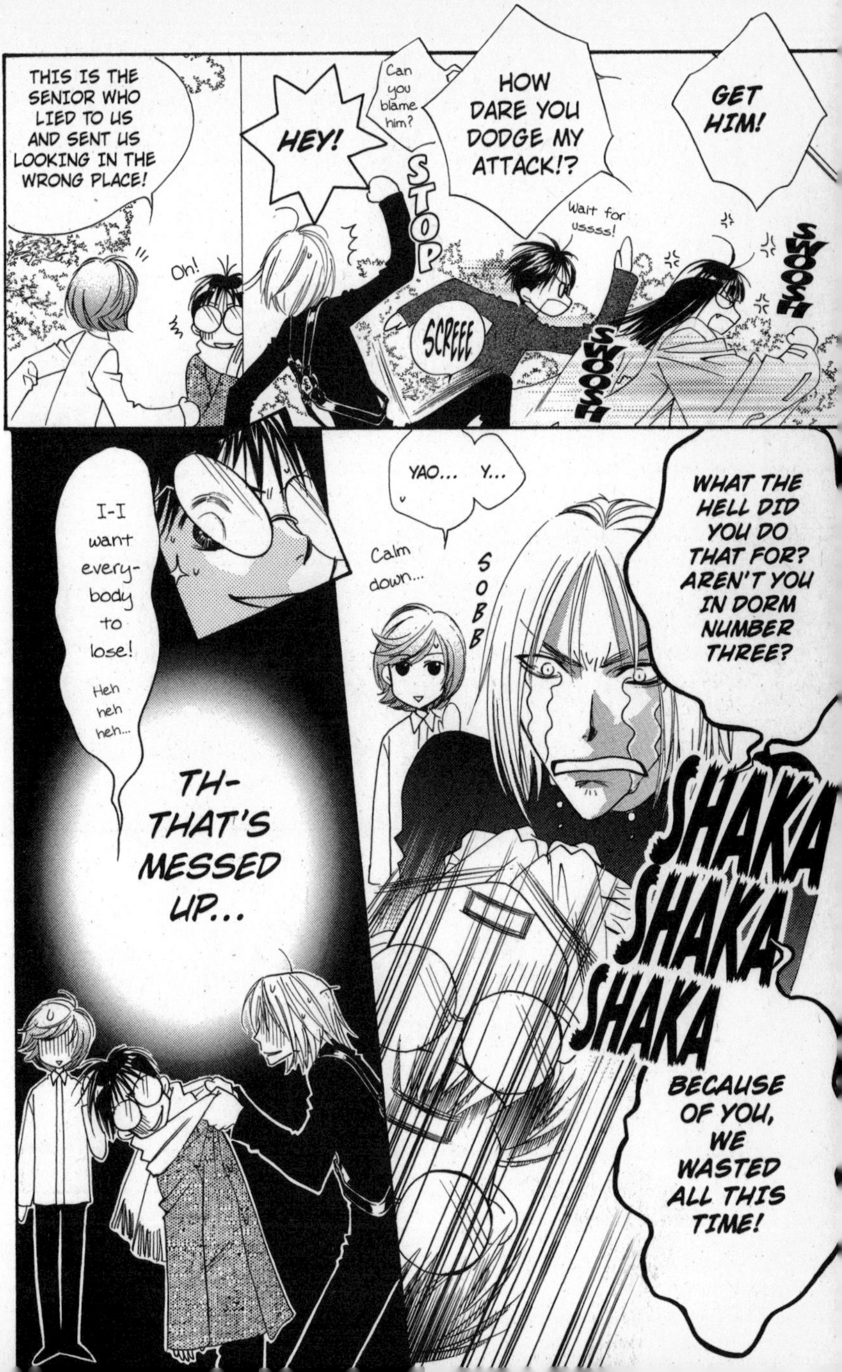
GET HIM!
HOW DARE YOU DODGE MY ATTACK!?
Can you blame him?
SWOOSH
Wait for ussss!
SWOOSH
STOP
HEY!
SCREEE
THIS IS THE SENIOR WHO LIED TO US AND SENT US LOOKING IN THE WRONG PLACE!
Oh!
WHAT THE HELL DID YOU DO THAT FOR? AREN'T YOU IN DORM NUMBER THREE?
SHAKA SHAKA SHAKA
BECAUSE OF YOU, WE WASTED ALL THIS TIME!
YAO... Y...
SOBB
Calm down...
I-I want every-body to lose!
Heh heh heh...
TH-THAT'S MESSED UP...

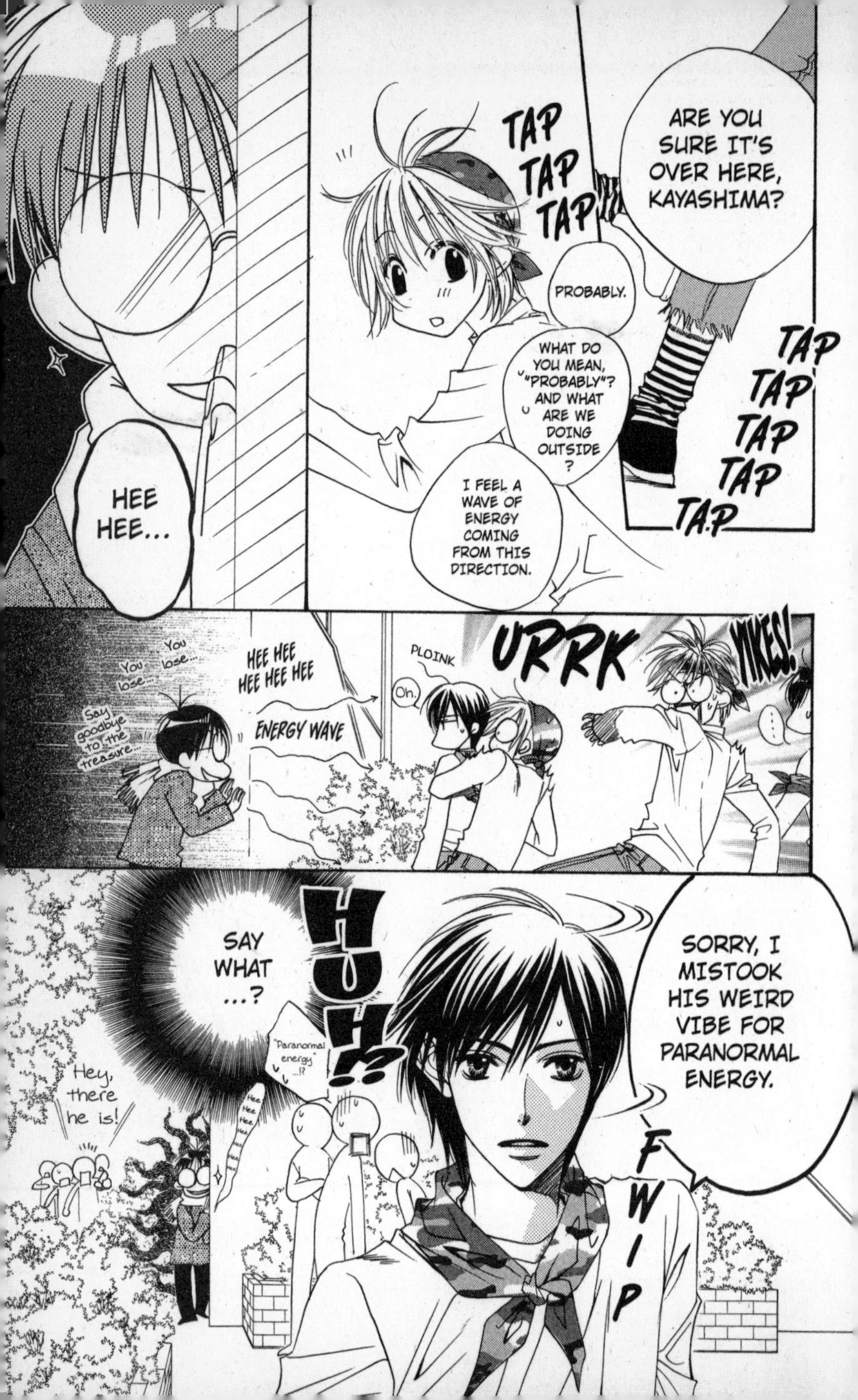
ARE YOU SURE IT'S OVER HERE, KAYASHIMA?
TAP TAP TAP TAP TAP
TAP TAP TAP
PROBABLY.
WHAT DO YOU MEAN, "PROBABLY"? AND WHAT ARE WE DOING OUTSIDE?
I FEEL A WAVE OF ENERGY COMING FROM THIS DIRECTION.
HEE HEE...
YIKES!
URRK
PLOINK
Oh.
HEE HEE HEE HEE HEE
ENERGY WAVE
You lose...
You lose...
Say goodbye to the treasure...
SORRY, I MISTOOK HIS WEIRD VIBE FOR PARANORMAL ENERGY.
FWIP
HUH!?
SAY WHAT ...?
"Paranormal energy" ...!?
Hee Hee Hee Hee
Hey, there he is!

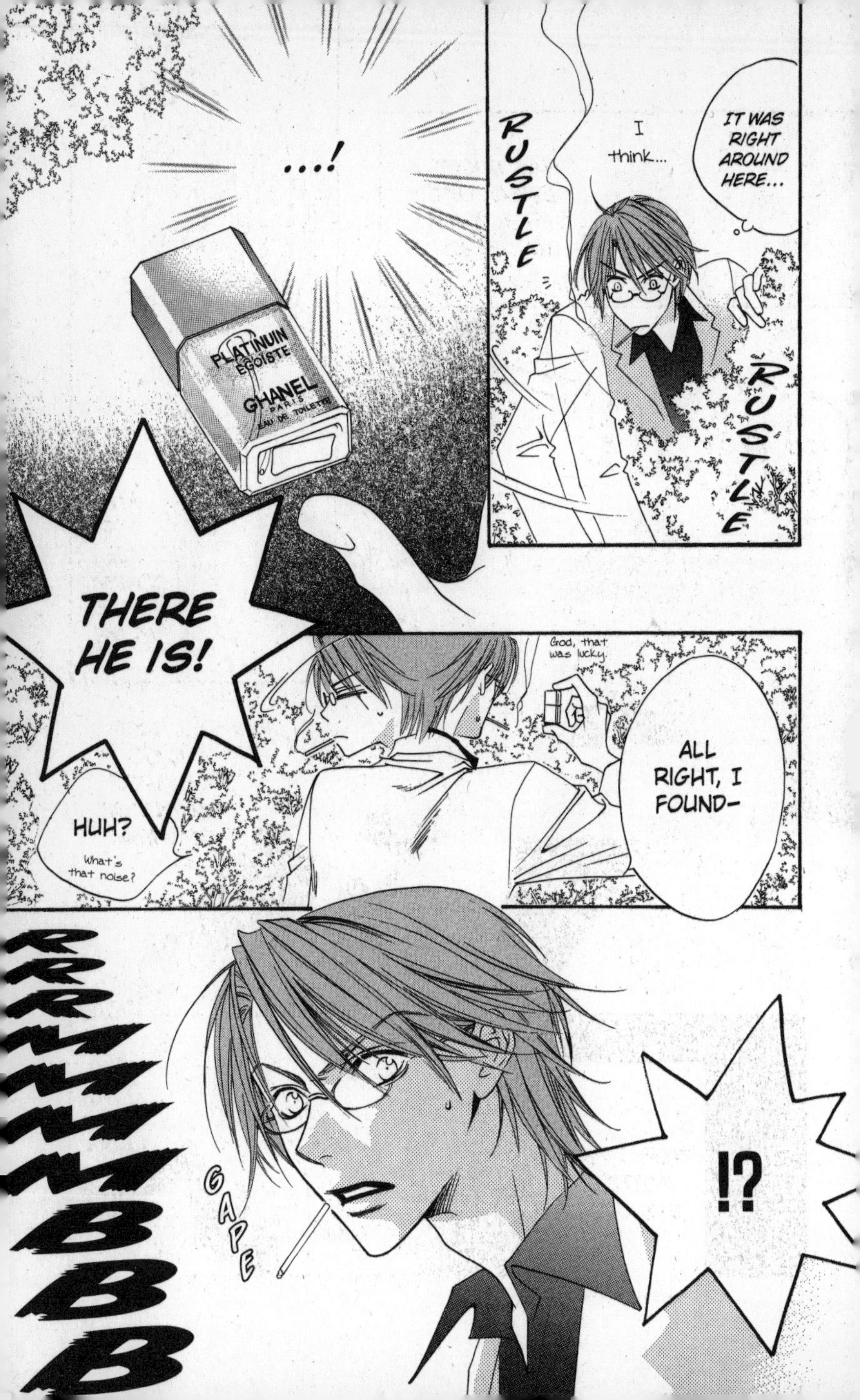
IT WAS RIGHT AROUND HERE...
I think...
RUSTLE
RUSTLE
...!
PLATINUIN EGOISTE
CHANEL PARIS
EAU DE TOILETTE
THERE HE IS!
God, that was lucky.
ALL RIGHT, I FOUND–
HUH?
What's that noise?
!?
GAPE
RRRMMMMBBB

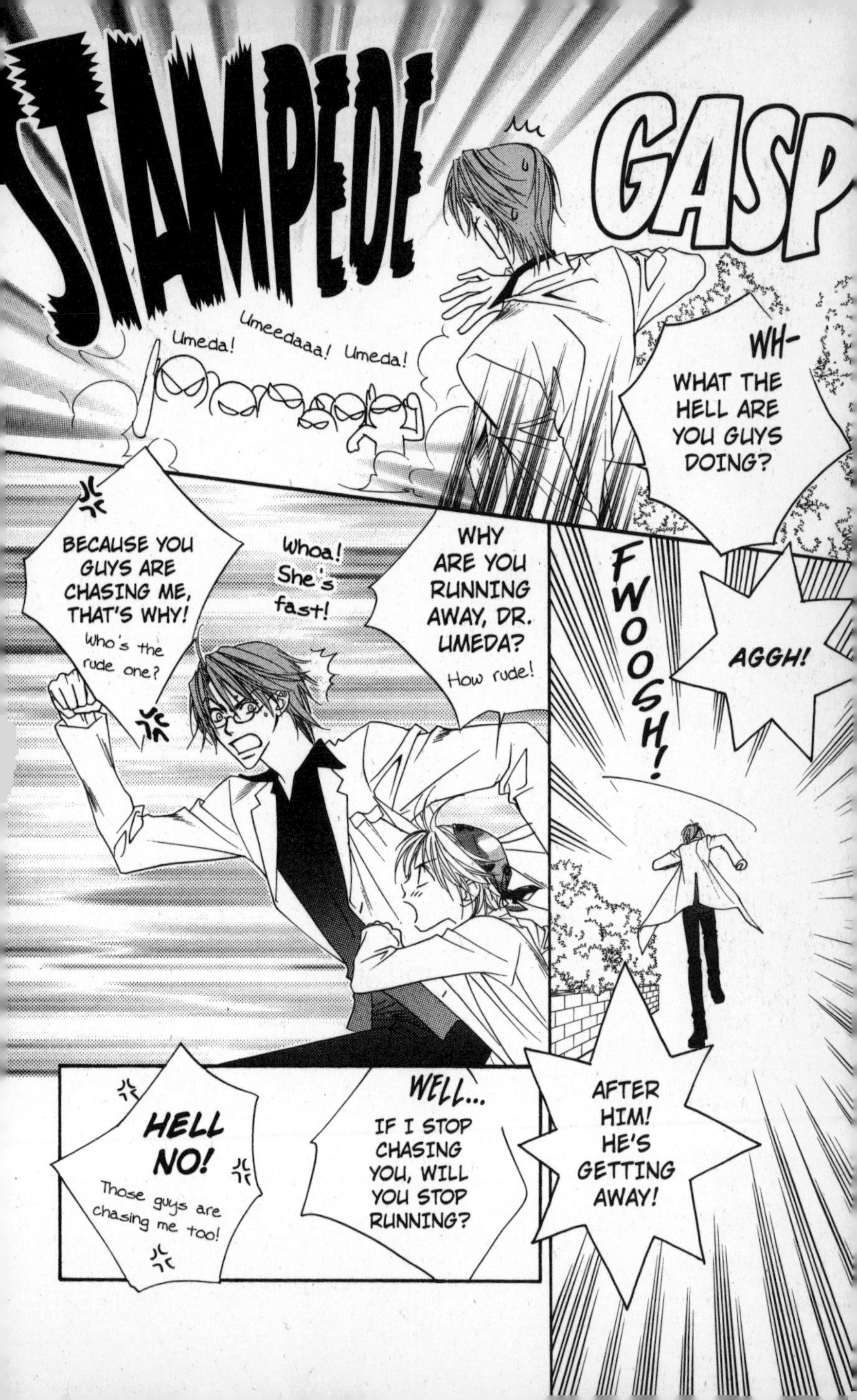
GASP
WH- WHAT THE HELL ARE YOU GUYS DOING?
STAMPEDE
Umeedaaa! Umeda!
Umeda!
AGGH!
FWOOSH!
AFTER HIM! HE'S GETTING AWAY!
WHY ARE YOU RUNNING AWAY, DR. UMEDA?
How rude!
Whoa! She's fast!
BECAUSE YOU GUYS ARE CHASING ME, THAT'S WHY!
Who's the rude one?
WELL... IF I STOP CHASING YOU, WILL YOU STOP RUNNING?
HELL NO!
Those guys are chasing me too!

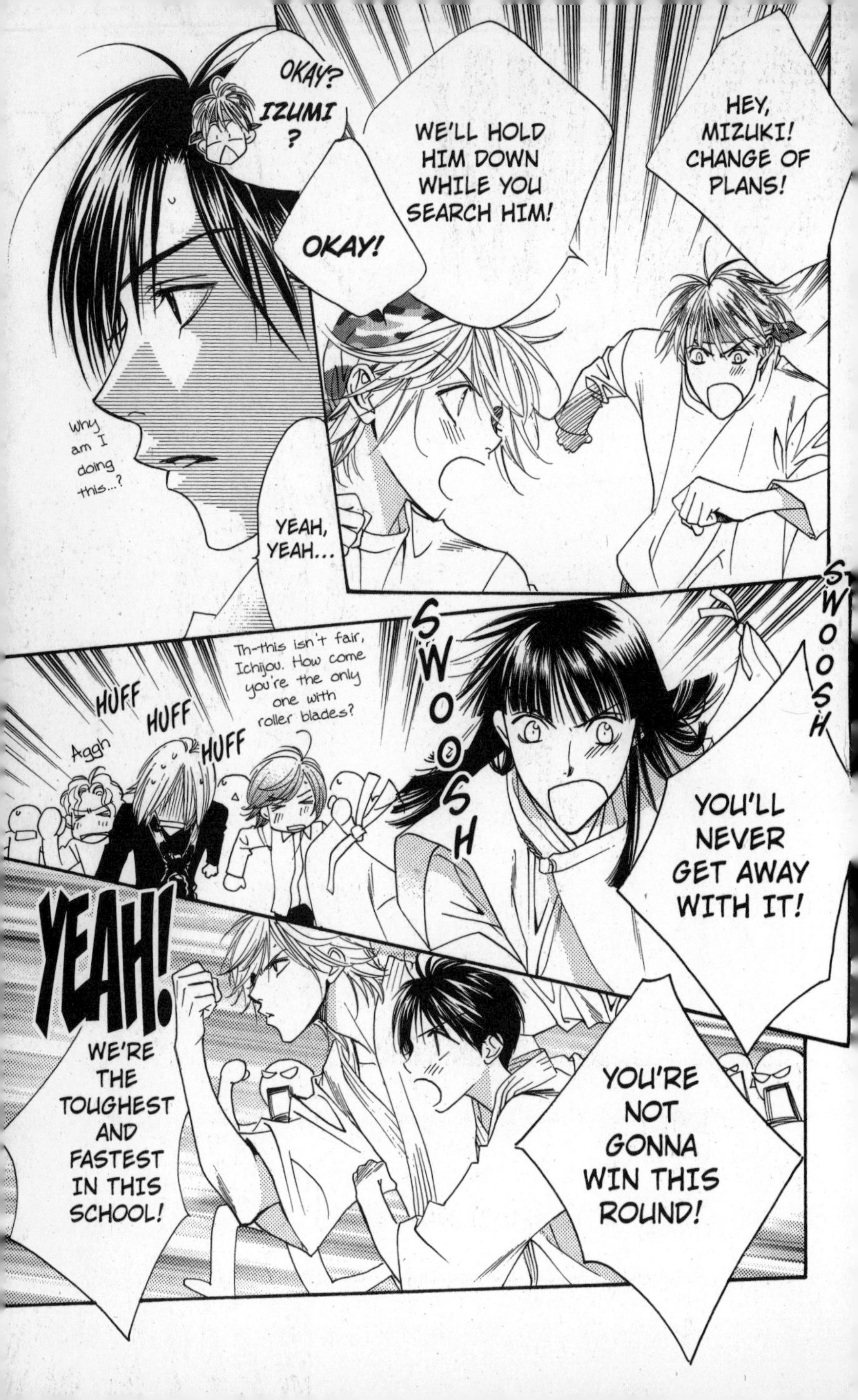
HEY, MIZUKI! CHANGE OF PLANS!
WE'LL HOLD HIM DOWN WHILE YOU SEARCH HIM!
OKAY!
OKAY? IZUMI ?
YEAH, YEAH...
Why am I doing this...?
SWOOSH
YOU'LL NEVER GET AWAY WITH IT!
SWOOSH
Th-this isn't fair, Ichijou. How come you're the only one with roller blades?
HUFF HUFF HUFF
Aggh
YOU'RE NOT GONNA WIN THIS ROUND!
YEAH!
WE'RE THE TOUGHEST AND FASTEST IN THIS SCHOOL!

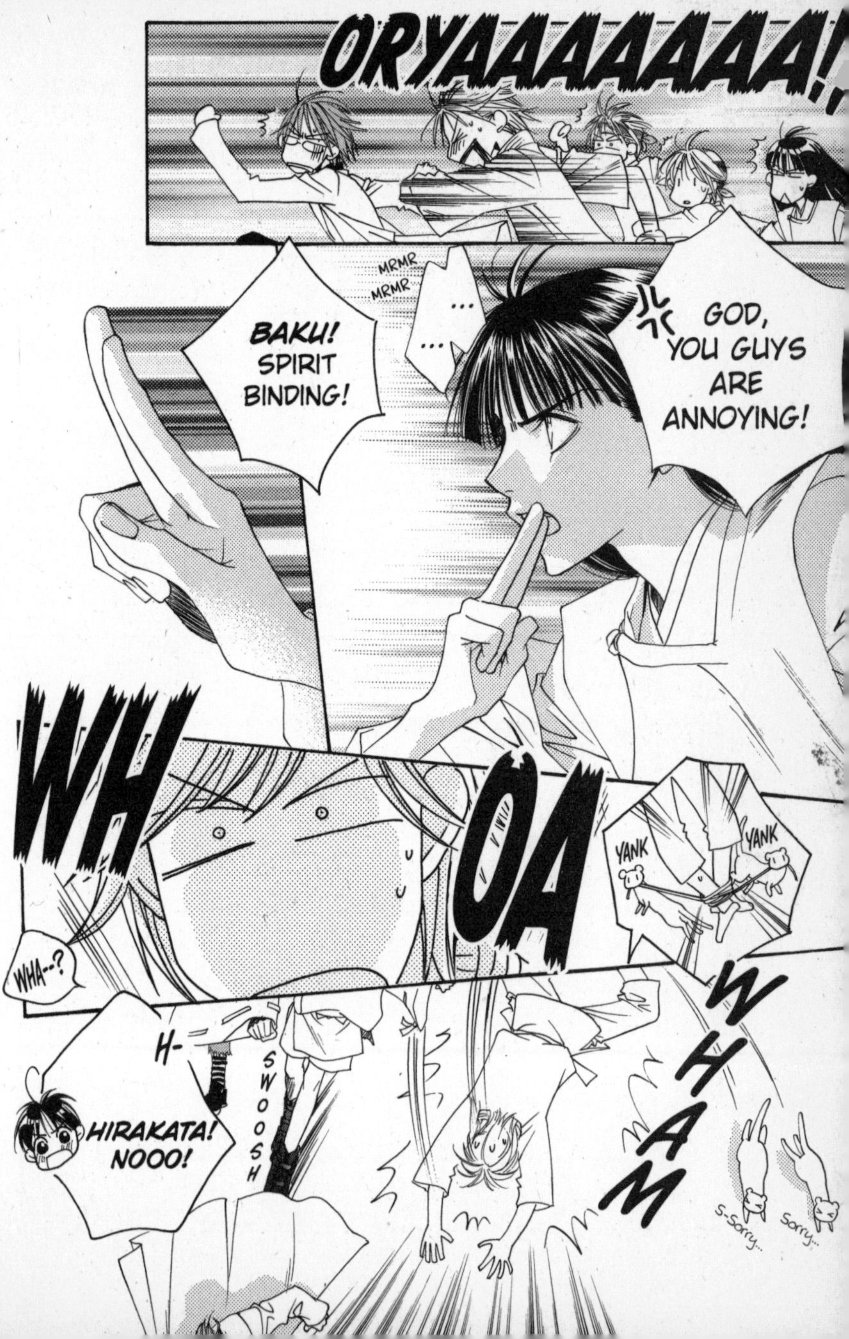
ORYAAAAAAA!!
GOD, YOU GUYS ARE ANNOYING!
...
...
MRMR MRMR
BAKU! SPIRIT BINDING!
YANK
YANK
WHOA
WHA--?
WHAM
Sorry...
S-Sorry...
SWOOSH
H-
HIRAKATA! NOOO!

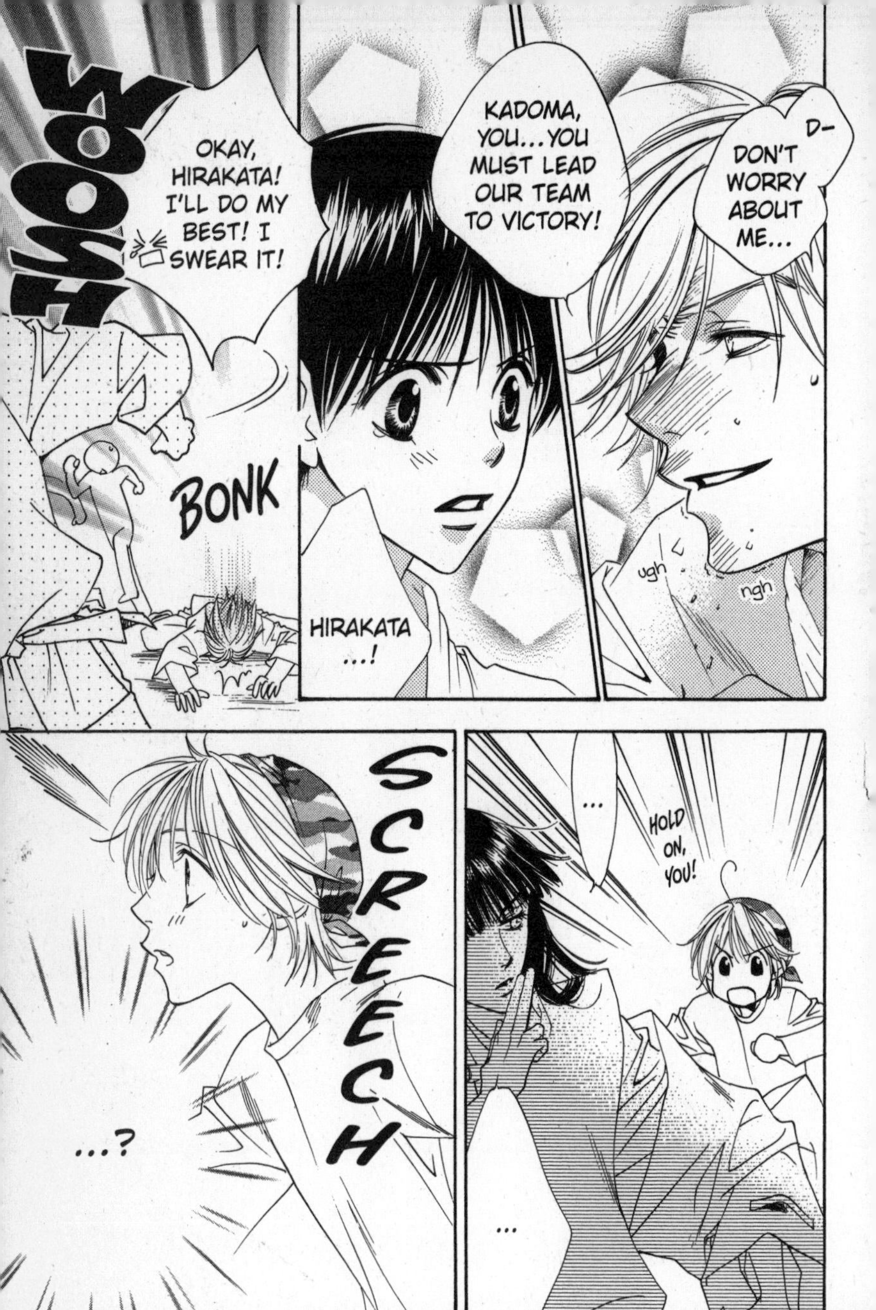

D- DON'T WORRY ABOUT ME...
ugh
ngh
KADOMA, YOU...YOU MUST LEAD OUR TEAM TO VICTORY!
HIRAKATA ...!
OKAY, HIRAKATA! I'LL DO MY BEST! I SWEAR IT!
WHOOSH
BONK
...
HOLD ON, YOU!
...
SCREECH
...?

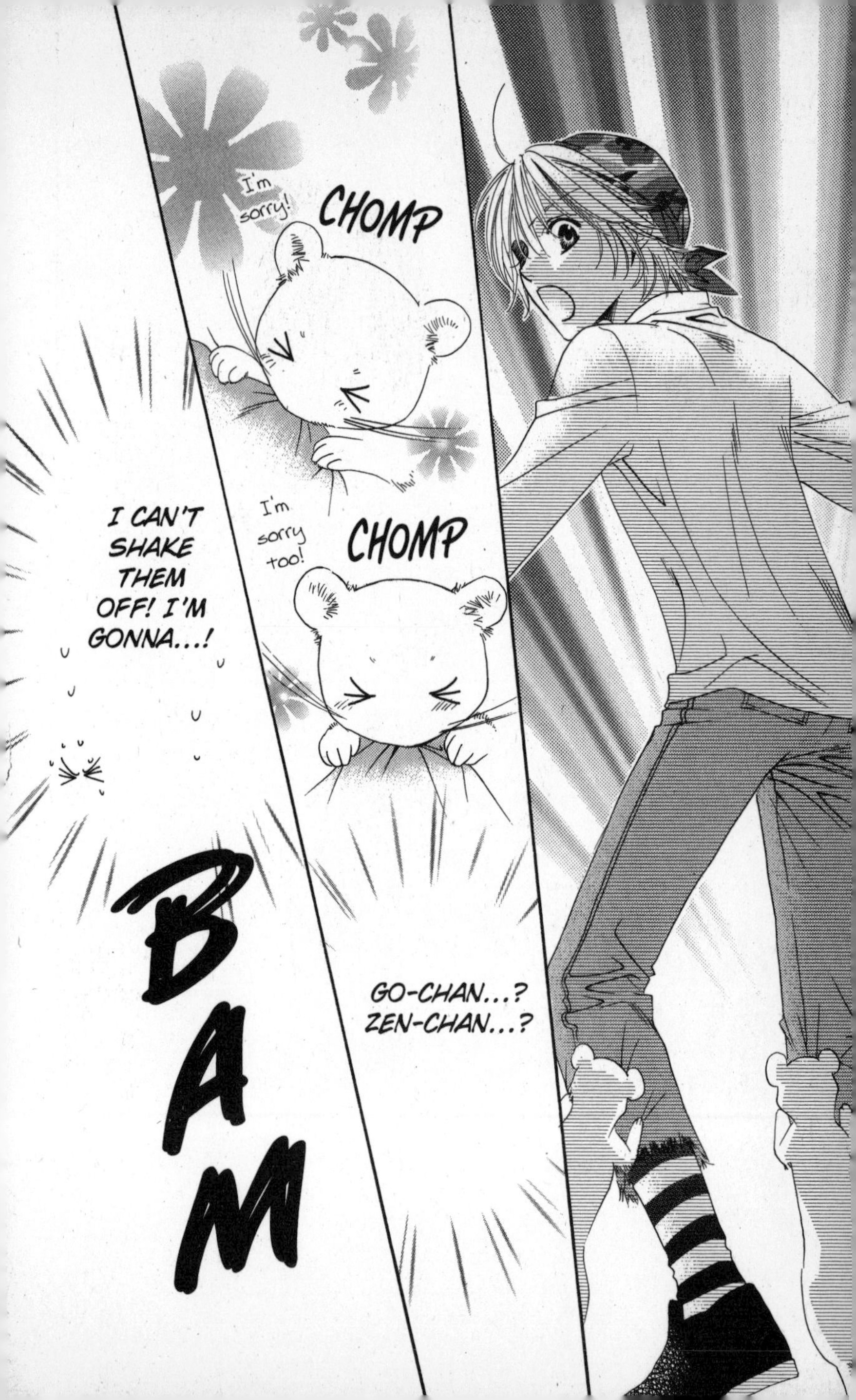
GO-CHAN...? ZEN-CHAN...?
CHOMP
I'm sorry!
CHOMP
I'm sorry too!
I CAN'T SHAKE THEM OFF! I'M GONNA...!
BAM

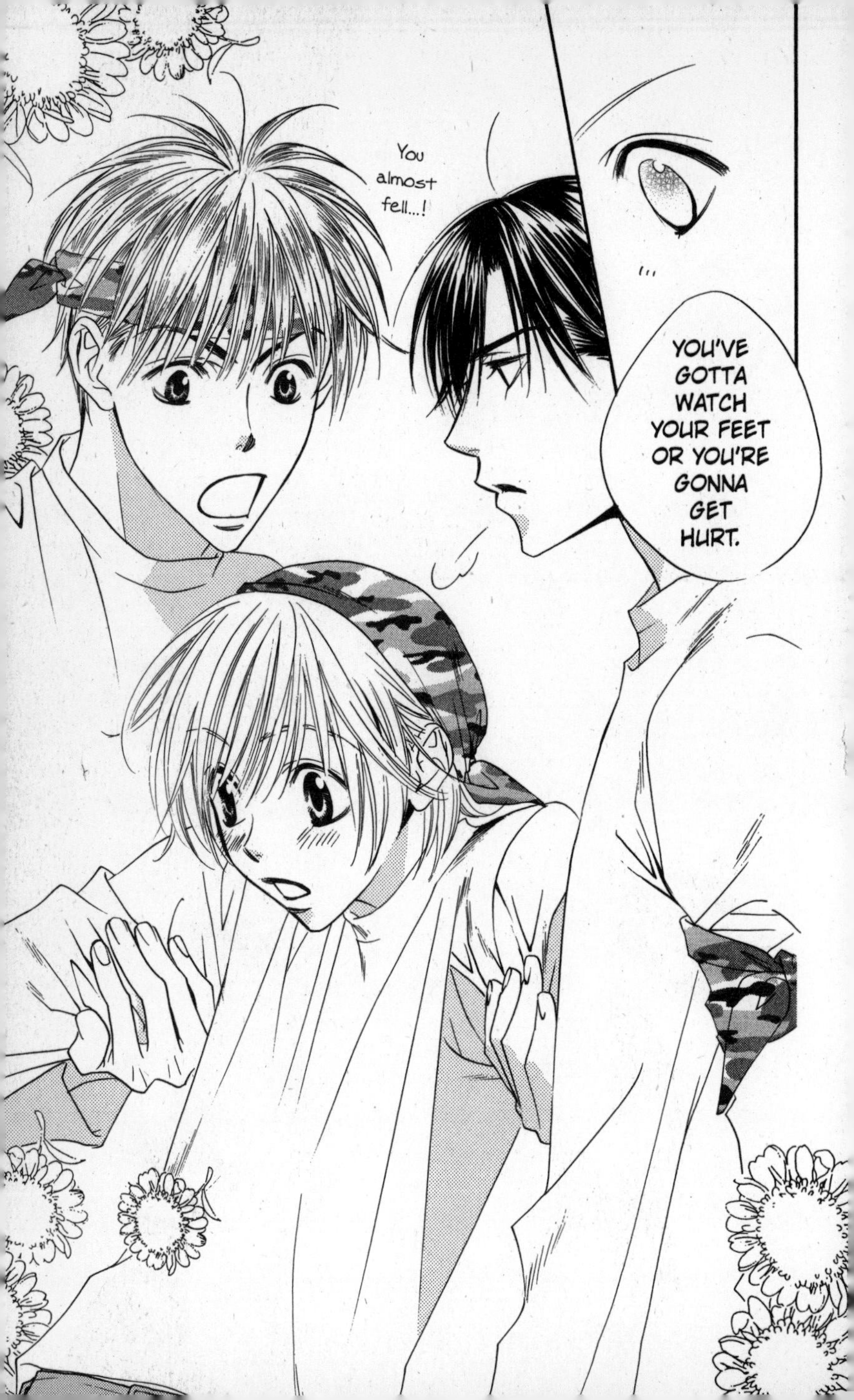
...
You almost fell...!
YOU'VE GOTTA WATCH YOUR FEET OR YOU'RE GONNA GET HURT.

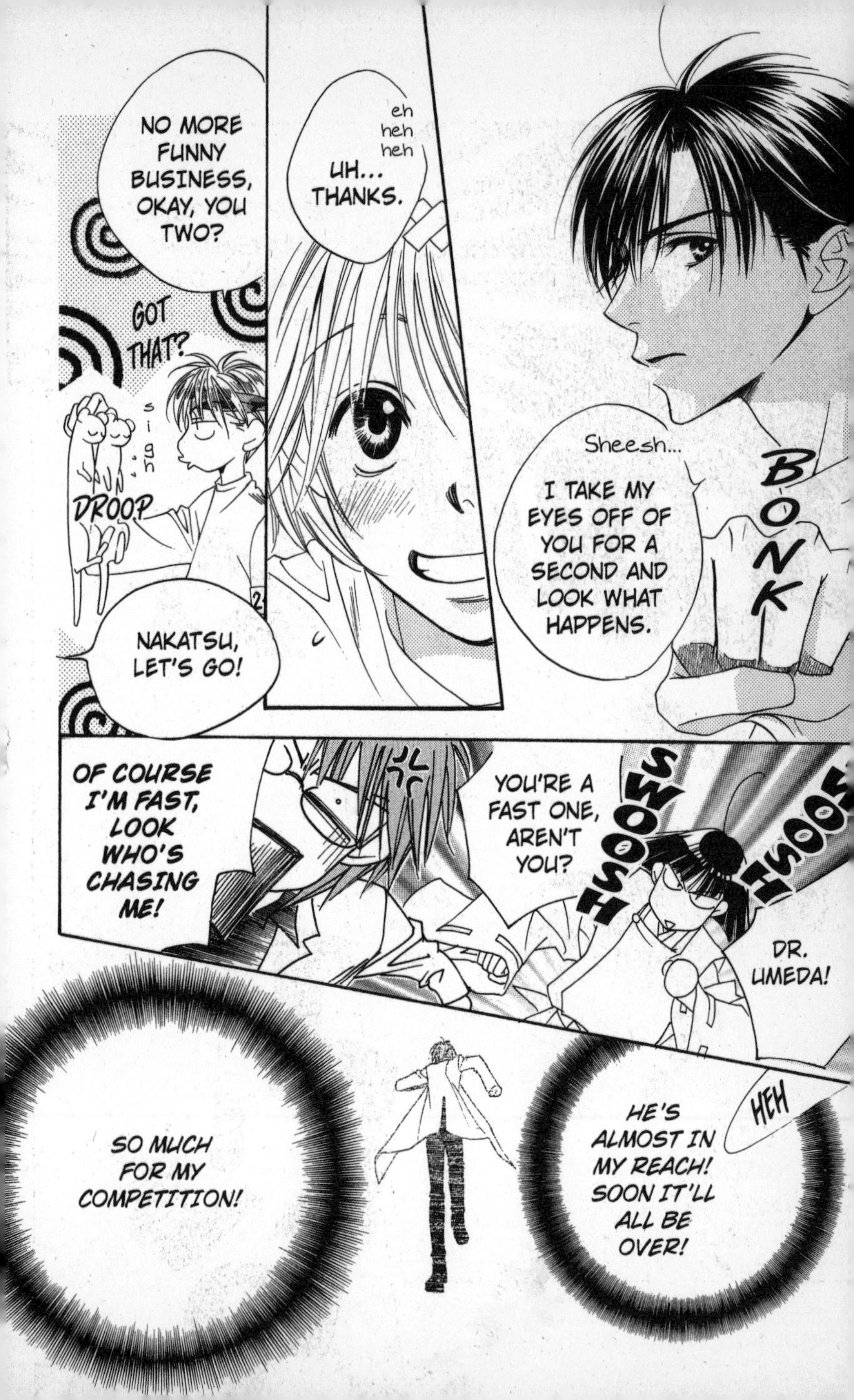
BONK
Sheesh...
I TAKE MY EYES OFF OF YOU FOR A SECOND AND LOOK WHAT HAPPENS.
eh heh heh
UH... THANKS.
NO MORE FUNNY BUSINESS, OKAY, YOU TWO?
GOT THAT?
sigh
DROOP
NAKATSU, LET'S GO!
SWOOSH
SWOOSH
DR. UMEDA!
YOU'RE A FAST ONE, AREN'T YOU?
OF COURSE I'M FAST, LOOK WHO'S CHASING ME!
HEH
HE'S ALMOST IN MY REACH! SOON IT'LL ALL BE OVER!
SO MUCH FOR MY COMPETITION!

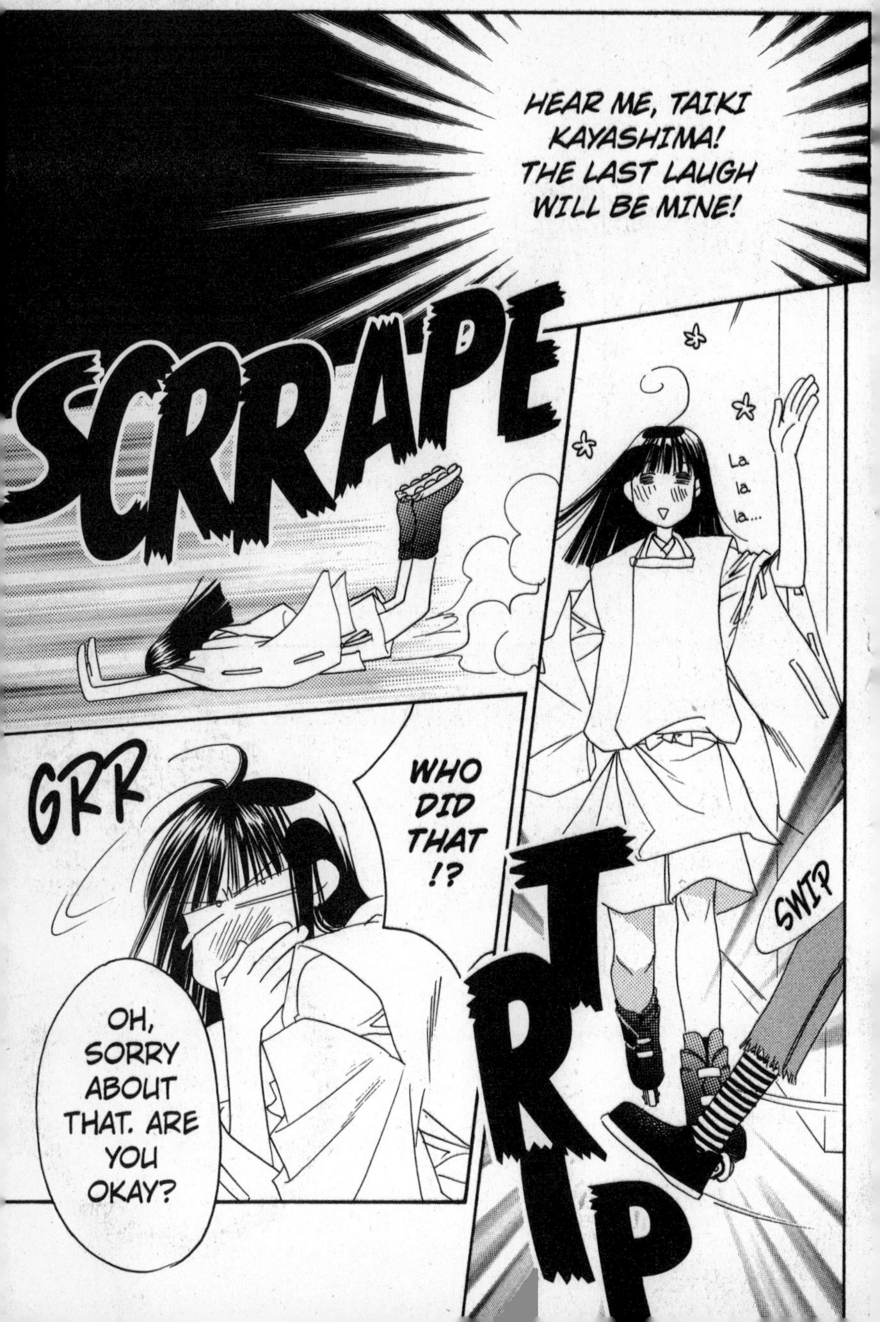
HEAR ME, TAIKI KAYASHIMA! THE LAST LAUGH WILL BE MINE!
La la la...
SWIP
TRIP
SCRRAPE
WHO DID THAT!?
GRR
OH, SORRY ABOUT THAT. ARE YOU OKAY?

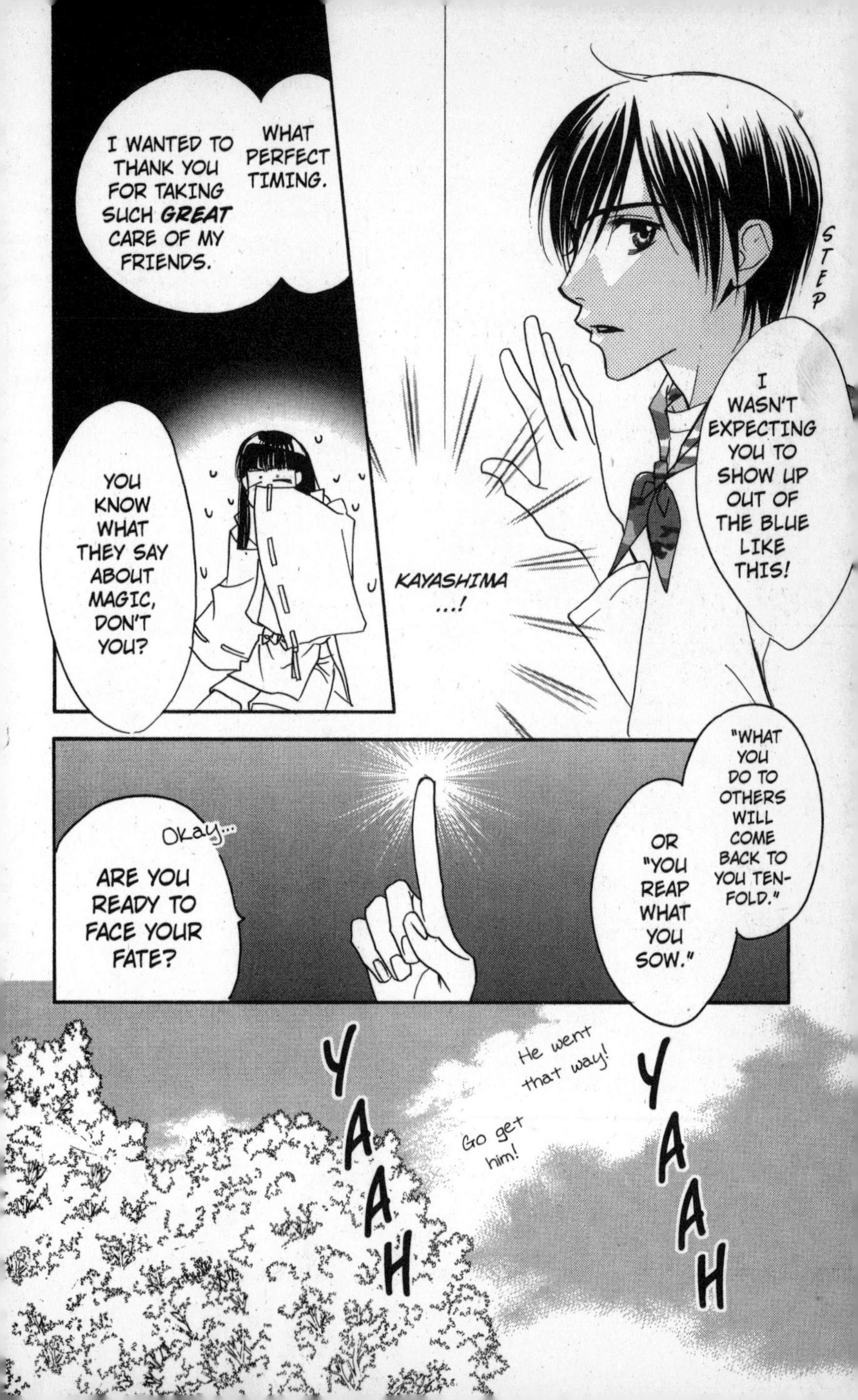
STEP
I WASN'T EXPECTING YOU TO SHOW UP OUT OF THE BLUE LIKE THIS!
KAYASHIMA ...!
WHAT PERFECT TIMING.
I WANTED TO THANK YOU FOR TAKING SUCH GREAT CARE OF MY FRIENDS.
YOU KNOW WHAT THEY SAY ABOUT MAGIC, DON'T YOU?
"WHAT YOU DO TO OTHERS WILL COME BACK TO YOU TEN-FOLD."
OR "YOU REAP WHAT YOU SOW."
Okay...
ARE YOU READY TO FACE YOUR FATE?
YAAAH
He went that way!
Go get him!
YAAAH

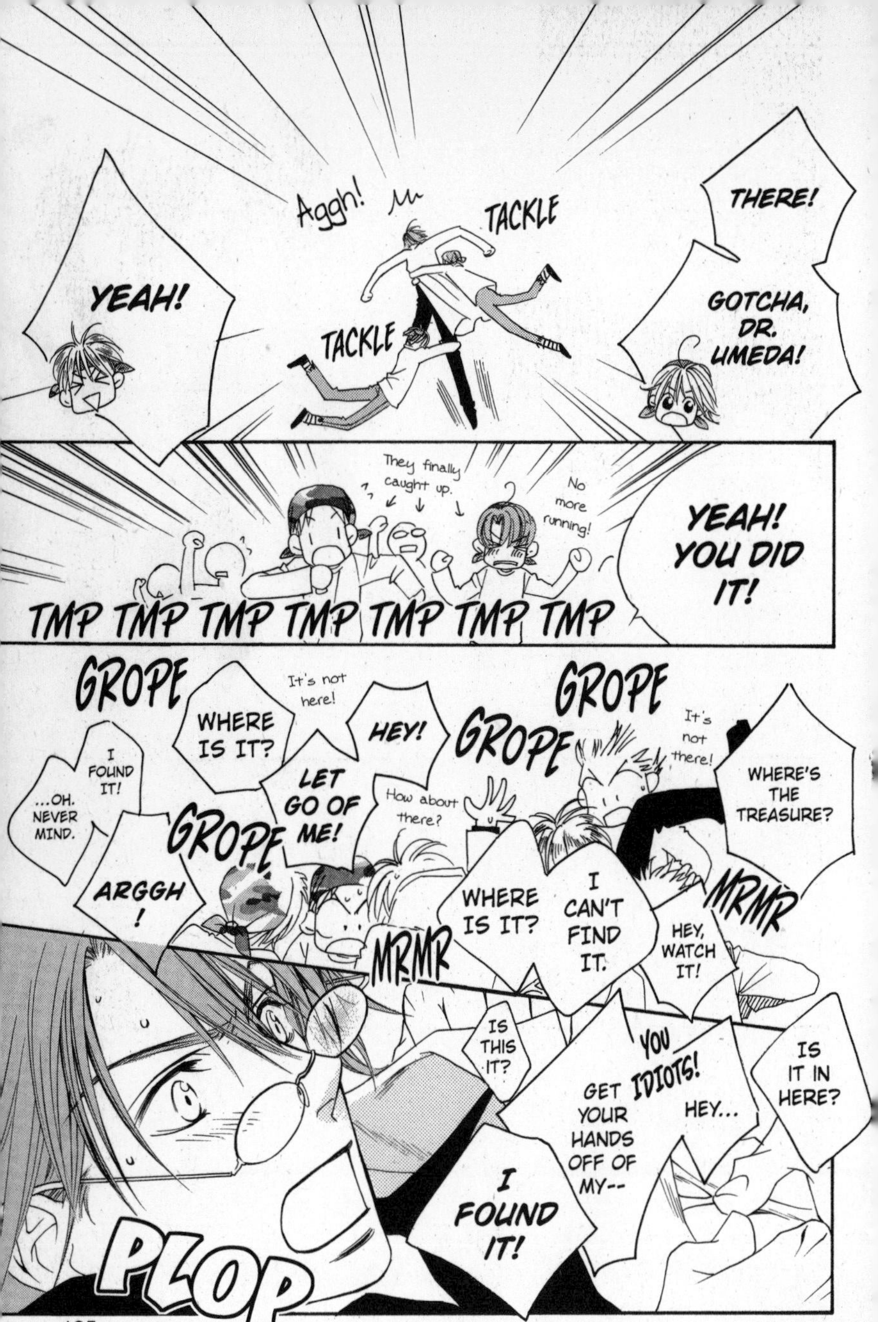
THERE!
GOTCHA, DR. UMEDA!
TACKLE
Aggh!
YEAH!
TACKLE
YEAH! YOU DID IT!
No more running!
They finally caught up.
TMP TMP TMP TMP TMP TMP TMP
WHERE'S THE TREASURE?
It's not there!
GROPE
GROPE
HEY!
It's not here!
WHERE IS IT?
GROPE
I FOUND IT!
...OH. NEVER MIND.
LET GO OF ME!
How about there?
GROPE
ARGGH!
MRMR
I CAN'T FIND IT.
WHERE IS IT?
HEY, WATCH IT!
MRMR
IS IT IN HERE?
HEY...
YOU IDIOTS!
GET YOUR HANDS OFF OF MY--
IS THIS IT?
I FOUND IT!
PLOP

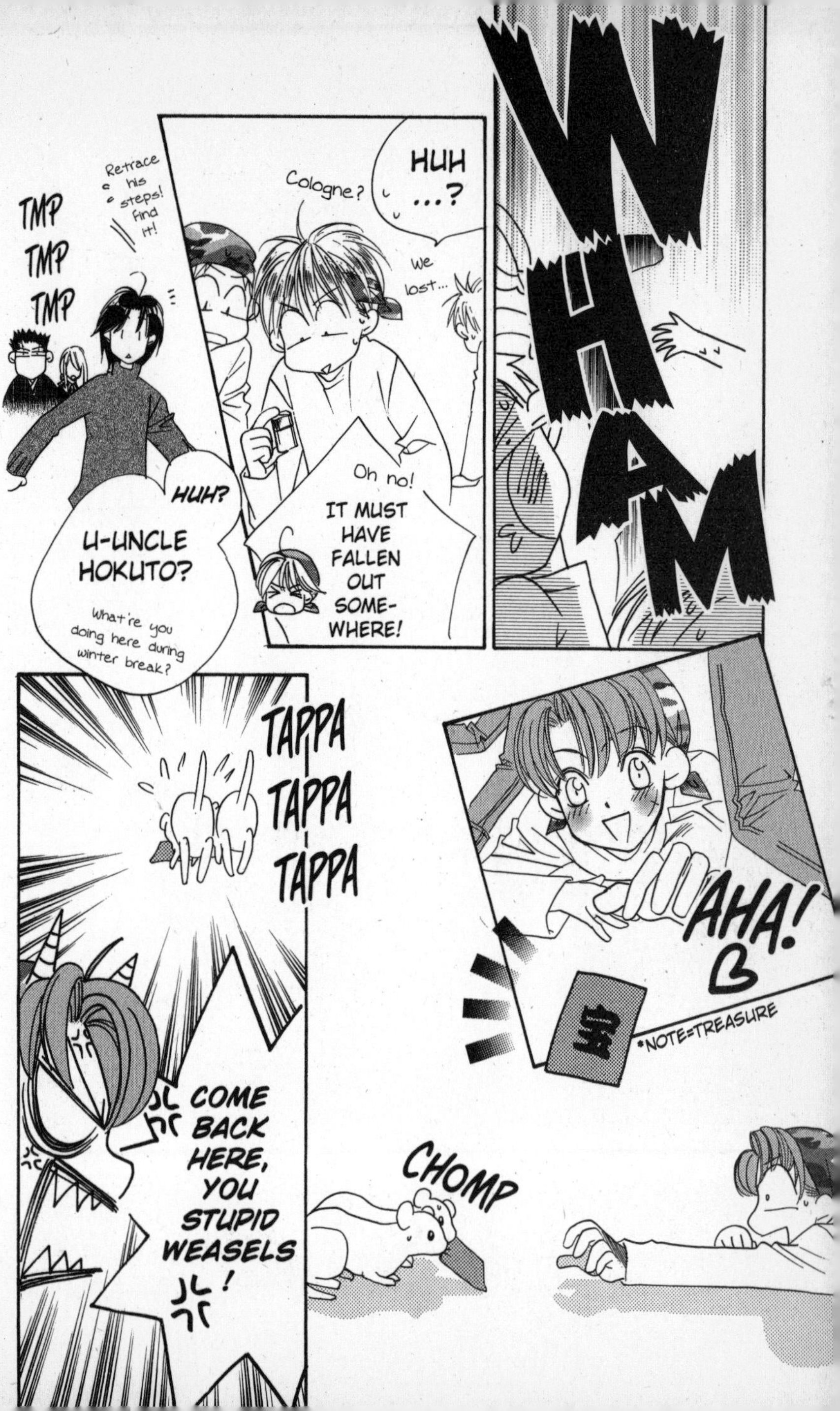
WHAM
HUH ...?
Cologne?
We lost...
Oh no!
IT MUST HAVE FALLEN OUT SOMEWHERE!
Retrace his steps! Find it!
TMP TMP TMP
HUH?
U-UNCLE HOKUTO?
What're you doing here during winter break?
AHA!
*NOTE=TREASURE
CHOMP
TAPPA TAPPA TAPPA
COME BACK HERE, YOU STUPID WEASELS!

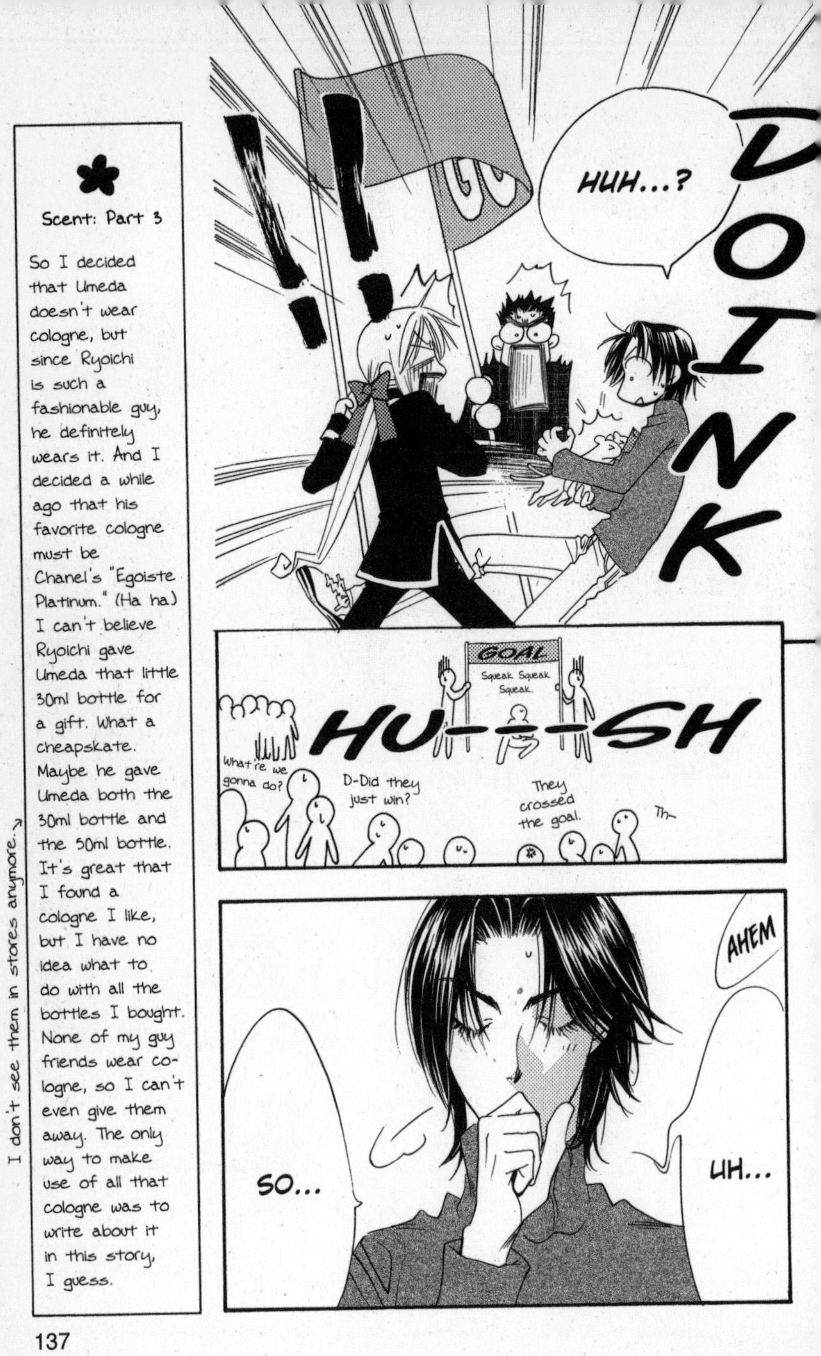
DOINK
HUH...?
GOAL
Squeak Squeak Squeak.
HU---SH
Th-
They crossed the goal.
D-Did they just win?
What're we gonna do?
AHEM
UH...
SO...

✿

Scent: Part 3

So I decided that Umeda doesn't wear cologne, but since Ryoichi is such a fashionable guy, he definitely wears it. And I decided a while ago that his favorite cologne must be Chanel's "Egoiste Platinum." (Ha ha) I can't believe Ryoichi gave Umeda that little 30ml bottle for a gift. What a cheapskate. Maybe he gave Umeda both the 30ml bottle and the 50ml bottle. It's great that I found a cologne I like, but I have no idea what to do with all the bottles I bought. None of my guy friends wear cologne, so I can't even give them away. The only way to make use of all that cologne was to write about it in this story, I guess.

I don't see them in stores anymore.→

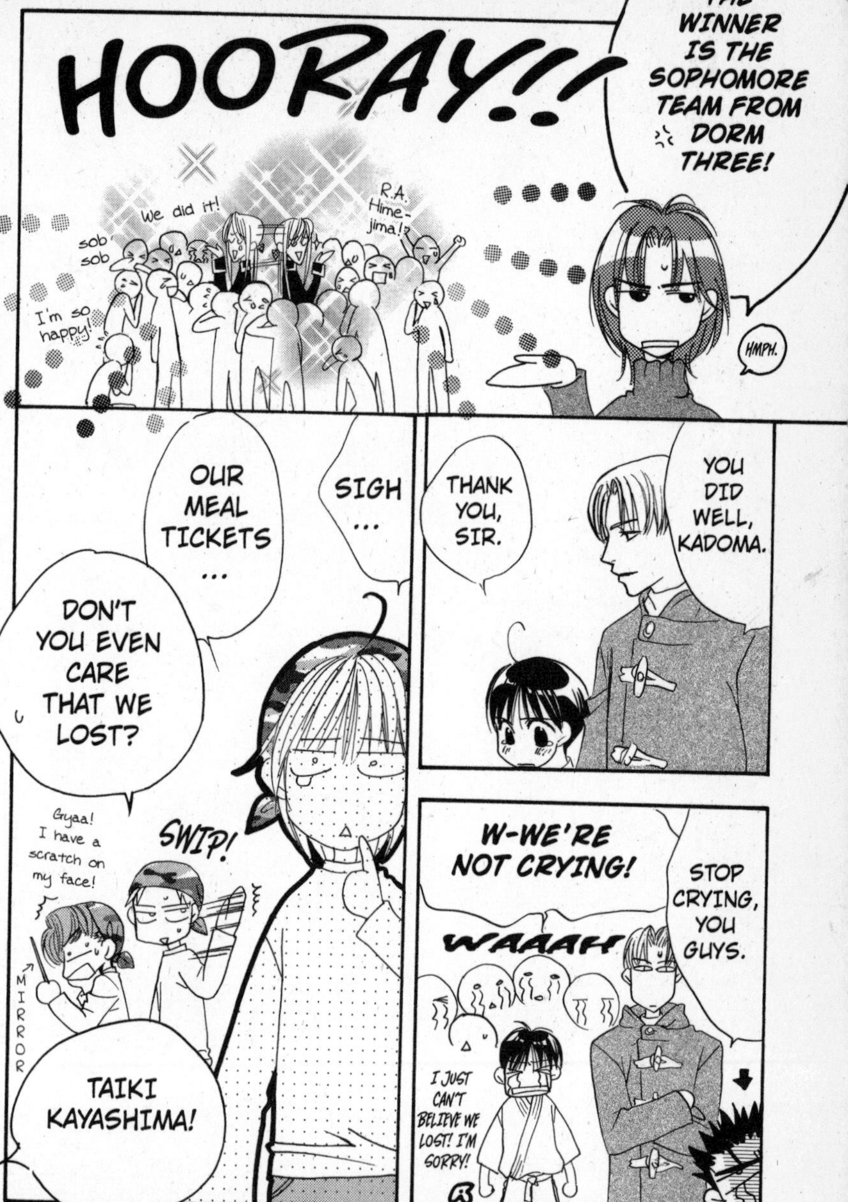
THE WINNER IS THE SOPHOMORE TEAM FROM DORM THREE!
HMPH.
HOORAY!!
R.A. Hime-jima!
We did it!
sob sob
I'm so happy!
YOU DID WELL, KADOMA.
THANK YOU, SIR.
STOP CRYING, YOU GUYS.
W-WE'RE NOT CRYING!
WAAAH
I JUST CAN'T BELIEVE WE LOST! I'M SORRY!
SIGH...
OUR MEAL TICKETS...
DON'T YOU EVEN CARE THAT WE LOST?
SWIP!
Gyaa! I have a scratch on my face!
MIRROR
TAIKI KAYASHIMA!

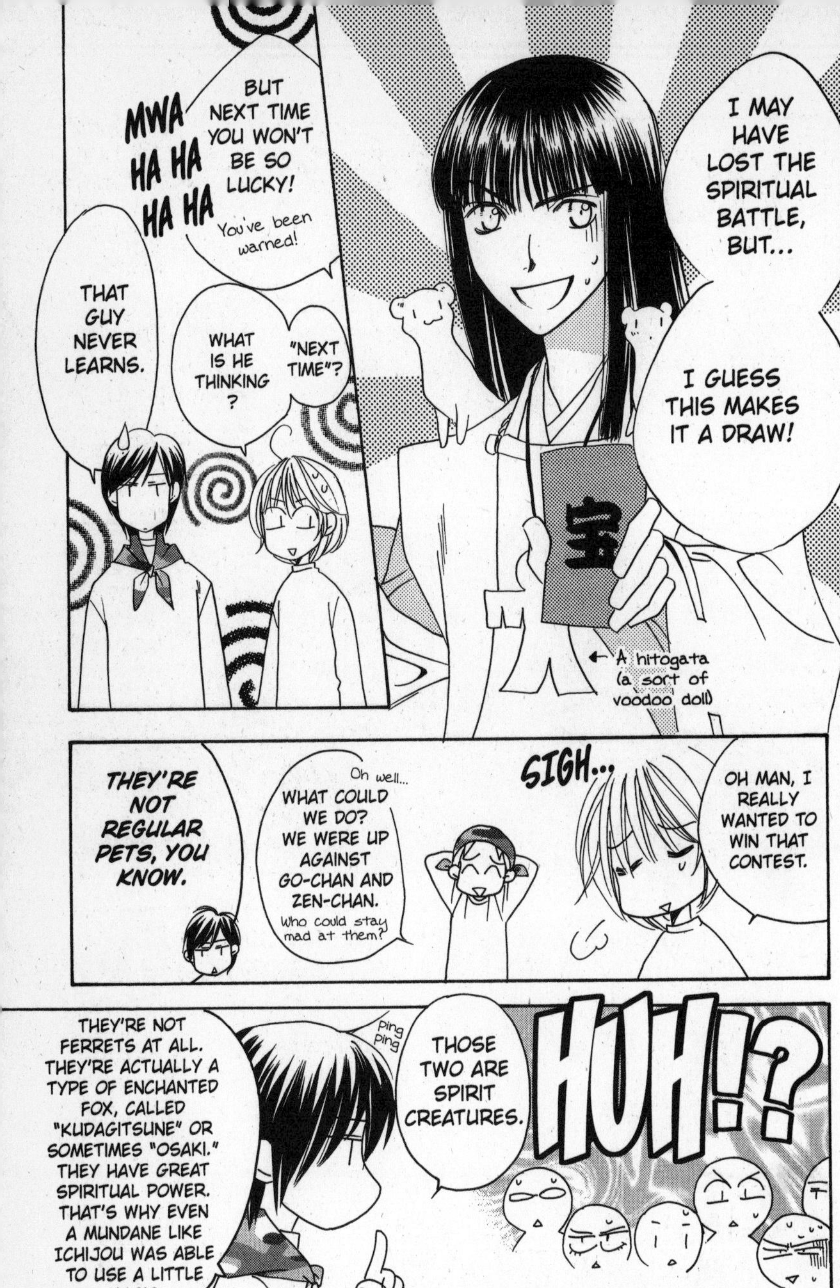
I MAY HAVE LOST THE SPIRITUAL BATTLE, BUT...
I GUESS THIS MAKES IT A DRAW!
← A hitogata (a sort of voodoo doll)
BUT NEXT TIME YOU WON'T BE SO LUCKY!
MWA HA HA HA HA
You've been warned!
"NEXT TIME"?
WHAT IS HE THINKING?
THAT GUY NEVER LEARNS.
OH MAN, I REALLY WANTED TO WIN THAT CONTEST.
SIGH...
Oh well...
WHAT COULD WE DO? WE WERE UP AGAINST GO-CHAN AND ZEN-CHAN.
Who could stay mad at them?
THEY'RE NOT REGULAR PETS, YOU KNOW.
HUH!?
THOSE TWO ARE SPIRIT CREATURES.
ping ping
THEY'RE NOT FERRETS AT ALL. THEY'RE ACTUALLY A TYPE OF ENCHANTED FOX, CALLED "KUDAGITSUNE" OR SOMETIMES "OSAKI." THEY HAVE GREAT SPIRITUAL POWER. THAT'S WHY EVEN A MUNDANE LIKE ICHIJOU WAS ABLE TO USE A LITTLE MAGIC.

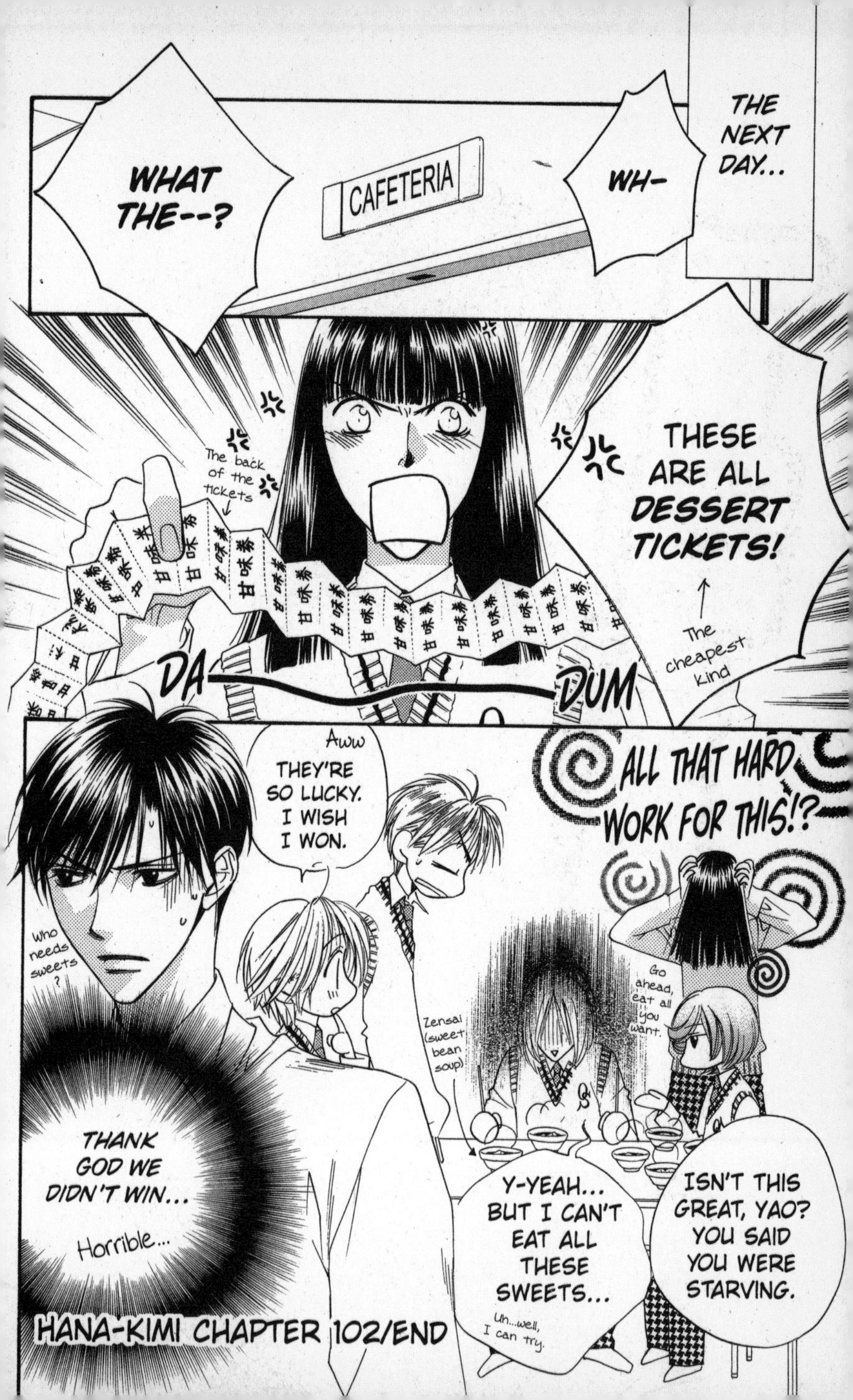
THE NEXT DAY...
WH-
CAFETERIA
WHAT THE--?
THESE ARE ALL DESSERT TICKETS!
The cheapest kind
The back of the tickets
DA—DUM
ALL THAT HARD WORK FOR THIS!?
Go ahead, eat all you want.
ISN'T THIS GREAT, YAO? YOU SAID YOU WERE STARVING.
Y-YEAH... BUT I CAN'T EAT ALL THESE SWEETS...
Uh...well, I can try.
Zensai (sweet bean soup)
Aww
THEY'RE SO LUCKY. I WISH I WON.
Who needs sweets?
THANK GOD WE DIDN'T WIN...
Horrible...
HANA-KIMI CHAPTER 102/END

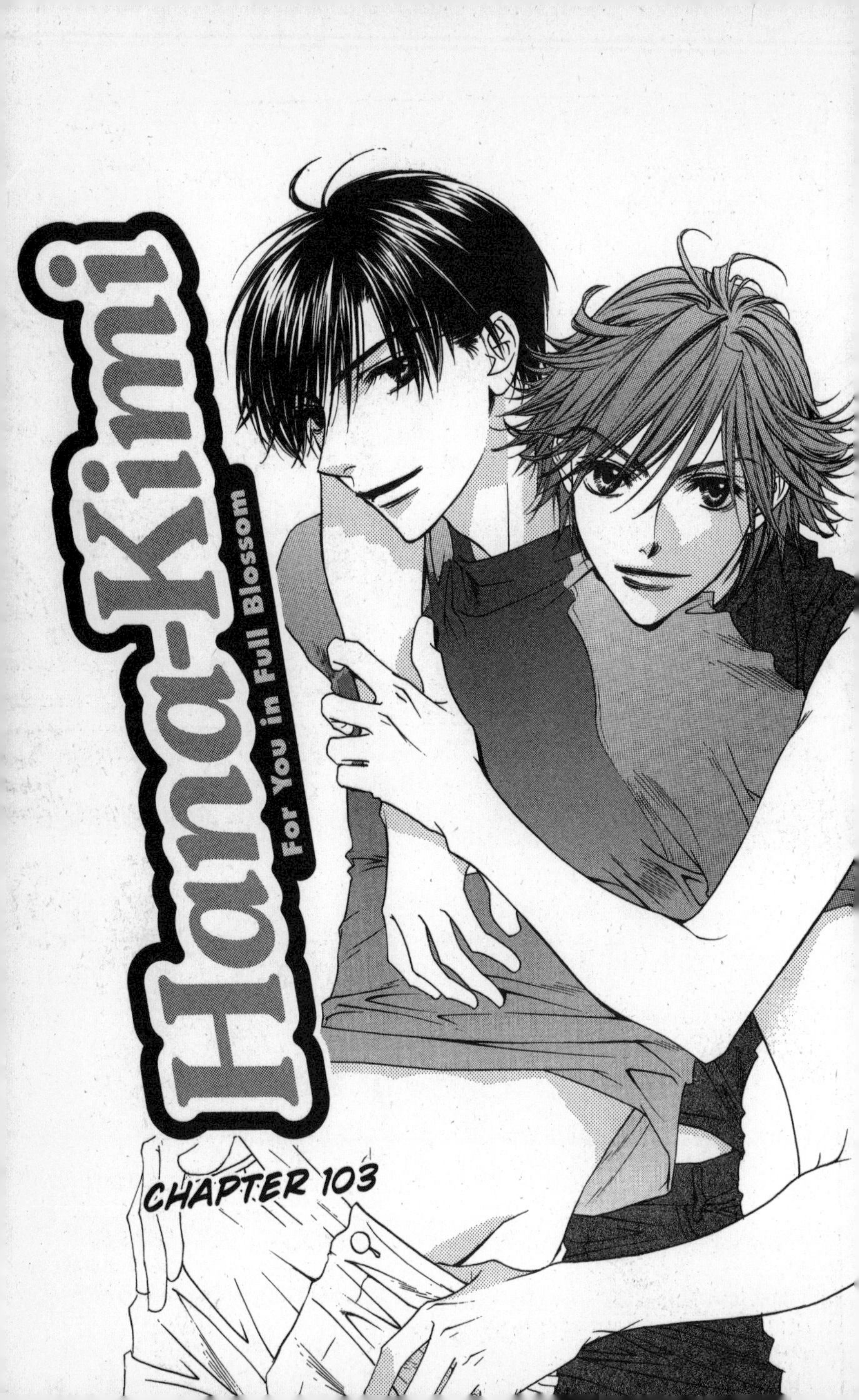
Hana-Kimi
For You in Full Blossom
CHAPTER 103

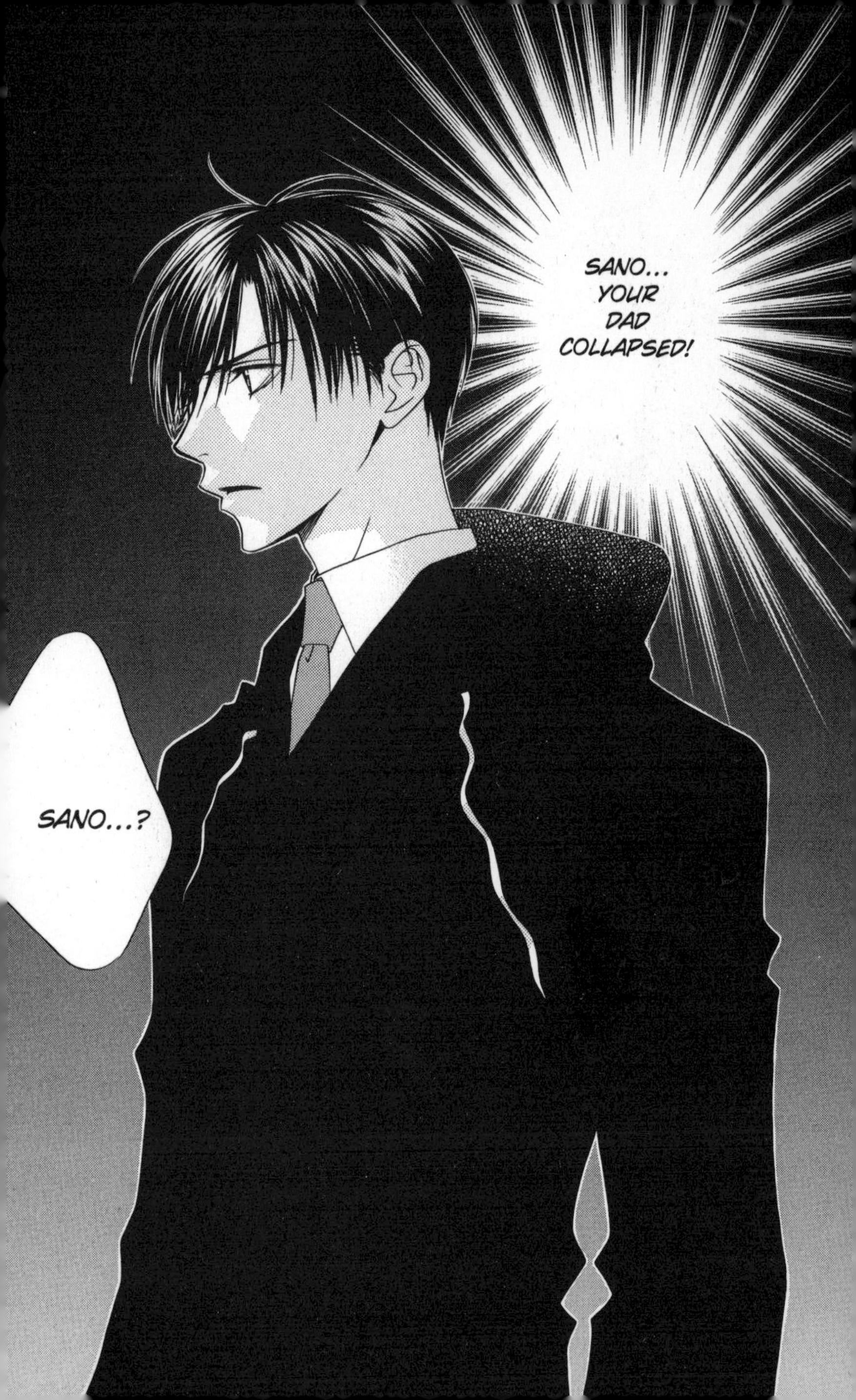
SANO... YOUR DAD COLLAPSED!
SANO...?

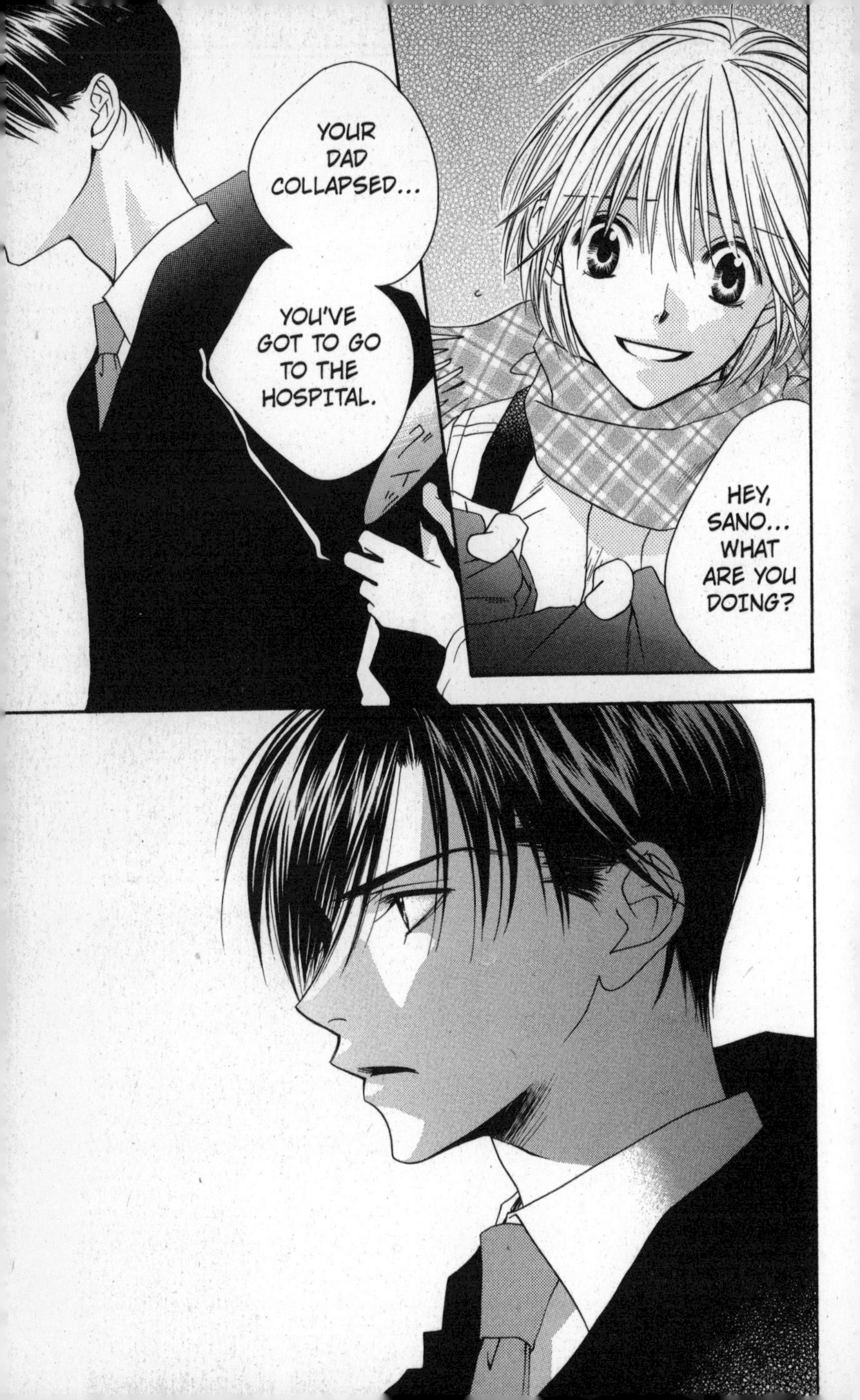
HEY, SANO... WHAT ARE YOU DOING?
YOUR DAD COLLAPSED...
YOU'VE GOT TO GO TO THE HOSPITAL.

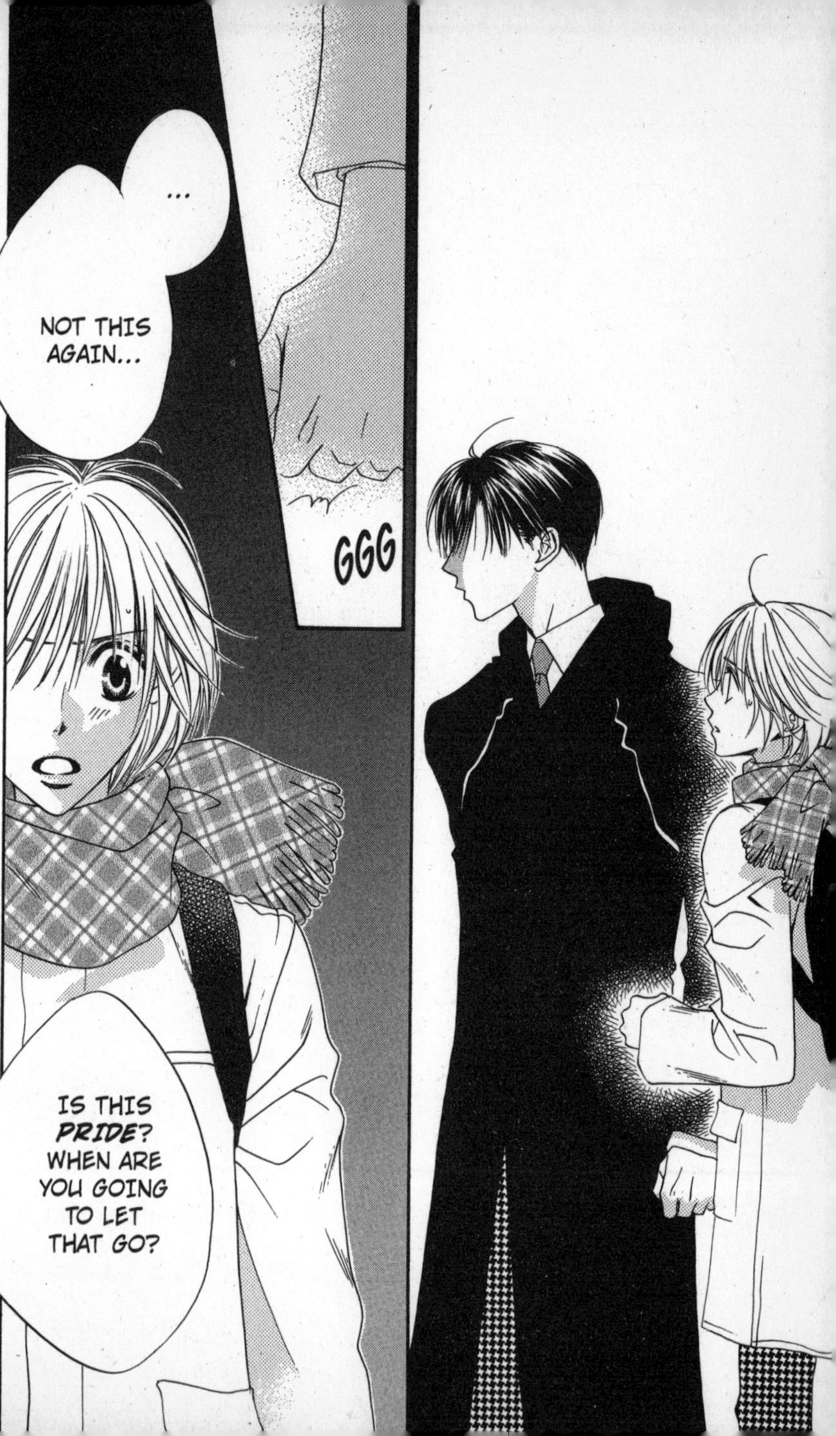
...
NOT THIS AGAIN...
GGG
IS THIS *PRIDE*? WHEN ARE YOU GOING TO LET THAT GO?

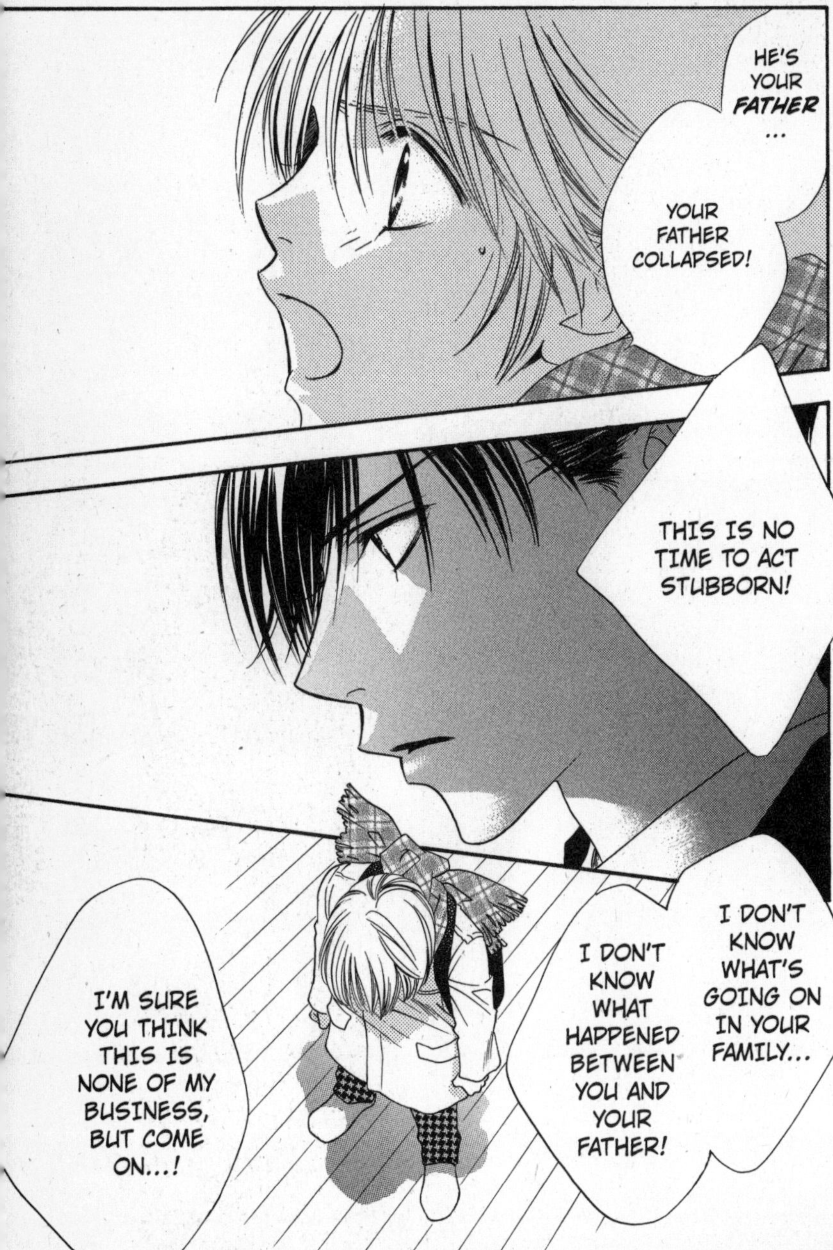
HE'S YOUR FATHER ...
YOUR FATHER COLLAPSED!
THIS IS NO TIME TO ACT STUBBORN!
I DON'T KNOW WHAT'S GOING ON IN YOUR FAMILY...
I DON'T KNOW WHAT HAPPENED BETWEEN YOU AND YOUR FATHER!
I'M SURE YOU THINK THIS IS NONE OF MY BUSINESS, BUT COME ON...!

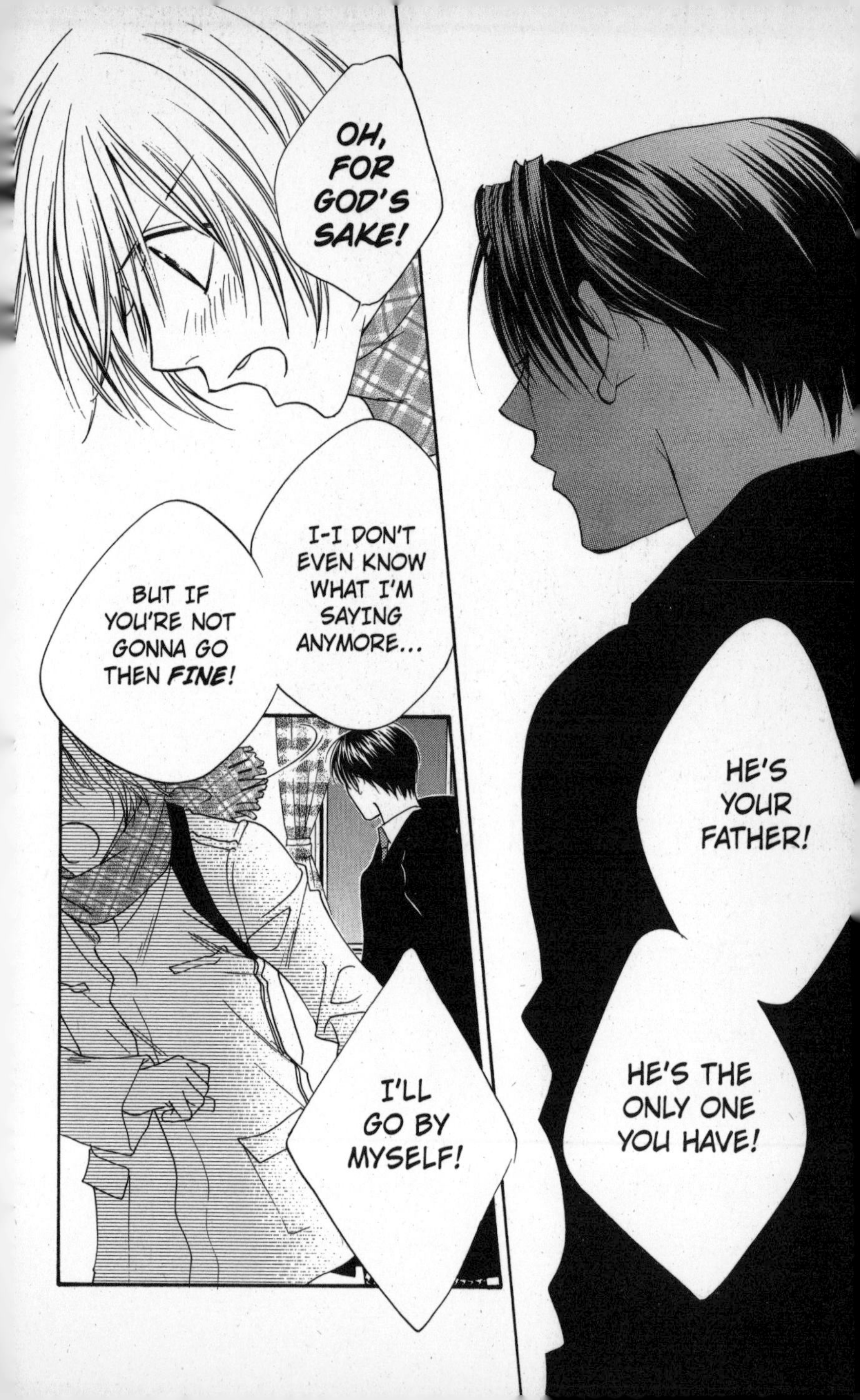
HE'S YOUR FATHER!
HE'S THE ONLY ONE YOU HAVE!
OH, FOR GOD'S SAKE!
I-I DON'T EVEN KNOW WHAT I'M SAYING ANYMORE...
BUT IF YOU'RE NOT GONNA GO THEN FINE!
I'LL GO BY MYSELF!

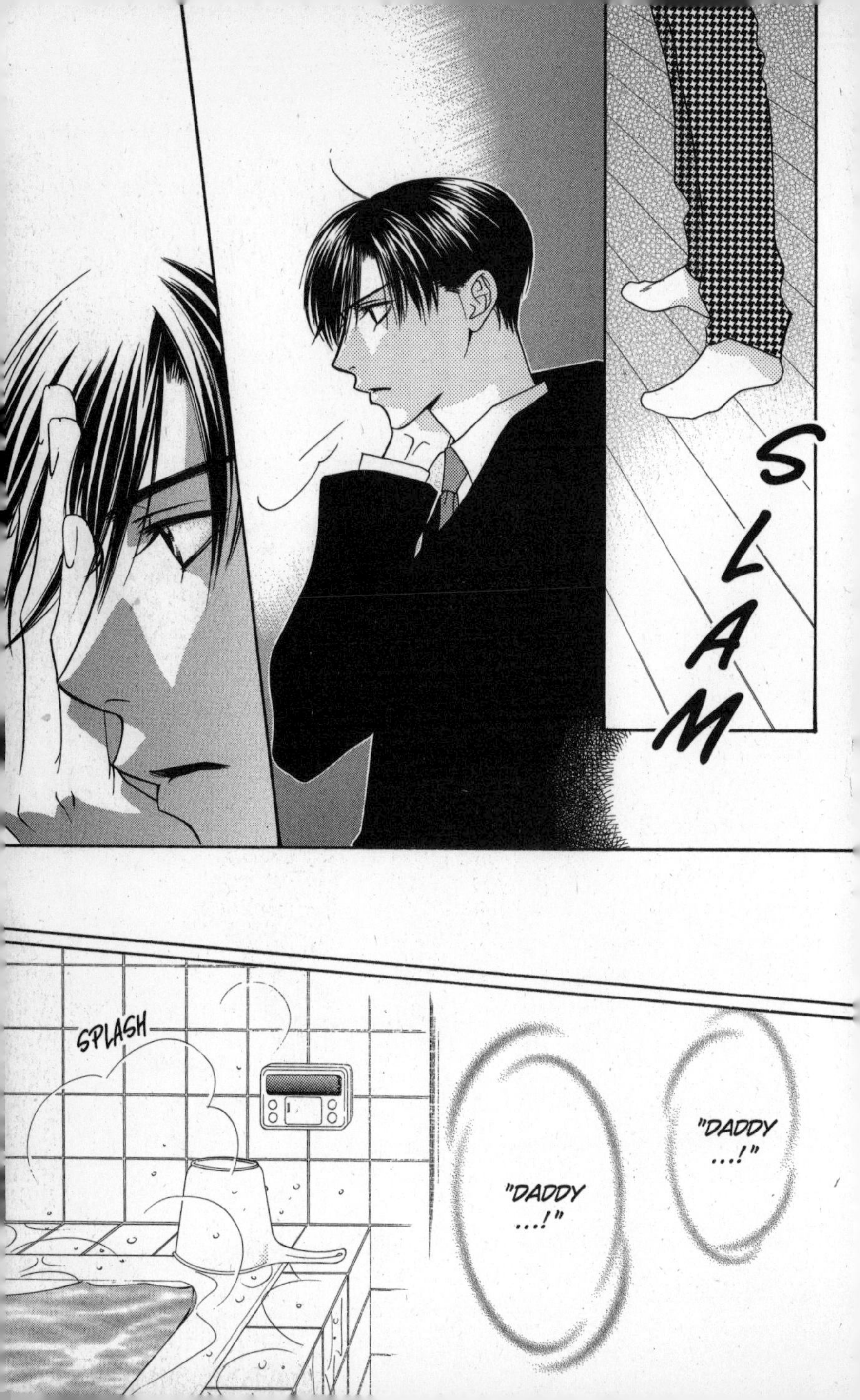
SLAM
"DADDY ...!"
"DADDY ...!"
SPLASH

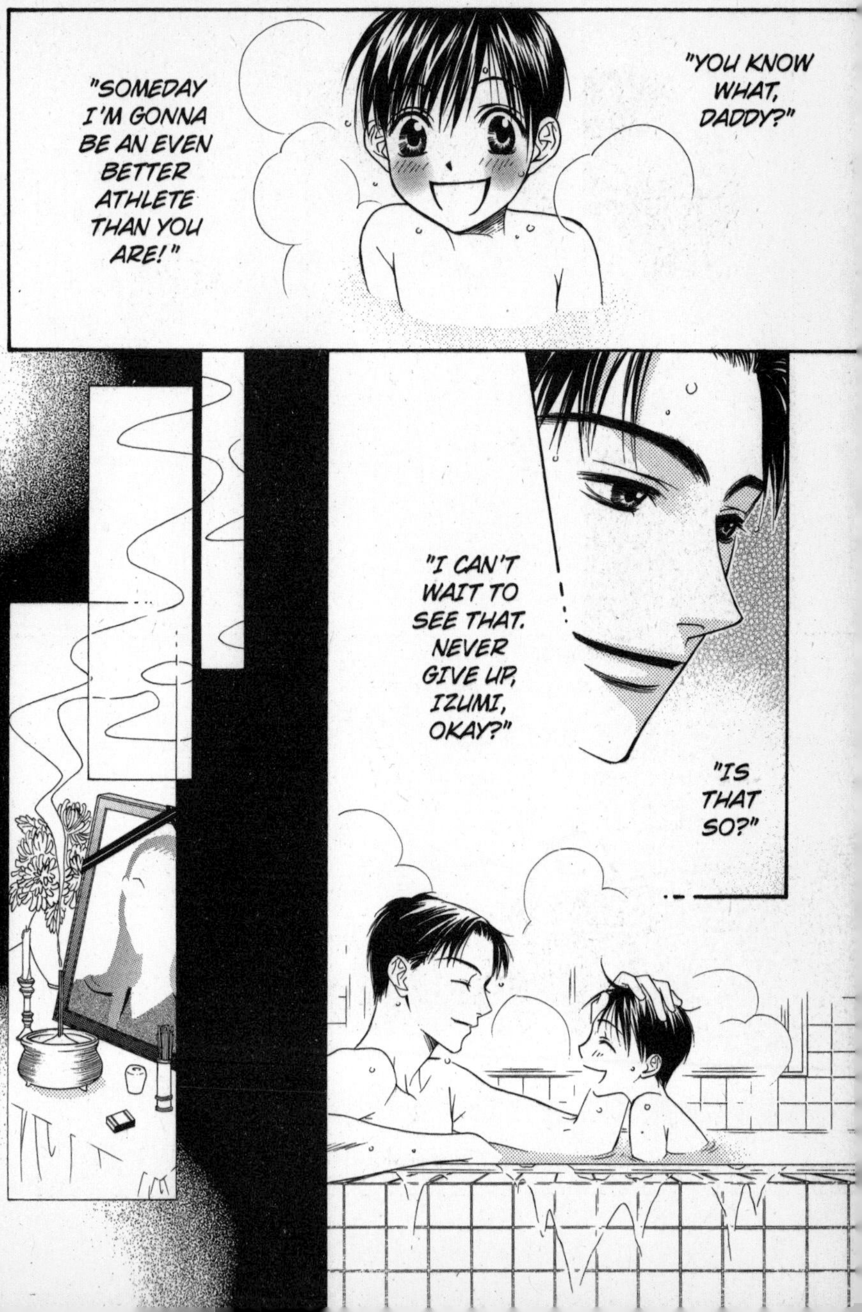
"YOU KNOW WHAT, DADDY?"
"SOMEDAY I'M GONNA BE AN EVEN BETTER ATHLETE THAN YOU ARE!"
"IS THAT SO?"
"I CAN'T WAIT TO SEE THAT. NEVER GIVE UP, IZUMI, OKAY?"

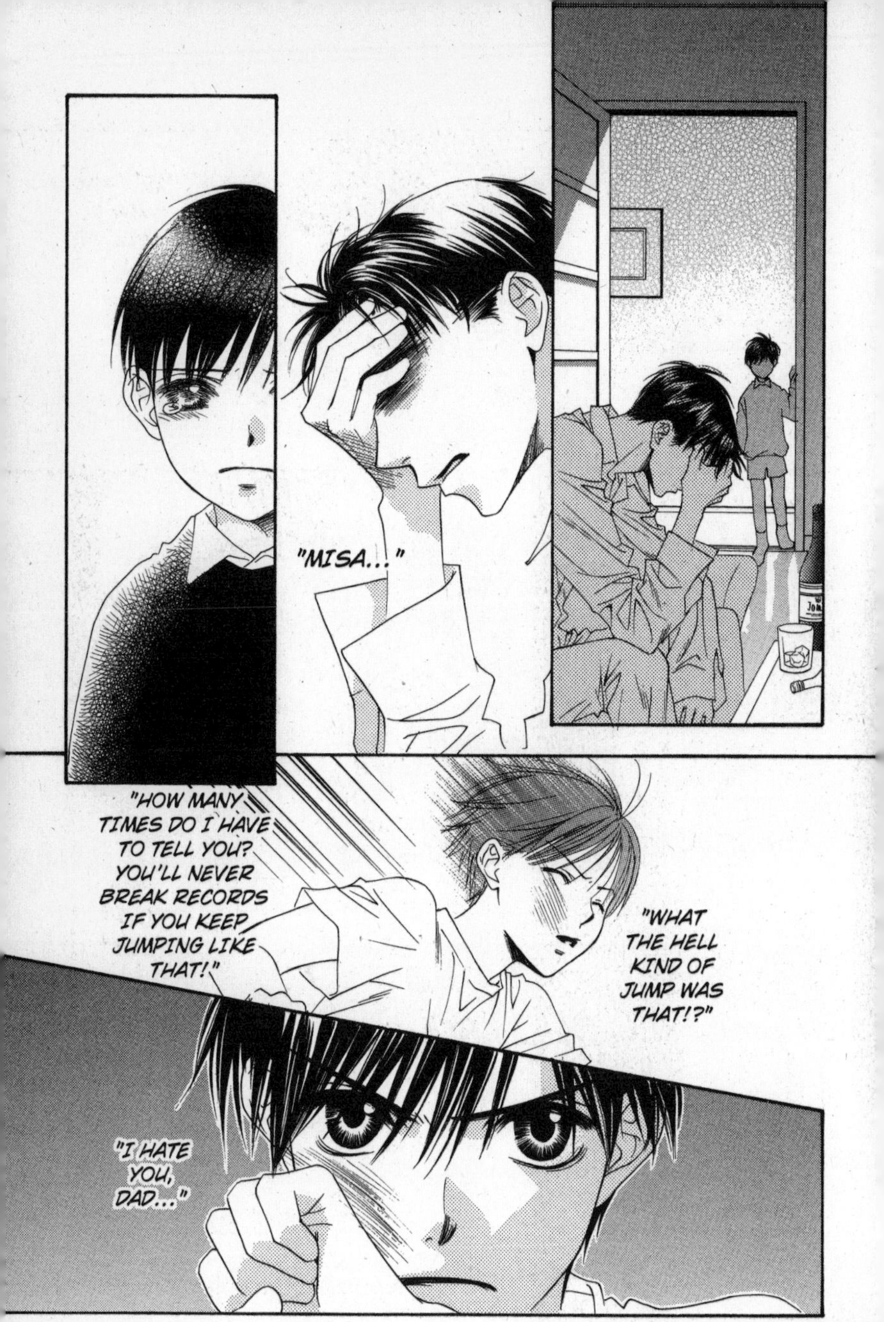
"MISA..."
"WHAT THE HELL KIND OF JUMP WAS THAT!?"
"HOW MANY TIMES DO I HAVE TO TELL YOU? YOU'LL NEVER BREAK RECORDS IF YOU KEEP JUMPING LIKE THAT!"
"I HATE YOU, DAD..."

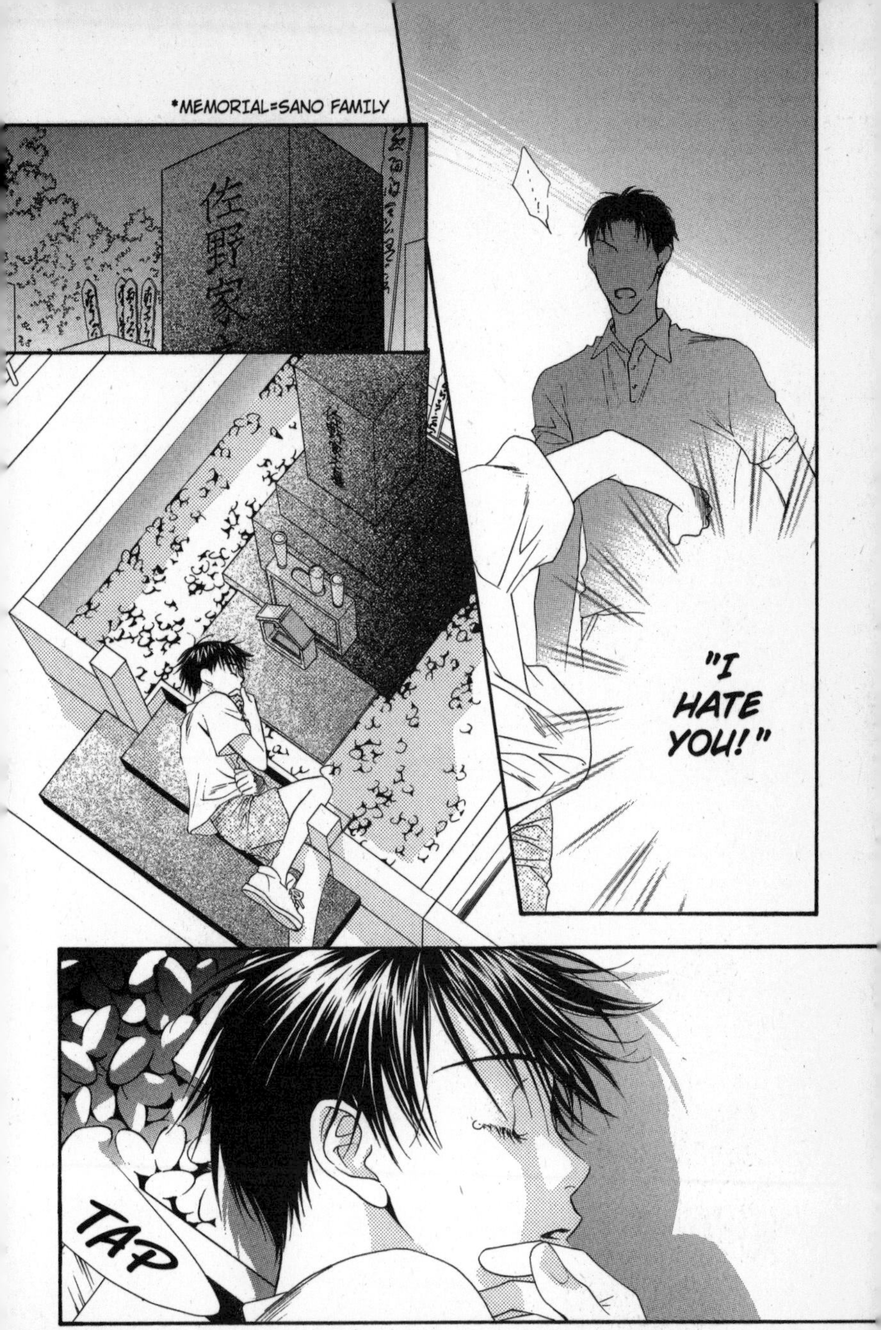
…!
"I HATE YOU!"
*MEMORIAL=SANO FAMILY
佐野家
TAP

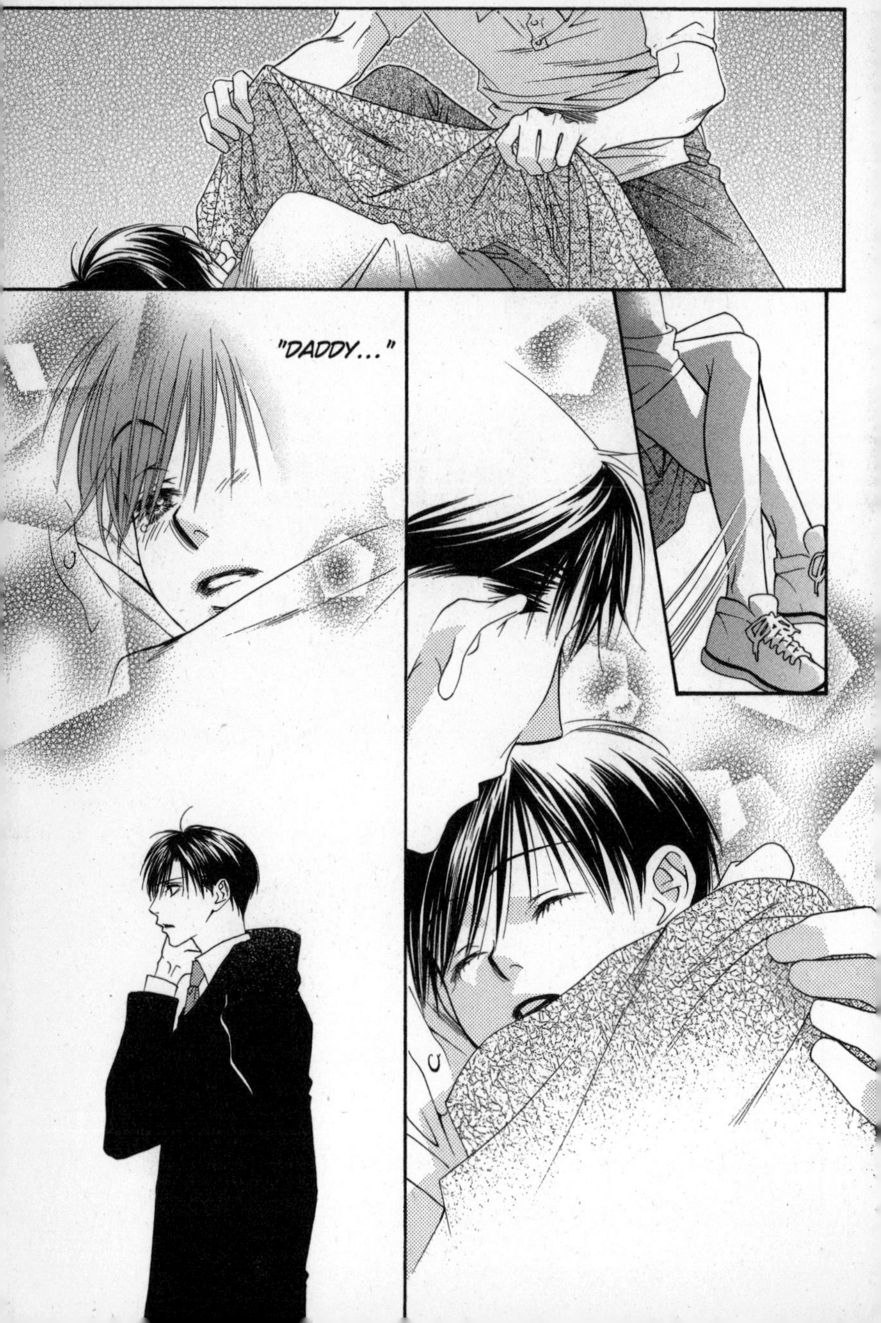
"DADDY..."

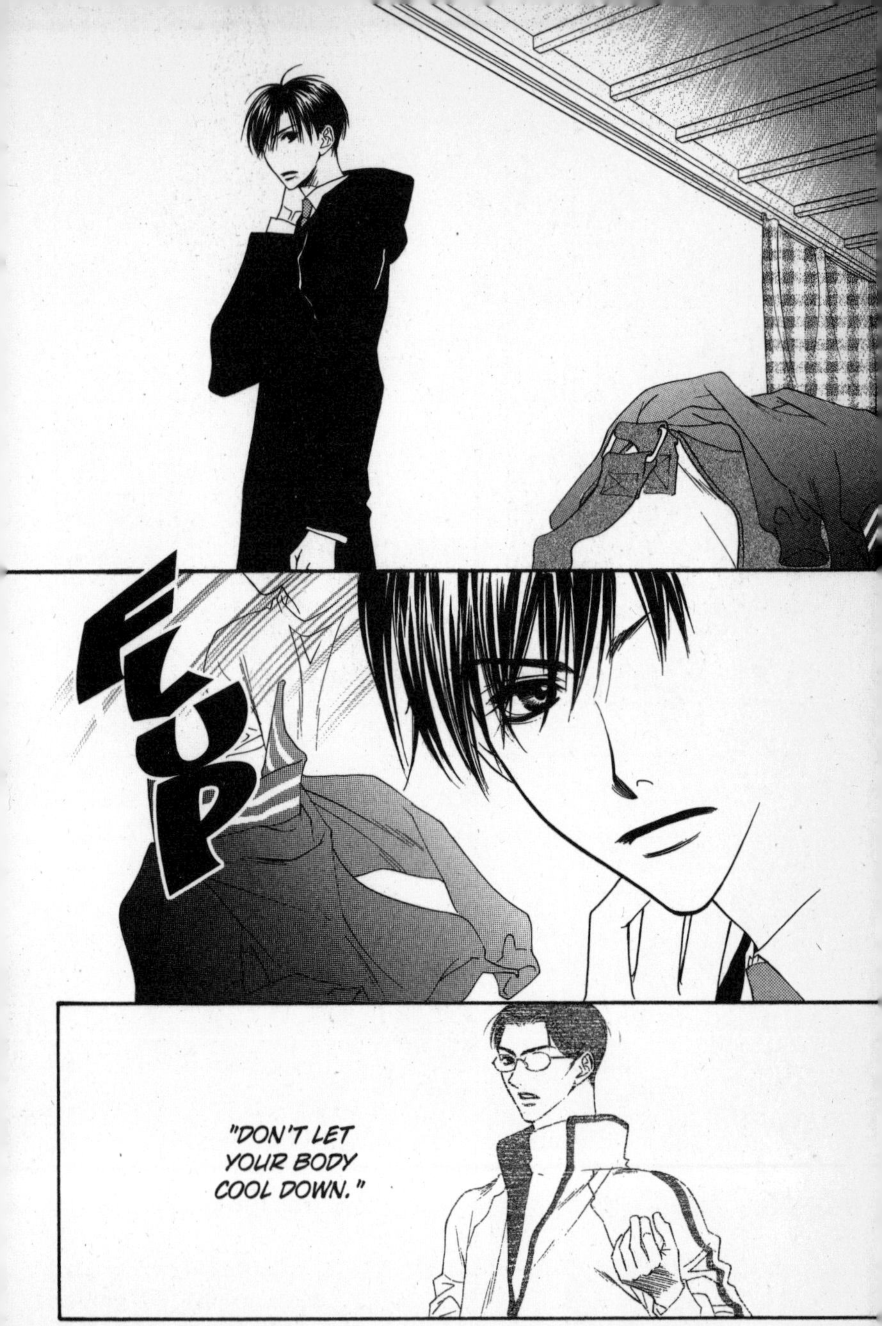
FLUP
"DON'T LET YOUR BODY COOL DOWN."

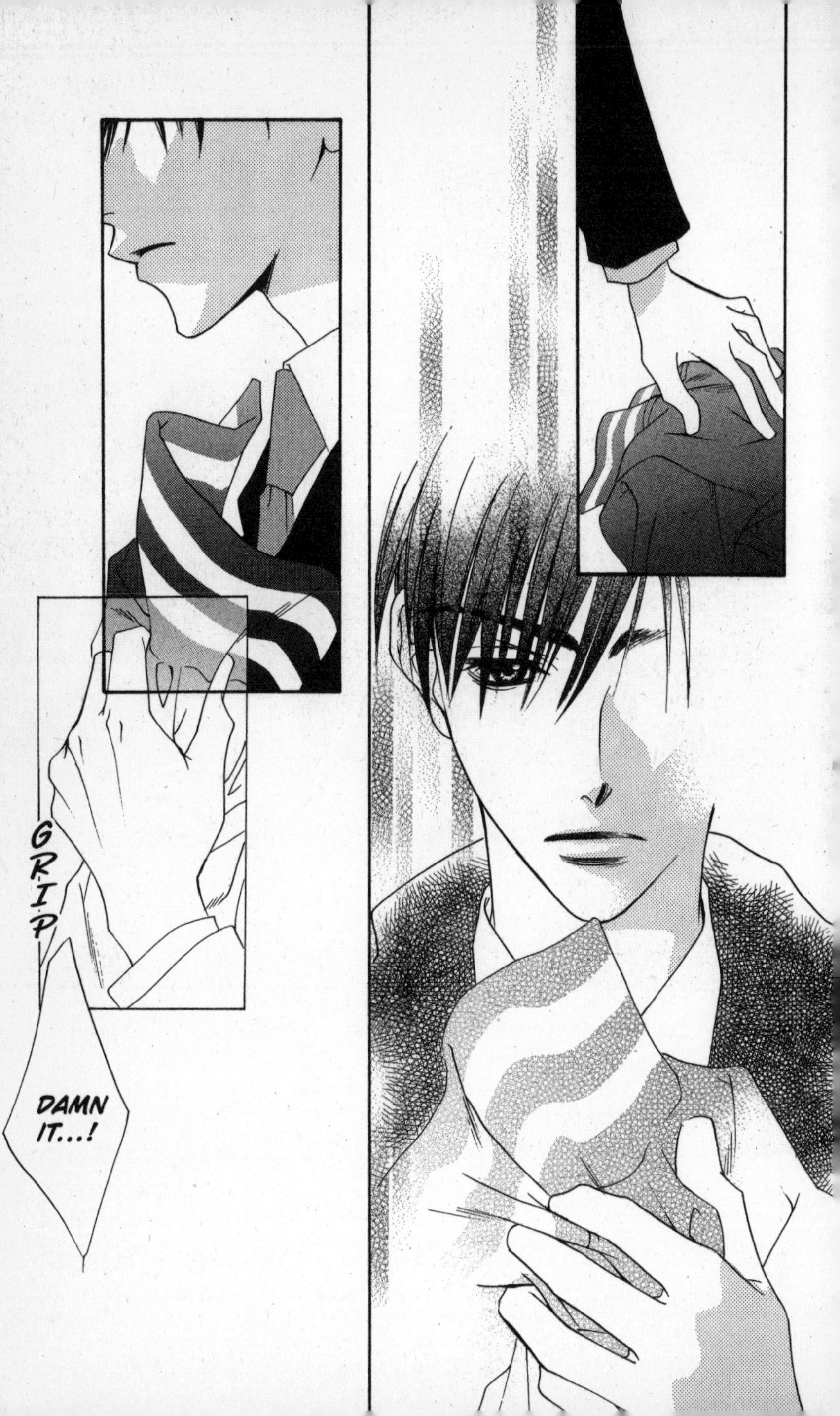
G.R.I.P
DAMN IT...!

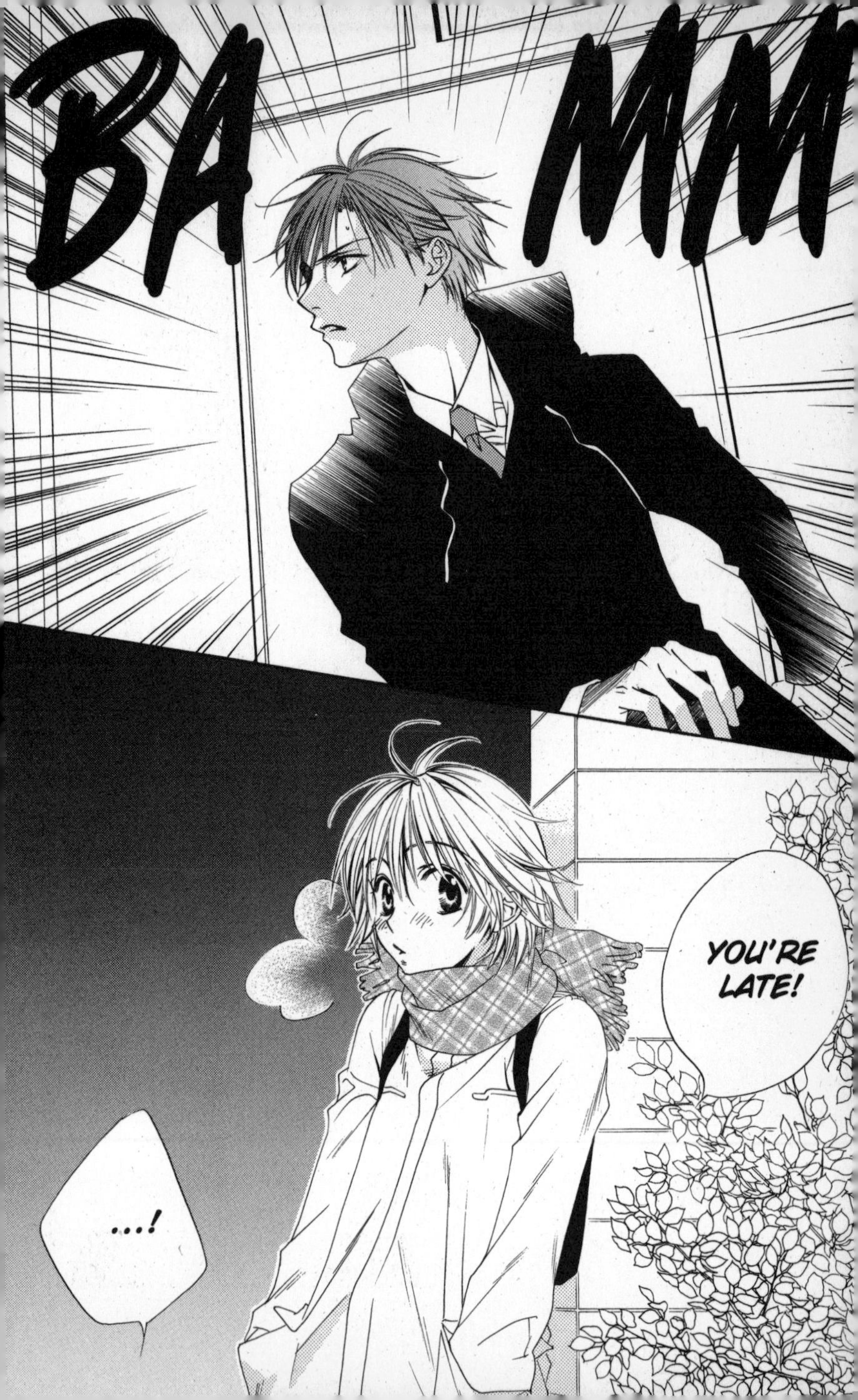
BAMM
YOU'RE LATE!
...!

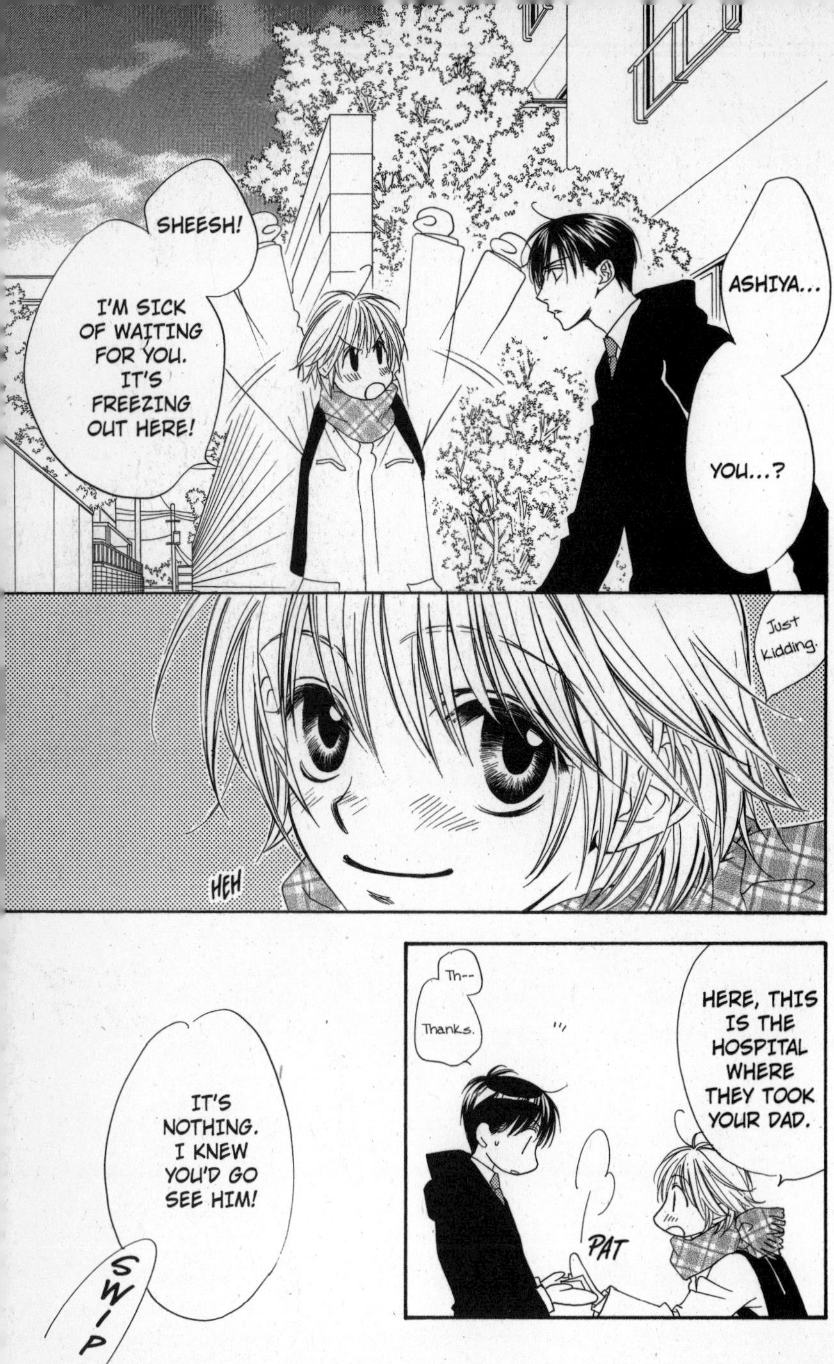
ASHIYA... YOU...?
SHEESH!
I'M SICK OF WAITING FOR YOU. IT'S FREEZING OUT HERE!
Just kidding.
HEH
HERE, THIS IS THE HOSPITAL WHERE THEY TOOK YOUR DAD.
Th-- Thanks.
PAT
IT'S NOTHING. I KNEW YOU'D GO SEE HIM!
SWIP

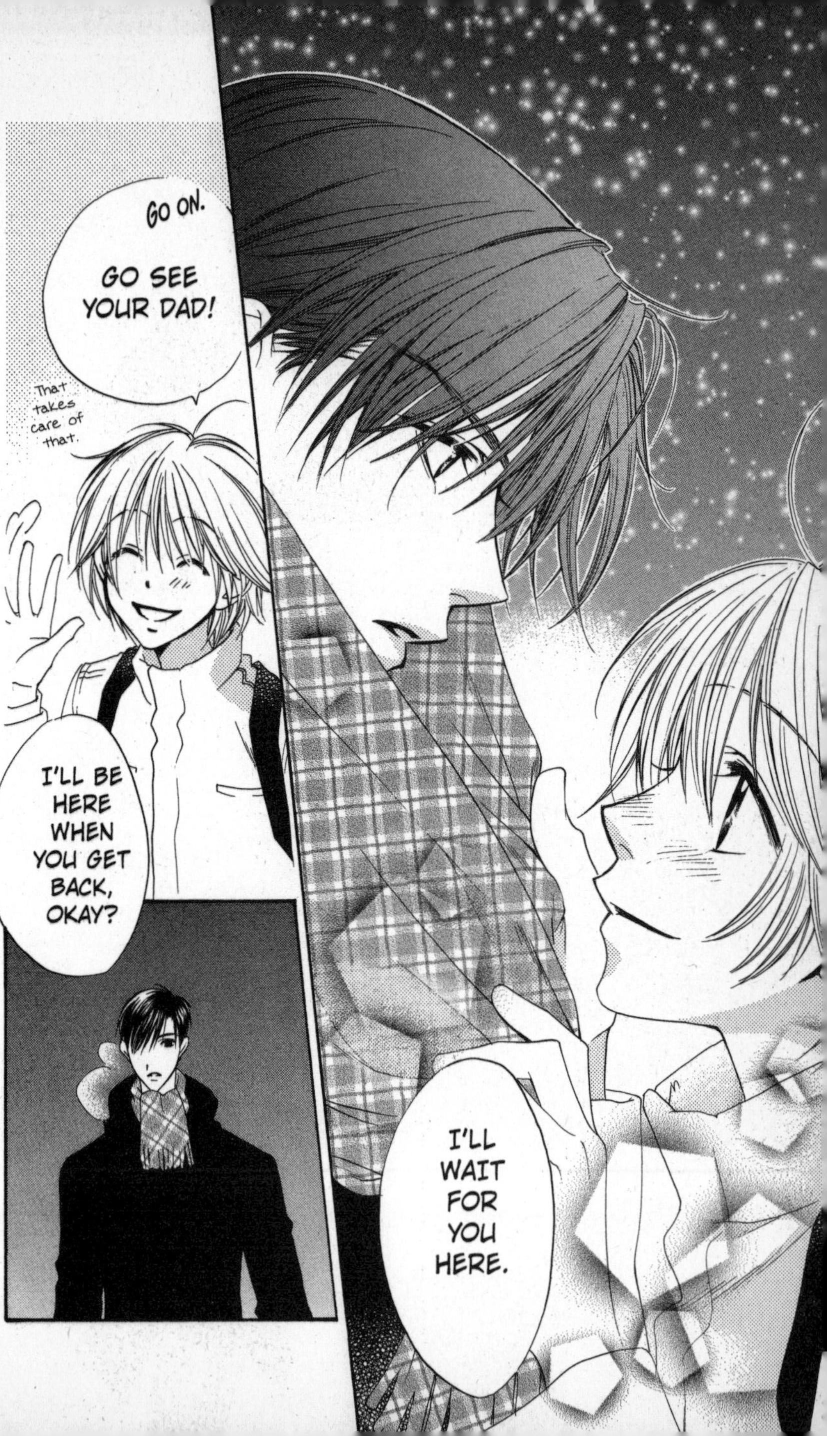
I'LL WAIT FOR YOU HERE.
GO ON.
GO SEE YOUR DAD!
That takes care of that.
I'LL BE HERE WHEN YOU GET BACK, OKAY?

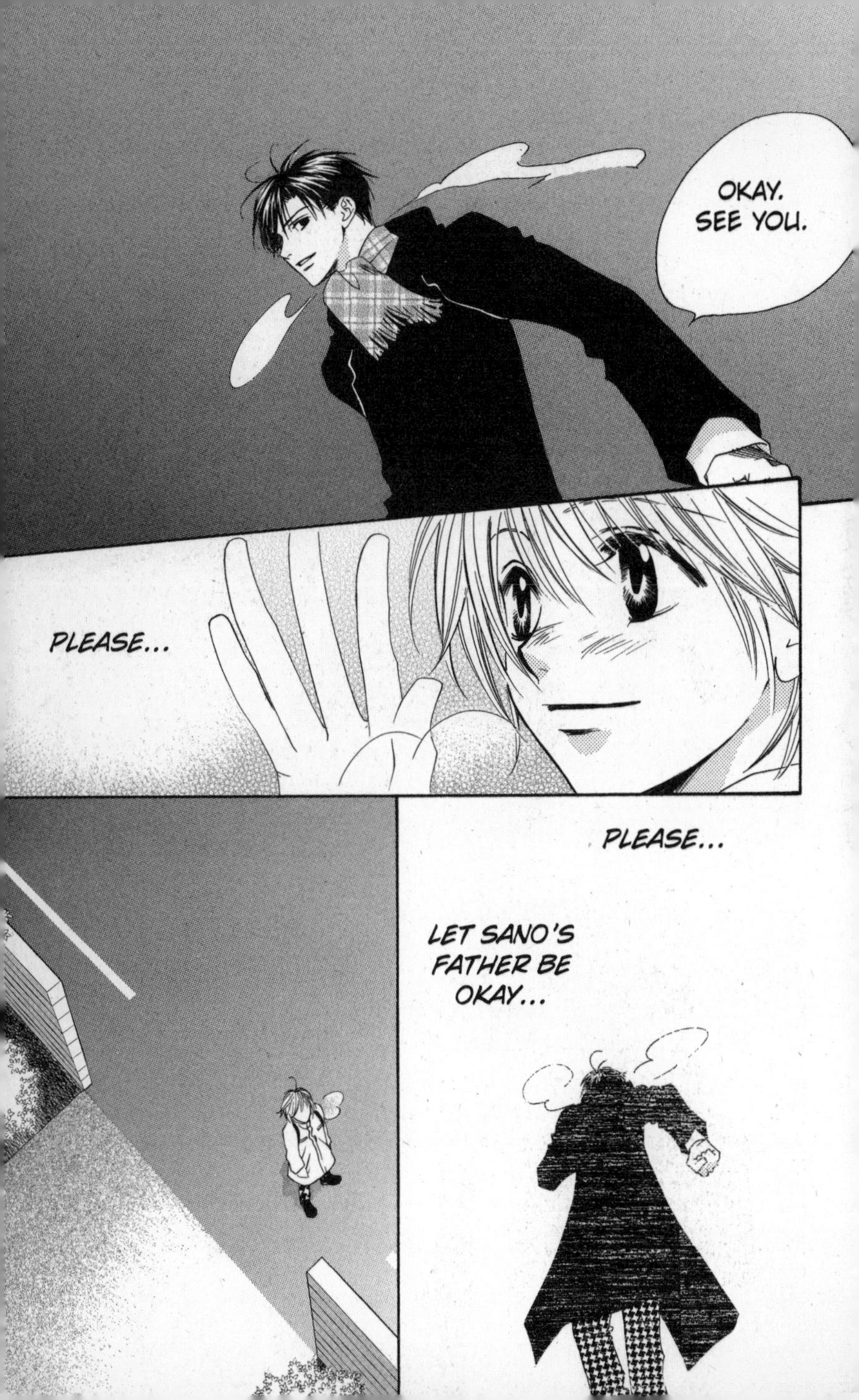
OKAY. SEE YOU.
PLEASE...
PLEASE...
LET SANO'S FATHER BE OKAY...

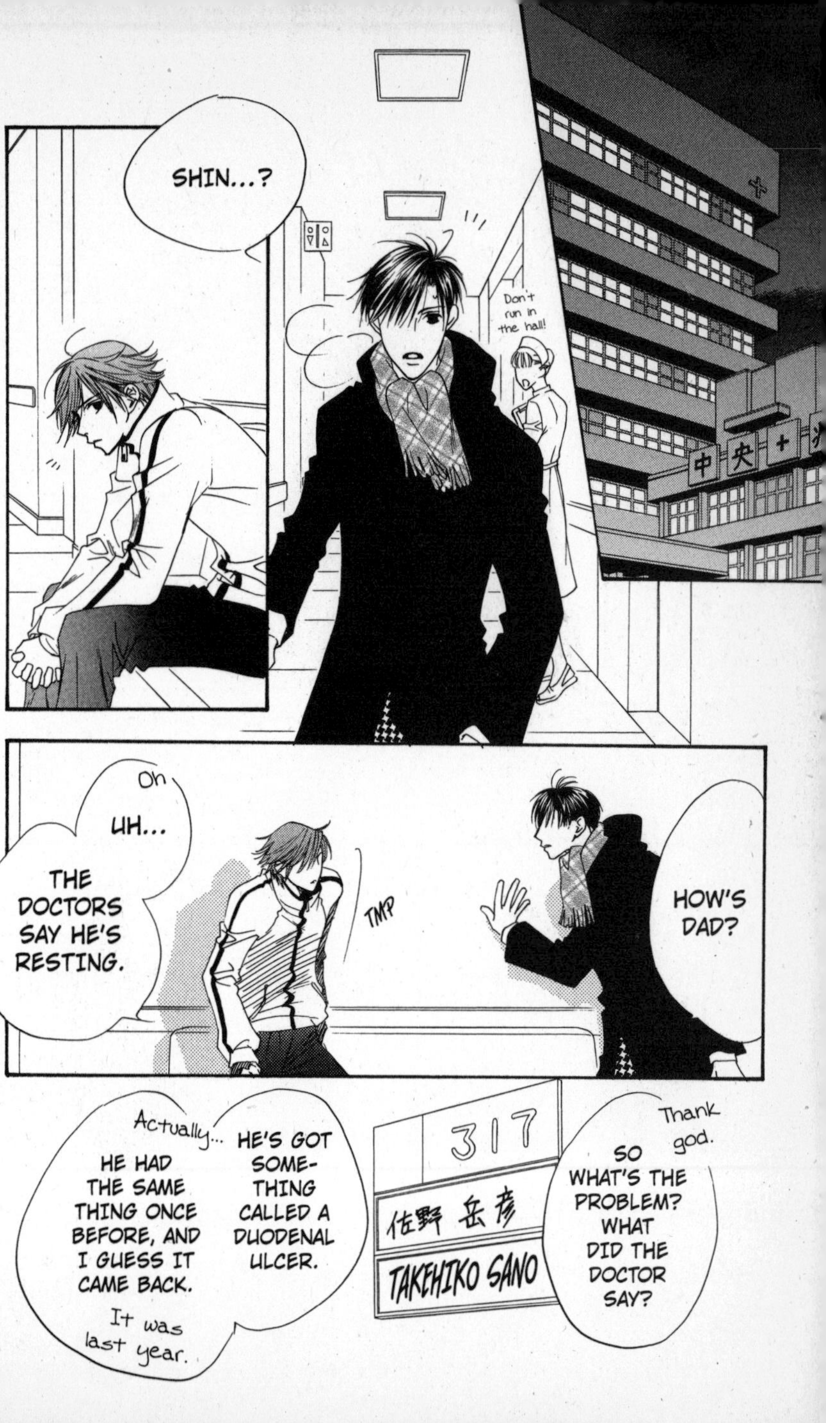

中央 +
Don't run in the hall!
SHIN...?
HOW'S DAD?
TMP
Oh
UH...
THE DOCTORS SAY HE'S RESTING.
Thank god.
SO WHAT'S THE PROBLEM? WHAT DID THE DOCTOR SAY?
317
佐野 岳彦
TAKEHIKO SANO
HE'S GOT SOMETHING CALLED A DUODENAL ULCER.
Actually...
HE HAD THE SAME THING ONCE BEFORE, AND I GUESS IT CAME BACK.
It was last year.

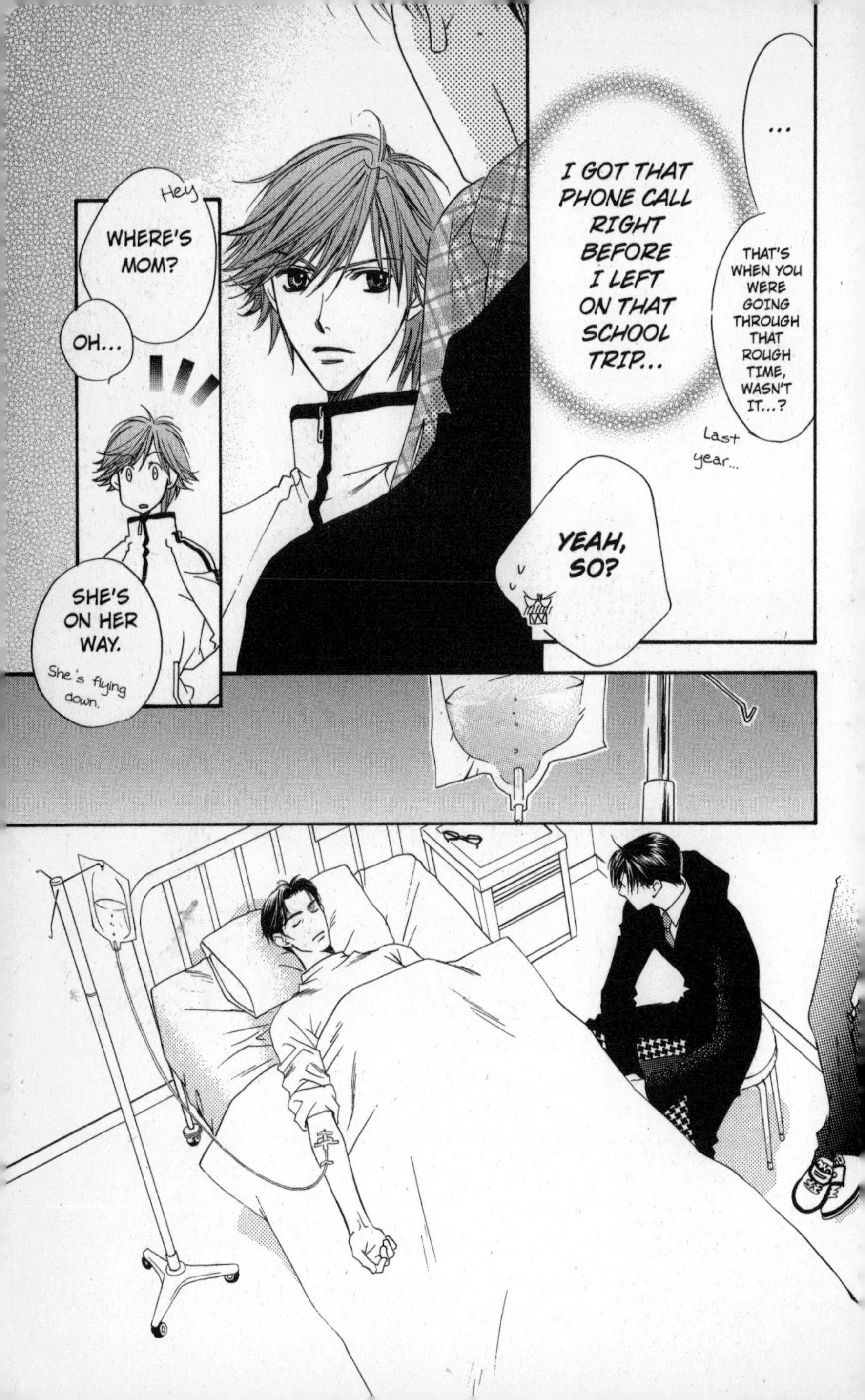
...
THAT'S WHEN YOU WERE GOING THROUGH THAT ROUGH TIME, WASN'T IT...?
Last year...
I GOT THAT PHONE CALL RIGHT BEFORE I LEFT ON THAT SCHOOL TRIP...
YEAH, SO?
Hey
WHERE'S MOM?
OH...
SHE'S ON HER WAY.
She's flying down.

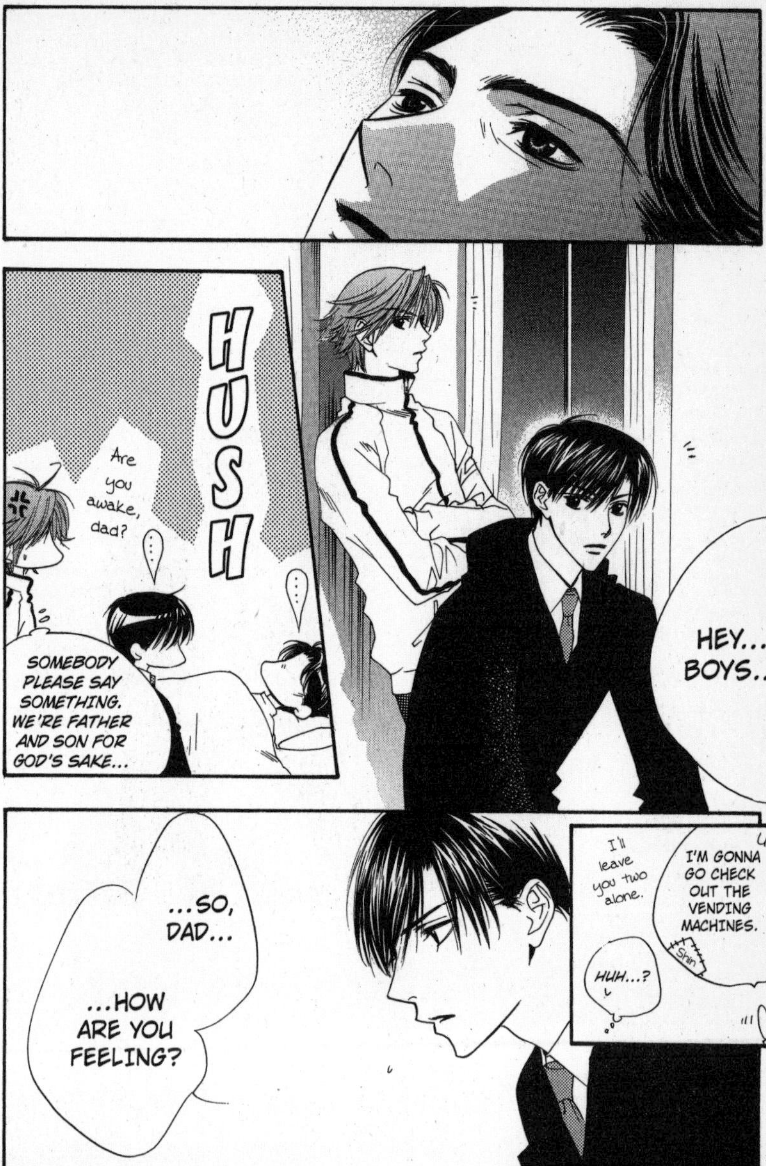
HEY... BOYS...
HUSH
Are you awake, dad?
SOMEBODY PLEASE SAY SOMETHING. WE'RE FATHER AND SON FOR GOD'S SAKE...
Uh...
I'M GONNA GO CHECK OUT THE VENDING MACHINES.
Shin
I'll leave you two alone.
HUH...?
...SO, DAD...
...HOW ARE YOU FEELING?

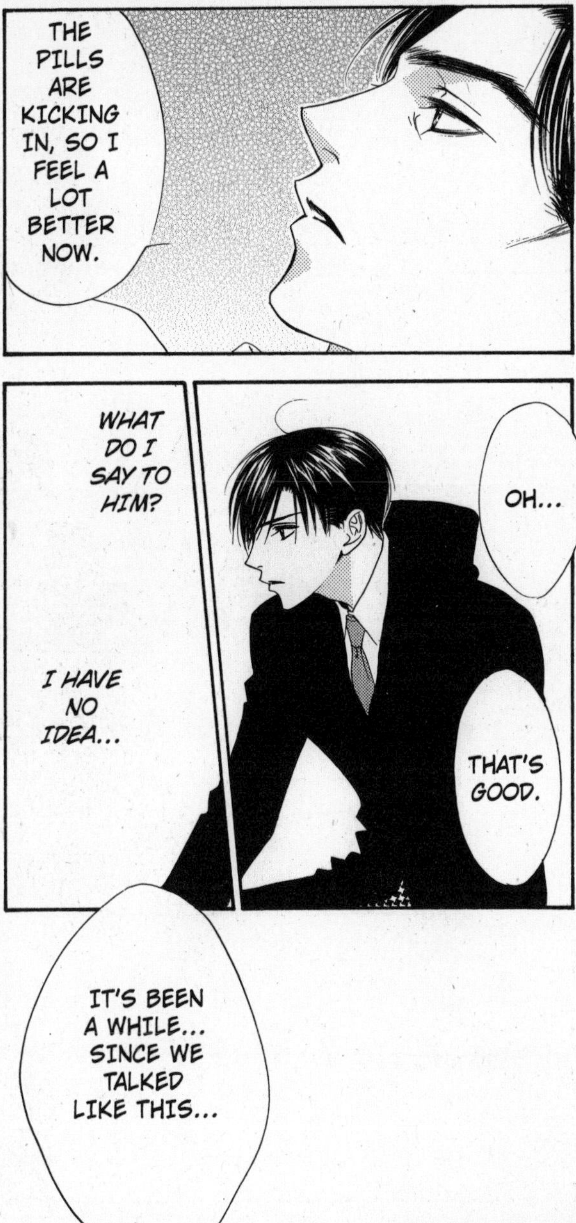
THE PILLS ARE KICKING IN, SO I FEEL A LOT BETTER NOW.
OH...
THAT'S GOOD.
WHAT DO I SAY TO HIM?
I HAVE NO IDEA...
IT'S BEEN A WHILE... SINCE WE TALKED LIKE THIS...

Scent: Part 4

I started out talking about cat's paws, and then I talked about men's cologne. Actually, I can't stand strong smells, and whenever I pass by a perfume counter I get a headache. But that doesn't mean that I don't like perfume. The bottles are so cute, and it makes me happy just putting them in my room, like decorations. The first perfume I ever bought was by Jean Paul Gaultier. It came in a can. I've been wearing Calvin Klein's "CKB" ever since I was in college. The cutest bottles are from Ana Sui, but most of my perfume is by Jeanne Arthes. (I like Co2 and Sultan.) My recent favorite is "Happy" from Clinique.

Readers often send me bottles of perfume. Thanks, everybody!

I also like "Green Tea" by Elizabeth Arden.

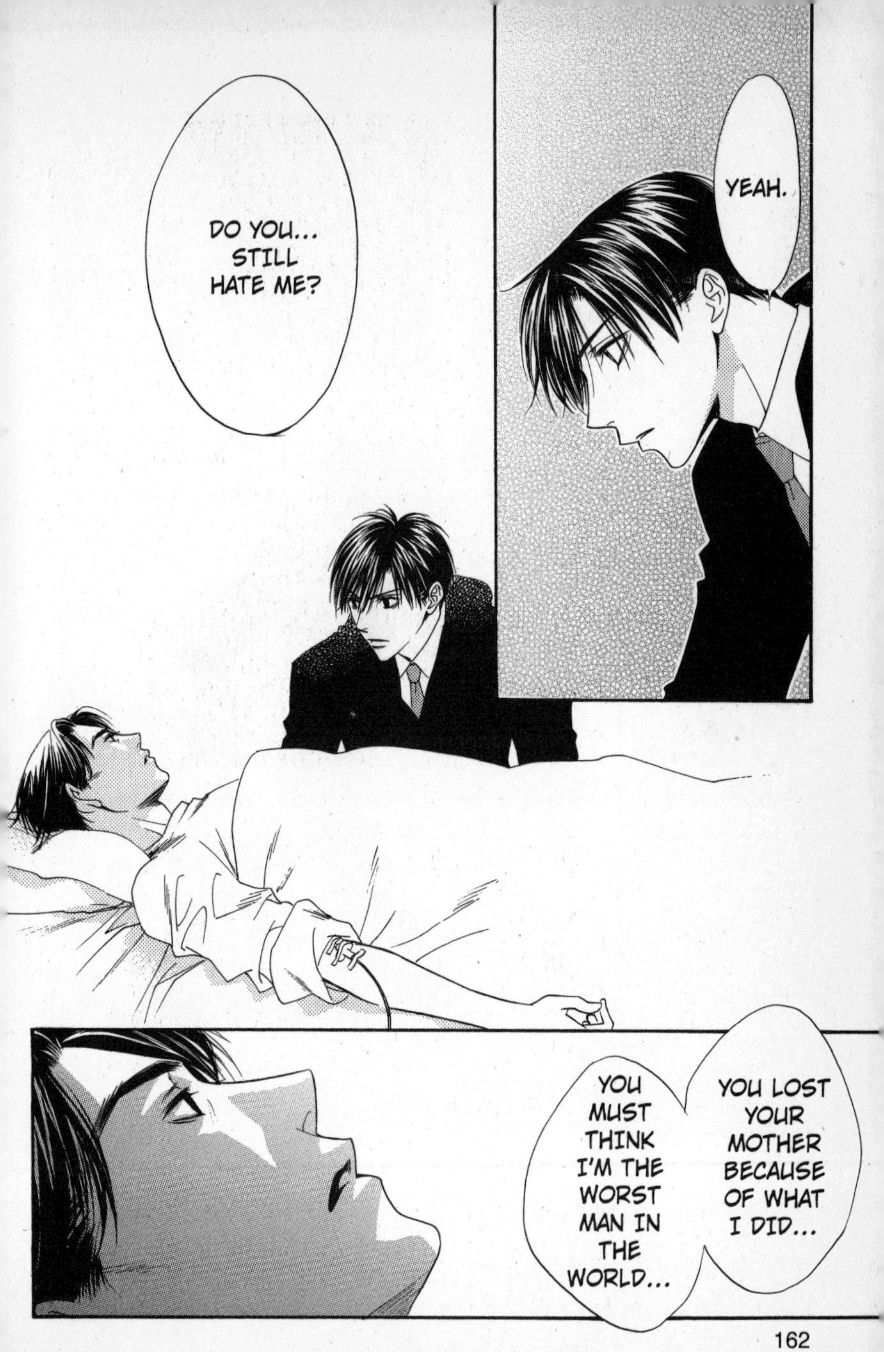
DO YOU... STILL HATE ME?
YEAH.
YOU LOST YOUR MOTHER BECAUSE OF WHAT I DID...
YOU MUST THINK I'M THE WORST MAN IN THE WORLD...

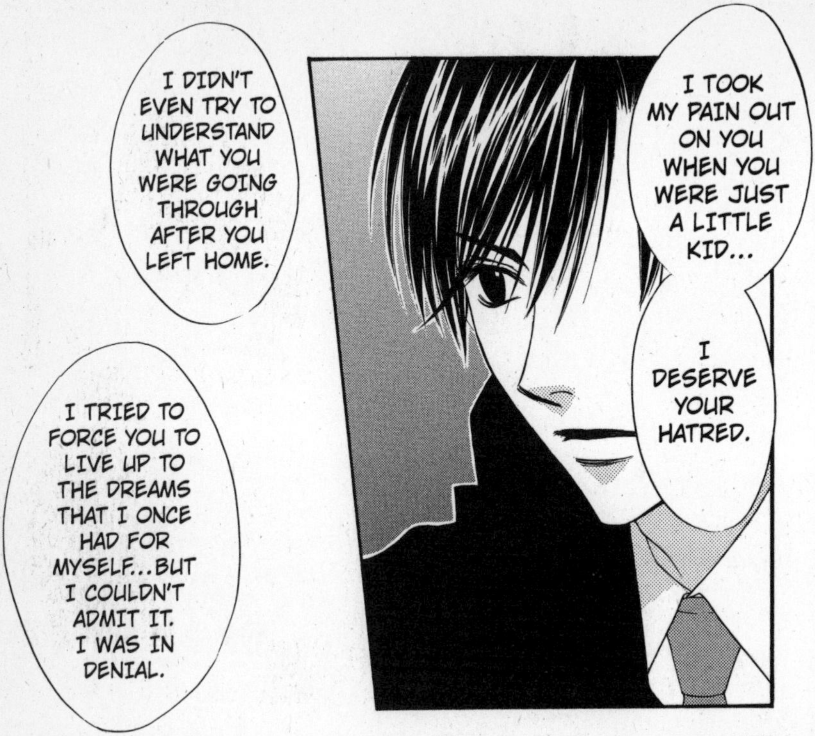
I TOOK MY PAIN OUT ON YOU WHEN YOU WERE JUST A LITTLE KID...
I DESERVE YOUR HATRED.
I DIDN'T EVEN TRY TO UNDERSTAND WHAT YOU WERE GOING THROUGH AFTER YOU LEFT HOME.
I TRIED TO FORCE YOU TO LIVE UP TO THE DREAMS THAT I ONCE HAD FOR MYSELF...BUT I COULDN'T ADMIT IT. I WAS IN DENIAL.

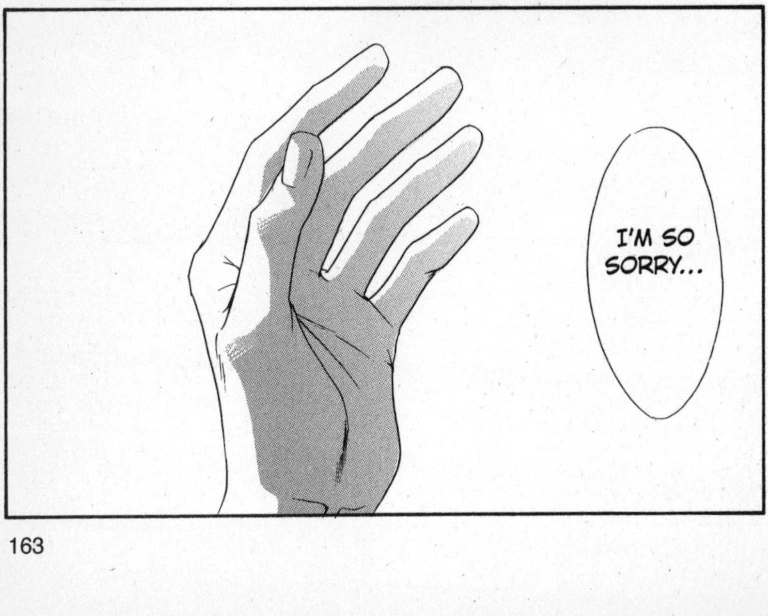
I'M SO SORRY...

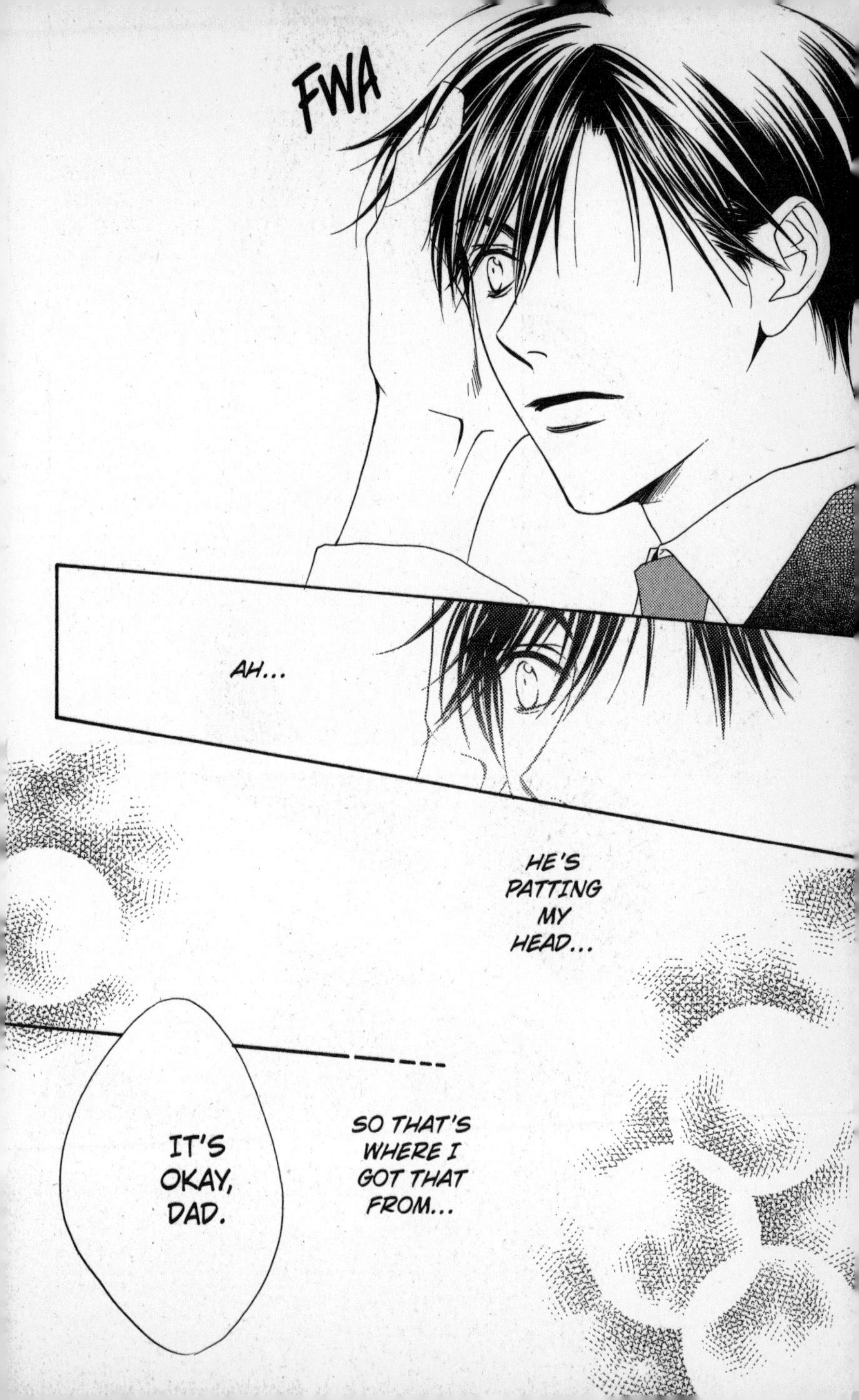
FWA
AH...
HE'S PATTING MY HEAD...
SO THAT'S WHERE I GOT THAT FROM...
IT'S OKAY, DAD.

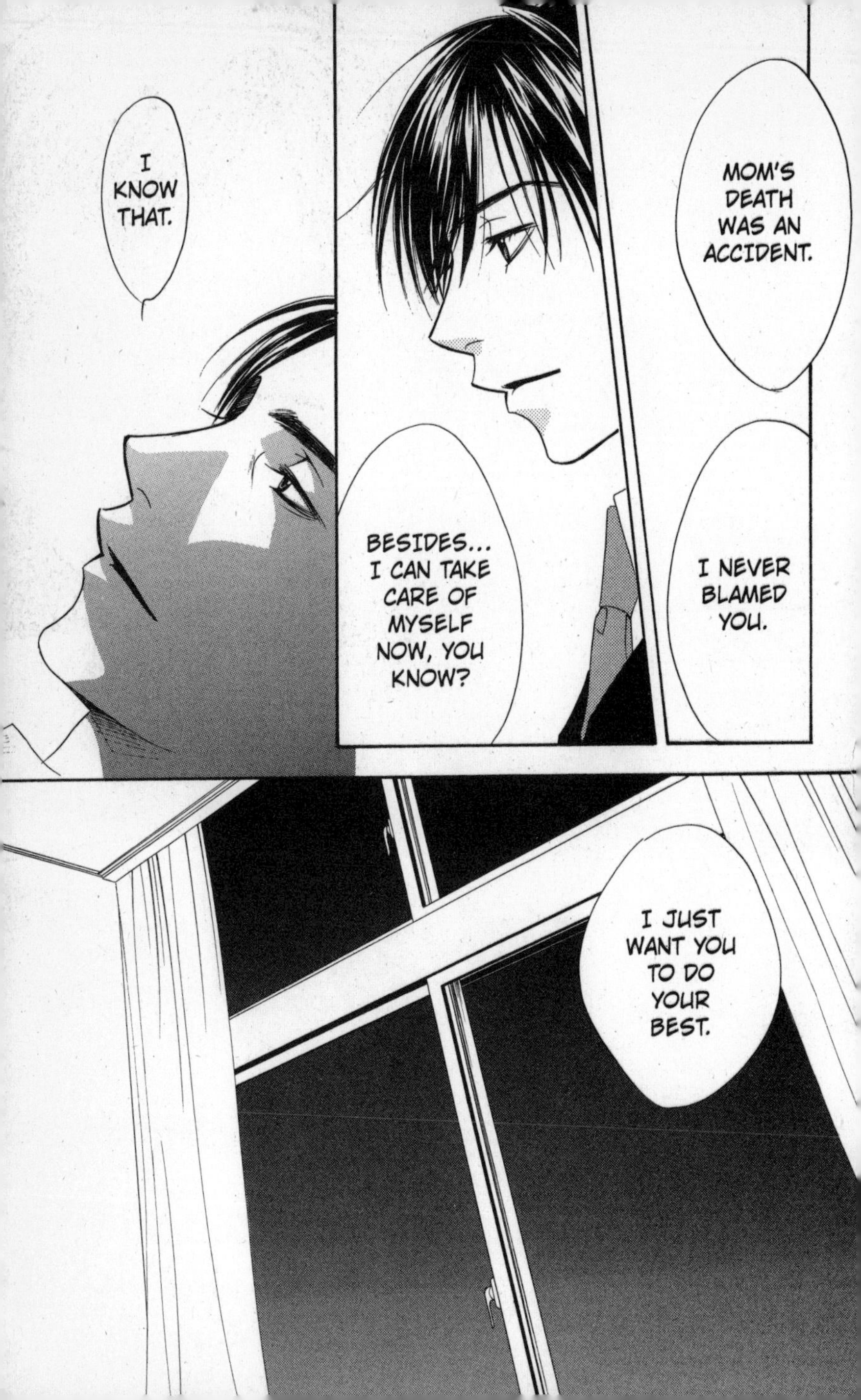
MOM'S DEATH WAS AN ACCIDENT.
I NEVER BLAMED YOU.
BESIDES... I CAN TAKE CARE OF MYSELF NOW, YOU KNOW?
I KNOW THAT.
I JUST WANT YOU TO DO YOUR BEST.

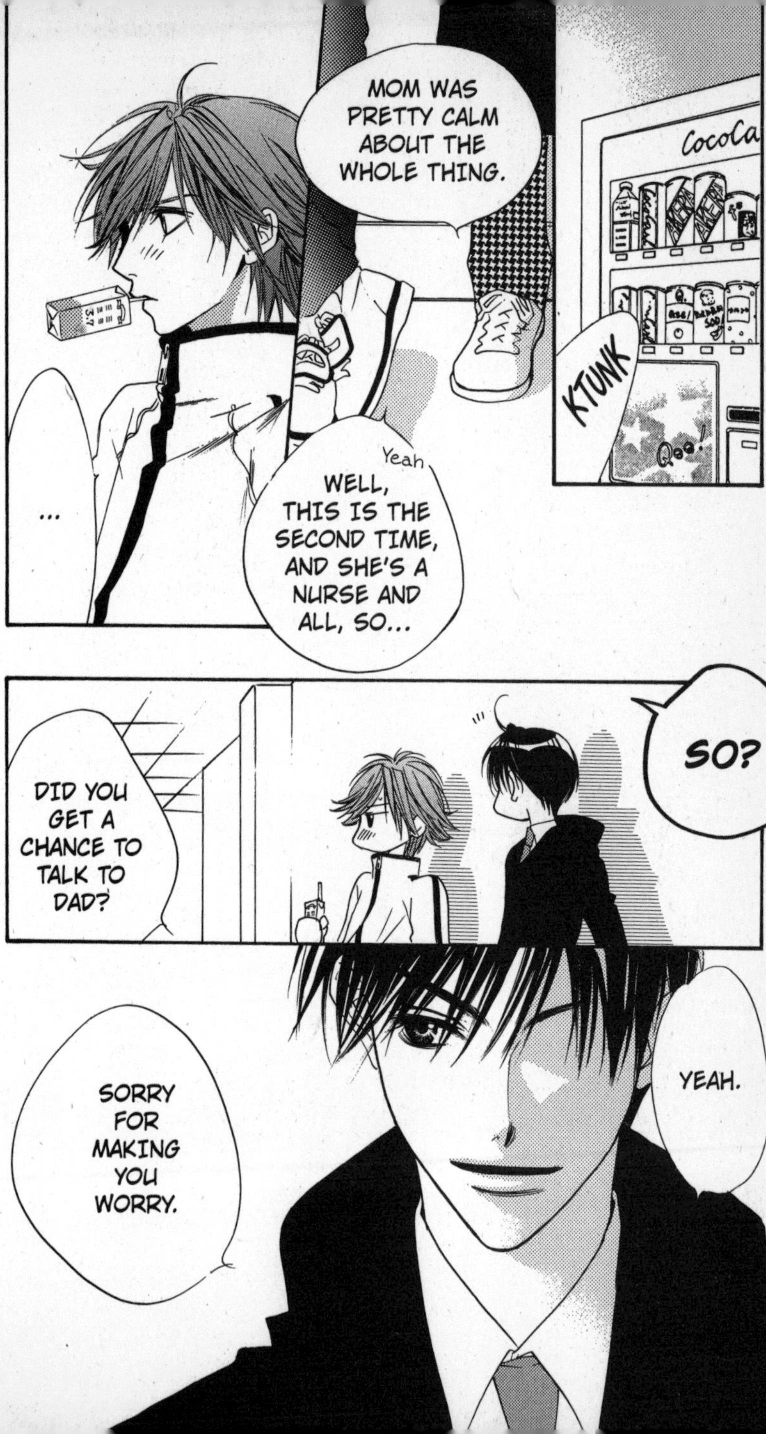
CocoCa
KTUNK
MOM WAS PRETTY CALM ABOUT THE WHOLE THING.
Yeah
WELL, THIS IS THE SECOND TIME, AND SHE'S A NURSE AND ALL, SO...
...
SO?
DID YOU GET A CHANCE TO TALK TO DAD?
YEAH.
SORRY FOR MAKING YOU WORRY.

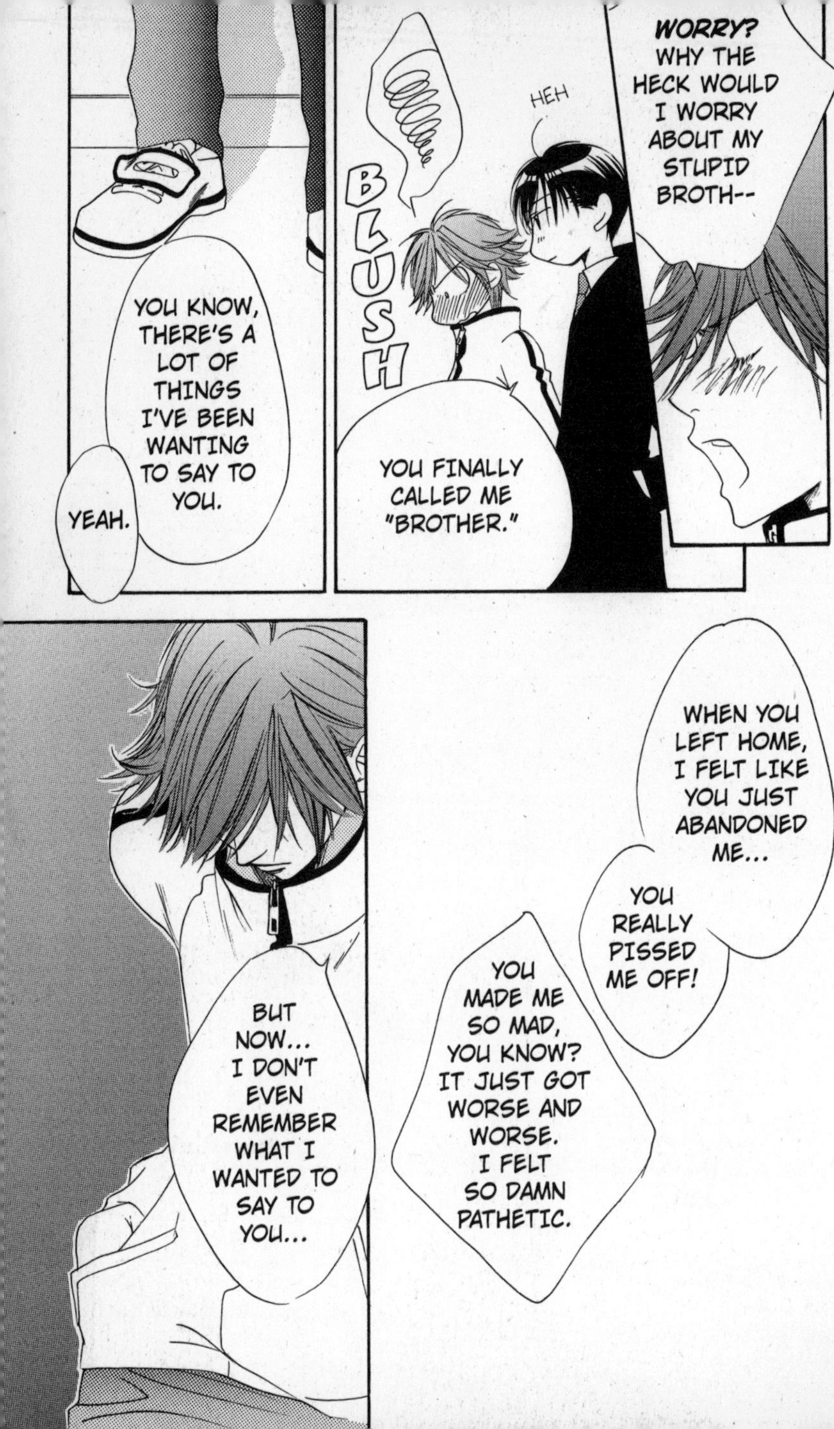
WORRY? WHY THE HECK WOULD I WORRY ABOUT MY STUPID BROTH--
HEH
BLUSH
YOU FINALLY CALLED ME "BROTHER."
YOU KNOW, THERE'S A LOT OF THINGS I'VE BEEN WANTING TO SAY TO YOU.
YEAH.
WHEN YOU LEFT HOME, I FELT LIKE YOU JUST ABANDONED ME...
YOU REALLY PISSED ME OFF!
YOU MADE ME SO MAD, YOU KNOW? IT JUST GOT WORSE AND WORSE. I FELT SO DAMN PATHETIC.
BUT NOW... I DON'T EVEN REMEMBER WHAT I WANTED TO SAY TO YOU...

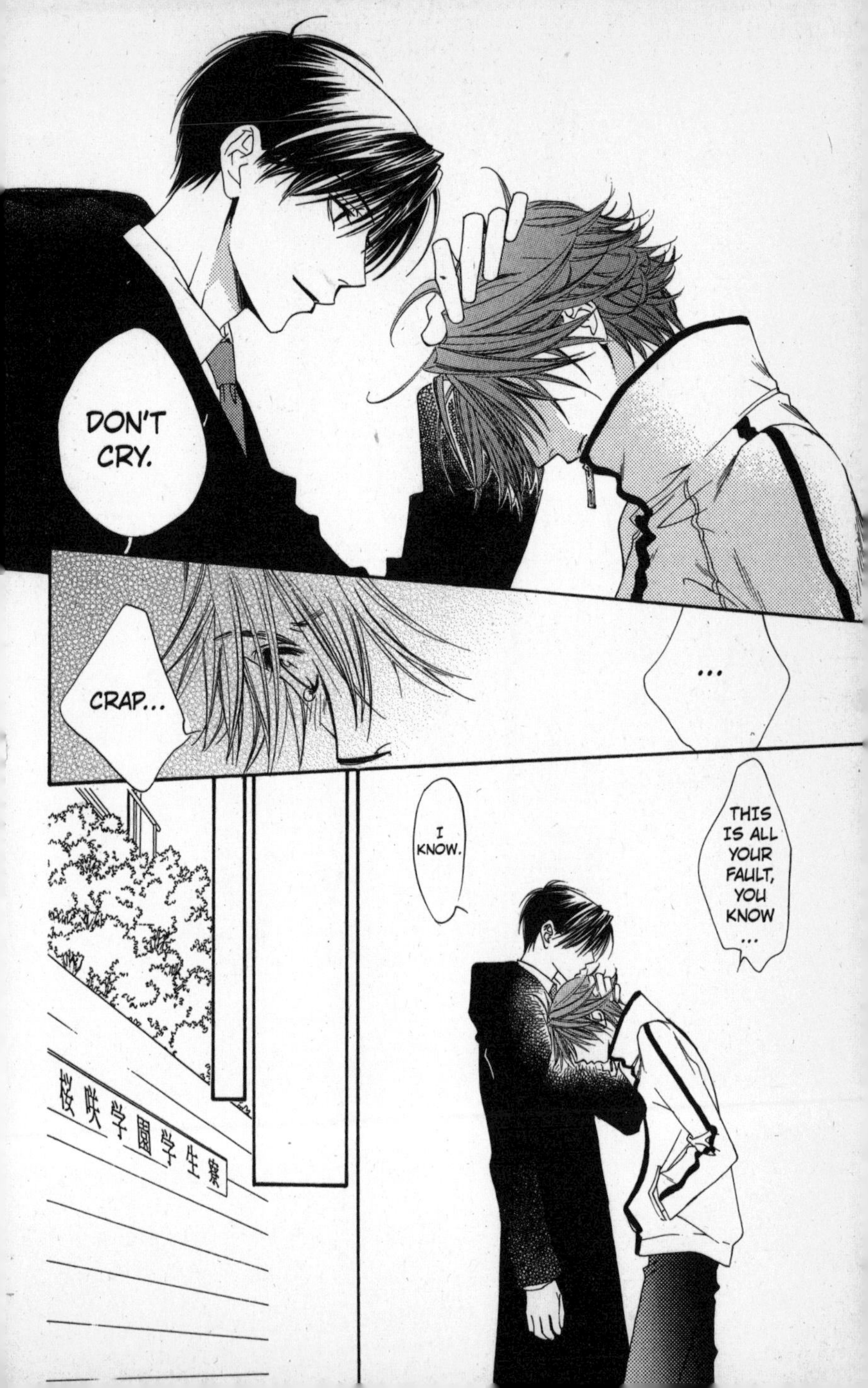
DON'T CRY.
...
CRAP...
THIS IS ALL YOUR FAULT, YOU KNOW...
I KNOW.
桜咲学園学生寮

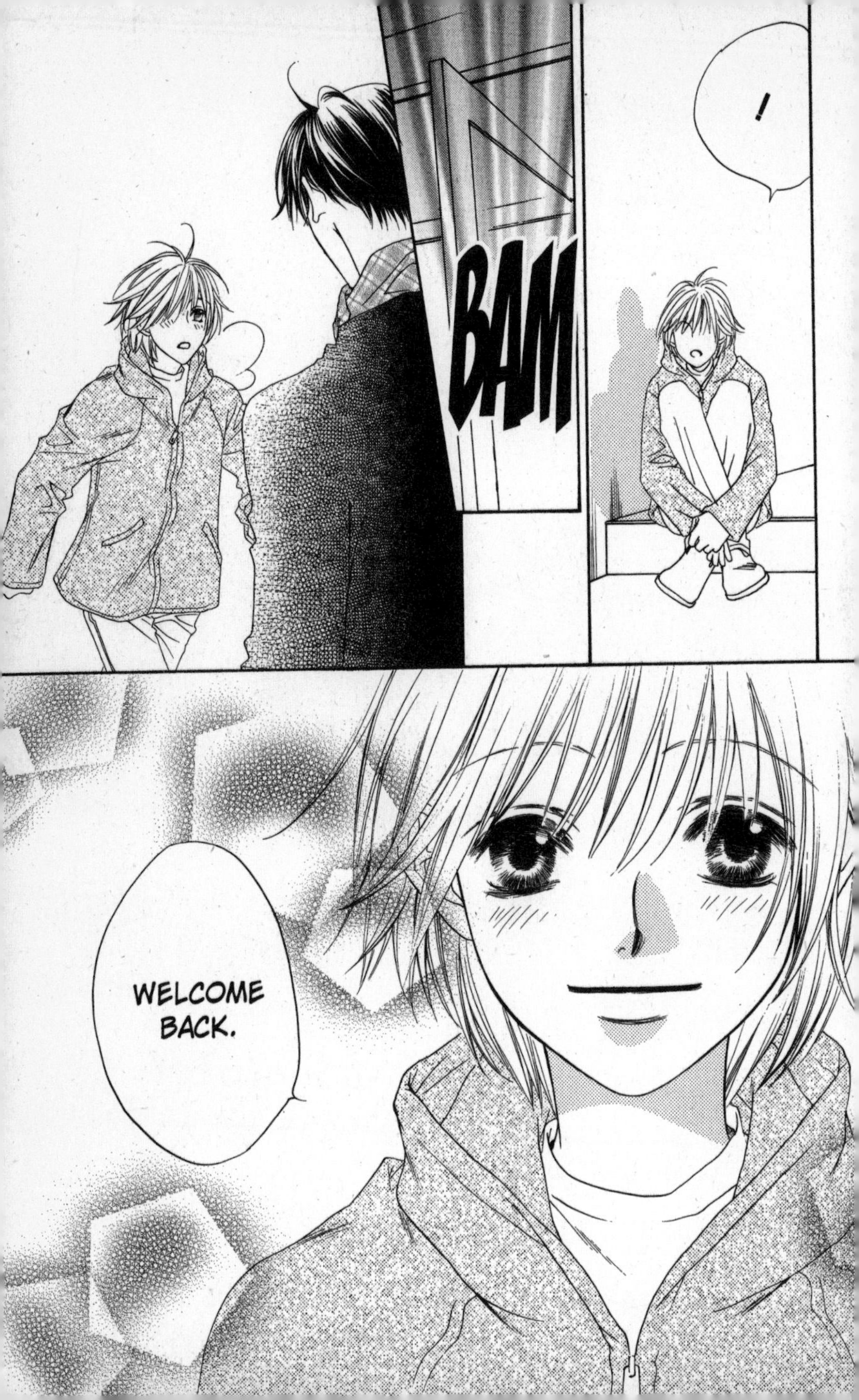
!
BAM
WELCOME BACK.

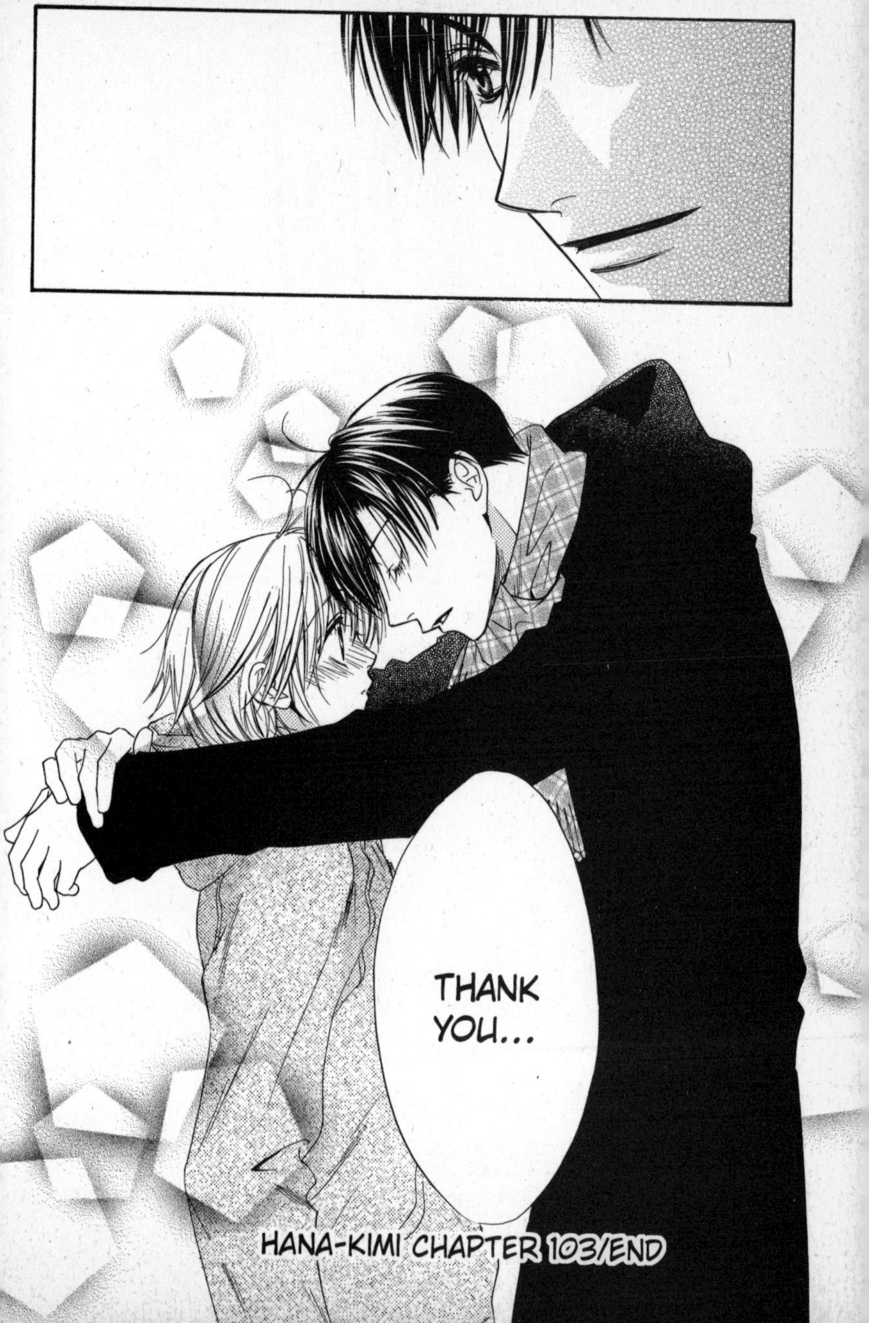
THANK YOU...

HANA-KIMI CHAPTER 103/END

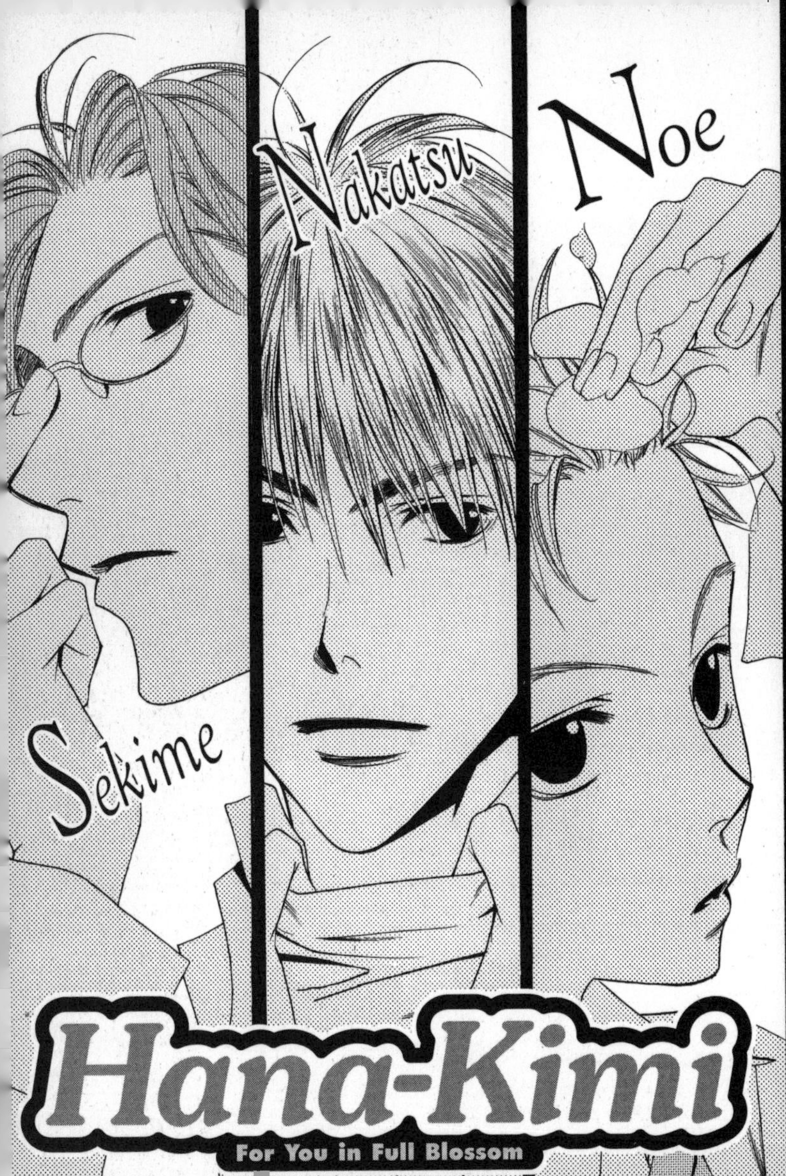
Noe
Nakatsu
Sekime
Hana-Kimi
For You in Full Blossom

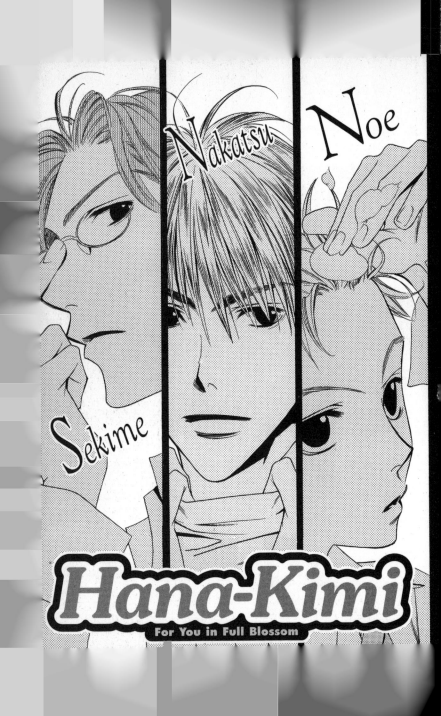

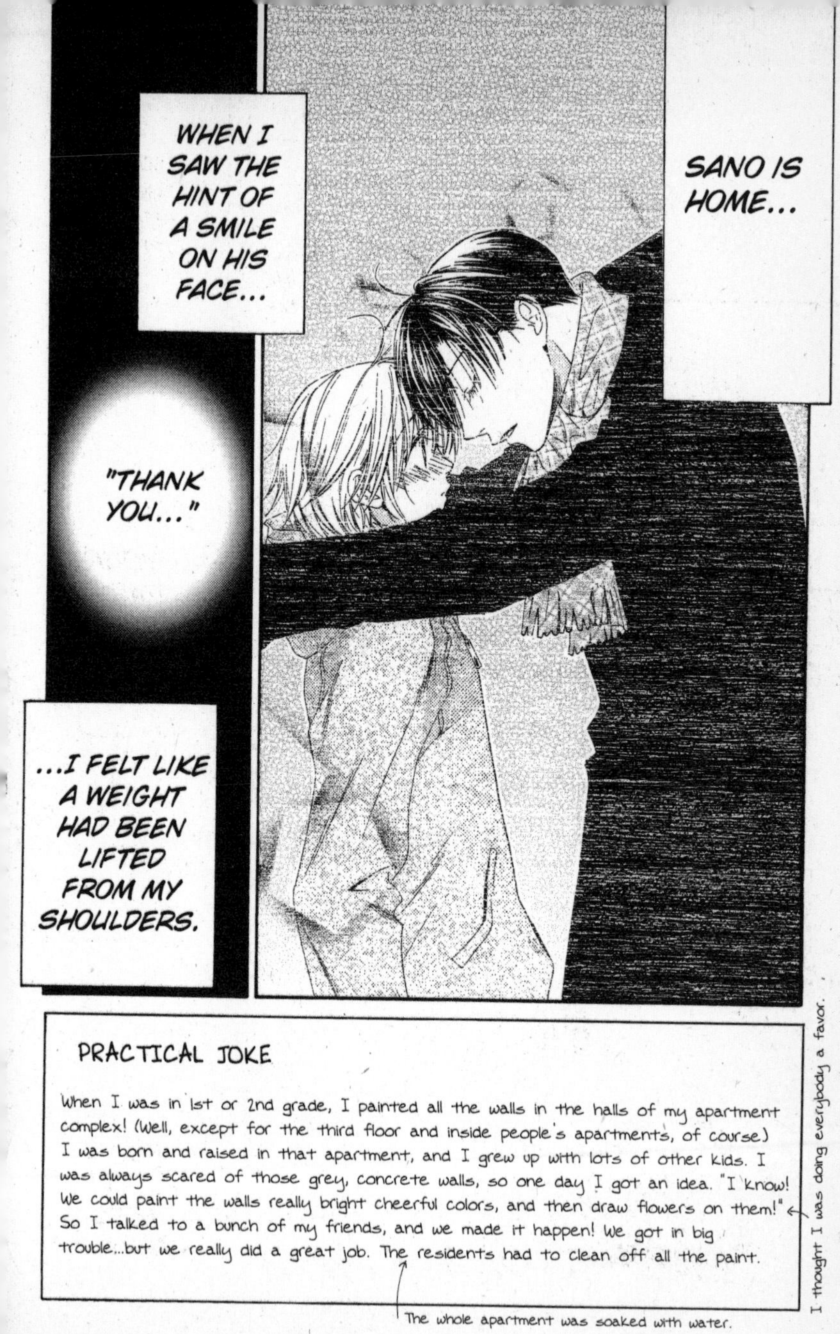
SANO IS HOME...
WHEN I SAW THE HINT OF A SMILE ON HIS FACE...
"THANK YOU..."
...I FELT LIKE A WEIGHT HAD BEEN LIFTED FROM MY SHOULDERS.

PRACTICAL JOKE

When I was in 1st or 2nd grade, I painted all the walls in the halls of my apartment complex! (Well, except for the third floor and inside people's apartments, of course.) I was born and raised in that apartment, and I grew up with lots of other kids. I was always scared of those grey, concrete walls, so one day I got an idea. "I know! We could paint the walls really bright cheerful colors, and then draw flowers on them!" So I talked to a bunch of my friends, and we made it happen! We got in big trouble...but we really did a great job. The residents had to clean off all the paint.

I thought I was doing everybody a favor.

The whole apartment was soaked with water.

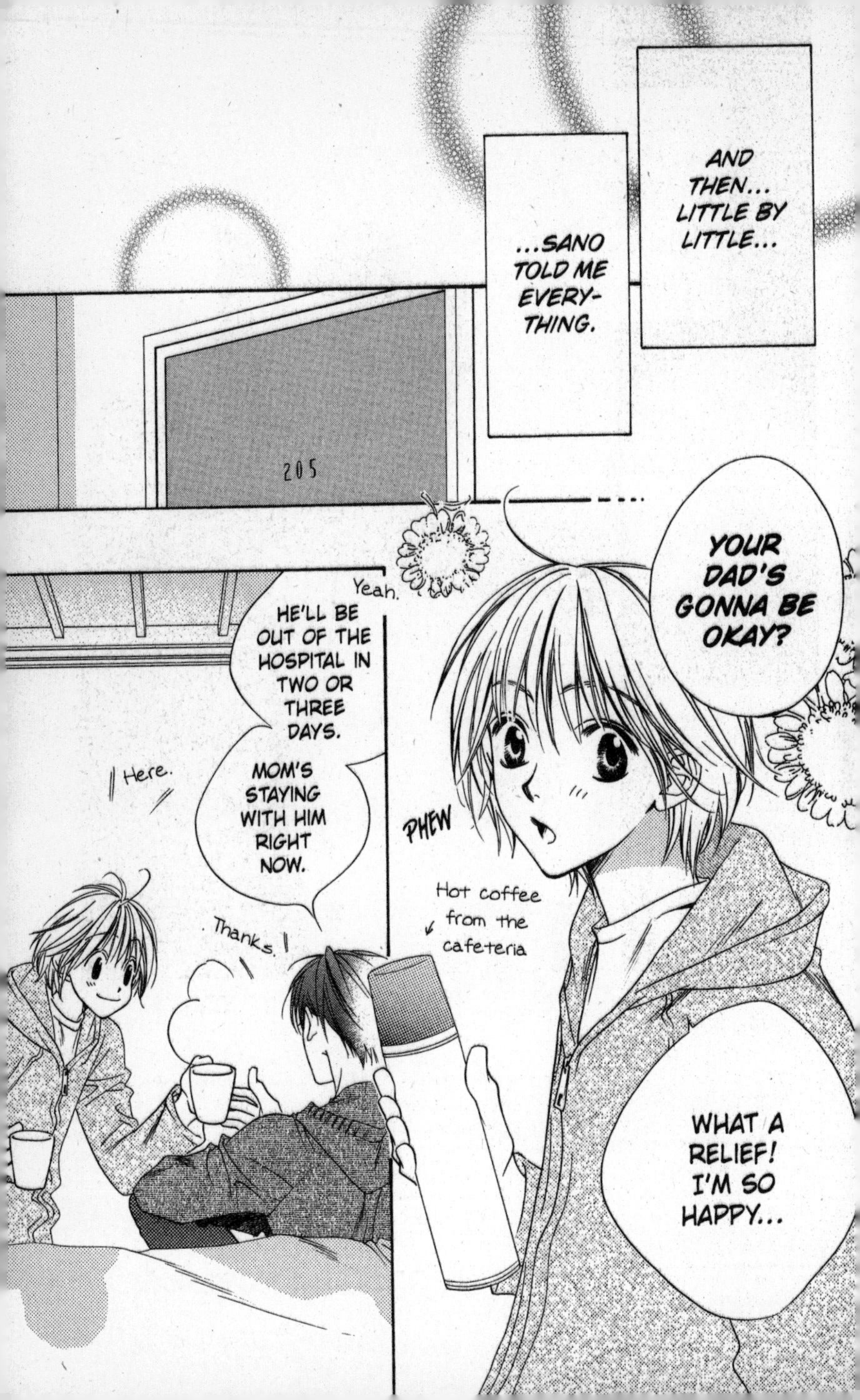
AND THEN... LITTLE BY LITTLE...
...SANO TOLD ME EVERY-THING.
205
YOUR DAD'S GONNA BE OKAY?
PHEW
WHAT A RELIEF! I'M SO HAPPY...
Hot coffee from the cafeteria
Yeah.
HE'LL BE OUT OF THE HOSPITAL IN TWO OR THREE DAYS.
MOM'S STAYING WITH HIM RIGHT NOW.
Here.
Thanks.

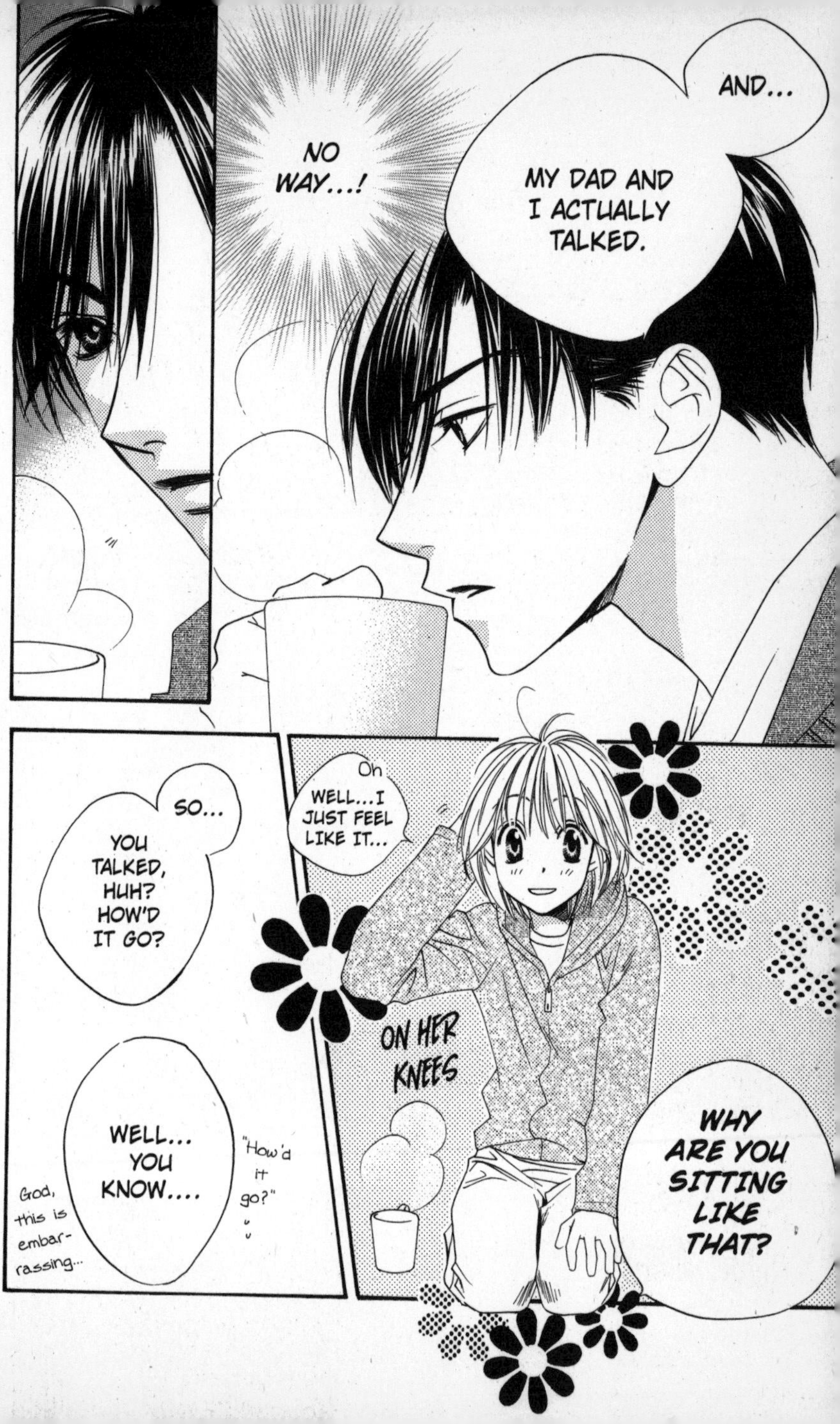
AND...
MY DAD AND I ACTUALLY TALKED.
NO WAY...!
WHY ARE YOU SITTING LIKE THAT?
ON HER KNEES
Oh WELL...I JUST FEEL LIKE IT...
SO... YOU TALKED, HUH? HOW'D IT GO?
"How'd it go?"
WELL... YOU KNOW....
God, this is embarrassing...

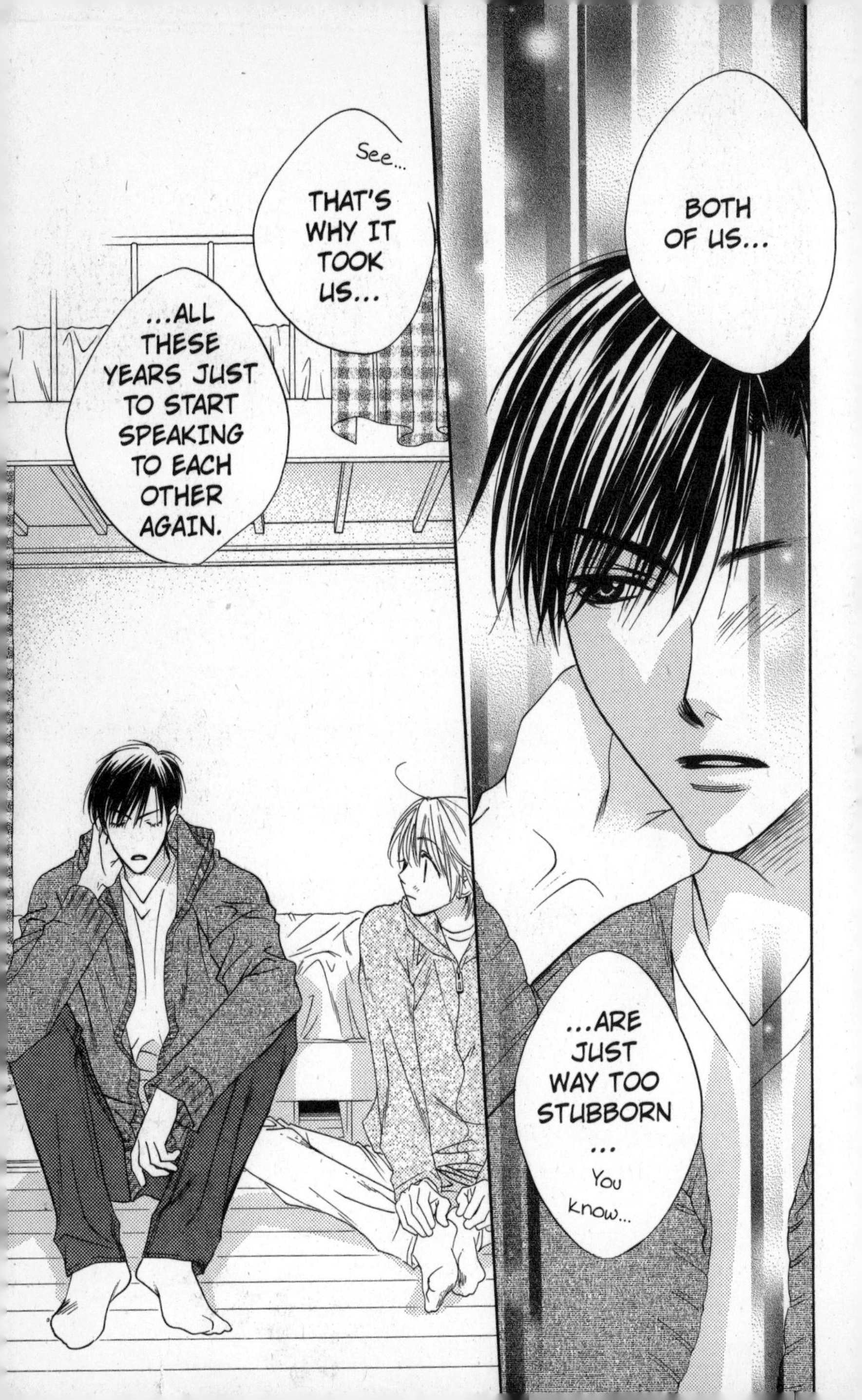
BOTH OF US...
...ARE JUST WAY TOO STUBBORN ...
You know...
See...
THAT'S WHY IT TOOK US...
...ALL THESE YEARS JUST TO START SPEAKING TO EACH OTHER AGAIN.

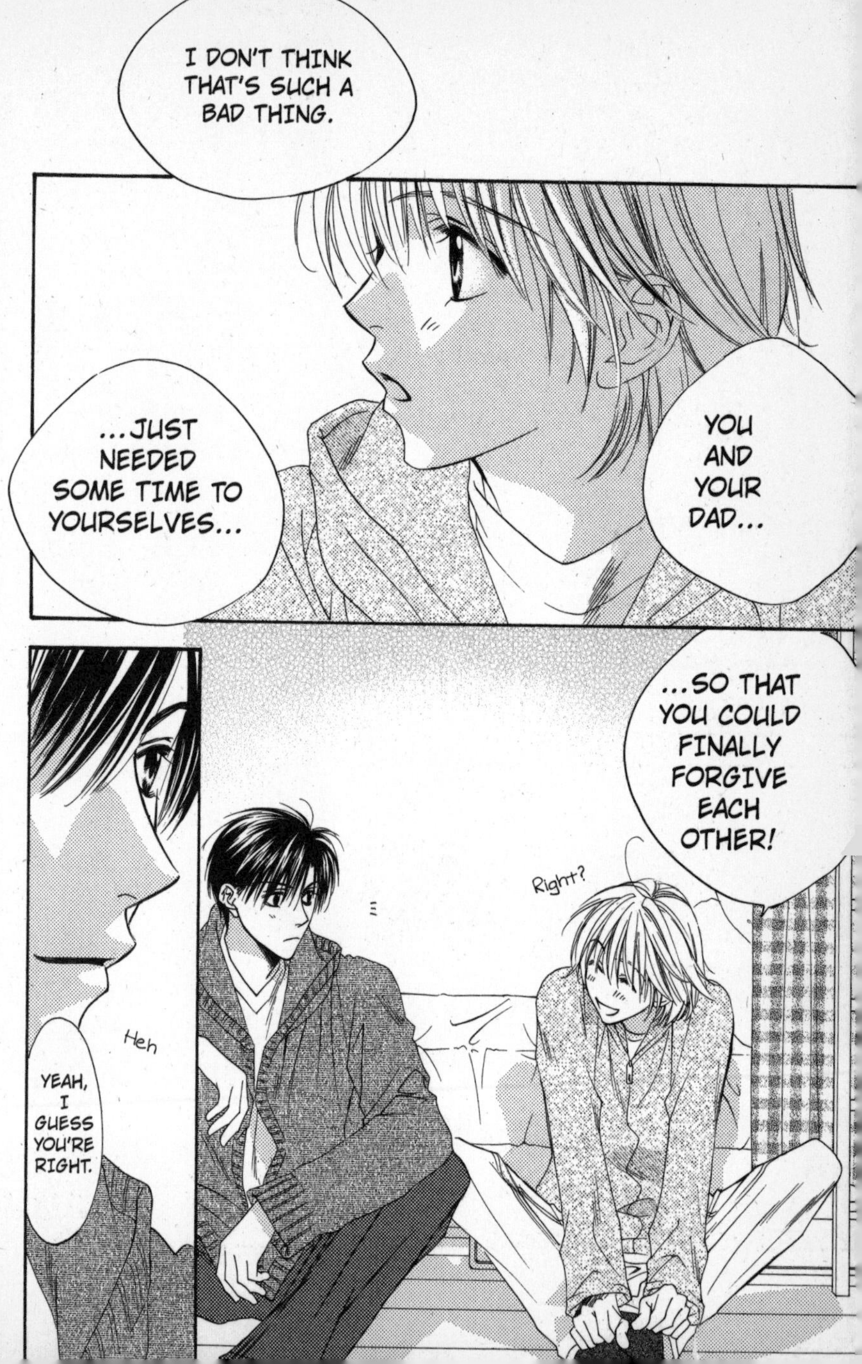
I DON'T THINK THAT'S SUCH A BAD THING.
YOU AND YOUR DAD...
...JUST NEEDED SOME TIME TO YOURSELVES...
...SO THAT YOU COULD FINALLY FORGIVE EACH OTHER!
Right?
Heh
YEAH, I GUESS YOU'RE RIGHT.

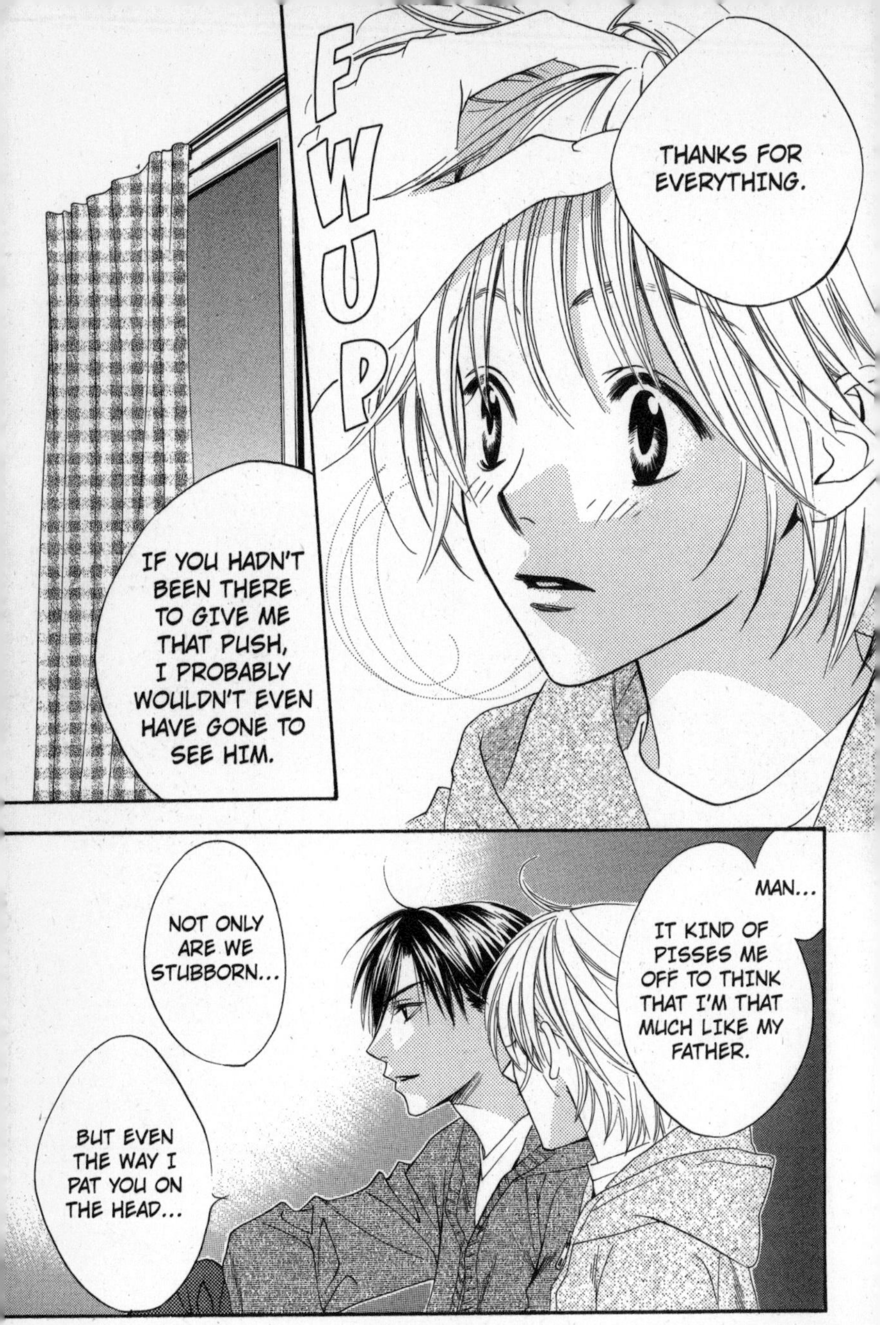
THANKS FOR EVERYTHING.
FWUP
IF YOU HADN'T BEEN THERE TO GIVE ME THAT PUSH, I PROBABLY WOULDN'T EVEN HAVE GONE TO SEE HIM.
MAN...
IT KIND OF PISSES ME OFF TO THINK THAT I'M THAT MUCH LIKE MY FATHER.
NOT ONLY ARE WE STUBBORN...
BUT EVEN THE WAY I PAT YOU ON THE HEAD...

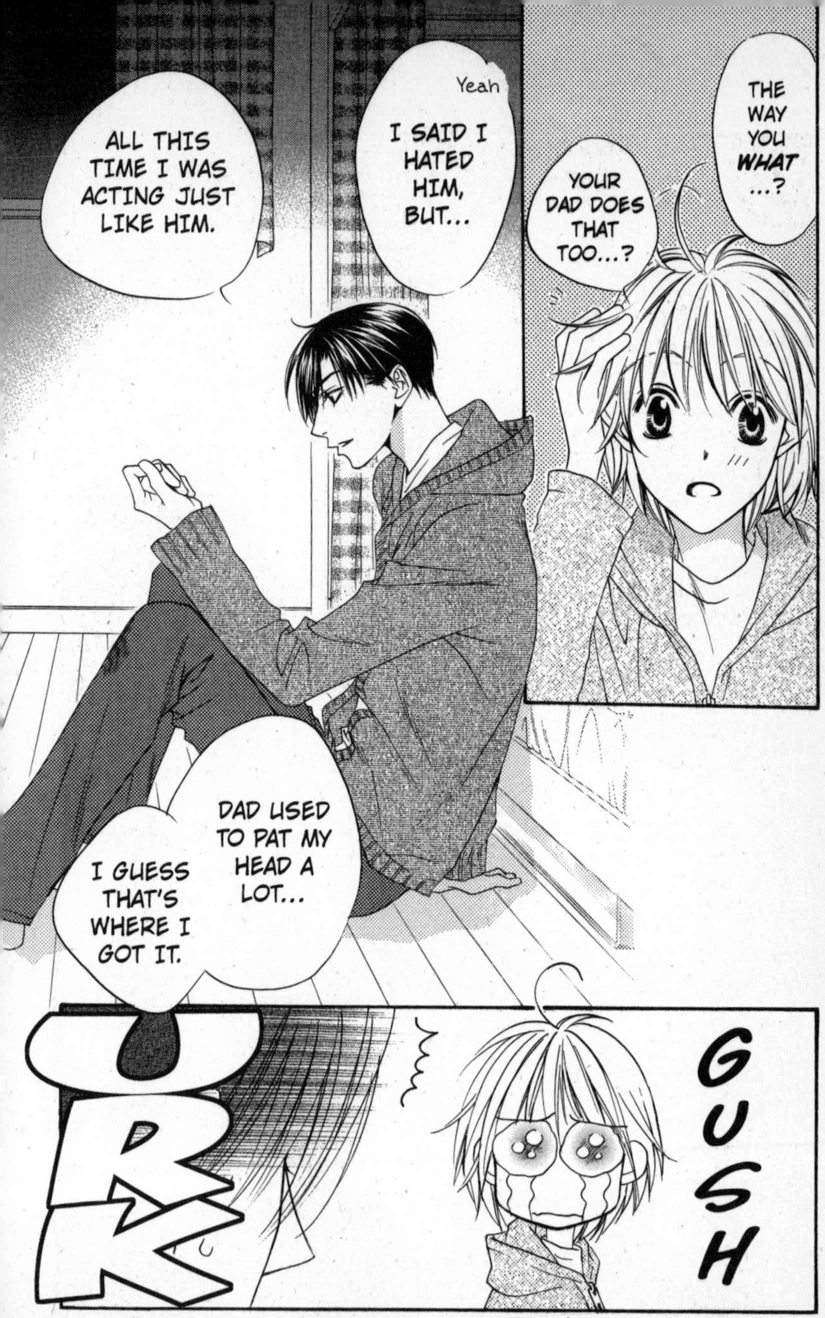
THE WAY YOU *WHAT*...?
YOUR DAD DOES THAT TOO...?
Yeah
I SAID I HATED HIM, BUT...
ALL THIS TIME I WAS ACTING JUST LIKE HIM.
DAD USED TO PAT MY HEAD A LOT...
I GUESS THAT'S WHERE I GOT IT.
GUSH
URK

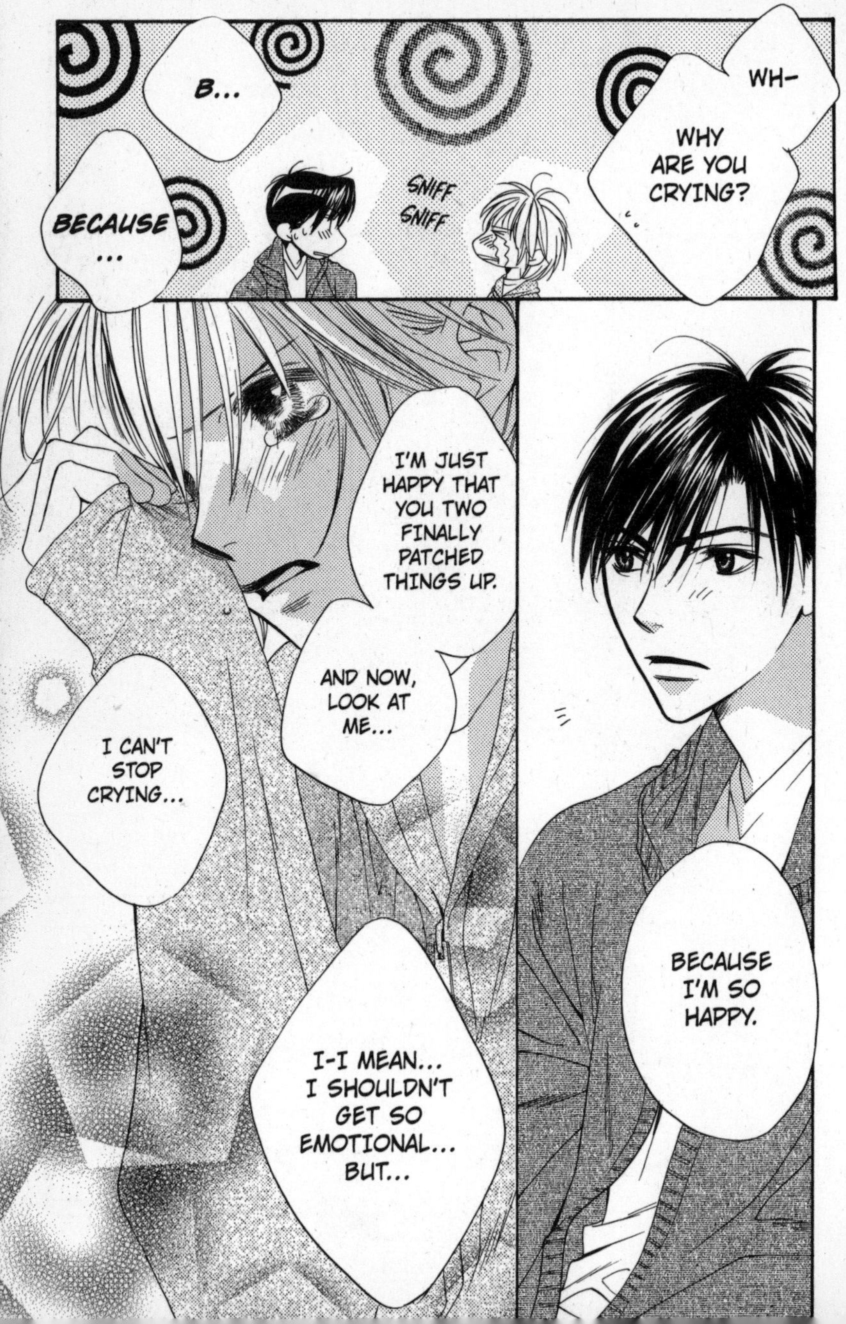
WH-
WHY ARE YOU CRYING?
SNIFF SNIFF
B...
BECAUSE ...
BECAUSE I'M SO HAPPY.
I'M JUST HAPPY THAT YOU TWO FINALLY PATCHED THINGS UP.
AND NOW, LOOK AT ME...
I CAN'T STOP CRYING...
I-I MEAN... I SHOULDN'T GET SO EMOTIONAL... BUT...

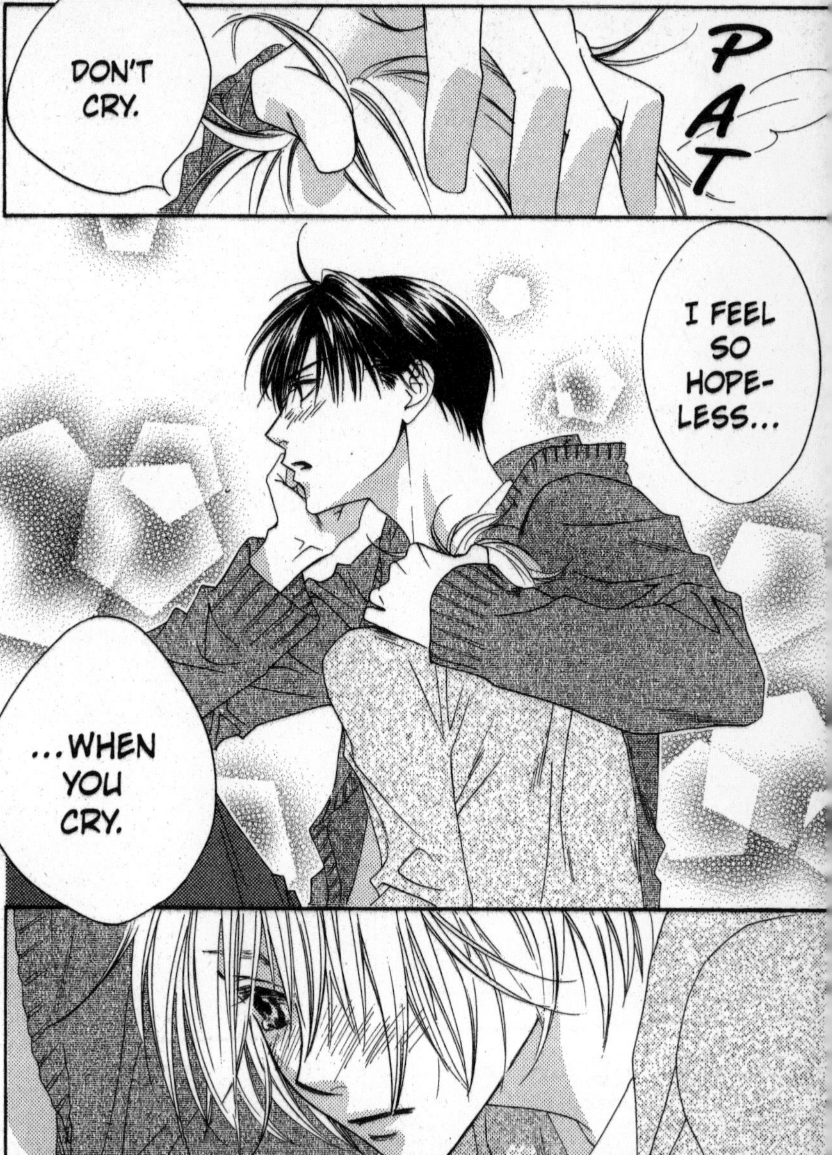
PAT
DON'T CRY.
I FEEL SO HOPE-LESS...
...WHEN YOU CRY.

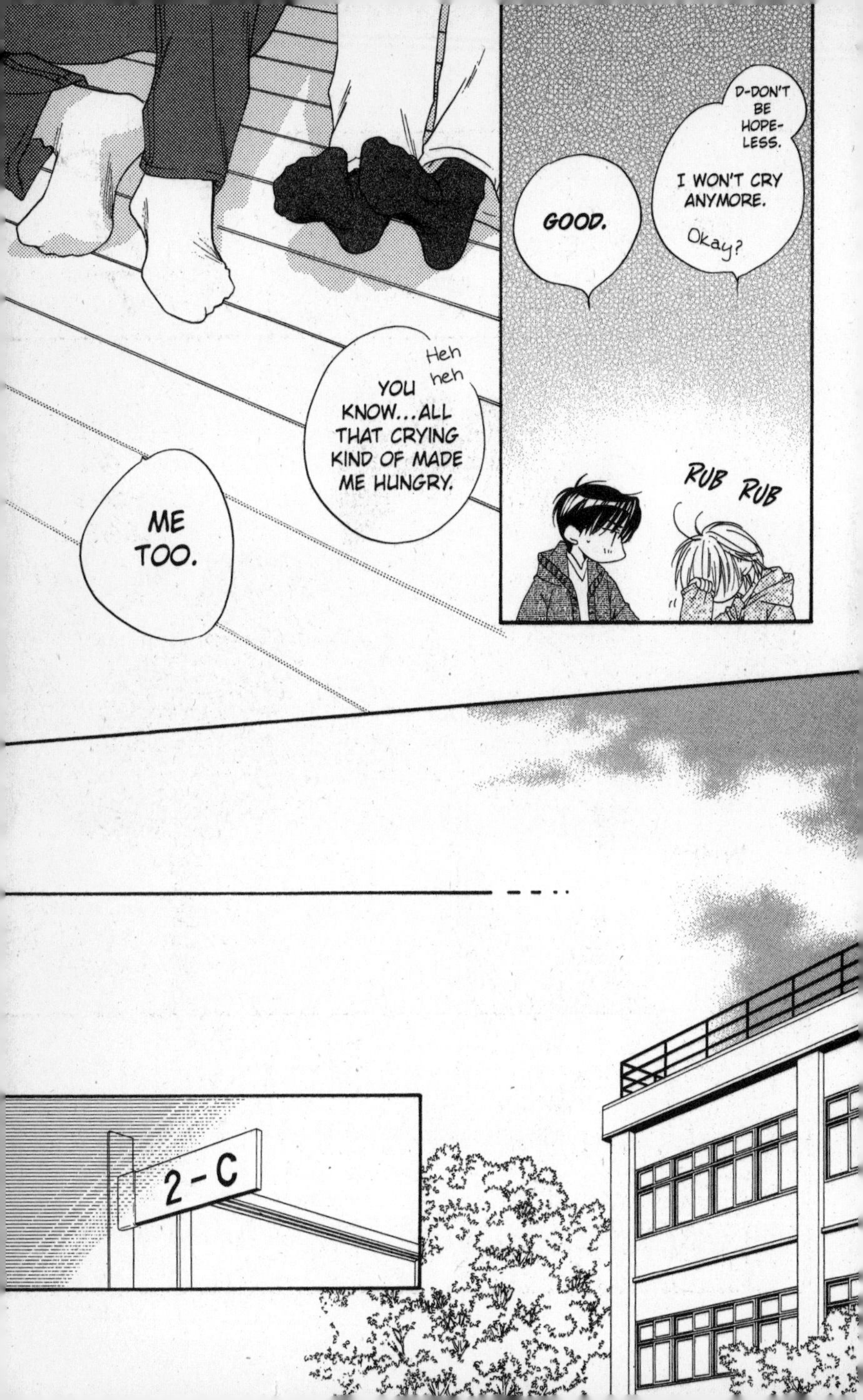
D-DON'T BE HOPE-LESS.
I WON'T CRY ANYMORE.
Okay?
GOOD.
RUB RUB
Heh heh
YOU KNOW...ALL THAT CRYING KIND OF MADE ME HUNGRY.
ME TOO.
2-C

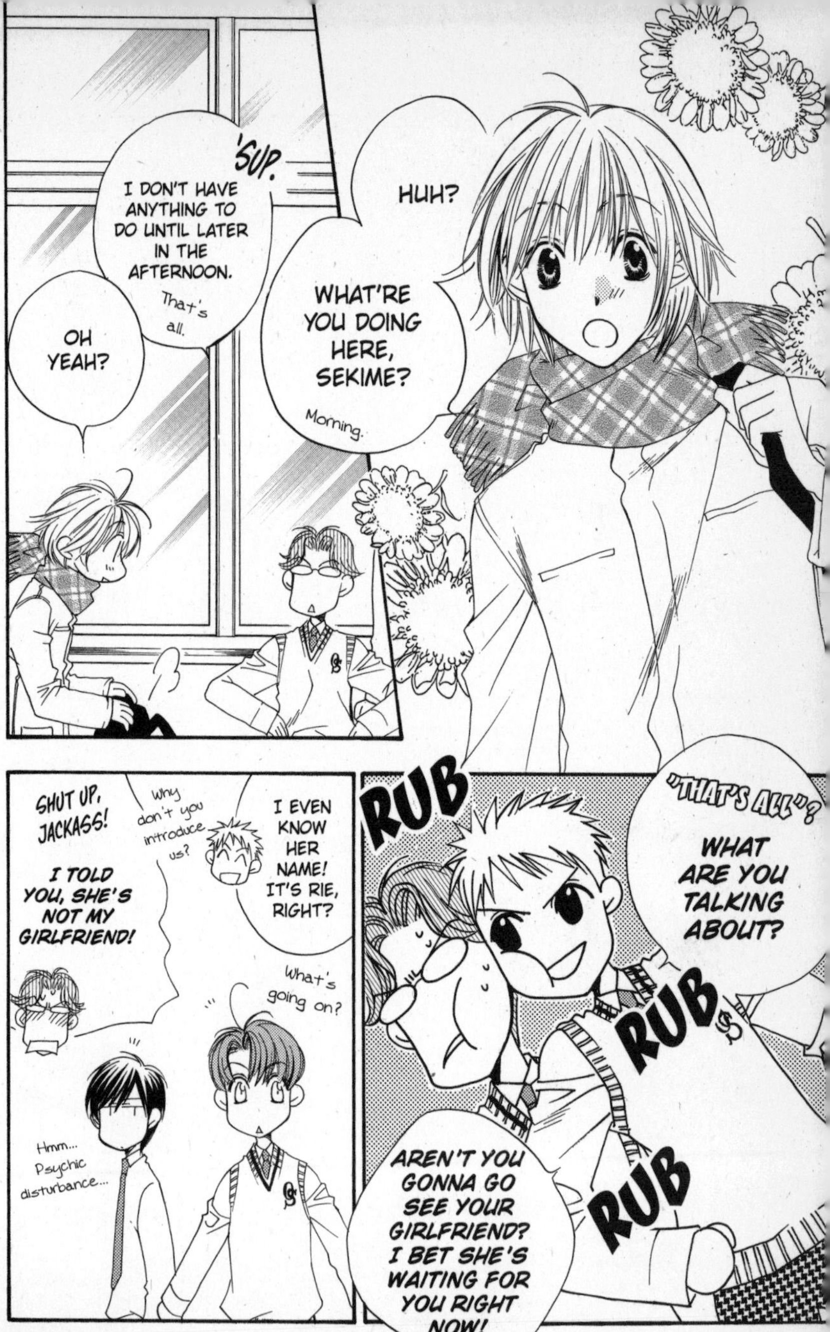
HUH?
WHAT'RE YOU DOING HERE, SEKIME?
Morning.
'SUP.
I DON'T HAVE ANYTHING TO DO UNTIL LATER IN THE AFTERNOON.
That's all.
OH YEAH?
"THAT'S ALL"? WHAT ARE YOU TALKING ABOUT?
RUB
RUB
RUB
AREN'T YOU GONNA GO SEE YOUR GIRLFRIEND? I BET SHE'S WAITING FOR YOU RIGHT NOW!
I EVEN KNOW HER NAME! IT'S RIE, RIGHT?
Why don't you introduce us?
SHUT UP, JACKASS!
I TOLD YOU, SHE'S NOT MY GIRLFRIEND!
What's going on?
Hmm... Psychic disturbance...

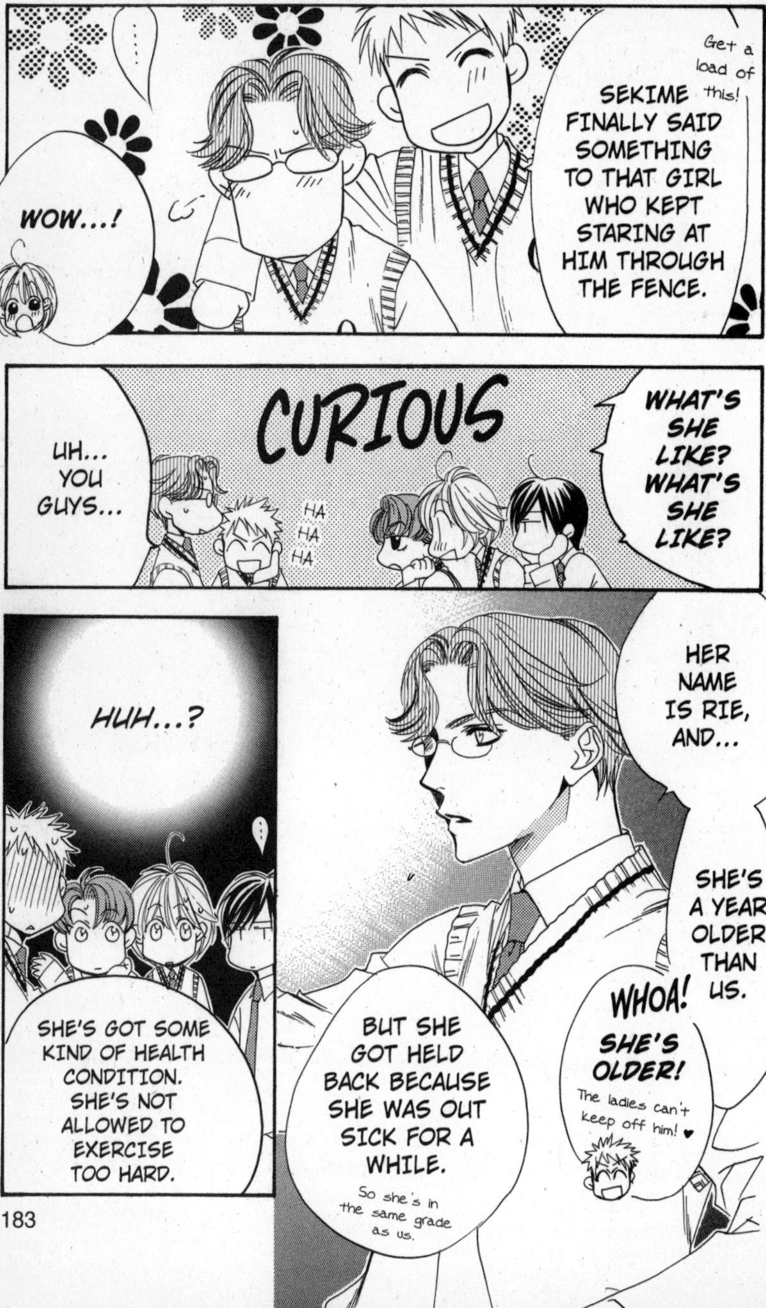

Get a load of this!
SEKIME FINALLY SAID SOMETHING TO THAT GIRL WHO KEPT STARING AT HIM THROUGH THE FENCE.
...
WOW...!
WHAT'S SHE LIKE? WHAT'S SHE LIKE?
CURIOUS
HA HA HA
UH... YOU GUYS...
HER NAME IS RIE, AND...
SHE'S A YEAR OLDER THAN US.
WHOA! SHE'S OLDER!
The ladies can't keep off him!
BUT SHE GOT HELD BACK BECAUSE SHE WAS OUT SICK FOR A WHILE.
So she's in the same grade as us.
HUH...?
!
SHE'S GOT SOME KIND OF HEALTH CONDITION. SHE'S NOT ALLOWED TO EXERCISE TOO HARD.

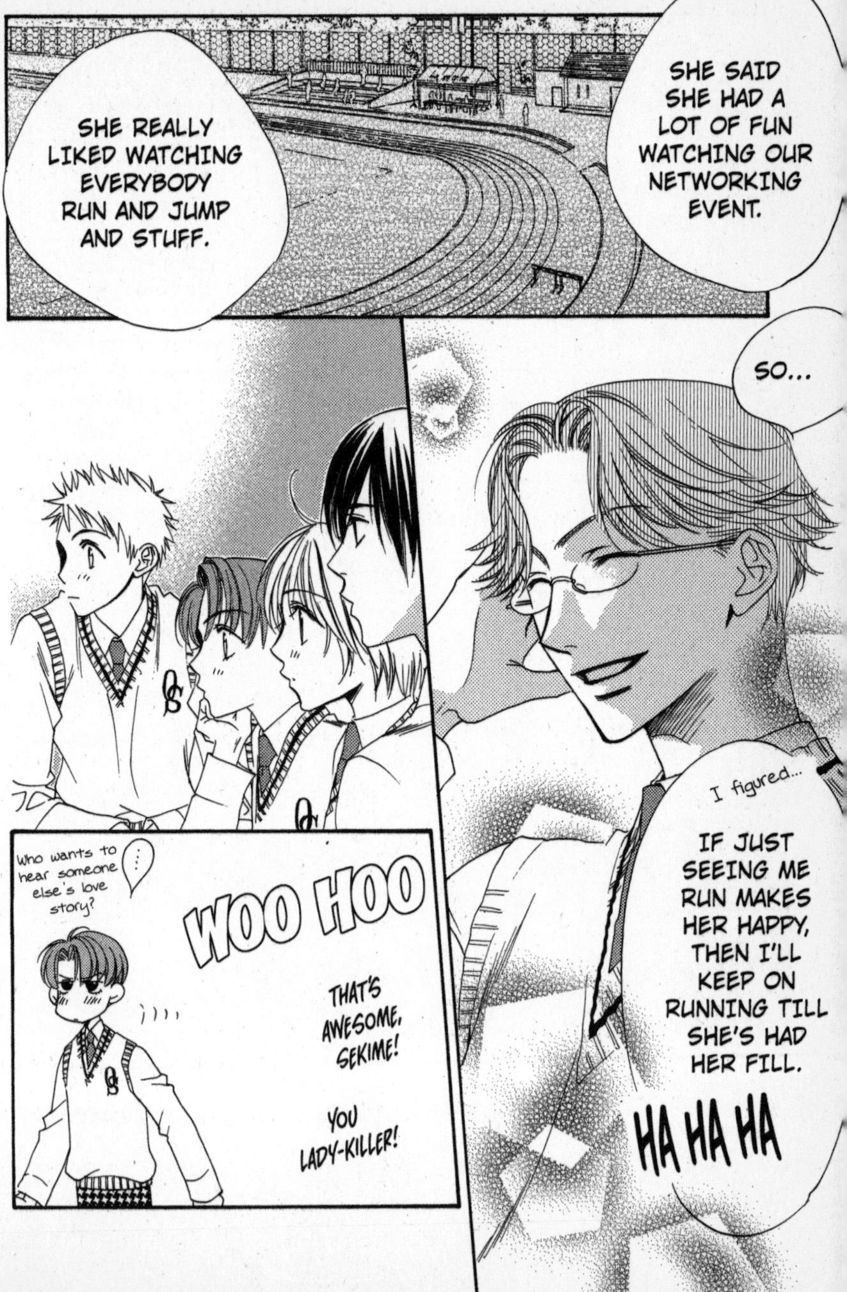

SHE SAID SHE HAD A LOT OF FUN WATCHING OUR NETWORKING EVENT.
SHE REALLY LIKED WATCHING EVERYBODY RUN AND JUMP AND STUFF.
SO...
I figured...
IF JUST SEEING ME RUN MAKES HER HAPPY, THEN I'LL KEEP ON RUNNING TILL SHE'S HAD HER FILL.
HA HA HA
WOO HOO
THAT'S AWESOME, SEKIME!
YOU LADY-KILLER!
Who wants to hear someone else's love story?
...

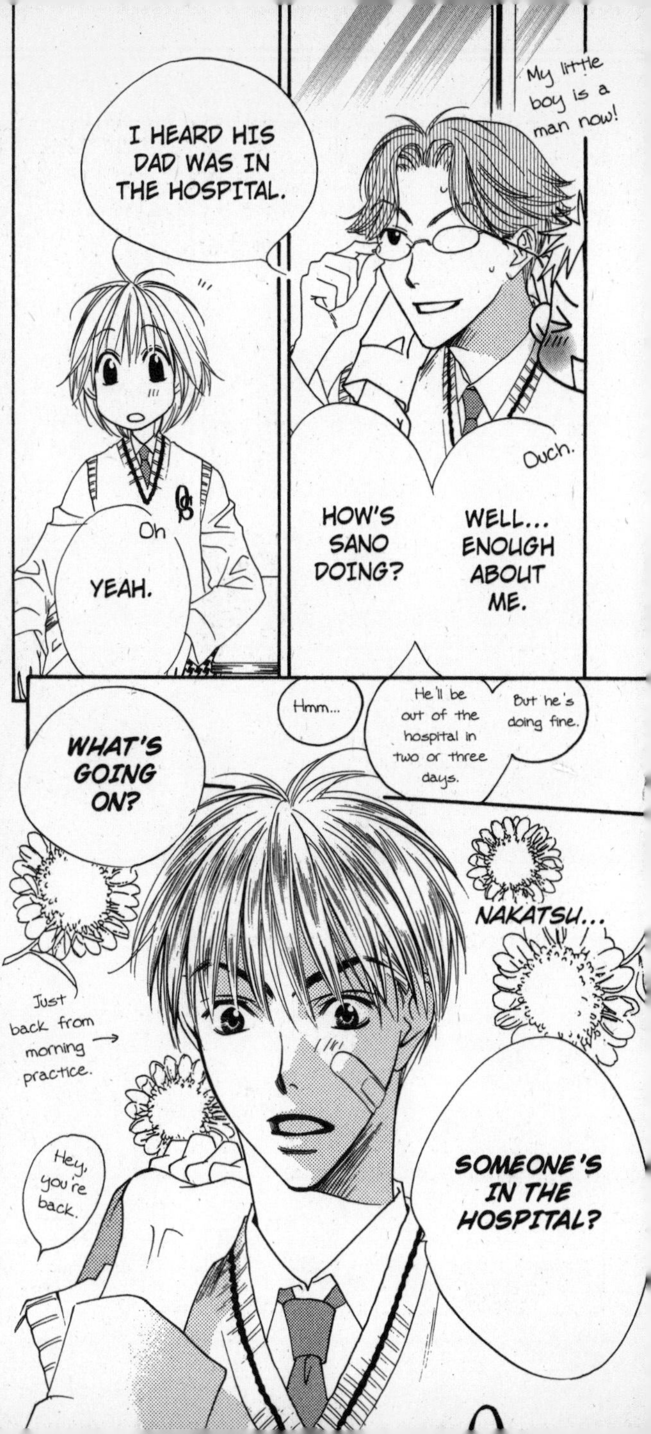
My little boy is a man now!
WELL... ENOUGH ABOUT ME.
Ouch.
HOW'S SANO DOING?
I HEARD HIS DAD WAS IN THE HOSPITAL.
Oh
YEAH.
But he's doing fine.
He'll be out of the hospital in two or three days.
Hmm...
WHAT'S GOING ON?
NAKATSU...
SOMEONE'S IN THE HOSPITAL?
Just back from morning practice.
Hey, you're back.

SEE YOU

Looks like I ended up filling most of this volume's notes with my "Scent" topic. I wanted to celebrate my 100th episode, but all I wrote about was smells and smelling...Do I have a smell fetish? Maybe I do. I tend to smell things a lot. Actually, I have a strict rule about wearing perfume: "Don't put too much on or you'll stink." If you overdo it because you think it smells nice you might end up annoying other people, so please be careful when you wear perfume.

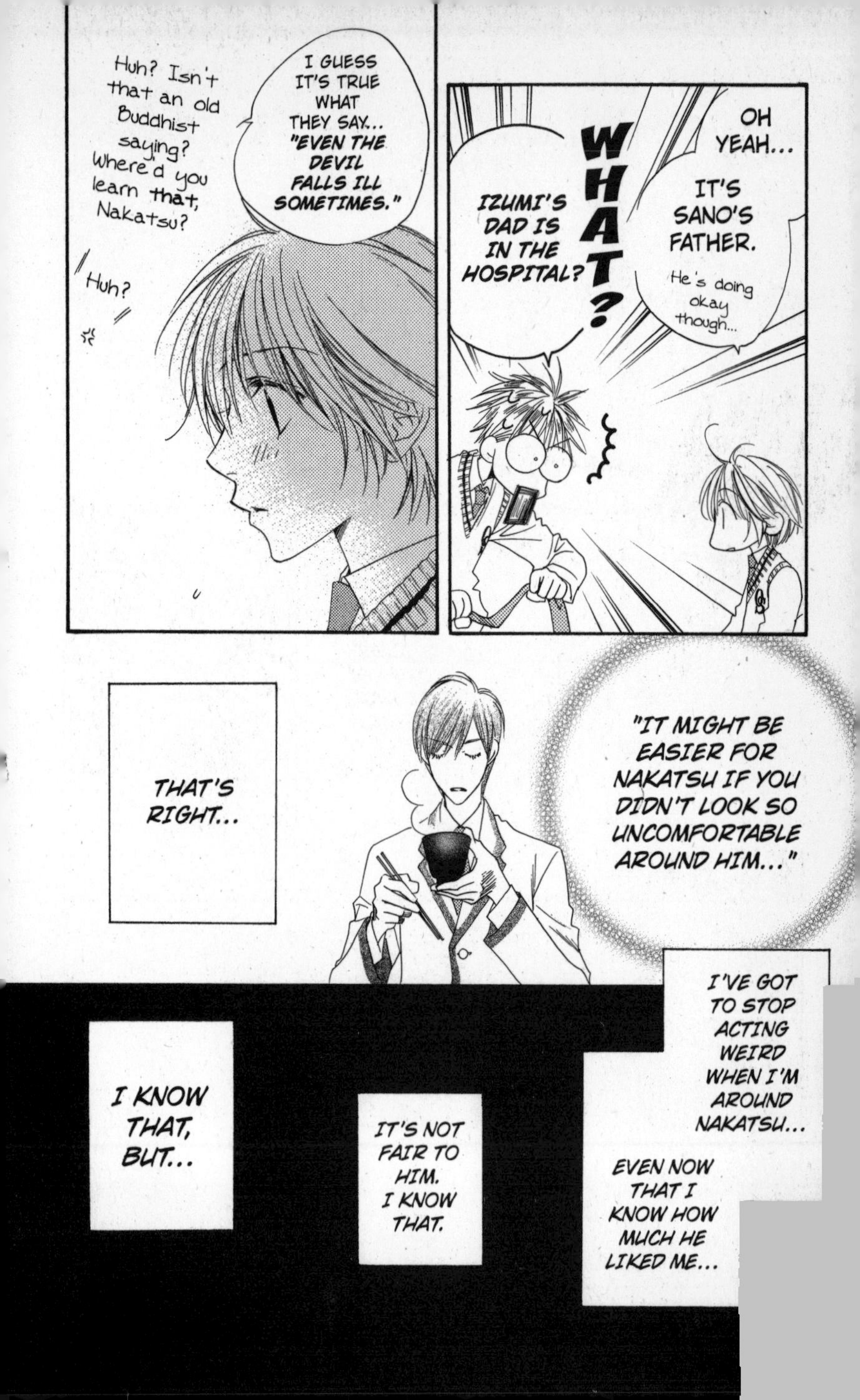
OH YEAH... IT'S SANO'S FATHER.
He's doing okay though...
IZUMI'S DAD IS IN THE HOSPITAL?
WHAT?
I GUESS IT'S TRUE WHAT THEY SAY... "EVEN THE DEVIL FALLS ILL SOMETIMES."
Huh? Isn't that an old Buddhist saying? Where'd you learn that, Nakatsu?
Huh?
"IT MIGHT BE EASIER FOR NAKATSU IF YOU DIDN'T LOOK SO UNCOMFORTABLE AROUND HIM..."
THAT'S RIGHT...
I'VE GOT TO STOP ACTING WEIRD WHEN I'M AROUND NAKATSU...
EVEN NOW THAT I KNOW HOW MUCH HE LIKED ME...
IT'S NOT FAIR TO HIM. I KNOW THAT.
I KNOW THAT, BUT...

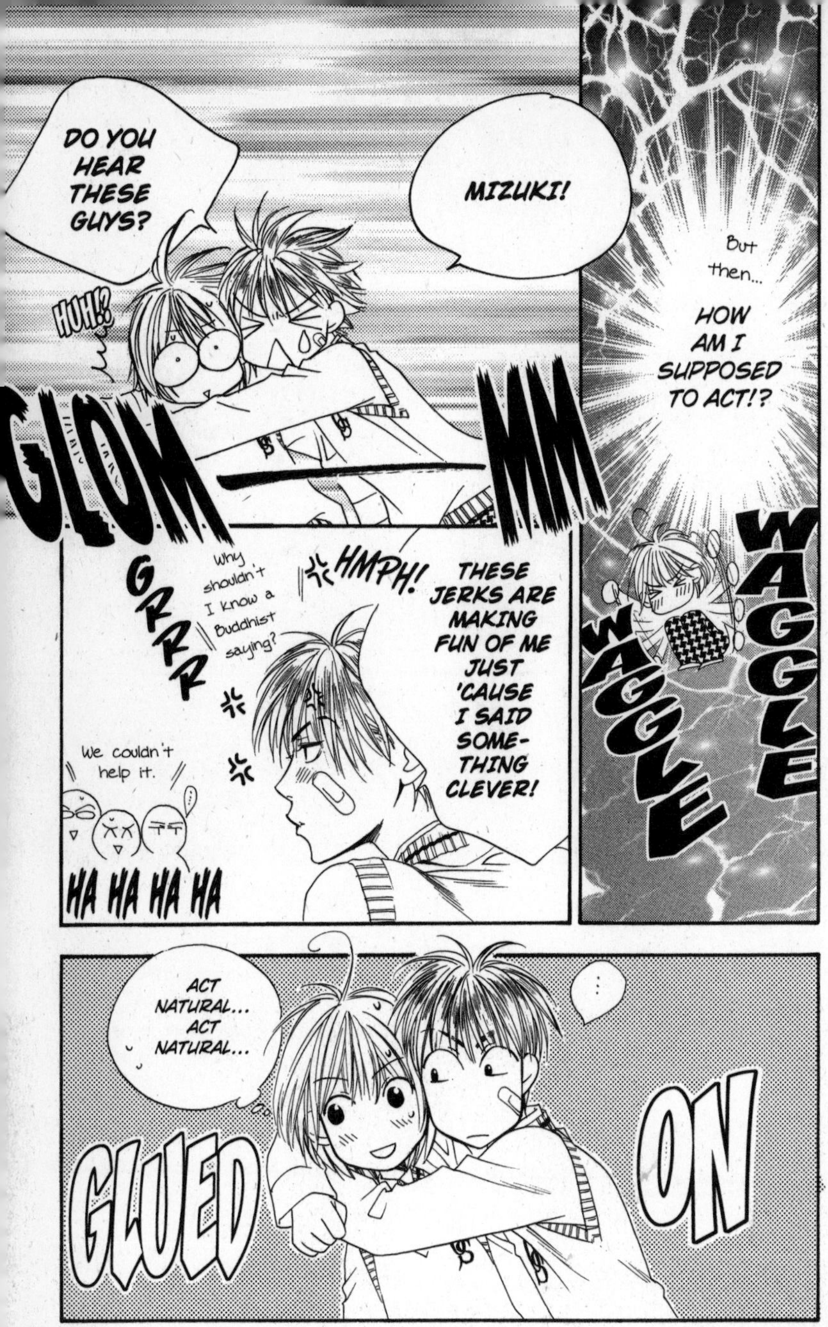
But then...
HOW AM I SUPPOSED TO ACT!?
WAGGLE
WAGGLE
MIZUKI!
DO YOU HEAR THESE GUYS?
HUH!?
GLOMM
THESE JERKS ARE MAKING FUN OF ME JUST 'CAUSE I SAID SOME-THING CLEVER!
HMPH!
Why shouldn't I know a Buddhist saying?
GRRR
We couldn't help it.
HA HA HA HA
...
ACT NATURAL... ACT NATURAL...
GLUED
ON

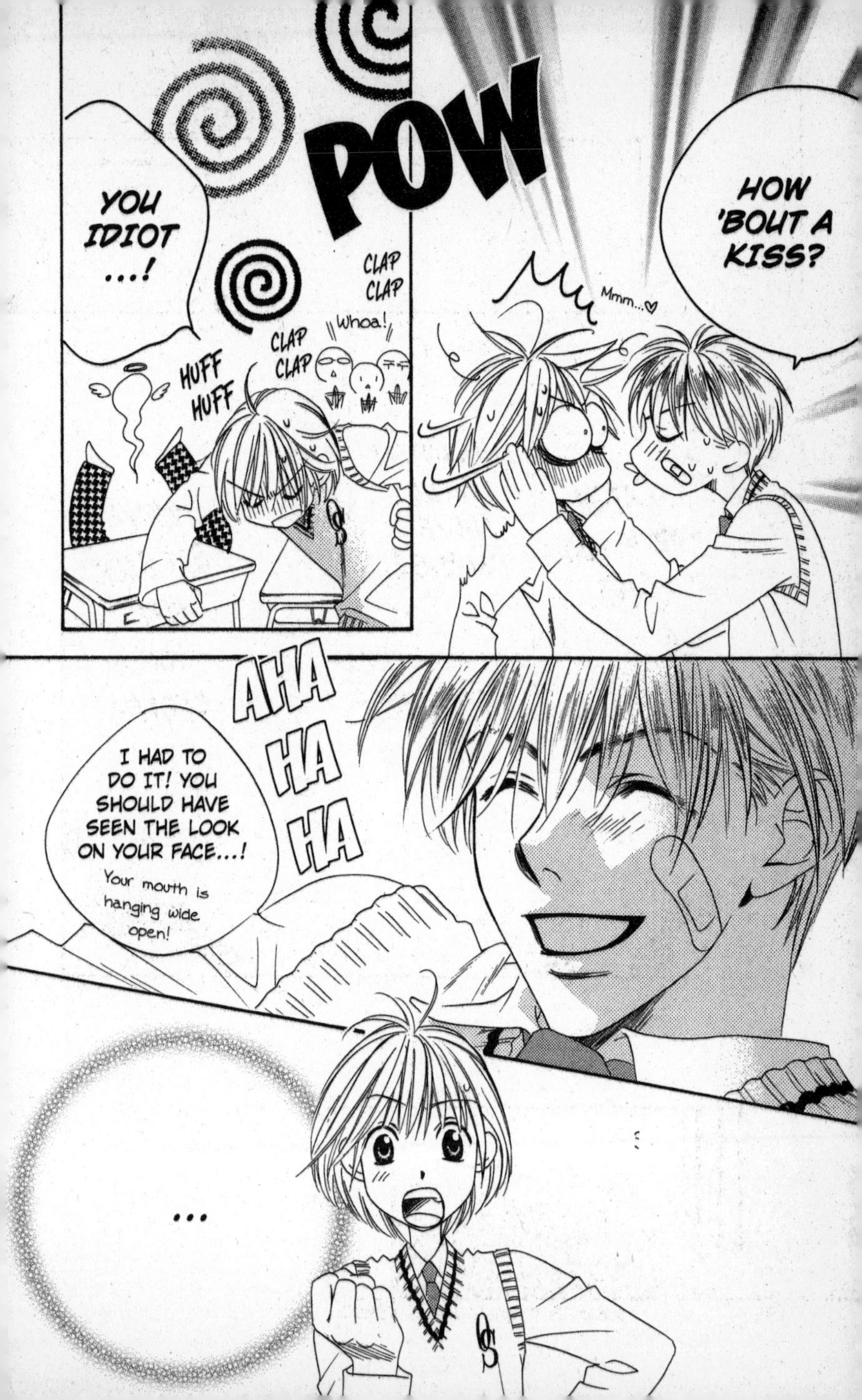
HOW 'BOUT A KISS?
Mmm...♥
POW
YOU IDIOT ...!
CLAP CLAP
Whoa!
CLAP CLAP
HUFF HUFF
AHA HA HA
I HAD TO DO IT! YOU SHOULD HAVE SEEN THE LOOK ON YOUR FACE...!
Your mouth is hanging wide open!
...

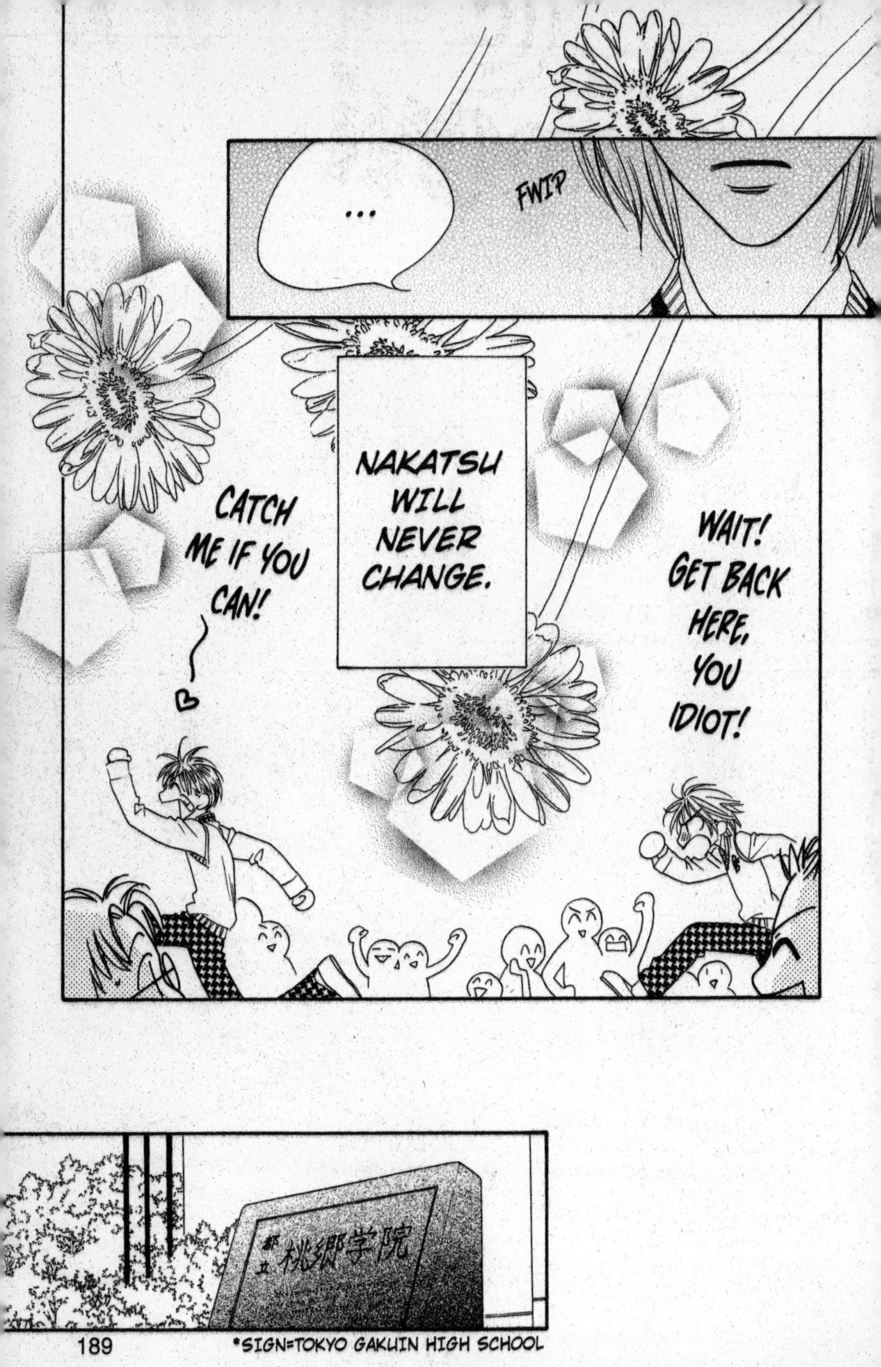
...
FWIP
WAIT! GET BACK HERE, YOU IDIOT!
CATCH ME IF YOU CAN! ♥
NAKATSU WILL NEVER CHANGE.
都立 桃郷学院

*SIGN=TOKYO GAKUIN HIGH SCHOOL

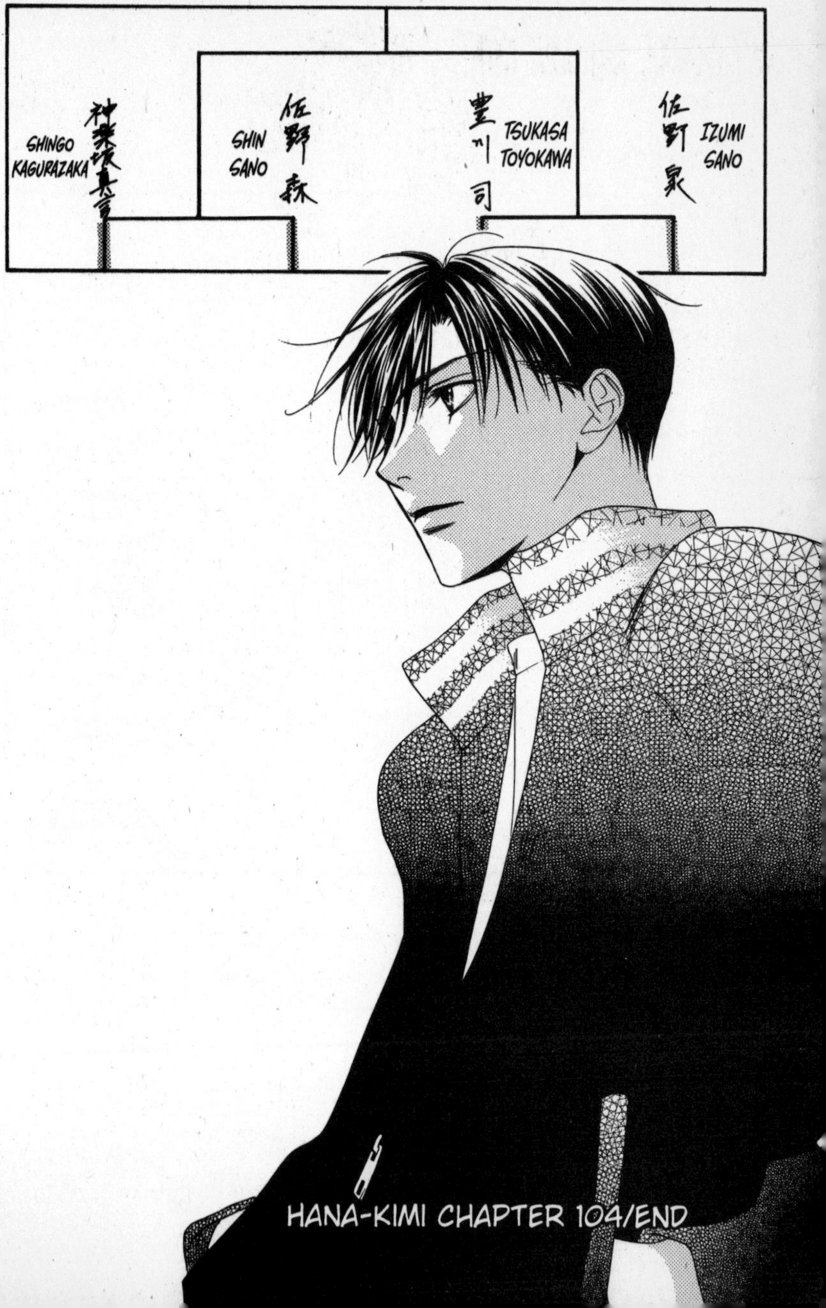
佐野泉
IZUMI SANO
豊川司
TSUKASA TOYOKAWA
佐野森
SHIN SANO
神楽坂真言
SHINGO KAGURAZAKA
HANA-KIMI CHAPTER 104/END

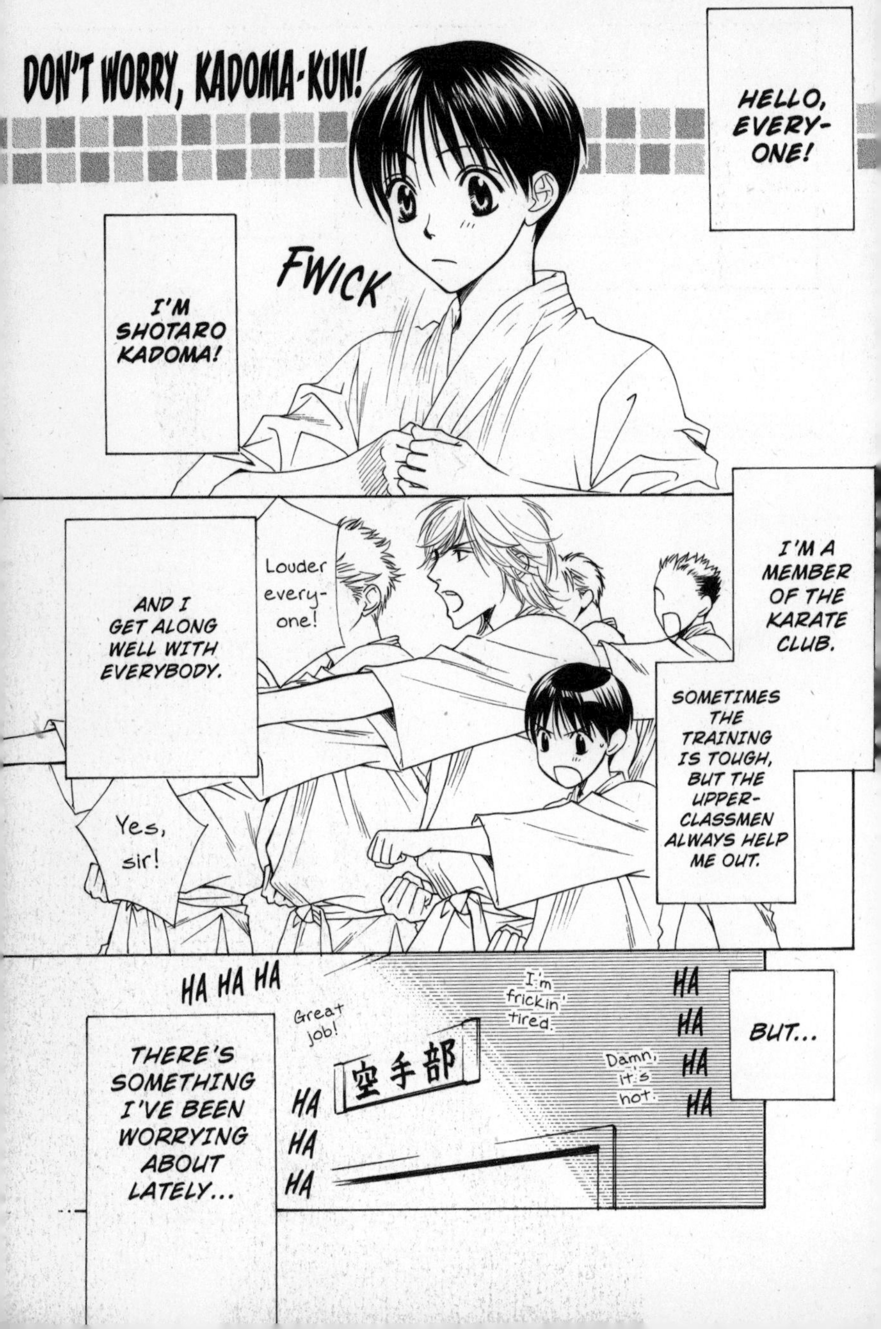
DON'T WORRY, KADOMA-KUN!
HELLO, EVERY-ONE!
I'M SHOTARO KADOMA!
FWICK
I'M A MEMBER OF THE KARATE CLUB.
SOMETIMES THE TRAINING IS TOUGH, BUT THE UPPER-CLASSMEN ALWAYS HELP ME OUT.
Louder every-one!
AND I GET ALONG WELL WITH EVERYBODY.
Yes, sir!
BUT...
HA HA HA HA
Damn, it's hot.
I'm frickin' tired.
Great job!
HA HA HA
空手部
HA HA HA
THERE'S SOMETHING I'VE BEEN WORRYING ABOUT LATELY...

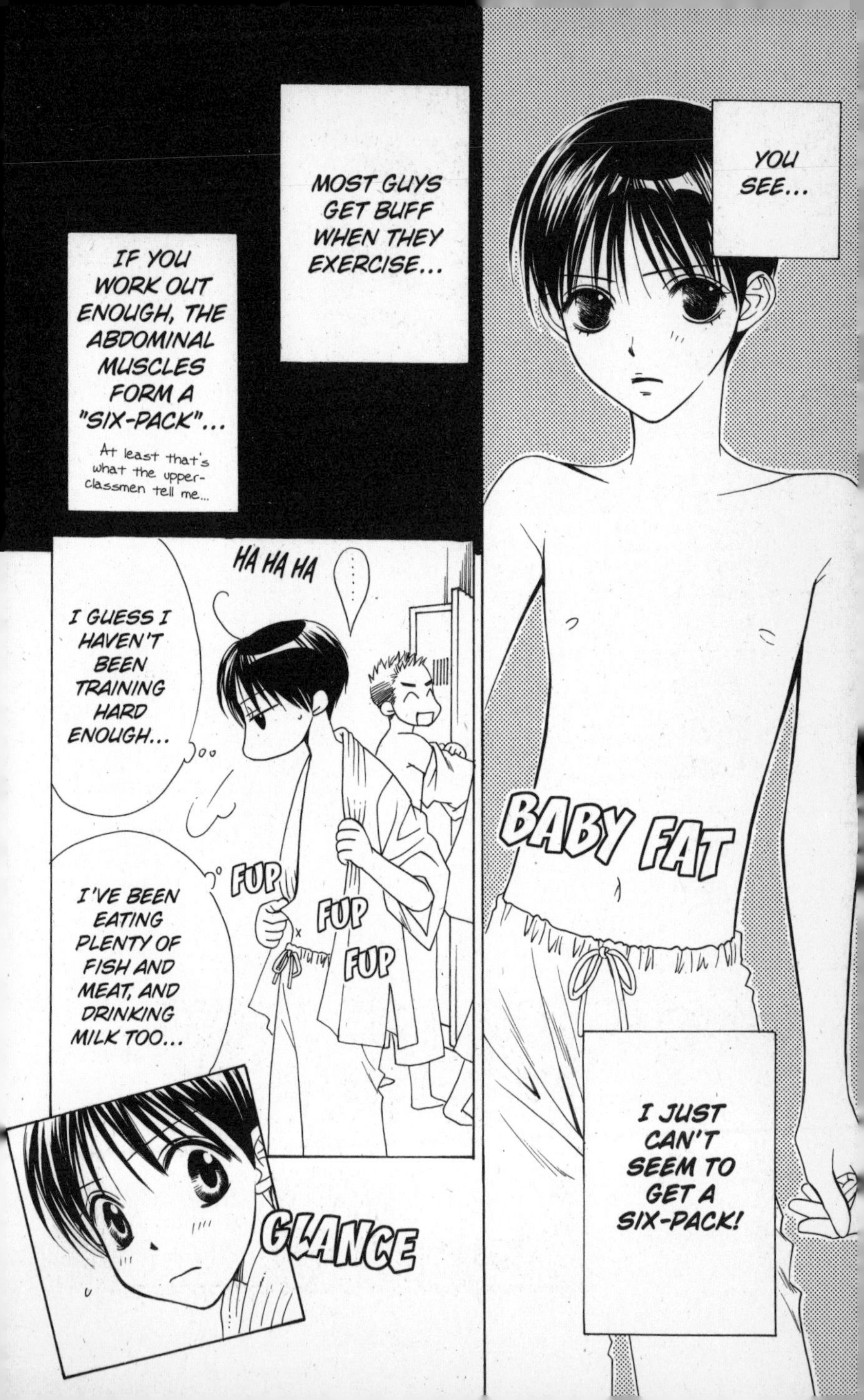

YOU SEE...
BABY FAT
I JUST CAN'T SEEM TO GET A SIX-PACK!
MOST GUYS GET BUFF WHEN THEY EXERCISE...
IF YOU WORK OUT ENOUGH, THE ABDOMINAL MUSCLES FORM A "SIX-PACK"...
At least that's what the upper-classmen tell me...
HA HA HA
...
I GUESS I HAVEN'T BEEN TRAINING HARD ENOUGH...
I'VE BEEN EATING PLENTY OF FISH AND MEAT, AND DRINKING MILK TOO...
FUP
FUP
FUP
GLANCE

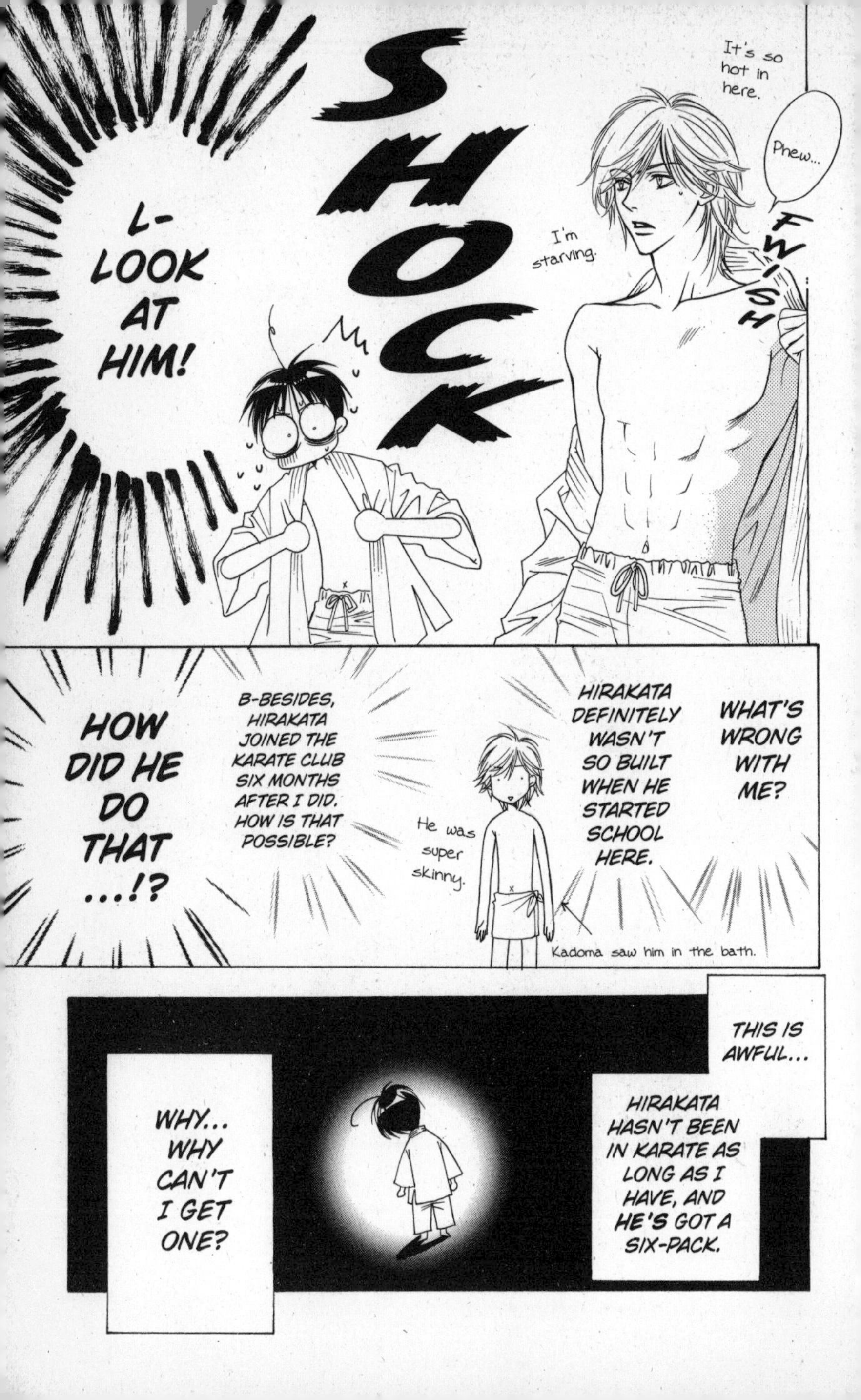

It's so hot in here.
Phew...
FWISH
SHOCK
I'm starving.
L-LOOK AT HIM!
WHAT'S WRONG WITH ME?
HIRAKATA DEFINITELY WASN'T SO BUILT WHEN HE STARTED SCHOOL HERE.
Kadoma saw him in the bath.
He was super skinny.
B-BESIDES, HIRAKATA JOINED THE KARATE CLUB SIX MONTHS AFTER I DID. HOW IS THAT POSSIBLE?
HOW DID HE DO THAT...!?
THIS IS AWFUL...
HIRAKATA HASN'T BEEN IN KARATE AS LONG AS I HAVE, AND HE'S GOT A SIX-PACK.
WHY... WHY CAN'T I GET ONE?

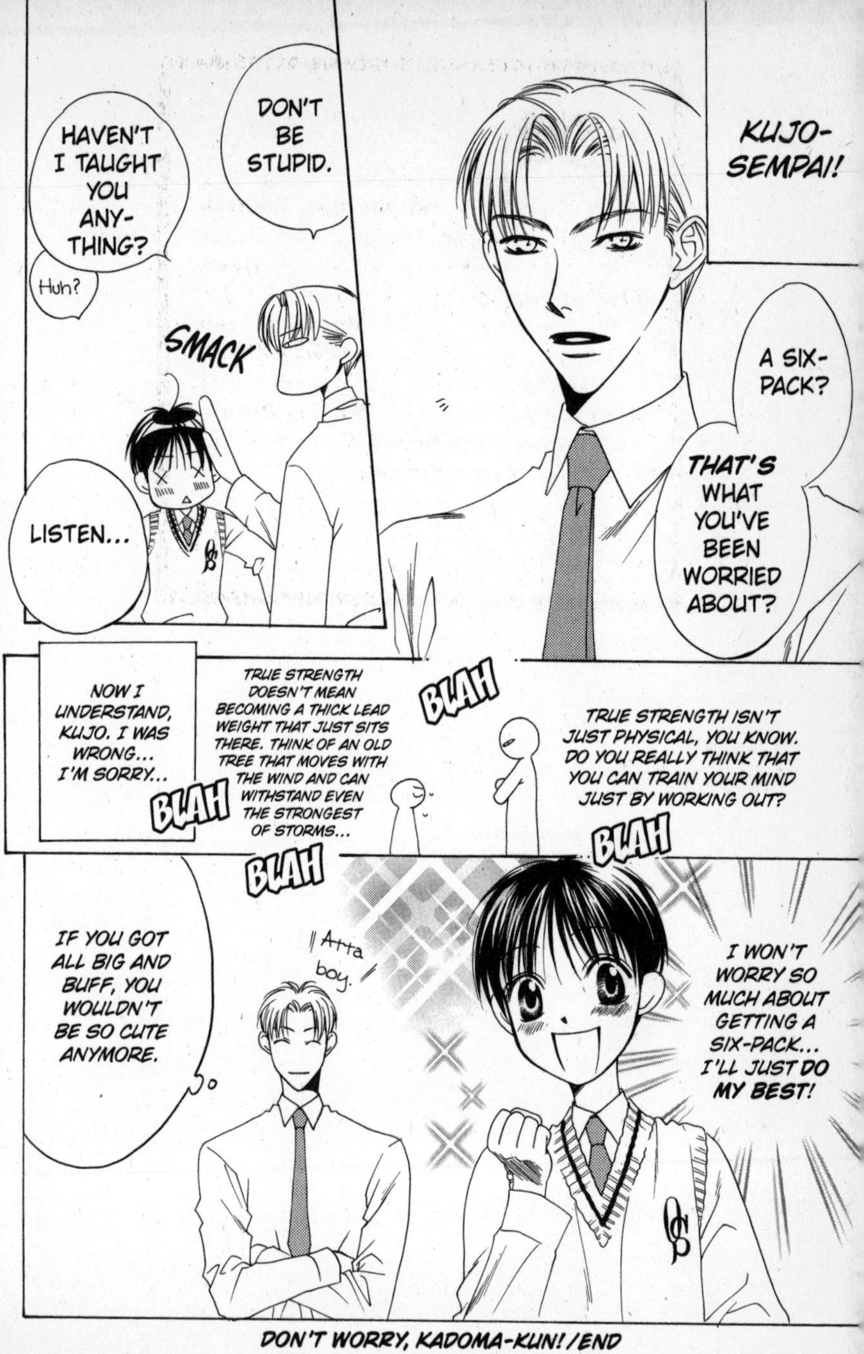
KUJO-SEMPAI!
A SIX-PACK?
THAT'S WHAT YOU'VE BEEN WORRIED ABOUT?
DON'T BE STUPID.
HAVEN'T I TAUGHT YOU ANYTHING?
Huh?
SMACK
LISTEN...
TRUE STRENGTH ISN'T JUST PHYSICAL, YOU KNOW. DO YOU REALLY THINK THAT YOU CAN TRAIN YOUR MIND JUST BY WORKING OUT?
BLAH
BLAH
TRUE STRENGTH DOESN'T MEAN BECOMING A THICK LEAD WEIGHT THAT JUST SITS THERE. THINK OF AN OLD TREE THAT MOVES WITH THE WIND AND CAN WITHSTAND EVEN THE STRONGEST OF STORMS...
BLAH
BLAH
NOW I UNDERSTAND, KUJO. I WAS WRONG... I'M SORRY...
I WON'T WORRY SO MUCH ABOUT GETTING A SIX-PACK... I'LL JUST DO MY BEST!
Atta boy.
IF YOU GOT ALL BIG AND BUFF, YOU WOULDN'T BE SO CUTE ANYMORE.

DON'T WORRY, KADOMA-KUN! /END

ABOUT THE AUTHOR

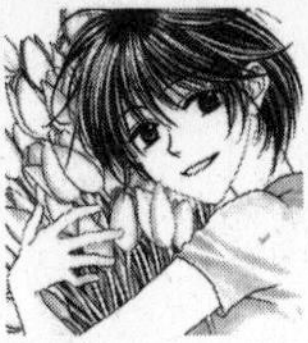

Hisaya Nakajo's manga series **Hanazakari no Kimitachi he** (For You in Full Blossom, casually known as **Hana-Kimi**) has been a hit since it first appeared in 1997 in the shôjo manga magazine **Hana to Yume** (Flowers and Dreams). In Japan, two **Hana-Kimi** art books and several "drama CDs" have been released. Her other manga series include **Missing Piece** (2 volumes), **Yumemiru Happa** (The Dreaming Leaf, 1 volume) and **Sugar Princess**.

Hisaya Nakajo's website:
www.wild-vanilla.com

IN THE NEXT VOLUME...

This is the moment it's all been building up to...the high-jump competition between Shin, Izumi and Kagurazaka! Then, does Sekime have a girlfriend? And what *Hana-Kimi* character gets a surprise visit from their relatives...?

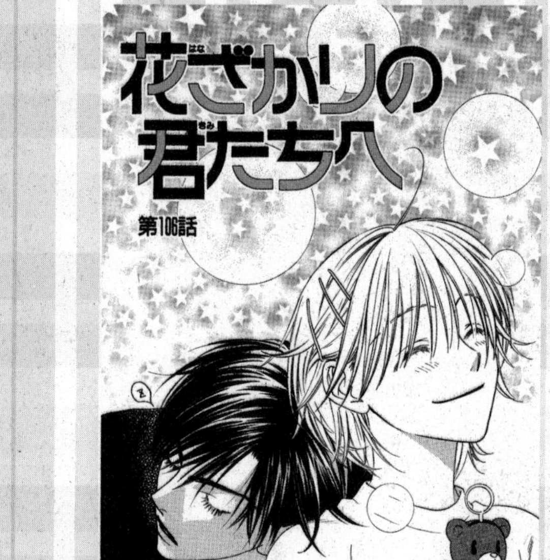
花ざかりの君たちへ
第106話
COMING AUGUST 2007!

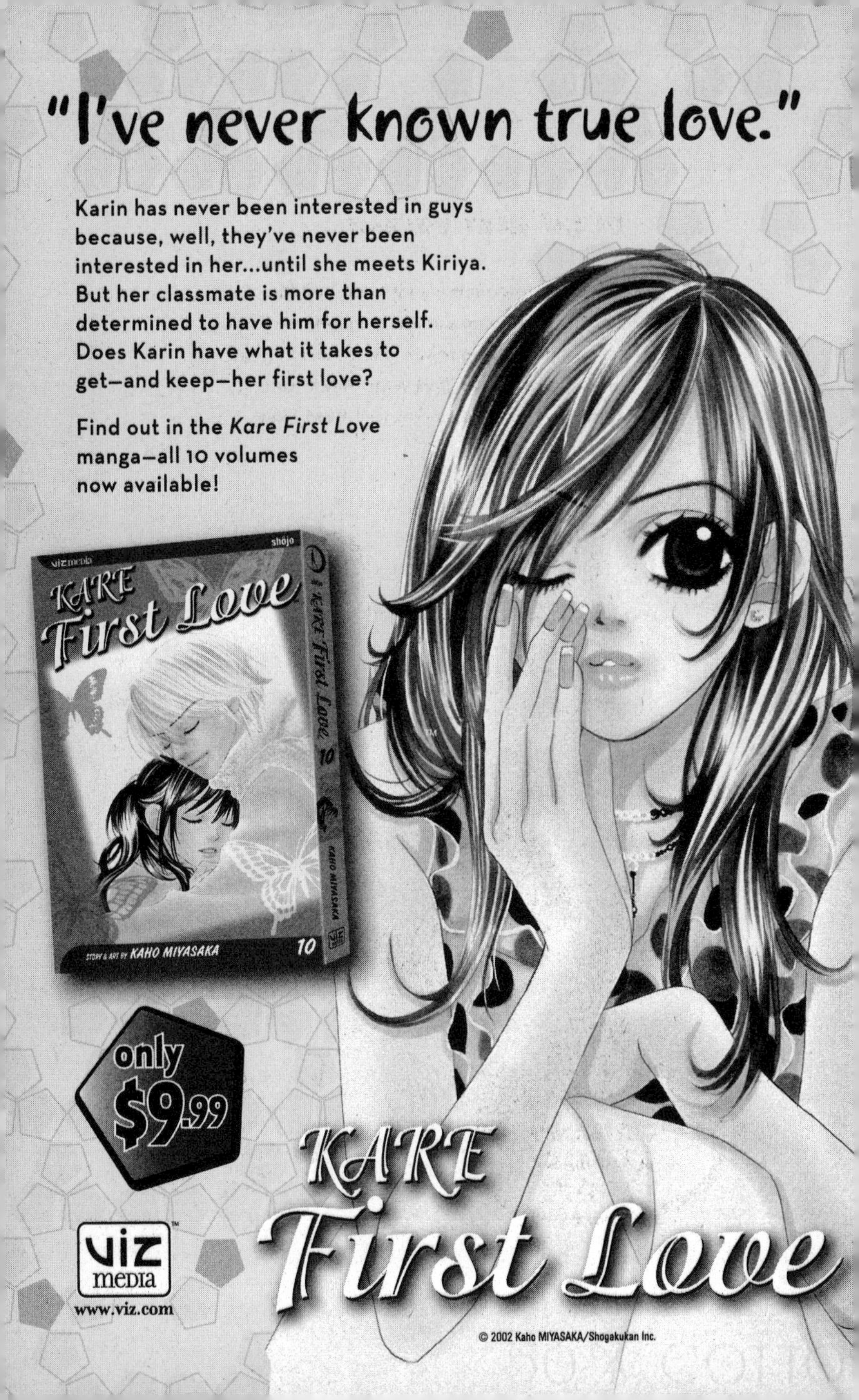
"I've never known true love."
Karin has never been interested in guys because, well, they've never been interested in her...until she meets Kiriya. But her classmate is more than determined to have him for herself. Does Karin have what it takes to get—and keep—her first love?
Find out in the Kare First Love manga—all 10 volumes now available!
viz media
shôjo
KARE First Love
KARE First Love 10
KAHO MIYASAKA
STORY & ART BY KAHO MIYASAKA
10
only $9.99
KARE First Love
VIZ media
www.viz.com
© 2002 Kaho MIYASAKA/Shogakukan Inc.

Hot Gimmick™

Will our hapless heroine ever figure out the game of love? Find out in *Hot Gimmick*— get the complete collection today!

Read the original manga—all 12 volumes available now

A novelization of the popular manga, with alternate ending and a bonus manga episode!

From the creator of *Tokyo Boys & Girls*— available from our Shojo Beat Manga line

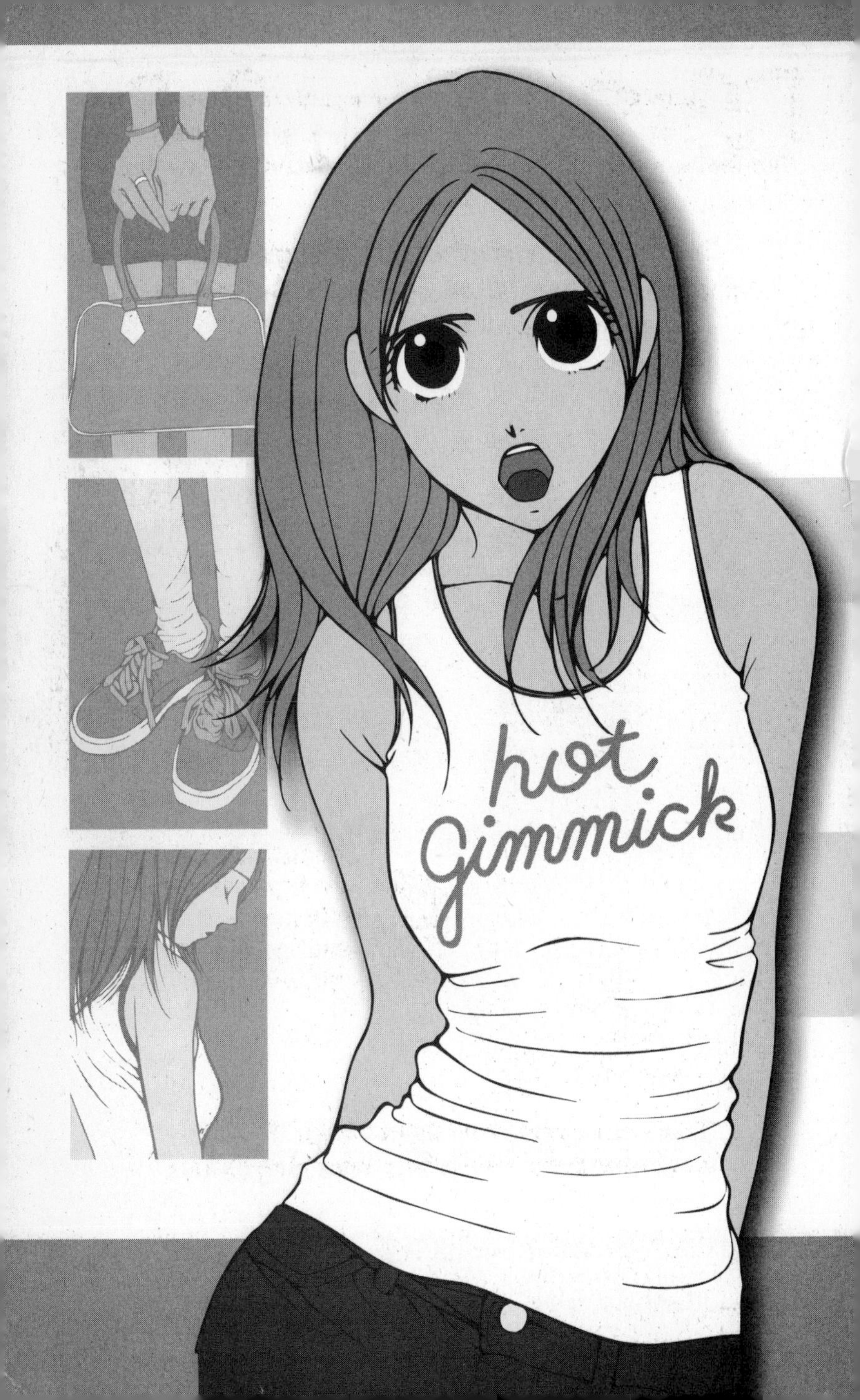
hot
Gimmick

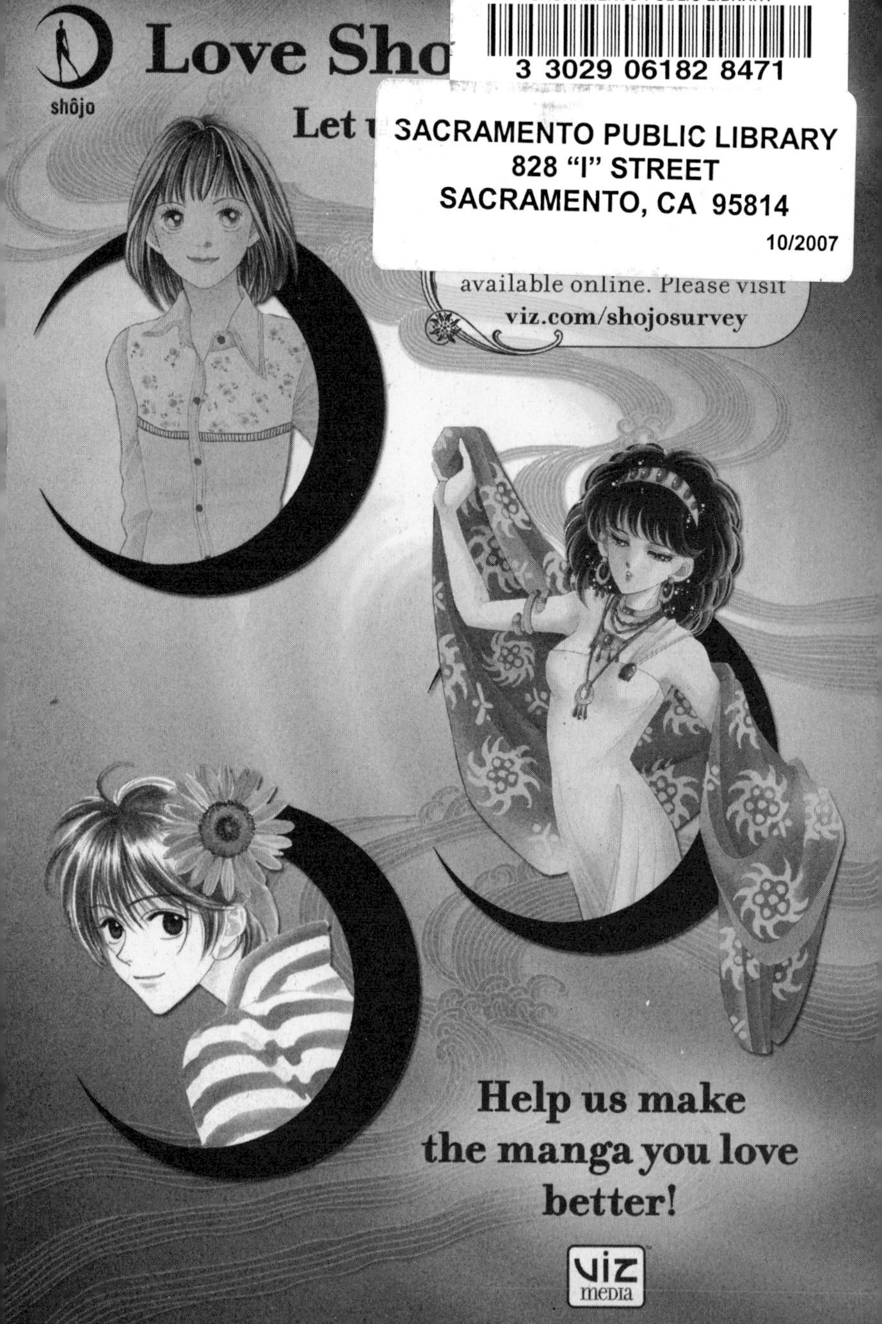
shôjo
Love Sho
Let u
available online. Please visit
viz.com/shojosurvey
Help us make
the manga you love
better!
VIZ media